HOUSEHOLD CREDIT USAGE

HOUSEHOLD CREDIT USAGE

PERSONAL DEBT AND MORTGAGES

Edited by
Sumit Agarwal and Brent W. Ambrose

Foreword by
John Y. Campbell

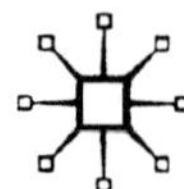

HOUSEHOLD CREDIT USAGE

First published in 2007 by
PALGRAVE MACMILLAN™
175 Fifth Avenue, New York, N.Y. 10010 and
Houndmills, Basingstoke, Hampshire, England RG21 6XS
Companies and representatives throughout the world.

PALGRAVE MACMILLAN is the global academic imprint of the Palgrave Macmillan division of St. Martin's Press, LLC and of Palgrave Macmillan Ltd. Macmillan® is a registered trademark in the United States, United Kingdom and other countries. Palgrave is a registered trademark in the European Union and other countries.

ISBN-13: 978–1–4039–8392–3
ISBN-10: 1–4039–8392–5

Library of Congress Cataloging-in-Publication Data

Household credit usage : personal debt and mortgages / edited by Sumit Agarwal and Brent W. Ambrose; foreword by John Y. Campbell.
p. cm.
Includes bibliographical references and index.
ISBN 1–4039–8392–5 (alk. paper)
1. Consumer credit. 2. Finance, Personal. I. Agarwal, Sumit. II. Ambrose, Brent W. (Brent William), 1964–

HG3755.H68 2007
332.7′43—dc22 2007007637

A catalogue record for this book is available from the British Library.

Design by Newgen Imaging Systems (P) Ltd., Chennai, India.

First edition: November 2007

10 9 8 7 6 5 4 3 2 1

Printed in the United States of America.

CONTENTS

LIST OF CHARTS, FIGURES, AND TABLES

Charts

Figures

Tables

FOREWORD

We live in an age of rapid innovation in consumer financial markets.

Households are being offered new ways to borrow, save, and purchase goods and services. Consumer credit markets have undergone particularly rapid change, and the households that are most affected are those that have had limited access to credit in the past. Such households, with low or moderate income, low financial assets, volatile income and expenditure, and poor credit histories, now have expanded access to secured credit through auto loans and sub-prime mortgages, and unsecured credit through payday loans and credit cards.

These new forms of consumer credit raise fascinating questions for economists and policy makers. How do observable characteristics of borrowers affect the cost of credit? How do lenders use the decisions of borrowers, such as the size of a loan or the type of asset that is used as collateral, to determine the interest rate that is charged? Do consumers choose loan instruments, such as adjustable or fixed rate mortgages, in accordance with economists' models of utility maximization under constraints, or do some households make decisions that reflect confusion or ignorance? Is there evidence that consumers value forms of credit that commit them to a savings plan? How should laws against discrimination be enforced in an increasingly complex environment where loans are priced to reflect lenders' estimates of each borrower's default risk?

The chapters in this volume explore these questions and provide a valuable overview of the contemporary U.S. consumer finance system. This and other household finance research is fundamentally important because it challenges economists to understand the limits of the traditional model of the sovereign consumer, it challenges policymakers to adapt consumer regulation to changing circumstances, and it challenges the financial services industry to use financial engineering and information technology for the benefit of all consumers.

John Y. Campbell
Morton L. and Carole S. Olshan Professor of Economics
Harvard University

NOTES ON CONTRIBUTORS

Sumit Agarwal is a financial economist at the Federal Reserve Bank of Chicago.

Brent W. Ambrose is Jeffery L. and Cindy M. King Faculty Fellow in Business and Professor of Real Estate at the Pennsylvania State University.

Sujit Chakravorti is a senior economist at the Federal Reserve Bank of Chicago.

Souphala Chomsisengphet is a senior economist at the Office of the Comptroller of the Currency, United States Department of the Treasury.

Shubhasis Dey is an economist at the Bank of Canada.

Jason Dietrich is a senior economist with the Office of the Comptroller of the Currency, United States Department of the Treasury.

Lucia Dunn is Professor of Economics at Ohio State University.

Tufan Ekici is instructor, Middle East Technical University, North Cyprus Campus.

Irene Fang is a senior economist with the Office of the Comptroller of the Currency, United States Department of the Treasury.

Michael Farrell is a student researcher assistant, Sauder School of Business, University of British Columbia.

Marc Anthony Fusaro is Assistant Professor of Economics, East Carolina University.

Robert M. Hunt is a senior economist at the Federal Reserve Bank of Philadelphia.

Kathleen W. Johnson is an economist, Board of Governors of the Federal Reserve System.

Yosh Kasahara is a student researcher assistant, Sauder School of Business, University of British Columbia.

Grace Kim is Assistant Professor of Economics, Michigan State University.

Tae Hyung Kim is a senior consultant, Deloitte & Touche.

Michael LaCour-Little is a Professor in the Department of Finance at California State University, Fullerton.

Andreas Lehnert is a senior economist with the Federal Reserve Board of Governors.

Dean Maki is a senior vice president at Barclays Capital.

Monica Paiella is an economist in the Bank of Italy's Research Department.

Anthony Pennington-Cross is Associate Professor in the Department of Real Estate, Marquette University.

Mark Pocock is an economist with the Office of the Comptroller of the Currency, United States Department of the Treasury.

Alberto Franco Pozzolo is Assistant Professor at the Università degli Studi del Molise, Dipartimento di Scienze Economiche Gestionali e Sociali.

Li Qiang is a student researcher assistant, Sauder School of Business, University of British Columbia.

Katherine A. Samolyk is a senior economist with the Federal Deposit Insurance Corporation.

C. Tsuriel Somerville is a Professor in the Department of Real Estate at The University of British Columbia.

Paulina Teller is a student researcher assistant, Sauder School of Business, University of British Columbia.

PART I

INTRODUCTION

CHAPTER 1

HOUSEHOLD FINANCE AND THE FINANCIAL DECISION-MAKING PROCESS

Sumit Agarwal and Brent W. Ambrose

Financial economists have long studied how corporations utilize financial instruments, yet relatively little is understood about how consumers and households utilize various credit alternatives in managing their consumption and savings objectives. However, with increasing interest in issues surrounding household behavioral finance, research into household financial decision-making processes is becoming increasingly important. For example, at the 2006 American Finance Association Presidential Address, Professor John Campbell raised a number of critical insights toward our understanding household participation and diversification decisions in the financial markets, as well as their mortgage refinancing decisions. However, Professor Campbell admittedly neglected many other important issues related to households' choice of credit, use or repayment of credit card debt, payday lending, and other relevant issues related to household credits.

The field of household finance seeks to understand how households select, use, and repay financial instruments. One of the reasons financial economists have avoided studying household credit decisions in the past has been due to the lack of micro-level data allowing for reliable empirical testing of theoretical models. However, recent advances in computerized record keeping have created a number of new databases that allow researchers to analyze questions concerning household use of financial credit. As a result, new research is emerging that examines the factors impacting consumer financial choices and the performance of household personal credits.

This book presents a collection of essays by leading researchers studying issues involving households' selection, use, and repayment of credit instruments. The chapters in this book provide readers with a greater understanding of what is currently known about important issues affecting household credit decisions and, should provide a guide for future research.

The Growth in Household Debt

According to the Federal Reserve's Flow of Funds, consumer credit outstanding jumped from $1.98 trillion in January 2000 to $4.01 trillion in November 2006. While overall household credit outstanding doubled over this six-year period, the majority of the growth resulted from real estate debt (first and second mortgages) increasing from $1.4 trillion to $3.2 trillion and consumer credit (credit cards, auto loans, unsecured loans, etc.) growing from $494 billion to $727 billion. In comparison, commercial credit outstanding rose by a modest 19 percent over the same time period.

Interestingly, the growth in consumer credit coincided with a period of modest economic growth. For example, between January 2000 and November 2006, the U.S. Gross Domestic Product (GDP), the general measure of economic activity, grew at a modest quarterly rate of 1.5 percent, the unemployment rate increased from 2.5 percent to 6 percent, and the large-cap stock market index (the S&P 500) ended the period at roughly the same level as at the beginning of the period while the small-cap stock index (the Nasdaq) suffered about a 20 percent decline. In contrast to the stock market, the housing market has experienced a period of remarkable growth and is the bright spot among the economic indicators. For example, over the six-year period, the national median house price index has increased an average of 8 percent per year, with some areas of the country (particularly the two coasts) experiencing considerably greater prices increases.

Another interesting feature of the growth in consumer credit during this decade is that delinquencies on consumer debt have been falling rather than rising. For example, the credit card delinquency rate has fallen from a peak of 5 percent in Q2 2001 to 4 percent in Q3 2006. Finally, recent changes in personal bankruptcy laws lead to a substantial rise in non-business bankruptcy filings prior to October 2005, yet the overall level of personal bankruptcies remained relatively constant. As a result, the past six years has seen a dramatic rise in consumer credit associated with a drop in delinquencies and bankruptcies.

A major concern among policy makers and market participants is that the recent near-record high level of household debt poses a threat to the future growth of the U.S. economy. To better understand the potential impact of the recent increase in household debt, this book contains eclectic chapters of interesting research that explore both the supply as well as the demand side of household credits. On the supply side, readers will gain insights into the use of collateral as well as the use of teaser rates by lenders to extend credit, as well as the risk that lenders face. On the demand side, readers will gain insights into the use and management of credit by households. In turn, the chapters in this book overall provide readers with a better understanding of the environment, options, and risks that households face in selecting, using, and repaying their financial instruments.

Households in Financial Distress

While the rise in household debt has been used to finance household consumption and thus has helped to sustain the U.S. economic growth over the last five years, real income of many American households has been increasing at a relatively slower pace than the increase in their debt holdings. Household debt in America has steadily increased at an annual rate of 5 percent in the last six years while the average real income has dropped slightly by 1.4 percent. Moreover, the Federal Reserve's Flow of Funds report that household debt to disposable income rose from 100 percent in 2001 to about 120 percent in 2005. Therefore, many are concerned with the financial vulnerability of American households to withstand adverse interest rate and/or income shocks, which in turn affects their debt repayment ability.

In Part 2, we present three chapters that provide additional insights into the issues surrounding household debt and financial distress. In Chapter 2, Kathleen Johnson takes a closer look at household's debt repayment ability by analyzing the financial obligations ratio (FOR), a statistics published by the Federal Reserve Board of Governors to broadly measure and track the financial position of American households. In addition to the monthly mortgage and consumer debt payments, the FOR also accounts for household's monthly payment on auto leases, rent, homeowner's insurance, and real estate taxes. Johnson looks into each individual component of the FOR and finds that the increase in the total FOR over the last few years can be attributed to the substantial increase in the revolving credit FOR. She concludes that to the extent that households take advantage of additional access to credit card debts, they may be able to ease their temporary financially distressed situation if the additional debt obligation is not at an unmanageable level.

While underwriting standards by lenders are more relaxed and consumers thereby have easier access to credit, there is also a growing concern that consumers are ill-prepared to make sound decisions in the face of financial distress and a complex financial environment. Many argue that financially less-savvy consumers are also more likely to error in their choice of financial instruments and debt level that is manageable by their disposable income. In addition, financially less-savvy consumers are more likely to incur high interest and fee payments. In chapter 3, Robert Hunt discusses credit counseling as a possible option for those borrowers attempting to manage their financially distressed situation. While credit counseling may seem like a win-win solution for both consumers and lenders, Hunt maintains that the effectiveness of credit counseling has not yet been empirically found

A common perception that grew popular recently is the notion that more and more households are taking advantage of generous bankruptcy exemption laws and are filing for bankruptcy to get out of their highly unmanageable unsecured debt. Recent statistics indicate that personal bankruptcy filings have been increasing at an annual rate of 5 percent since 2001, except for the 30.1 percent increase in bankruptcy filing in 2005 due to a change in the bankruptcy law that stimulated bankruptcy filings just before the new bankruptcy law went into effect in October 2005. In the chapter 4, Andreas Lehnert and Dean Maki empirically test and find that on average states with higher bankruptcy exemptions are more likely to encounter higher bankruptcy rate. In addition, Lehnert and Maki find that households in states with higher bankruptcy exemptions are less likely to use low-return liquid assets to pay off their high-interest unsecured debt.

Household Credit and Payment: Supply, Demand, Usage, and Risk

With advances in the data collection and credit scoring technology, lenders are now able to better assess credit risk as well as credit needs of consumers. In turn, lenders are able to better price individual borrower risk and provide an array of credit options based on consumer needs. Hence, the market has seen a significant increase in competition by lenders to provide consumers with credit. In this section, we take a closer look into the supply and demand as well as the usage and repayment patterns of household credits.

Given the significant rise in home prices as well as the low interest rate environment in recent years, the market for home equity credit has been of the fastest growing credit market these past five years. We begin this section with two chapters that look at the role of collateral on risk and pricing of consumer credit. In chapter 5, Shubhasis Dey and Lucia Dunn look at the role of collateral in lenders' pricing of and borrowers' demand for home equity line of credits. Dey and Dunn empirically find that borrowers with larger collateral in their home are more likely to choose a lower loan-to-value (LTV) contract, thus providing a signal to lenders that they are less risky. In turn, Dey and Dunn consistently find that borrowers with higher LTV ratios are charged higher interest rates because lenders consider higher LTV borrowers hold greater credit risk. In chapter 6, Sumit Agarwal, Brent Ambrose, and Souphala Chomsisengphet empirically analyze the repayment behavior of auto loans to demonstrate how borrowers with higher LTV ratio loans are riskier on average. Agarwal, Ambrose, and Chomsisengphet estimate the prepayment and default risks of automobile loans and find that automobile loans experiencing significant decline in the value of the car (higher current LTV) have higher risk of default and lower risk of prepayment.

Chapters 7 and 8 turn to look at the supply, demand, and usage of credit cards. In chapter 7, Tufan Ekici, Lucia Dunn, and Tae Hyung Kim enlighten readers with the recent phenomenon of aggressive solicitations by credit card lenders. Specifically, Ekici, Dunn, and Kim look at the behaviors of consumers to accept introductory credit card offers and switch card balances. The authors find that riskier as well as younger, less educated, and lower-income borrowers are more likely to accept an introductory credit card. Conditional on having an introductory card, borrowers who are more educated, have higher income, and who are homeowners are more likely to switch a card balance. Their results allow us to better understand how American cardholders are managing their credit cards. In chapter 8, Grace Kim explores the use of credit card by small business owners. Kim finds that small business owners' educational background and management role significantly affects the use of personal credit card.

This section also provides readers with additional insights into the consumer payment market that experienced higher growth than the credit card market in recent years—debit cards. The debit card industry has enjoyed a 20 percent annual growth rate from 1998 to 2004, compared to a 10 percent annual growth rate in the credit card industry. Chapter 9 by Mar Fusaro argues that self-control is the main reason why borrowers prefer to use debit cards over credit cards. Chapter 10 by Sujit Chakravorti explores the growth of consumer credit from an entirely different perspective. Chakravorti argues that over the years, merchants have shifted away from accepting paper-based payments (checks) to electronic payment (credit or debt cards). The decline in paper-based payment instruments is due to the high processing cost, and increased acceptance of electronic instruments is due to consumer preference for electronic payment instruments.

Finally, we conclude this section with chapter 11, which examines a different kind of household credit known as alternative financial service (AFS)—payday loans. In this chapter, Kathleen Samolyk gives readers an overview of the payday industry, a small, unique, and relatively unknown credit market that has dramatically grown since the 1990s. Payday lending provides consumers with a convenient and quick method of obtaining cash that is at a high cost and is partially secured by their checking account. However, the payday industry is relatively unknown and regulations vary by state legislation. Hence, Samolyk's chapter is an important contribution to our understanding of a nonmainstream consumer credit market.

Household Use of Mortgage Debt

As discussed in section 1, home purchasing is the largest and most complex financial decision most consumers ever make. The complexity of the decision process begins with the housing tenure decision, long before any asset is purchased. The housing tenure decision centers on the choice of whether to rent or to buy. Most U.S. households have long held the goal of homeownership and increasing homeownership is stated public policy for many politicians. Yet, few households recognize the implications of the rent/buy decision on their financial wealth later in life. After the housing tenure decision, most households face a highly complex financing decision involving the use of debt and personal capital (equity). The maturation of the U.S. mortgage market has opened up a vast menu of debt products—many containing sophisticated features. Finally, after negotiating the financing decision, the household now faces an ongoing optimization problem involving the embedded option in the debt contract.

Since real estate is a long duration asset and the capital required is often staggering, the repercussions from the home purchase decision can reverberate over decades. Wise (or lucky) housing decisions early in life can lead to great wealth and financial freedom while unwise (or unlucky) decisions can quickly destroy household savings and negatively impact future generations. Thus, research on topics related to the use of mortgage debt can serve the dual purpose of (1) providing policy makers with tools needed to help households make wise financial decisions regarding the largest asset in their portfolio and (2) providing financial institutions with information regarding the use of these products and ways to make them more efficient and profitable.

Part IV contains four chapters devoted to significant issues surrounding the home purchase and financing decision. In chapter 12, Tsur Somerville analyzes the issue of wealth accumulation with respect to the housing tenure decision. Rather than simply take for granted the conventional wisdom that in order to achieve financial independence households should become homeowners, Somerville examines the actual wealth accumulation for a set of Canadian renters and owners over a 25-year period. Contrary to the conventional wisdom, Somerville finds a number of scenarios where households could have achieved significantly greater wealth by renting rather than buying. However, his analysis indicates that a household would have to be a disciplined saver in order to achieve this result. Somerville's analysis drives home the point that homeownership often provides households with an enforced savings program (via the monthly principle paydown of mortgage debt) and it is the systematic enforced saving that drives much of the wealth accumulation effect.

As mentioned earlier, after the housing tenure decision, households face a highly complex menu of mortgage products to finance their home purchase. Monica Paiella and Alberto Pozzolo provide a new analysis of the decision to originate a fixed versus adjustable mortgage contract in chapter 13. The adjustable-rate mortgage (ARM) versus fixed-rate mortgage (FRM) decision can have dramatic consequences on housing affordability. Paiella and Pozzolo analyze a novel dataset of Italian households in order to show that household mortgage choice depends critically on household liquidity and the relative pricing of the mortgage contracts. This result contrasts with previous research indicating that borrower risk aversion is one of the primary factors driving borrower mortgage choice.

One of the recent growth areas in the U.S. mortgage market that coincides with the growth in the U.S. homeownership rate to record levels and the financial market expansion of mortgage product offerings is the advent of the sub-prime borrowing market. Although not well defined, the term sub-prime has come to encompass the origination of mortgages to households that traditionally were unable to obtain traditional mortgage debt products. Typically, these households had poor credit history, unverifiable income, or had insufficient capital for traditional downpayment levels. Chapter 14 by Souphala Chomsisengphet and Anthony Pennington-Cross examines the trends in pricing these new products. Their analysis reveals that the sub-prime mortgage market is characterized by a high degree of risk-based pricing, reflecting borrower credit history and downpayment funds.

Finally, after the housing tenure decision and the mortgage choice decision, households face the monthly (or daily) financial decisions of how to optimize the embedded options in their mortgage contract. The academic literature on this subject is voluminous. Michael LaCour-Little tackles this literature in chapter 15 in order to provide the reader with a synthesis of the current research on residential mortgage default and prepayment. LaCour-Little effectively summarizes the recent findings and offers his perspective on remaining unanswered research questions. As a result, readers of this chapter will gain insights into the complex problem facing each mortgage borrower and perhaps find a spark for future research that may help households manage this most difficult and complex financial instrument.

Regulatory Prospective of Consumer Credit

Ever since the publication of the "Fed Boston Study" there has been a considerable debate on the issue of discrimination in consumer lending (Munnell et al.

1996). Discrimination can occur whenever the terms of a transaction are affected by personal characteristics of the applicant that are not relevant to the transaction. The most commonly considered characteristics of discrimination in application processing are those of race and gender. In the household credit market, this might translate to loan approvals differing across racial or ethnic groups with otherwise similar credit risk characteristics. The Fair Housing Act (FHA) of 1968 and the Equal Credit Opportunity Act (EAOC) of 1974 prohibit discrimination on the basis of protected characteristics, such as race, gender, age, marital status, religion, receipt of public assistance, and handicap. As a result, regulators routinely conduct fair lending exams to ensure enforcement of the above regulations. In chapter 16, Mark Pocock, Irene Fang, and Jason Dietrich outline the regulator's perspective and methodology on modeling and testing for possible fair lending violations in the context of national bank fair lending examination. They also share some of the new statistical tools that the regulator is using to detect fair lending violations. As a result, readers, particularly bankers and community activists, will find this chapter highly valuable to understanding the role of a bank regulator in enforcing fair lending standards.

Reference

A.G. Munnell, L.E. Browne, J. McEneaney, and M.B. Tootell. 1996. "Mortgage Lending in Boston: Interpreting HMDA Data." *American Economic Review* (March) 86(1): 25–53.

PART II

HOUSEHOLD CREDIT—DEMAND AND SUPPLY

CHAPTER 2

RECENT DEVELOPMENTS IN THE CREDIT CARD MARKET AND THE FINANCIAL OBLIGATIONS RATIO

Kathleen W. Johnson

Introduction

Over the past 17 years, U.S. households in the aggregate have devoted an increasing share of their after-tax income to the payment of financial obligations. Part of the increase is attributable to a rise in the level of credit card debt, which has raised the share of households' aggregate after-tax income that is devoted to credit card payments. Much of the rising share of credit card debt in overall financial obligations may stem from several notable changes in the credit card market over this period.

Financial obligations such as credit card debt and housing costs require monthly payments whose level relative to income is, of course, a vital concern to the individual household. A household's choice to take on obligations that increase these payments may represent an accurate assessment by the household of its ability to make payments on its obligations. However, devoting more income to required debt payments and other obligations will make the household more likely to default in the event of job loss or illness.

Likewise, an aggregate measure of payments on household financial obligations relative to income is of interest to economic policy makers because of potential concerns about the vulnerability of the household sector as a whole. In 1980, the Federal Reserve Board began calculating and tracking the ratio of households' aggregate required monthly payments on mortgage and consumer debt to their aggregate after-tax (that is, disposable) income, a measure called the debt service ratio (DSR). To gain a broader picture of households' financial position, the Federal Reserve Board in 2003 introduced a new measure, called the financial obligations ratio (FOR).[1] The new measure added other types of obligations to those of the DSR, namely payments on auto leases and housing expenses for rent, homeowner's insurance, and real estate taxes. As with the DSR, the obligations in the FOR are presented as a share of aggregate, after-tax income.

For a given level of aggregate income, no clear line separates an appropriate level of payments on financial obligations from an excessive one, but the current level of the FOR is elevated relative to historical experience. It stood at 18.75 percent in the first quarter of 2006, a level noticeably above its value 15 years earlier (chart 2.1). Of the major components of the FOR, the ratio of credit card payments to disposable income rose notably over this period. Mortgage payments also rose significantly as a share of income, but payments on other types of debt obligations fell (chart 2.2).

This chapter argues that three important developments in the credit card market over the past 17 years account for most of the rise in credit card payments relative to income. First, improvements in credit-scoring technology and the advent of risk-based pricing of credit card debt have increased the share of households—particularly lower-income households—with a credit card. Second, in the 1990s, credit card interest rates began to vary with changes in broader market interest rates, which in turn led to an especially pronounced decline in credit card interest rates when, beginning in 2001, market rates turned sharply lower; the decline in credit card rates raised the demand for credit card debt. Finally, households have increased their use of credit cards as a convenient means of paying for daily purchases.

Chart 2.1 Household financial obligations ratio (FOR), 1980–2006:Q1

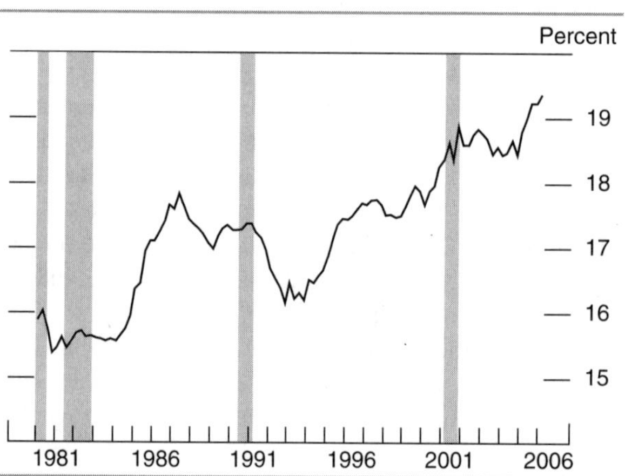

Note: The data are quarterly. Shaded bars are periods of recession as defined by the National Bureau of Economic Research. The FOR consists of the aggregate required monthly payments of the household sector on consumer debt, mortgages, homeowner's insurance, real estate taxes, rent, and auto leases as a percent of aggregate after-tax personal income.

Source: Federal Reserve Board (www.federalreserve.gov/releases/housedebt).

Chart 2.2 Selected components of the financial obligations ratio, 1989–2006:Q1

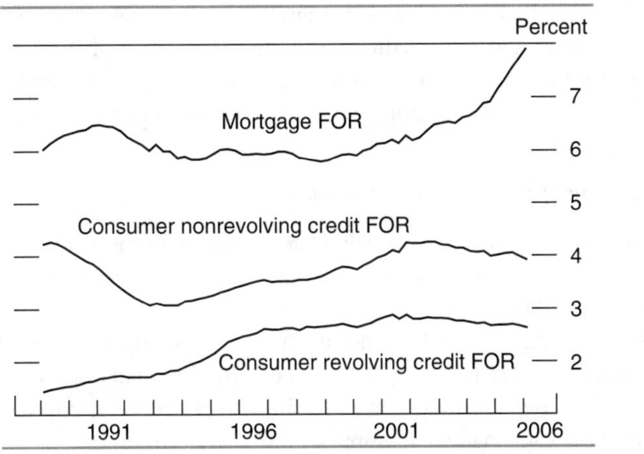

Note: The data are quarterly. For a description of consumer revolving credit, see text note 2. Nonrevolving debt consists of credit accounts that terminate when the balances are paid off; such accounts include loans for motor vehicles, household goods, and education. Data shown for each type of debt are the aggregate required monthly payments for that type as a percent of aggregate after-tax income. See also note to chart 2.1.

Source: Federal Reserve Board.

This chapter estimates the quantitative effect of each of these three developments on the revolving consumer (i.e., nonmortgage) credit portion of the FOR—the ratio of required minimum payments on revolving consumer credit relative to disposable income.[2] The analysis indicates that these three developments in the credit card market together accounted for most of the rise of the revolving credit FOR and played a strong role in the rise of the total FOR.

In the concluding section, this chapter considers these findings in relation to the possible economic implications of the rise in the revolving credit FOR. For example, a rise in required credit card payments stemming from a greater use of credit cards to pay for day-to-day purchases may not signal greater financial vulnerability if households are willing and able to pay off these card charges each month. In addition, the rise in payments associated with the increase in credit availability due to credit scoring may be accompanied by some benefits: More widespread access to credit may help more households maintain their consumption during temporary income disruptions and in turn contribute to the stability of the macroeconomy.

Developments in the Credit Card Market

Three developments in the credit card market likely accounted for much of the rise in household financial obligations over the past 17 years: an expansion in the prevalence of credit cards among lower-income households, the widespread adoption of variable-rate cards, and a greater willingness of households to use their credit cards for day-to-day purchases of goods and services. The available data—from the Federal Reserve Board's triennial Survey of Consumer Finances—allow a comprehensive analysis of the importance of each development for the period. The survey conducted nearest the beginning of the 17-year period was in 1989, and the survey for which the most recent data are available was conducted in 2004. Hence, the period of analysis for this chapter is framed by these two years.

The Expansion of the Credit Card Market

More and more households have gained access to credit cards over the past decade and a half. The share of households with at least one credit card rose from about 70 percent in 1989 to about 75 percent in 2004 (table 2.1). Determining which group of cardholders in 2004 would not have been cardholders in 1989 will help us estimate the effect that the expansion in cardholding had on household financial obligations. Broadly speaking, an expansion of cardholding could arise through two channels. First, changes in supply or demand conditions in the credit card market, holding the characteristics of households fixed, could increase the share of households with credit cards. Such developments may include changes in credit card underwriting standards or a general increase in households' desire for credit cards. Second, changes in household characteristics may increase the percentage of households who qualify for a credit card under a given set of underwriting standards.

The analysis presented later suggests that much if not most of the rise in cardholding over the 1989–2004 period came from an expansion of supply to riskier households—those that would not have qualified for a card in 1989. In the mid-1990s, card issuers began ranking applicants according to their probability of default; instead of denying cards to all those who posed too great a risk for a given

Table 2.1 Proportion of households with at least one credit card, by income quintile, selected years, 1989–2004

Income Quintile	*1989*	*1992*	*1995*	*1998*	*2001*	*2004*	*Percent Increase 1989–2004 (1)*
All	69.5	71.9	74.4	72.7	76.3	74.9	7.7
Lowest	29.3	33.0	38.2	34.7	42.9	41.6	42.1
Second lowest	57.1	66.9	63.9	64.4	67.4	63.7	11.6
Middle	75.9	74.2	78.3	77.7	82.1	79.3	4.5
Second highest	87.1	88.8	91.5	88.5	88.5	91.1	4.6
Highest	95.5	94.6	98.0	96.6	97.1	96.8	1.4

(1) Computed from unrounded data.

Note: For types of credit cards considered and definition of concepts of household and head of household used in the tables, see text note 3.

Source: Here and in the following tables, Federal Reserve Board's Survey of Consumer Finances and author's calculations.

interest rate on the card, they began issuing cards to some of the higher-risk applicants and set the interest rate on these riskier accounts high enough to compensate the lenders for the greater risk.[3] The practice of issuing cards to higher-risk household was a significant change in the supply conditions in the credit card market.

Credit Scoring and Risk-Based Pricing

Lenders can rank applicants according to their likelihood of default through a measure called a credit score, which aggregates the factors in a potential borrower's credit history that are associated with a willingness and ability to pay. The higher the credit score, the more likely is the applicant to pay as agreed on a new credit account. The adoption of flexible, or risk-based, pricing allows creditors to issue cards to less-qualified applicants in exchange for a higher interest rate on the card. Credit scoring was considered by providers of consumer credit as early as the late 1930s, but the practice did not become widespread until the 1990s, when computers capable of processing large amounts of data became widely used.[4]

Risk-based pricing has increased the availability of credit cards for all households, but its effect has been the greatest among riskier households. In particular, the rate of cardholding among households in the lowest quintile of the income distribution rose nearly half, from 29 percent to 42 percent, between 1989 and 2004 (table 2.1), whereas the rate of cardholding rose less than 10 percent in the general population, from 70 percent to 75 percent. Among households in the lowest-income decile (not shown in table 2.1), the rate of cardholding about doubled over the period, from 18 percent to 36 percent. The rate among households who reported having been previously denied credit also rose more than did the overall rate.

These patterns are consistent with an expansion of cardholding through the first channel—in this case, a higher supply of cards through the use of credit scoring. The possibility remains, however, that the increase in cardholding may have also arisen, at least in part, through the second channel—that is, the characteristics of these new cardholders may have improved over the period. For example, they may have demonstrated a better employment history or a better record of paying rent and utility bills; in this case, a rise in creditworthiness could have produced more widespread cardholding among lower-income households rather than a change in underwriting standards. We can sort out the relative influence of the two channels with a statistical model.

Who Are the New Cardholders?

I apply this model to data from the Federal Reserve Board's triennial Survey of Consumer Finances (SCF). Each SCF obtains detailed demographic and financial information from a statistically representative national sample of approximately 3,000 households. The model used here links the characteristics of households in the survey to the probability that they hold at least one credit card.

The characteristics used to predict cardholding were income, wealth, number of children, the age of the household head, and indicators for the sex, marital status,

Table 2.2 Selected characteristics of households, by whether they hold a credit card, 1989 (Percent except as noted)

	Mean	
Characteristic	*Holds a Credit Card*	*Does Not Hold a Credit Card*
Income (thousands of dollars)	63.2	20.0
Wealth (thousands of dollars)	317.8	60.6
Number of children	0.7	0.8
Recently delinqueut (1)	3.3	10.0
Head of household		
Age (years)	48.4	46.9
No high school degree	15.7	44.4
College graduate	36.5	8.1
Married	64.0	35.0
Male	77.3	59.2

Note: (1) Delinquent 60 days or more in the past year.

and education of the household head.[5] The predictors also included an indicator for whether a household was two months or more behind in debt payments in the past year (table 2.2).

These characteristics differ significantly between those households with credit cards and those without and thus serve as good predictors of cardholding. For example, in the 1989 SCF, households that held credit cards had significantly higher wealth and income than non-cardholders (table 2.2, first and second columns). In addition, the heads of cardholding households were more often college-educated, married, or male. Finally, cardholding households were less likely to have been behind on a loan payment in the preceding year.

The statistical model can determine which of these characteristics had an independent effect on cardholding, holding the other characteristics constant.[6] Estimates suggest that all the selected characteristics except age and marital status of the household head had a large and statistically significant influence on the probability that a household held a credit card in 1989 (table 2.2, third column). For example, the results imply that a 1 percent rise in a household's income raised the probability that it held a card 0.32 percentage point, while a 1 percent rise in a household's wealth raised the probability 0.11 percentage point.

The model can also shed light on the extent to which changes in supply factors (lenders' willingness to issue a card to a given household) and demand factors (a given household's interest in holding one) together contributed to the rise in cardholding between 1989 and 2004.[7] Any portion of the rise in credit card availability not attributable to supply and demand factors may be attributable to changes in the financial characteristics that have increased the creditworthiness of households. To separate these effects, I estimated the model first with data from the 1989 SCF and then with data from the 2004 SCF. Using the two sets of estimates and the characteristics of households in the two years, I first calculated the overall change in the estimated probability of cardholding between 1989 and 2004 (table 2.3, first row, first column). To isolate the effect of changes in supply and demand conditions between these years, I calculated a hypothetical probability of cardholding in 2004 based on the 1989 household characteristics and the 2004 estimation results. In other words, I predicted which households would have been holding cards in 2004 if there had been no changes in the characteristics of households over time. The difference between this hypothetical probability for 2004 and the estimated probability for 1989 corresponds to the effect of changes in supply and demand conditions from 1989 to 2004 (table 2.3, second column). The part of the overall change in the estimated probability not explained by changes in supply and demand is that associated with changes in household characteristics (table 2.3, third column).

For the general population, the results imply that changes in supply and demand conditions account for none of a 5 percentage point *overall* rise in the estimated probability of cardholding. But, in the lowest quintile of income, where the estimated probability of cardholding rose far more than the average, all of the effect is attributable to supply and demand factors. Although the model cannot distinguish changes in supply from changes in demand, the result is certainly consistent with an increase in the supply of credit cards for the lowest-income households.[8]

The model can also be used to identify the likely households in each survey who acquired cards most recently. Such households are termed "new cardholders" and are defined as those households with the lowest estimated probability of holding a credit card. An examination of changes in the characteristics of these households over time again suggests an increase in the supply of credit cards to riskier households (table 2.4). New cardholders in later surveys are more likely to have been delinquent on a loan in the preceding six months and are also younger and have more children; these patterns suggest that new cardholders now are likely less creditworthy than those in the past (table 2.4). Work by other researchers, who

Table 2.3 Change in the estimated probability that a household holds a credit card, and source of change, by income quintile, selected years, 1989–2004 (Percent except as noted)

		Source of Change	
Income Quintile	*Change in Probability*	*Change in Supply and Demand Conditions*	*Change in Household Characteristics*
All	5	0	5
Lowest	18	19	−1
Second lowest	5	2	3
Middle	5	−2	7
Second highest	1	−4	5
Highest	−1	−3	2

Note: For details, see text.

Table 2.4 Financial and demographic characteristics of existing and new cardholders, selected years, 1992–2004 (Percent except as noted)

	1992	*1995*	*1998*	*2001*	*2004*
Estimated existing cardholders					
Income (thousands of dollars)	56.8	61.4	69.7	85.3	80.2
Wealth (thousands of dollars)	288.5	318.8	394.4	534.1	558.1
Number of children	0.7	0.7	0.7	0.6	0.6
Recently delinquent (1)	2.5	3.2	4.2	2.4	4.2
Head of household					
Age (years)	48.7	48.7	49.3	49.7	50.8
No high school degree	9.7	9.1	7.4	5.9	5.2
College graduate	41.7	40.0	43.8	45.2	47.4
Married	64.1	62.4	61.9	63.2	60.9
Male	77.7	77.6	78.0	79.4	77.3
Estimated new cardowners					
Income (thousands of dollars)	8.6	11.4	12.5	16.1	13.7
Wealth (thousands of dollars)	21.0	24.9	8.4	23.8	23.6
Number of children	0.7	0.7	1.1	0.9	1.0
Recently delinquent (1)	9.3	12.9	24.1	19.2	20.5
Head of household					
Age (years)	50.8	52.3	44.6	46.1	44.3
No high school degree	54.8	53.8	50.6	43.2	40.1
College graduate	0.3	5.1	6.2	2.1	10.1
Married	18.5	23.6	16.5	20.7	12.8
Male	62.5	53.5	66.2	60.5	52.8

Note: (1) Delinquent 60 days or more in the past year.

examined the 1989–1995 period, corroborates the view that the average cardholder has become riskier—the average cardholder had less job seniority, had lower income, had lower liquid assets, was more willing to use debt to finance consumption (an attitude considered to be a "riskier" view of credit), and was more likely to be single and be a renter.[9]

The credit card debt taken on by these new cardholders probably raises the ratio of aggregate measured revolving credit payments to aggregate income. The effect on the overall FOR may be damped, however, if these households substituted credit card debt for other measured forms of credit, such as personal loans and installment loans. But given that access to these forms of credit for these new cardholders was likely limited in the past, substitution (to the degree it occurred) was probably out of unmeasured forms of debt. For example, in a survey of households in low- and moderate-income areas of Los Angeles, Chicago, and Washington, 53 percent of respondents said they would rely on friends or family to borrow $500 for three months, and 15 percent said they had obtained financing from institutions not captured by aggregate statistics, such as pawn shops, payday lenders, and rent-to-own establishments.[10]

Closer Relation of Credit Card Interest Rates to Broader Market Rates

The second important development in the credit card market is the closer relation of credit card interest rates to broader market rates. In particular, this development allowed credit card interest rates to move down when market rates began to fall in 2001, which in turn significantly boosted the demand for credit card debt and the payments required to service this debt.

One might expect credit card interest rates to vary with the cost of funds, given the important role of these costs in lenders' credit card expenses.[11] But, in the 1980s and early 1990s, credit card interest rates changed little, showing a correlation with the prime rate (a good measure of the cost of funds) of only about 0.09 (see appendix 1 "Theories of Credit Card Interest Rate 'Stickiness'" for a discussion of some possible reasons for this early unresponsiveness). The correlation subsequently rose sharply, and it has averaged 0.8 during the past ten years. The average credit card interest rate in real terms (i.e., adjusted for inflation) declined in tandem with the real prime rate from the first quarter of 2001 to the second quarter of 2004, when the real prime rate hit its most recent low (chart 2.3).

The rapid growth of variable-rate cards since 1989 materially contributed to the increase in the flexibility in interest rates on credit cards. A variable-rate credit card carries an interest rate that maintains a constant margin, or spread, over a stated market reference rate such as the prime rate or the LIBOR (the London interbank offered rate). In 1989, variable-rate credit cards accounted for only about 3 percent of credit card accounts. By 1994, this share had grown to about 60 percent; it is now probably close to 75 percent.[12]

Chart 2.3 Average real credit card interest rate and the real prime rate, 1989–2006:Q1

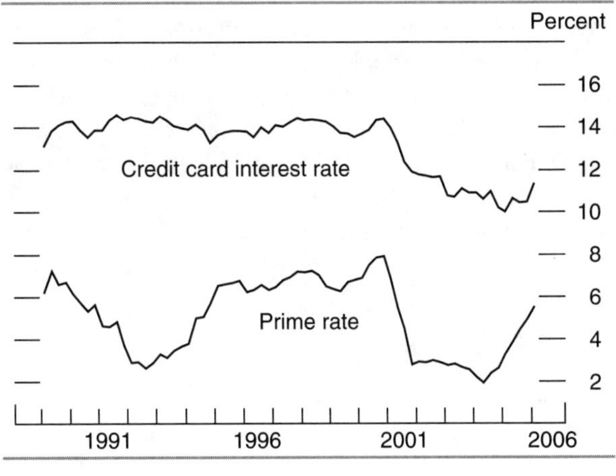

Note: The data are quarterly.

Source: Federal Reserve Board.

A key to the lender's choice of variable-rate versus fixed-rate pricing lies in the behavior of cardholders who are the most profitable to card issuers.[13] In general, the most profitable cardholders are those who carry large amounts of debt on their cards because they pay more interest than other cardholders (although this benefit is offset by the fact that some high-debt cardholders may have a higher likelihood of default). Several factors have increased the odds that profitable cardholders will switch to lower-rate cards; these factors have thus increased the incentive for lenders to lower credit card interest rates when their cost of funds allows it.

The first of these factors is that households may have become better able to predict how much credit card debt they will carry from month to month in the future and how much in interest costs they will incur. According to recent research, most consumers who were presented with a choice between two credit card contracts chose the contract that was optimal given their actual future borrowing.[14] This realistic assessment by cardholders of their borrowing needs implies that a large proportion of borrowers who carry debt will respond to an offer of a card with a lower rate.

A second reason that consumers with relatively large amounts of credit card debt may be more responsive to changes in credit card interest rates is that the cost of searching for a lower-rate card has declined. For example, a dramatic increase in advertising by credit card companies may have made it easier to compare rates across cards. The number of credit card solicitations jumped from about 12 per U.S. household in 1989 to about fifty-four in 2005.[15] In addition, the Internet has become a potent source of information about credit card terms; a recent online search of the term "compare credit card interest rates" yielded about 18,000 results. Changes in federal law have probably also made it easier for households to compare credit card terms. In 1988, the Congress amended the Truth in Lending Act to require that all credit card solicitations include information about the annual percentage rate, annual fee, minimum finance charge, transaction charge, grace period, balance computation method, cash advance fee, late payment fee, over-the-limit fee, and balance transfer fee.[16]

Lastly, credit card lenders have invested in information technology that allows them to better identify the least risky households with high levels of credit card debt. As a result, lenders can make offers to only those high-debt consumers who are expected to be profitable. Thus, although consumers with high levels of credit card debt are more likely than others to be turned down for a credit card, the gap in probabilities is narrowing.[17] All told, these developments have likely increased the share of switching done by profitable households with high levels of credit card debt and in turn have increased the incentive for lenders to adjust credit card interest rates.

Credit Cards as a Payment Method

A third important development in the credit card market is an increase in the transactions demand for credit cards. Such demand harks back to the purpose of the original third-party charge card, which was issued in 1950 by Diners' Club for use in restaurants.[18] Charges had to be paid in full each month, so the card represented only a convenient payment method rather than a way to obtain longer-term financing. American Express cards were launched in 1958, also as transaction cards, but Bank of America followed in the same year with the first general-purpose credit card on which only a portion of the balance needed to be paid each month.

Over time, many financial institutions began offering cards that offered the option of paying only a portion of the balance each month. Although the long-term-loan component of credit card debt came to exceed the transactions component, the transactions demand for credit cards has nonetheless continued to grow. For transactions, credit cards have several advantages over cash. First, unlike cash, a credit card may offer consumers protection when it is lost or stolen. Second, credit cards permit households to earn interest on their funds during the period between the transaction and the payment of the credit card bill (the interest earned in this way is known as "float"). Indeed, researchers have found that households with credit cards tend to have lower balances in their transactions accounts than do households without credit cards, suggesting that households may be holding funds in accounts that offer higher yields until they need to pay off their credit cards.[19] Credit cards also offer the consumer an advantage over checks in that it is faster to swipe a card through a terminal than to write a check.

In more recent years, transactions demand for credit cards has been spurred by card issuers that have responded to increasingly intense competition by offering rewards for heavy credit card use. Such rewards include cash-back rebates on purchases, discounts on merchandise, and "mileage" programs that cover travel expenses. These programs, which add to the benefits of using cards over cash, encourage the transactions use of cards because they generally do not require the cardholder to carry the balance from month to month to receive the rewards.[20]

Transactions demand has also grown because opportunities for credit card transactions have risen in the past decade.[21] According to the Census Bureau, sales over the Internet and by mail-order have increased considerably in recent years, and credit cards likely are used for many of these transactions. Sales in these categories have increased close to 28 percent per year since 1999, the first year for which e-commerce data were collected.[22] Even traditional brick-and-mortar stores have increased their acceptance of credit cards. In 1989, about 2.75 million merchants accepted Visa cards; by 2005, that number had reached 6.33 million.[23]

Increased transactions demand raises the aggregate level of credit card debt outstanding as currently measured. Suppose, for example, that a consumer charges $500 on the fifteenth day of one month and pays it off on the fifteenth day of the next month. Aggregate credit is measured as the stock of debt at the end of each month; so the measured estimates will capture the $500 owed at the end of the month in which the charge was made. Thus, measured aggregate credit includes debt that will be paid off in the next month (transactions demand) as well as debt that will be paid off over a longer period. If transactions demand rises more rapidly than the demand for longer-term debt, then measured aggregate debt will also grow faster than the demand for debt.

According to recent research, transactions demand as a share of measured revolving debt rose from about 6 percent in 1992 to 11 percent in 2004.[24] This analysis also suggests that the growth in transactions demand was particularly rapid in the latter part of the 1990s. Had transactions demand remained constant from

1992 to 2001, the growth of measured credit card debt during that period would have been slower by about 1 percentage point per year, and the level of credit card debt in 2001 would have been 7.5 percent lower than it actually was. These results are roughly consistent with data from a quarterly Federal Reserve survey of banks, which suggest that transactions demand accounted for about 10 percent of measured credit card debt over the past decade and a half.[25]

Developments in the Credit Card Market and the Revolving Credit FOR

The 1.25 percentage point rise in the revolving consumer credit portion of the financial obligations ratio between 1989 and 2004 is almost as large as the rise in the total FOR over that period.[26] How much of the increase in the revolving credit FOR is attributable to the developments in the credit card market discussed earlier? One can estimate the contribution by comparing actual financial obligations with those associated with "counterfactual" scenarios in which the effect of changes in the credit card market are removed from the data. The following sections present a counterfactual scenario for each of the three credit card market developments and one for all three together.

The Effect of the Increase in Cardholding

The effect of new cardholders on the revolving credit FOR can be estimated by calculating the ratio under the counterfactual scenario that the proportion of households holding at least one card remained at its 1989 level. Using the statistical model described earlier, cardholders were divided into one group that probably acquired cards after 1989, called new cardholders, and another group that probably had credit cards before 1989, called existing cardholders. The counterfactual revolving credit FOR was based on the debt of only the latter group, and the difference between the counterfactual and actual revolving credit FOR represents the effect of new cardholders.

New cardholders are defined as those households with the lowest probability of holding a credit card (see also table 2.2). For each triennial SCF from 1992 to 2004, enough new cardholders were removed from the group of cardholders to reduce the share of households with cards to its 1989 value.[27] The growth in credit card debt associated with the households who acquired cards after 1989 accounted for about 9 percent of the growth in total credit card debt between 1989 and the first quarter of 2006.[28]

The counterfactual revolving credit FOR with the debt of the new cardholders removed is below the actual level (chart 2.4). The results imply that had the share of households with credit cards remained at its 1989 level, the rise in the FOR would have been about 10 basis points smaller than it actually was. A general substitution toward credit cards from other types of consumer loans and, more recently, away from credit cards toward mortgages also affected the amount of credit card debt, although the effect on overall household financial obligations is ambiguous (see appendix 2 "Substitution between Credit Cards and Other Forms of Credit").

Chart 2.4 Effect on the revolving credit FOR of an increasing share of households that own credit cards, 1989–2006:Q1

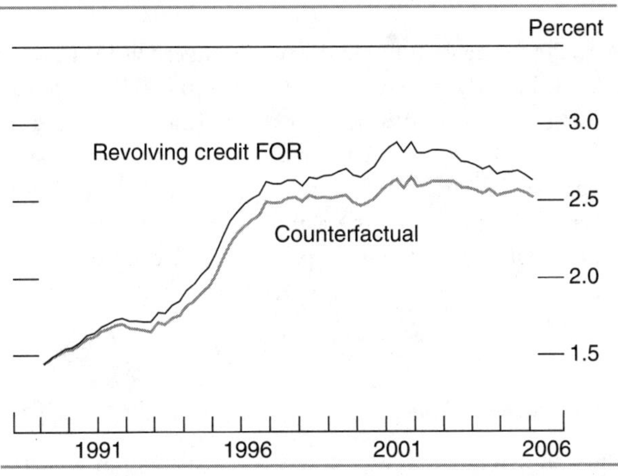

Note: The data are quarterly. The counterfactual data consist of the consumer revolving credit FOR only for households that had a credit card in 1989. For details, see text; see also note to chart 2.2.

Source: Federal Reserve Board and author's calculations.

The Effect of Variable Interest Rates

The greater responsiveness of credit card interest rates to market rates, combined with a significant change in market rates in the early part of this decade, had a substantial effect on household financial obligations. The average real credit card interest rate fell more than 3 percentage points from the fourth quarter of 2001 to the second quarter of 2004, when it reached its low point, about 11.25 percent. When credit card interest rates fall, households demand significantly more credit card debt. For example, researchers have estimated that a 1 percent decline in interest rates on bank-issued credit cards leads to a 1.33 percent rise in the demand for credit card debt.[29]

A decline in credit card interest rates that leads to a smaller margin over the cost of funds could also cause lenders to reduce their supply of credit card debt, which in turn could damp the amount of credit card debt outstanding. However, in the short run, the effect seems unlikely to be large because credit cards are open-ended credit contracts that specify only a credit limit. Most lenders are unwilling to reduce the credit line extended to existing customers in good standing. In a recent survey, 53 percent of banks reported reducing cardholder credit limits but usually only because the borrower had become riskier in some way. Hence, the responsiveness of demand to a change in rates would likely be the dominant determinant of the response of revolving debt outstanding to such a change.

To gauge the effect of changes in credit card interest rates on the revolving credit FOR, a counterfactual level of revolving credit was estimated under the assumption that interest rates on credit cards remained at their level in the first quarter of 1989. In particular, the change in real credit card debt predicted by the change in real credit card interest rates was subtracted from the actual level of debt.

From 1989 to 2000, the counterfactual revolving credit FOR follows the actual revolving credit FOR fairly closely (chart 2.5); this tracking is not surprising given that the real interest rate moved little over this period. Beginning in 2001, when the real credit card interest rate began to decline, the counterfactual revolving credit FOR began to lag the actual. By mid-2004, the counterfactual series was about 1/3 percentage point below the actual. This gap implies that the decline in real credit card interest rates in the early part of this decade accounts for a material part of the rise in the revolving credit FOR between 1989 and the first quarter of 2006.[30]

The Effect of Transactions Demand

As noted earlier, transactions-related credit card balances as a share of measured revolving debt rose from about 6 percent in 1992 to 11 percent in 2004. To estimate the effect of this increase in transactions demand on the revolving credit FOR, a counterfactual ratio was calculated under the assumption that the transactions demand for credit cards did not grow as a fraction of total revolving credit after 1989. In the first quarter of 2006, the counterfactual level of the revolving credit FOR was a little more than a quarter percentage point lower than the actual

Chart 2.5 Effect on the revolving credit FOR of a falling real interest rate, 1989–2006:Q1

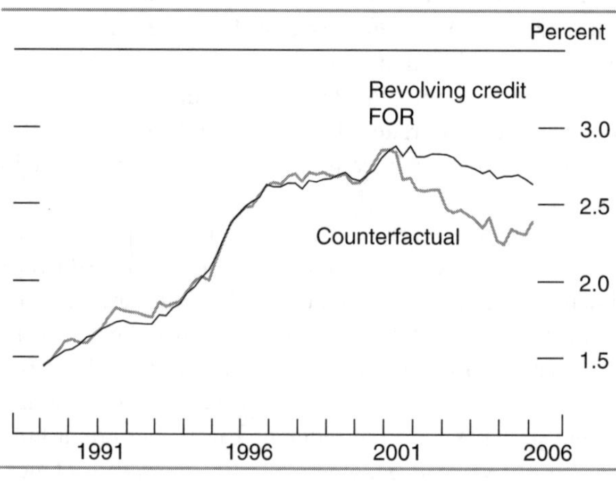

Note: The data are quarterly. The counterfactual data consist of the consumer revolving credit FOR predicted if the average real credit card interest rate had remained at its 1989:Q1 level. For details, see text; see also note to chart 2.2.

Source: Federal Reserve Board and author's calculations.

Chart 2.6 Effect on the revolving credit FOR of rising transactions-related use of credit cards, 1989–2006:Q1

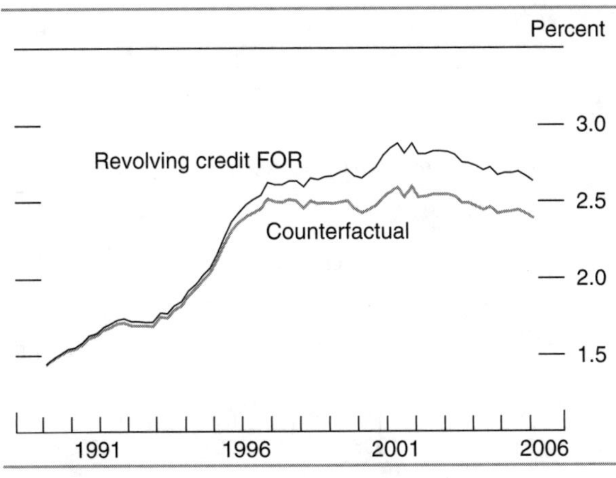

Note: The data are quarterly. The counterfactual data consist of the consumer revolving credit FOR predicted if the proportion of credit card debt arising from transactions-related use had remained at its 1989 level. For details, see text; see also note to chart 2.2.

Source: Federal Reserve Board and author's calculations.

revolving credit FOR (chart 2.6); this gap represents the cumulative effect of the rise in transactions demand since 1989.

The Combined Effect of the Three Credit Card Market Developments

A simple combination of the estimated effects of the increase in the share of households that hold credit cards, the fall in real credit card interest rates, and the rise in transactions demand explains a large portion of the net increase in the overall revolving credit FOR since 1989 (chart 2.7). However, these effects may not be entirely independent of one another; as a result, the sum of the three effects should be considered an upper bound. For example, a decline in the interest rate may cause an increase in debt partly because it may prompt households to apply for a first credit card; in this case, the sum of the influences captures the interest rate effect twice. Yet, the overlap may be limited by the fact that these effects, to some degree, pertain to different segments of the credit card market. For example, transactions demand has grown mainly among upper-income households that have held credit cards for a long time and are not sensitive to interest rates because they pay off their credit card balances each month.

Conclusion

Three developments in the credit card market contributed to the rise in the overall household FOR during the past 17 years. Had the share of households with

Chart 2.7 Combined effects on the revolving credit FOR of developments in the credit card market, 1989–2006:Q1

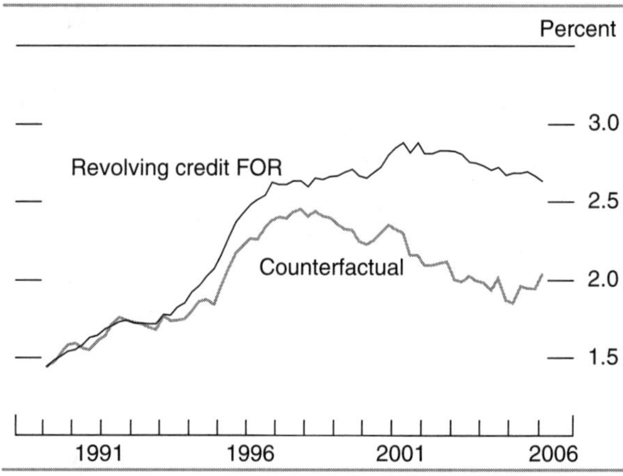

Note: The data are quarterly. The counterfactual data combine the effects of the developments shown in charts 4–6. For details, see text; see also note to chart 2.2.

Source: Federal Reserve Board and author's calculations.

credit cards, the level of credit card interest rates, and the transactions-related demand for credit cards all remained at their 1989 levels, credit card debt outstanding would have been significantly lower. In the absence of other changes, the rise in the total FOR would have been as much as two-thirds of a percentage point smaller than it actually was (chart 2.8).

The various sources of the rise in the revolving credit FOR have differing implications for the health of the household sector and the broader financial system. For example, the part of the rise stemming from a greater use of credit cards to pay for day-to-day purchases will not necessarily signal greater financial vulnerability among households if they are willing and able to pay off these card charges each month. As a related matter, the growth of transactions demand as a share of new borrowing may lessen the exposure of credit card issuers to defaults if households are more likely to pay off transaction balances than they are longer-term balances.

However, the implications of the rise in financial obligations associated with the decline in credit card interest rates in the early part of this decade are more complicated. A key issue would be the effect on households as interest rates rise. An increase in interest rates would likely damp demand for credit card debt, leading to some reversal of the rise in the revolving credit FOR. At the same time, rising rates could make it more difficult for some households to repay their existing debt.

Whether the rise in the share of households with a credit card is a cause for concern at the aggregate level depends on whether the benefits to the macroeconomy of the expansion of credit card availability outweigh the risks. New cardholders

Chart 2.8 Household financial obligations ratio, 1980–2006:Q1

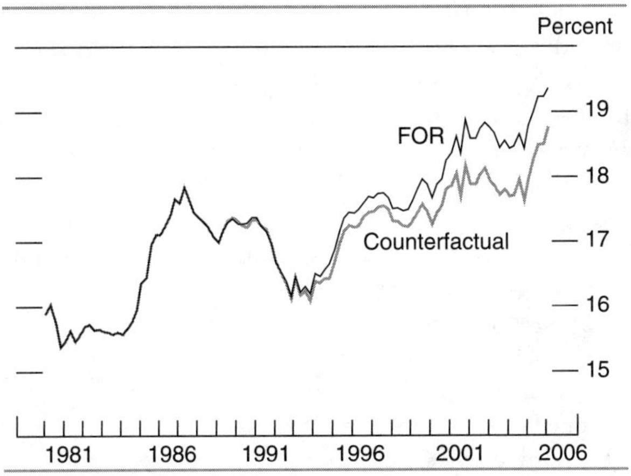

Note: The data are quarterly. The counterfactual series assumes that the level of revolving debt equals the level used to calculate the counterfactual revolving credit FOR. For details, see text; see also note to chart 2.7.

Source: Federal Reserve Board and author's calculations.

may be less adept at managing their credit than existing cardholders, and ready access to credit may make them more prone to taking on unmanageable levels of financial obligations. However, this ready access to credit may also help them maintain their consumption during temporary income disruptions, which could help smooth macroeconomic fluctuations.[31]

All told, an important implication of the analysis here is that researchers should exercise caution when comparing levels of the financial obligations ratio over long periods. Specifically, the factors behind an increase in the FOR should be identified and evaluated before one concludes that the increase implies greater financial fragility for the U.S. household sector or for the macroeconomy more broadly.

Appendix 1: Theories of Credit Card Interest Rate "Stickiness"

Credit card interest rates did not respond to changes in the cost of funds before the mid-1990s. The causes of this interest rate "stickiness" have been debated in the economics literature. Many authors have asserted that when the cost of funds declined, credit card lenders did not reduce their interest rates because doing so seemed likely to attract borrowers who were less profitable.[32]

One theory posited three types of credit card consumer to explain why only less profitable consumers were likely to switch to cards with lower interest rates.[33] The first type used a credit card only to transact (make day-day-purchases) and did not carry a balance. The second type used a card to borrow and planned to carry a balance. The third type did not plan on borrowing for the long term but ultimately was likely to carry a balance. The first and third types would not switch cards when a lower interest rate alternative was presented because they did not think they would borrow and pay interest; only consumers who knew they would borrow would decide to switch. If those who planned to carry a balance were less profitable than other consumers (perhaps because they have higher default rates), firms would be reluctant to reduce their interest rates.

Another theory explained sticky interest rates by asserting that the most profitable customers had higher costs both of searching for a new card and of switching to that card.[34] In this argument, consumers with high amounts of debt were the most profitable for the credit card lenders.[35] But these consumers were also the least likely to search for a card with a lower interest rate because they were more impatient (which is why they borrowed so much) and because they were more likely to be turned down for a new card owing to their high debt. All told, these factors implied that a firm that lowered its rates would have its pool of borrowers shift toward less profitable ones (those with less debt) because they were the most likely to switch to a lower-rate card.

A third theory asserted that credit card interest rates appeared sticky because borrowers switched from credit cards to other forms of financing when the cost of funds declined.[36] In response to the loss of borrowers, credit card lenders lent to riskier households and charged them higher interest rates to compensate for their higher probability of default. This change in the composition of credit card borrowers offset the effect of a lower cost of funds; thus, credit card interest rates did not decline with the cost of funds.

Appendix 2: Substitution between Credit Cards and Other Forms of Credit

Over the past 17 years, households appear to have substituted some forms of credit for others. The rise in the share of household debt associated with credit card loans mirrored a decline in so-called personal loans and loans tied specifically to the purchase of durable goods other than vehicles in the early part of this period. Trends in more recent years suggest that households may have been using mortgage loans as an alternative to credit card debt. The effect of this substitution on household financial obligations depends on the different terms associated with the different forms of debt.

Credit card loans have, in some respects, a significant advantage over personal loans (defined as unsecured, closed-end loans used to finance unspecified expenditures) and the installment loans from department stores and finance companies that traditionally have been used to purchase large durable goods other than vehicles. In particular, the open-ended nature of credit card loans implies a lower fixed cost of borrowing: Households may draw on their credit card accounts to obtain needed funds (as long as borrowing remains below a preset limit) as opposed to taking out an entirely new loan.

In deciding what form of credit to use, households weigh this cost advantage of credit cards against other traits of alternative loan types. One important feature is the interest rate. Because neither credit card loans nor personal loans are backed by collateral, interest rates are relatively high on both types of credit. All else equal, interest rates on installment loans backed by nonvehicle durable goods tend to be lower because they are secured. On balance, households appear to find the convenience of credit card loans to be appealing, as the ratio of nonvehicle non-revolving loans to consumer loans dropped from 12 percent in 1989 to 6 percent in 2001.

The substitution of credit cards for other types of consumer loans may not have a large effect on the amount of consumer debt outstanding if households are simply replacing one form of credit for an equal amount of credit card debt. However, substitution can affect households' regular debt-related financial obligations if the terms of credit card debt are different from the terms of the debt it replaced. For example, at current interest rates, the minimum required payment on a credit card loan would be 13 percent less than the payment on a personal loan of the same size. Even though the interest rates are similar, the credit card loan has a payment equivalent to a personal loan with a maturity almost one year longer than that of the typical personal loan.

In the past couple of years, households may have been substituting mortgage debt for credit card debt. For example, in 2005, outstanding mortgage debt increased about 14 percent, while credit card loans grew only about 4 percent. Mortgage loans can be an attractive alternative to credit card borrowing because they have lower interest rates and mortgage interest payments are tax deductible. Indeed, in surveys, households report using a significant share of the proceeds from cash-out mortgage refinancing transactions—which involve liquidating home equity by taking out a larger mortgage loan—to pay down credit card loans.[37] All told, substitution toward first-lien mortgages tends to lower required payments on financial obligations because they have lower interest rates and longer maturities. However, substitution toward mortgage debt does not always reduce required debt payments; for example, the terms on home equity lines of credit (generally a junior lien) are usually similar to those on credit card debt. The transfer of consumer debt to mortgage debt may be limited by the higher costs of defaulting on a mortgage (which could involve loss of the home) and the fact that only homeowners have access to mortgage credit.

Notes

This work is an updated version of an article originally published as "Recent Developments in the Credit Card Market and the FOR." Federal Reserve Bulletin, Fall 2005. www.federalreserve.gov/pubs/bulletin/default.htm. I thank Tsz-Yan Doris Sum for research assistance and Gregg Forte for editing assistance. The views expressed in this work do not necessarily reflect those of the Board of Governors of the Federal Reserve System or of its Staff.

1. See Dynan, Johnson, and Pence (2003).
2. A credit card account is a type of consumer (i.e., nonmortgage) revolving credit. Generally, revolving credit extensions can be made at the customer's discretion, provided that they do not cause the outstanding balance of the account to exceed a prearranged credit limit. Revolving credit repayments are also at the customer's

discretion, subject to a prearranged minimum, and may be made in one or more installments. More than 90 percent of consumer revolving debt is credit card debt.

3. Edelberg (2003).
4. McCorkell (2002).
5. See Bucks, Kennickell, and Moore (2006) for a presentation of results of the 2004 SCF (the most recent survey for which data are available); see page 30 of that work for a definition of the terms *household* and *head of household* used here. The types of cards considered in the surveys include bank-issued cards, store cards and charge accounts, gasoline company cards, and so-called travel and entertainment cards such as American Express and Diners' Club (p. 24, note 27).
6. This technique, called a probit model, has been used by Klee (2004) and Duca and Whitesell (1995). The model does a fairly accurate job of predicting whether each household in the 1989 data set held a credit card. It correctly predicts actual card-holding for 91 percent of households with at least one card and 56 percent of households with no card, for an overall correct prediction rate of 81 percent.
7. The model cannot identify supply factors separately from demand factors.
8. See also Bostic (2002).
9. Black and Morgan (1998).
10. Siedman, Hababou, and Kramer (2005). Rent-to-own establishments offer consumers the option to acquire the ownership of merchandise by renting it for a specified period of time.
11. One industry source found that the cost of funds accounted for 43 percent of the cost of credit extended through credit cards between 1990 and 1993 (*Credit Card News*, May issue of various years).
12. Stango (2002) and author's calculations.
13. The greater prevalence of variable-rate cards can also be explained by an increase in market concentration (see Stango, 2000), and, indeed, the ten largest card issuers doubled their market share from 40 percent in 1989 to about 80 percent in 2004.
14. Agarwal and others (2005). The data used in this work cannot demonstrate a change from the early to late 1990s in households' ability to assess their borrowing needs.
15. http://core.synovate.com/MAILVOL.asp.
16. One might argue that profitable, high-debt consumers are indifferent to changes in search costs because they tend to be impatient. Analyses of SCF data by Calem and Mester (1995) do show a negative relationship between high credit card debt and willingness to shop for better credit card terms; however, work by Calem, Gordy, and Mester (2005), Crook (2002), and the present author indicate that the relationship has weakened since then.
17. This assertion is based on an analysis of 1989 and 2001 SCF data by the present author that builds on work by Calem and Mester (1995).
18. See Evans and Schmalensee (1999).
19. See, e.g., Duca and Whitesell (1995); White (1976); and Mandell (1972). Transactions accounts are checking, savings, and money market accounts as well as cash accounts at brokerages.
20. Card issuers can benefit from an increase in transactions demand because they receive revenue from the fees they levy on the merchant for each transaction.
21. However, the increase in these opportunities has also enabled the growth of a substitute for the transaction demand for credit cards—the use of debit cards. Zinman (2005) provides evidence that households that cannot take advantage of float because they carry a balance on their credit cards tend to use debit cards. Klee

(2004) identifies several factors that may have led to an increase in debit card use, perhaps at the expense of credit cards.

22. The Census Bureau defines e-commerce sales as "sales of goods and services where an order is placed by the buyer or price and terms of sale are negotiated over an Internet, extranet, Electronic Data Interchange (EDI) network, electronic mail, or other online system. Payment may or may not be online." U.S. Department of Commerce (2005).
23. http://www.usa.visa.com/.
24. Johnson (2004).
25. Quarterly Report of Credit Card Interest Rates (FR 2248) http://*www.federalreserve.gov*/boarddocs/reportforms/ReportDetail.cfm.
26. The revolving consumer credit portion of the FOR—the level of monthly payments on such credit relative to disposable income—is calculated from the level of revolving credit balances. Payments on revolving credit balances—the numerator of the revolving credit FOR—are assumed to be 2.5 percent of those balances. This assumption corresponds to the average minimum required payment implied by responses to the Federal Reserve System's January 1999 Senior Loan Officer Survey on Bank Lending Practices. In that survey, loan officers also indicated that minimums had not changed substantially over the previous decade. Responses to the 2003 Consumer Action survey of banks also implied an average minimum payment of between 2 and 3 percent (*Consumer Action News*, "Annual Credit Card Survey 2003").

    More recently, some lenders have changed their payment formula so that minimum payments equal current finance charges and fees plus some small amount of the outstanding balance (*Consumer Action News*, "Annual Credit Card Survey 2005"). This new formula could raise or lower required payments depending on the interest rate and the amount of balance repaid. (For the *Consumer Action News* surveys, see www.consumer-action.org/English/library/credit_cards/index.php.)
27. About 2.5 percent of cardholders were removed in 1992, 6.5 percent in 1995, 4 percent in 1998, 8.5 percent in 2001, and 6 percent in 2004. To extend the analysis through the first quarter of 2006, the share of credit card debt held by new cardholders was held constant at its 2004 value.
28. This estimated effect is slightly smaller than that calculated by Yoo (1997, 1998), who assumes that new cardholders have the same amount of debt as existing holders. However, new cardholders appear to have a bit less debt than existing holders; e.g., in 2001, the average credit card balance of a new cardholder was about $2,180, whereas the average balance of an existing cardholder was $2,332.
29. Gross and Souleles (2002). This effect was estimated without accounting for households switching balances between cards as interest rates change. Accounting for this switching reduces the rise in demand to about 1 percent.
30. This analysis ignores the point that interest rates on mortgages fell as well over this period, a development that likely induced households to borrow more against their homes and use the proceeds to pay down credit card debt, which is more costly. See appendix "Substitution between Credit Cards and Other Forms of Credit" for a more complete discussion of this potential effect.
31. See Dynan, Elmendorf, and Sichel (2006).
32. Because they were written at a time when general market rates were declining, these papers do not address the causes of upward stickiness, that is, the reasons why credit card interest rates did not rise with general market rates.
33. Ausubel (1991).

34. Calem and Mester (1995).
35. This assertion is plausible: According to *Credit Card News* (May issue, various years) interest charges on borrowing accounted for an average of 73 percent of the revenue of credit card lenders between 1990 and 1993. However, some portion of the profits from interest charges levied on high-debt consumers would be offset by their greater propensity to default.
36. Brito and Hartley (1995).
37. Canner, Dynan, and Passmore (2002).

References

Agarwal, Sumit, Souphala Chomsisengphet, Chunlin Liu, and Nicholas S. Souleles. 2005. "How Well Do Consumers Forecast Their Future Borrowing?" Paper presented at the conference "Recent Developments in Consumer Credit and Payments," sponsored by the Federal Reserve Bank of Philadelphia, September 29–30.

Ausubel, Lawrence M. 1991. "The Failure of Competition in the Credit Card Market," *American Economic Review* 81 (March): 50–81.

Black, Sandra E., and Donald P. Morgan. 1998. "Risk and the Democratization of Credit Cards." Research Paper 9815. New York: Federal Reserve Bank of New York, June.

Bostic, Raphael. 2002. "Trends in Equal Access to Credit Products." In Thomas A. Durkin and Michael E. Staten, eds., *The Impact of Public Policy on Consumer Credit.* Boston: Kluwer, pp. 171–93.

Brito, Dagobert L., and Peter R. Hartley. 1995. "Consumer Rationality and Credit Cards." *Journal of Political Economy* 103 (April): 400–33.

Bucks, Brian K., Arthur B. Kennickell, and Kevin B. Moore. 2006. "Recent Changes in U.S. Family Finances: Evidence from the 1998 and 2004 Survey of Consumer Finances." *Federal Reserve Bulletin* (March 22): 1–38.

Calem, Paul S., and Loretta J. Mester. 1995. "Consumer Behavior and the Stickiness of Credit-Card Interest Rates." *American Economic Review* 85 (December): 1327–36.

Calem, Paul S., Michael B. Gordy, and Loretta J. Mester. 2005. "Switching Costs and Adverse Selection in the Market for Credit Cards: New Evidence." Working Paper 05–16. Philadelphia: Federal Reserve Bank of Philadelphia, July.

Canner, Glenn, Karen Dynan, and Wayne Passmore. 2002. "Mortgage Refinancing in 2001 and Early 2002." *Federal Reserve Bulletin* 99 (December): 469–90.

Crook, Jonathan. 2002. "Adverse Selection and Search in the Bank Credit Card Market." Credit Research Centre. Working Paper 01/2. Edinburgh: University of Edinburgh, www.crc.man.ed.ac.uk/papers2002.html.

Duca, John V., and William C. Whitesell. 1995. "Credit Cards and Money Demand: A Cross-Sectional Study." *Journal of Money, Credit, and Banking* 27 (May): 604–23.

Dynan, Karen, Douglas Elmendorf, and Daniel Sichel. 2006. "Can Financial Innovation Explain the Reduced Volatility of Economic Activity?" *Journal of Monetary Economics* 53 (January): 123–50.

Dynan, Karen, Kathleen W. Johnson, and Karen Pence. 2003. "Recent Changes to a Measure of U.S. Household Debt Service." *Federal Reserve Bulletin* 89 (October): 417–26.

Edelberg, Wendy. 2003. "Risk-Based Pricing of Interest Rates in Household Loan Markets." Finance and Economics Discussion Series 2003–62. Washington: Board of Governors of the Federal Reserve System, December.

Evans, David S., and Richard Schmalensee. 1999. *Paying with Plastic: The Digital Revolution in Buying and Borrowing.* Cambridge, Mass.: MIT Press. 2nd ed., 2005.

Gross, David S., and Nicholas S. Souleles. 2002. "Do Liquidity Constraints and Interest Rates Matter for Consumer Behavior? Evidence from Credit Card Data." *Quarterly Journal of Economics* 117 (February): 149–85.

Johnson, Kathleen W. 2004. "Convenience or Necessity? Understanding the Recent Rise in Credit Card Debt," Finance and Economics Discussion Series 2004–47. Washington: Board of Governors of the Federal Reserve System, September.

Klee, Elizabeth. 2004. "Retail Payments 1995–2001: Findings from Aggregate Data and the Survey of Consumer Finances." unpublished paper. Board of Governors of the Federal Reserve System, Division of Monetary Affairs, May.

Mandell, Lewis. 1972. *Credit Card Use in the United States.* Ann Arbor, MI.: Institute for Social Research.

McCorkell, Peter L. 2002. "The Impact of Credit Scoring and Automated Underwriting on Credit Availability." In Thomas A. Durkin and Michael E. Staten, eds., *The Impact of Public Policy on Consumer Credit.* Boston: Kluwer, pp. 209–19.

Siedman, Ellen, Moez Hababou, and Jennifer Kramer. 2005. "A Financial Services Survey of Low- and Moderate-Income Households." Paper presented at the Federal Reserve System Community Affairs Research Conference "Promises and Pitfalls: As Consumer Finance Options Multiply, Who is Being Served and at What Cost?" Washington, D.C., April 7–8, www.chicagofed.org/ cedric/ promises_pitfalls_2005_conference.cfm.

Stango, Victor. 2000. "Competition and Pricing in the Credit Card Market." *Review of Economics and Statistics* vol. 82 (August): 499–508.

U.S. Department of Commerce. 2006. "Quarterly Retail E-Commerce Sales: 2nd Quarter 2006." *U.S. Census Bureau News*, August 17.

White, Kenneth J. 1976. "The Effect of Bank Credit Cards on the Household Transactions Demand for Money." *Journal of Money, Credit, and Banking* 8 (February): 51–61.

Yoo, Peter S. 1997. "Charging Up a Mountain of Debt: Accounting for the Growth of Credit Card Debt." Federal Reserve Bank of St. Louis, *Review* 79 (March–April): 3–14.

———. (1998). "Still Charging: The Growth of Credit Card Debt between 1992 and 1995." Federal Reserve Bank of St. Louis, *Review* 80 (January–February): 19–28.

Zinman, Jonathan. 2005. "Debit or Credit?" Unpublished paper, Dartmouth College, Department of Economics, October.

CHAPTER 3

WHITHER CONSUMER CREDIT COUNSELING

Robert M. Hunt

Introduction

The availability and use of consumer credit in the United States has grown dramatically over the last 50 years. While this is undoubtedly beneficial, one consequence is that, at any time, there are a million or more consumers having difficulties in managing their unsecured debts. For a half century, nonprofit credit counseling organizations have offered financial education and budget counseling sessions for free or at nominal cost to borrowers. They also negotiate comprehensive repayment plans (debt management plans) with a borrower's unsecured creditors. These repayment plans provide an alternative to bankruptcy that is valuable to many consumers.

But credit counseling is not without controversy. The older counseling organizations rely primarily on creditors for their revenues, and this may create the appearance of a conflict of interest. More recently, many new debt counseling organizations have appeared on the scene. This new breed relies less on creditors for revenues because they charge borrowers significantly more for their services. If these higher fees are drawn from a borrower's limited reserves, he or she may have additional difficulty completing the repayment plan. In addition, creditors worry that at least some of these new organizations are not screening their clients—proposing concessions for borrowers who could have paid their debts on the original terms. This has affected how creditors work with counselors. These concerns and others have triggered significant legislative and regulatory activity in recent years.

The credit counseling industry is an important one, but its activities and effects are not widely understood. Still the available research does give us some insight into the effects of consumer credit counseling and debt management plans on borrower behavior and the implications for the industry and regulation.

Any conclusions, unfortunately, must be tentative. There are few formal studies of the contribution of credit counseling organizations, and they must wrestle with a difficult methodological problem: Do borrowers who seek credit counseling perform better because of the counseling (a treatment effect) or because they are somehow different from borrowers who do not seek counseling (a selection effect)?

Background

Credit counseling organizations typically provide four types of services to consumers: (1) they offer consumer financial education; (2) they offer budget counseling to individual households; (3) they negotiate *debt management plans* with creditors on behalf of borrowers; and (4) when appropriate, they refer consumers to other support organizations or recommend that they seek advice about a bankruptcy filing.

A debt management plan is a schedule for repaying all of the borrower's *unsecured* debts over three to five years.[1] Ideally, the credit counselor is able to include all of the borrower's unsecured creditors in the plan. While the principal is repaid in full, creditors typically reduce interest rates and other charges. Creditors are sometimes willing to *re-age* accounts in a debt management plan. In other words, assuming plan payments are made, the creditor considers the account as current and reports it this way to credit bureaus. This improves the borrower's payment history and credit rating.

An essential feature of the benefit credit counselors offer is the ability to coordinate the concessions made by a borrower's creditors. Of course, borrowers can negotiate with individual creditors, but they must overcome each creditor's concern that any concession it makes benefits the borrower's other creditors at its expense. Winton Williams coined a phrase for this phenomenon—the *creditor's dilemma.*[2] All creditors would likely benefit if they all agreed to refrain from legal action and allow the borrower more time to repay. But if all creditors agree to this approach, any individual creditor might do better by insisting on being repaid from the proceeds of the concessions offered by other creditors. If creditors distrust each other, they will refuse to make concessions and possibly race to secure claims on the borrower's cash flow (by garnishing wages) or assets (by placing liens on the borrower's property). If this happens, the borrower is more likely to file for bankruptcy, and all the unsecured creditors are likely to recover very little.

Credit counselors can often avoid this outcome. Through repeated interactions with creditors, they have established a reputation for securing the agreement of most or all of a borrower's creditors and establishing repayment plans that put each creditor on more or less the same footing in terms of the borrower's resources. This reduces the risk of a run against the borrower, which, in turn, increases the chances of the creditors being repaid.

Note that participation in debt management plans is entirely voluntary. Borrowers need not seek a credit counselor, and they may abandon a repayment plan if they so choose. Similarly, creditors cannot be forced to agree to a debt management plan, and they are free to resort to collections activity or other legal activity at any time. Clearly, what makes these plans work, when they do work, is a good deal of trust that is fostered by the credit counselor.

Origins of the Nonprofit Credit Counseling Industry

The traditional nonprofit credit counseling organizations emerged in the 1950s and 1960s, partially in response to the rapid growth in unsecured consumer debt during that time. Many were organized by or with the support of creditors. During this same period, many states enacted legislation to regulate or simply ban the operation of the existing for-profit debt counselors (sometimes called debt poolers or proraters) on consumer protection grounds. Most states deliberately exempted nonprofit counseling organizations from these laws in the hope that they would continue to develop.[3]

A national trade organization, what is now called the National Foundation for Credit Counseling (NFCC), became active in 1951. At its peak, NFCC membership included about 200 organizations with about 1,500 offices around the country.[4] Today, NFCC member organizations counsel 1.5 million borrowers each year. They administer nearly 600,000 debt management plans, which pay unsecured creditors at least $2.5 billion a year. To put these numbers into perspective, very roughly speaking, each year NFCC member agencies counsel about 1 percent of American bankcard holders, and there is one debt management plan for every two personal bankruptcy filings.

These nonprofit credit counselors rely primarily on contributions from creditors for their revenues. Under a norm called *fair share*, creditors would return to the credit counselor about 12 percent of debt payments it helped to facilitate. These contributions accounted for two-thirds or more of the revenues of traditional credit counselors, but the share has fallen in recent years.[5] In the past, fair share receipts exceeded the cost of administering debt management plans, which afforded resources for the agencies' consumer education and budget counseling programs.

Some argue that a dependence on creditors for revenues creates at least a potential conflict of interest. For example, does a credit counselor that relies on fair share payments have an adequate incentive to suggest that a consumer seek legal advice about bankruptcy?[6] About 6 percent of borrowers who contact an NFCC member agency are referred to legal assistance, while 30–35 percent are enrolled in a debt management plan.[7] While these numbers suggest that counseling agencies might steer some borrowers away from bankruptcy, we need to know a good deal more about borrowers' circumstances and preferences to conclude that this pattern is inappropriate from the standpoint of borrowers or society.

Options Available to Distressed Borrowers

Why do borrowers enter into debt management plans? Why are unsecured creditors willing to accept these plans? The answer is that participating in the plans is better than the alternatives for some borrowers (see table 3.1). Depending on the resources available, borrowers can choose between repaying on the original terms,

Table 3.1 Pros and cons of options available to borrowers

Option	*Borrowers*	*Unsecured Creditors*
Repayment on original terms	Preserves access to credit on better terms *Assumes sufficient cash flow to pay principal and interest*	Principal repaid in full Earns interest and fee income
Informal bankruptcy	Preserves cash flow for other expenses *Little or no access to new credit* *Little protection from legal action by creditors*	*Lose most or all principal* *Collections and legal action are costly*
Chapter 7 bankruptcy filing	Unsecured debts typically discharged Future income unencumbered by debt payments Prevents collections and legal action by creditors *Borrower must undergo credit counseling prior to filing and obtain financial education prior to the discharge* *Non-exempt property sold to pay debts* *Filing and attorney fees* *Bankruptcy flag on credit report for 10 years* *Cannot file again for Chapter 7 bankruptcy for 8 years*	*Stay against collections and legal action* *Lose most or all principal*
Chapter 13 bankruptcy filing	Borrower retains his or her property Repayment plan based on future income (3–5 years) Unsecured debts are not repaid in full Prevents collections and legal action by creditors *Part of future income devoted to debt payments* *Filing, attorney, and trustee fees*	*Stay against collections and legal action* *Planned payments typically cover a small portion of original principal* *Many repayment plans fail*

Continued

Table 3.1 Continued

Option	*Borrowers*	*Unsecured Creditors*
	Bankruptcy flag on credit report for 10 years *Cannot obtain a Chapter 13 discharge within 2 years of a previous Chapter 13 discharge, or within 4 years of a discharge under another chapter*	
Debt management plan	Creditors *voluntarily* abstain from collections and legal action Lower interest and fees Improved credit history should assure access to new credit sooner than bankruptcy *Diverts cash flow from payments on secured debts* *Must pay entire principal* *Plan fees (see text)*	If successful, principal repaid in full *Part of repayment (fair share) goes to counselor* *Lower interest and fee income* *Many repayment plans fail*

Note: Cons of options available to borrowers are set in italics in the table. Under the Bankruptcy Abuse Prevention and Consumer Protection Act of 2005, access to a Chapter 7 discharge is subject to a means test. For details, see the January–March 2005 issue of the Federal Reserve Bank of Philadelphia's *Banking Legislation and Policy* (http://www.phil.frb.org/ econ/blp/index.html).

not paying but not filing for bankruptcy either (informal bankruptcy), and formal bankruptcy. Creditors can be either more or less aggressive in their collection efforts, or they may take legal action, such as obtaining an order to garnish wages.

One factor that influences borrowers' choice is the effect on their future access to credit. Obviously, timely repayment on the original terms preserves the borrower's credit history and is most likely to ensure future access to credit on good terms. Under the informal or formal bankruptcy options, borrowers will have difficulty obtaining new credit on affordable terms for a long time. A bankruptcy flag remains on a borrower's credit report for ten years.

Another factor that influences borrowers' choice is the size of the payments they make and how creditors respond. Payments are typically largest if the debt is paid on the original terms. Alternatively, the consumer can simply stop making payments (informal bankruptcy). But this option affords borrowers few protections from debt collectors. They cannot prevent repossession of their car or foreclosure on their house. They cannot prevent creditors from placing liens against the real property they own. They have few ways of avoiding garnishment of their wages. Still, many distressed borrowers choose not to repay and not to file for bankruptcy.[11]

Two Forms of Bankruptcy for Consumers

Most borrowers can choose between two forms of bankruptcy: Chapter 7 [liquidation] or Chapter 13 [a wage-earner plan].[9] Both chapters impose a stay on collections and legal actions by creditors. In the case of Chapter 13, this may allow the borrower to catch up on mortgage payments and avoid foreclosure.

Under Chapter 7, the borrower's assets (except for certain exempt property) are used to pay some portion of the debts owed to unsecured creditors.[10] The remaining unsecured debt is discharged, so the consumer's future income is unencumbered. In practice, borrowers filing under this chapter rarely have assets to surrender; so unsecured creditors receive little or nothing. The claims of secured creditors are unaffected, so they can eventually foreclose on those assets if they choose. It is not uncommon for borrowers to *reaffirm* their secured debts in order to retain the collateral (such as the car or the house).

Alternatively, the borrower can file under Chapter 13 of the bankruptcy code. Under this Chapter, the borrower can keep his or her assets but must propose a repayment plan financed by a significant share of his or her future income over the next several years. The plan must offer unsecured creditors at least as much as they would obtain under a Chapter 7 filing, but, as noted earlier, this is typically not very much. Creditors cannot reject the terms of a plan if the borrower has pledged his or her entire *disposable* income over the next three to five years for debt payments. Disposable income here means income after taxes, basic living expenses, and tuition. Upon completion of the plan, the remaining unsecured debts are discharged. In practice, unsecured creditors typically receive a fraction of the outstanding principal (see later). General unsecured creditors received about $815 million from Chapter 13 plans during the 2001 fiscal year.[11]

Debt Management Plans Are Not the Same as Chapter 13

While debt management plans are similar in many ways to a Chapter 13 bankruptcy filing, there are several important differences.[12] Borrowers who participate in a debt management plan should be able to improve their credit history more quickly than if they default or file for bankruptcy. This should mean they are able to gain access to new credit more rapidly.[13] Unlike most Chapter 13 plans, debt management plans expect the borrower to repay the entire principal owed. A number of protections afforded in bankruptcy are absent in a debt management plan. For example, participation in a debt management plan does not protect the borrower from legal action by his or her creditors. Nor are creditors compelled to accept a proposed debt management plan.

Debt management plans also do not address secured credit. If consumers have important assets, financed by secured loans, which they are also having trouble paying, a bankruptcy filing may be the better option. In this situation, a borrower who enters a debt management plan might increase the risk of losing the house because he or she has pledged income to pay unsecured debts that would probably be discharged in bankruptcy. In short, while debt management plans are useful for many distressed borrowers, they are not suitable for all borrowers in trouble, and they are not simply a substitute for a Chapter 13 filing.

Why Do Creditors Agree to Participate in Debt Management Plans?

From the creditor's standpoint, the net benefit of agreeing to a debt management plan depends on what they think the borrower will do in the absence of the plan. If the creditor thinks a borrower will otherwise stop paying altogether or enter bankruptcy, the creditor might recover more if it agrees to a debt management plan than if it refuses. But if the creditor thinks a borrower would otherwise continue to pay, agreeing to a debt management plan would likely reduce the payments the creditor will receive. After all, longer repayment terms, lower interest charges and fees, plus fair share payments come at the expense of the creditor.

What's more, creditors' expectations depend significantly on what they expect a borrower's other creditors will do. As explained earlier, if it is likely that another creditor will push a borrower into bankruptcy, every creditor has less incentive to offer concessions or to refrain from collections activity.

What do Credit Counselors Accomplish?

Once again, it is important to recognize the very difficult problem of selection: Do borrowers who seek out credit counseling perform better because of the counseling or because they are somehow different from borrowers who do not seek counseling? It is at least possible that any measured differences between these groups is due to a selection effect (perhaps only highly motivated borrowers seek out counseling) rather than a treatment effect (the counseling itself helps borrowers to manage their debts).

Debt Management Plans

According to data from NFCC members, a typical debt management plan included $16,000 in unsecured debts, roughly 40 percent of the annual income of the participating borrowers.[14] Despite this remarkable degree of leverage, about one-quarter of plan participants remain in the plans until all their debts are paid off. In many other cases, borrowers pay down some of their debts and exit the plans to manage the remainder on their own. Still, approximately one-half of debt management plans fail after about six months. In some instances, borrowers have pledged more cash flow than they can afford. In others, one or more creditors refuse to accept the terms of a plan and take actions (such as garnishment) that push the borrower into bankruptcy.

Anecdotal evidence suggests that the completion rate of debt management plans is a bit higher than that of Chapter 13 plans (which is only about 33 percent). But the criterion for success is different under debt management plans, where the entire principal is expected to be repaid. Even in successful Chapter 13 plans, unsecured creditors receive only about 35 percent of the original principal.[15] Chapter 13 plans are also costly to administer. The average attorney's and trustee's fees for a Chapter 13 case in 2003 were $1,500, or about 14 percent of the amount repaid.[16]

A 1999 study conducted by Visa provides some insights into the success or failure of debt management plans. Borrowers who dropped out were more likely to be unemployed or to lose their jobs. Similarly, borrowers with lower income were less likely to complete their plans. Almost a third of borrowers who dropped out of a debt management plan had filed for bankruptcy. Compared to a separate survey of borrowers who filed for bankruptcy, participants in debt management plans appear to enjoy better access to unsecured and secured credit. Those successfully completing a debt management plan were more likely to hold a credit card than those who could not. Borrowers who successfully completed a debt management plan were more likely to buy a house than those who did not complete the plan.

Visa asked borrowers why they sought credit counseling. Respondents were three times as likely to mention a desire to get out of debt, or concerns about being overextended, than to cite creditors' collection tactics or the desire to avoid a bankruptcy filing.[17] This may suggest that borrowers who enter into debt management plans are different from other distressed borrowers.

Is there any evidence that creditors do better with accounts in debt management plans than for accounts held by borrowers with similar observable characteristics? Creditors obviously believe they do, or they would not be willing to participate in the plans. Ralph Spurgeon describes the results of comparison between two sets of cardholders at a large store chain: One group enrolled in debt management plans, and the other group did not.[18] The chain lost money on both groups of accounts, but it lost 32 percent less on the accounts in debt management plans. Taking into account fair share payments to the credit counseling organizations, the chain's net losses were 17 percent lower.

Consumer Financial Education

There is some evidence of significant effects for the counseling programs offered by NFCC member organizations. In one study, only 7 percent of consumers counseled filed for bankruptcy, compared with 25 percent in a comparable control group. In another study, economists Gregory Elliehausen, Christopher Lundquist, and Michael Staten examined the effect of budget counseling (not debt management plans) on borrower credit quality, as measured by data contained in credit bureau files for about 6,000 borrowers just before and 3 years after the counseling session (i.e., in 1997 and in 2000). Improvements among this group were compared to changes in the creditworthiness of a comparable control group—comparable in the sense that individuals with similar credit scores were drawn from the same geographic areas as those who were counseled.[19]

The authors report significant improvements in a wide variety of measures of creditworthiness among borrowers who sought credit counseling. Relative to the control group, counseled borrowers increased their credit scores and decreased their total indebtedness and the number of accounts with balances. They also experienced a significant decline in the number of delinquent accounts. The effects were the largest among borrowers with the lowest credit scores around the time they sought out credit counseling.

There remains the concern that the borrowers who sought out credit counseling are somehow different from other borrowers. In their analysis, Ellihausen, Lundquist, and Staten try to control for this by first attempting to predict, using data contained in credit bureau files, which borrowers would seek out counseling. That makes this study superior to most other studies, but we still cannot be entirely sure the authors' technique has fully controlled for selection bias.

A Revolution in the Credit Counseling Industry

Around 1990, there were about 200 nonprofit credit counseling organizations in the United States. It took 30 years to reach that number. But this process of gradual increase changed dramatically in the 1990s. After 1994, at least 1,200 new organizations began counseling borrowers; three-quarters of these became active after 1999.[20] This *new breed* has been very successful, taking market share away from NFCC member organizations. Several of the new organizations are the largest in the field, managing roughly $7 billion in outstanding debts.[21]

The new breed is different from the previous generation of counseling agencies. For example, they are more automated, and they invest much more heavily in advertising. They also focus almost exclusively on debt management plans. They offer little budget counseling or financial education. They rely more on borrowers, and less on creditors, for their revenues. They do this by charging borrowers significantly higher fees than the traditional counseling agencies. It can cost a borrower $1,000 or more in fees to complete a debt management plan with some of the new counseling organizations.[22]

Some members of the new breed have been accused of engaging in egregious trade practices, similar to those attributed to the for-profit debt counseling organizations of the 1950s and 1960s.[23] Some organizations apply the first month of debt payments to plan fees rather than payments to creditors, but they don't disclose this information to borrowers. As a result, these borrowers fall further behind with their creditors. Other counseling organizations charge borrowers large upfront fees. Some deduct significant fees ($50 or more) from borrowers' monthly debt payments. Some counselors do not include all unsecured creditors in the plan, increasing the risk of legal action against the borrower and ensuring the failure of the plan. The completion rate on plans administered by some of the largest of the new counseling organizations is rather low—only 2 percent in one instance.[24]

Why the Influx of New Counseling Organizations?

Several factors explain the influx of new organizations into the counseling industry. For one, demand for these services has increased significantly. Consider the case of general purpose credit cards issued by banks. In the 11 years between 1992 and 2003, the number of bankcard holders increased by nearly 33 million. Among this group, the share that was seriously delinquent rose gradually until 1999 and then rose rapidly as the United States entered into recession. The combination of these two trends contributed to a tripling of the number of delinquent cardholders (figure 3.1).[25] This also corresponds with a period of rapid increase in bankruptcy filings and in active debt management plans relative to the population (figure 3.2). The subsequent decline in the use of debt management plans may be due in part to rising house prices (and low interest rates), which helped many consumers to pay down their unsecured debts using home equity loans.[26]

Figure 3.1 Delinquent bank cardholders (1,000s)

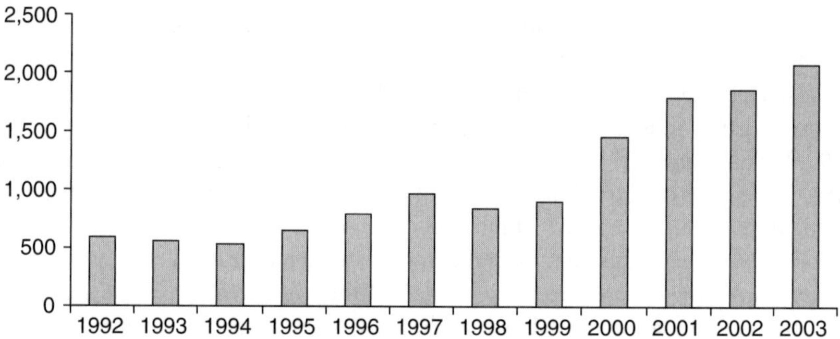

Note: Delinquency refers to cardholders who are 90 more days late on their payments.

Sources: Author's calculations based on data from the *Statistical Abstract of the United States, The Nilson Report* and TransUnion's *Trendata.*

Figure 3.2 Bankruptcy and debt management plans per thousand of population aged 16+

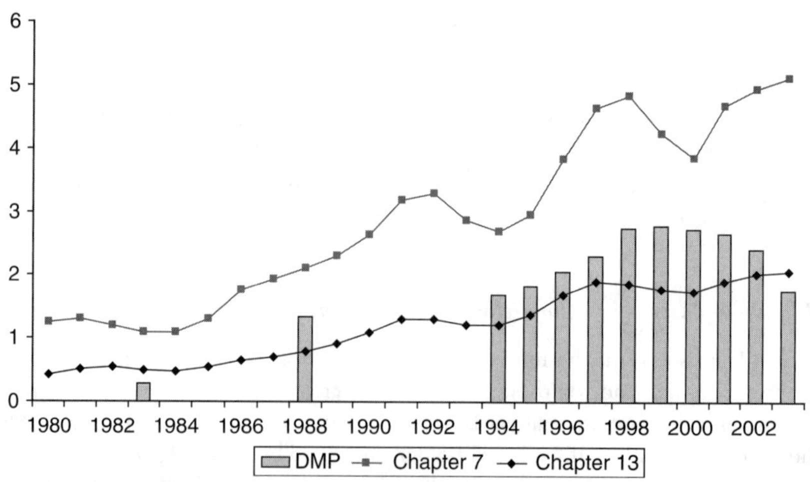

Note: Data on debt management plans refer only to NFCC member organizations.

Sources: Author's calculations using data from NFCC and the Administrative Office of the U.S. Courts.

A second factor is that barriers to entry into the credit counseling business fell, at least temporarily. There are a number of reasons for this. For one, nonprofit credit counseling organizations are lightly regulated at the state and local level, and there is no federal regulation that directly addresses this industry.[27] Another is that advances in technology (call centers, the Internet, data processing, and electronic payments) reduced the upfront cost of setting up debt management plans and the ongoing cost of administering them. But these technologies also require significant investment, and that is one reason newer counseling organizations seek the business of borrowers around the country rather than in a particular local market, as was common with the older counseling organizations.

Another reason barriers to entry were at least initially low is the amount of trust established between credit counselors and creditors over the previous 30 years. Creditors expected counselors to properly screen borrowers and were willing to provide generous fair share payments. At least initially, creditors treated the new organizations much as they did the initial ones.[28] The success of the existing institutions also invited entry. If fair share payments could be used to subsidize education and budget counseling, profits could be earned by organizations willing to focus on just debt management plans, assuming they are successful in attracting borrowers.

The Relationship with Creditors

Credit counselors no longer enjoy the same relationship with creditors. One reason is that the out-of-pocket costs for debt management plans have become quite large. The share of large credit card portfolios that consist of accounts in debt management plans is now about 2 to 3 percent. About a quarter of the collections budget of major credit card lenders is spent on fair share payments.[29]

While it has always been difficult to quantify the benefit to creditors of participating in debt management plans, creditors suspect that the benefits to them may have fallen. With the entry of the new breed, creditors are convinced that at least some consumers that would otherwise pay their unsecured debts are simply seeking more advantageous terms.

At the same time, creditors began to reduce their fair share payments from the 12 to 15 percent typical of 20 years ago to half this amount, or even lower, today. Among NFCC members, fair share payments currently average about 6 percent of payments made to creditors. Revenue compression has contributed to consolidation among NFCC members and the near failure of others.[30] In contrast, the new breed is less affected because they rely more on fees paid by the borrowers and are more willing to raise those fees.

In addition, creditors have reduced the concessions (such as lower interest rates) they offer to borrowers enrolled in debt management plans, making them more difficult to complete.[31] This has a significant effect on borrowers, since balances take longer to pay off when the interest rates are higher. As a result, borrowers pay down less debt over the typical three- to five-year length of a debt management plan. In addition, borrowers are more likely to become discouraged and drop out of the plan altogether

Counselors, Creditors, and Regulators Respond

More recently, there are signs that established credit counselors and creditors are responding to the influx of counseling organizations. For example, the NFCC has established new standards for its member organizations, including accreditation of counselors, licensing and bonding requirements, annual audits of accounts, educational and counseling requirements, and disclosure of financing sources and fees. In addition, the NFCC prohibits the payment of bonuses to credit counselors, charging consumers fees in advance of providing services, and "prescreening" consumers to be solicited for debt management plans.

Credit counselors are seeking alternative funding sources for their financial education and budget counseling efforts. They are also participating in studies to demonstrate the efficacy of these programs. NFCC members are also making significant investments in IT to improve their productivity.

Creditor Action

Lenders are changing their relationship with counseling organizations. For example, they now play a more active role in determining which consumers should be eligible for debt management plans. Some creditors make fair share payments only to counseling organizations that meet specific standards, for example, by limiting fees charged to borrowers.

Creditors are adopting back-loaded fair share payments and other pay-for-performance formulas. For example, when a borrower starts a debt management plan, the creditor may return only 2 percent to the counseling organization. If the borrower remains current on the plan for a year, the creditor may return an additional 7 percent of plan payments to the counseling organization. Other lenders are replacing fair share contributions altogether with charitable contributions made to nonprofit counseling organizations that apply for support.[32] In short, large creditors are concentrating their fair share payments on a smaller number of counseling organizations—ones that can demonstrate their effectiveness. These changes are relatively new; so creditors and credit counselors continue to hone the measures of effectiveness used to determine fair share payments,

Legislation

The most significant changes affecting the credit counseling industry are those contained in the recently enacted bankruptcy law.[33] The Bankruptcy Abuse Prevention and Consumer Protection Act of 2005 limits access to Chapter 7 for some high-income borrowers, leaving them to consider either a workout under Chapter 13 or a debt management plan negotiated by a credit counseling organization. The act also lengthens from six to eight the number of years before a borrower can obtain another Chapter 7 discharge. Borrowers will now be required to obtain credit counseling from an approved nonprofit organization before filing for bankruptcy. To obtain a discharge of their debts in bankruptcy, borrowers must first complete a course in personal financial management.

The law specifies minimum standards to be used by U.S. trustees or the courts to determine whether a nonprofit credit counseling organization is approved for the purposes of the mandatory counseling requirement. Assuming these standards are sufficiently rigorous, such a certification process could make it easier for consumers to identify reputable credit counselors. The law also requires the Executive Office for U.S. trustees to develop standards for the required consumer financial education programs and to evaluate the effectiveness of those efforts.

This law includes a provision designed to encourage unsecured creditors to accept debt management plans proposed by credit counselors. If such a plan would repay 60 percent of the original principal (under current practice these plans return 100 percent of the principal), and the creditor refuses to participate, a borrower filing for bankruptcy can petition the court to reduce the outstanding debt by up to 20 percent. The likely effect of this provision is unclear. If a borrower is able to file under Chapter 7, most or all of his or her unsecured debts will be discharged anyway. Most Chapter 13 repayment plans offer unsecured creditors some portion of the original principal, but it is typically small and even less is usually repaid. A 20 percent reduction in such amounts may be insufficient to influence the decisions of unsecured creditors.

There are a number of other legislative proposals at the federal level. A 2003 bill, the Debt Counseling, Debt Consolidation, and Debt Settlement Practices Act (H.R. 3331), would make explicit that credit counseling organizations, irrespective of their nonprofit status, can be sued for unfair and deceptive trade practices. There are also proposals to revise the 1996 Credit Repair Organizations Act with credit counselors in mind. This law currently does not apply to nonprofit organizations. A recent federal court case, however, makes clear that the act will apply to tax-exempt charities that are, in fact, operated as for-profit organizations.[34]

The National Consumer Law Center, together with the Consumer Federation of America, has proposed a model state law to regulate credit counselors. The National Conference of Commissioners on Uniform State Laws is also working on a draft Uniform Consumer Debt Counseling Act that would, among other things, regulate fees charged to consumers for debt management plans and require that counselors spend at least as much on education as they do on advertising.

Regulatory Action

Since 2003, the Internal Revenue Service has initiated investigations into the nonprofit status of 59 credit counseling organizations, which collectively account for approximately 50 percent of the industry's revenues. It has sued one large organization and denied applications for nonprofit status to four others. That same year, the FTC sued a number of the newer counseling organizations for engaging in unfair and deceptive trade practices and operating as for-profit enterprises. In 2005, the FTC concluded a number of settlements, effectively shutting some of these organizations down. Others have announced changes in their organization and business practices.[35]

Conclusion

In the United States, credit counseling organizations are playing an increasingly important role in the functioning of the market for unsecured consumer credit. Credit counselors make it possible for some borrowers to repay their unsecured debts. This, in turn, offers borrowers the chance to reestablish access to credit more rapidly than if they file for bankruptcy.

Credit counselors are also important providers of consumer financial education and budget counseling, which, until recently, was indirectly subsidized through fair share payments made by creditors. If these programs are indeed effective, but creditors are now less willing to fund them, perhaps the public should. In other words, these activities may represent an important public good. A lender may well benefit when its customers become more sophisticated about credit, but the lender does not enjoy all the benefits. Some of the benefits are enjoyed by the customer and his or her other creditors. Thus, lenders may have an inadequate incentive to fund such efforts. While customers may benefit from receiving budget counseling and financial education, they are presumably unable to afford it at their time of greatest need.

There is evidence that credit counseling organizations are effective in helping some consumers regain access to credit and better manage their finances. But it is difficult to interpret these results. Are they due to selection or treatment effects? Relatively little formal research has been done, and there is a lot more to do.

In recent years, changes in technology and in the market for consumer credit have induced major changes in what had been a quiet life for nonprofit credit counseling organizations. There has been a dramatic increase in the number of counseling organizations and in the observable costs of debt management plans among unsecured creditors. Creditors are not so sure they are benefiting from the increased use of debt management plans.

Creditors and traditional counseling organizations are beginning to respond to these new conditions, but it is too early to tell how effective these changes will be. There is also growing interest, both at the state and federal levels, in additional regulation of credit counselors. The idea is to make it easier for consumers to make an informed choice *among* credit counselors.

But distressed borrowers must also decide between their different options. Is it better to file for bankruptcy than to participate in a debt management plan? If so, is it better to file under Chapter 7 or Chapter 13? How well do borrowers understand these options? What organizations are in the best position, and have the right incentives, to educate consumers about these options? More generally, how can we quantify the effect of credit counselors' activities on consumers' access to unsecured credit and the price they pay for it? These are just a few of many important questions that require further study.

Notes

This article was inspired by two workshops organized by the Philadelphia Fed's Payment Cards Center in 2001 and 2003. See Stanley (2001) and Furletti (2003). I thank Patti Hasson for many helpful discussions. Chris Ody and Paul Weiss helped me compile the data for this article.

The views expressed here are those of the author and do not necessarily represent the views of the Federal Reserve Bank of Philadelphia or the Federal Reserve System.

1. An unsecured debt is one in which the borrower does not pledge collateral (e.g., a house or car) that may be taken by the creditor in the event the borrower defaults on the loan. Credit card debts are almost always unsecured.
2. See Williams (1998).
3. See Hall (1968); section V of the Northwestern University Law Review Consumer Credit Symposium; Sniderman-Milstein and Ratner (1981); and Kabot Schiller (1976). For a recent review of state regulations, see the report by the California Department of Corporations (2003) and the report by Deanne Loonin and Heather Packard (2004).
4. Not all credit counseling organizations are NFCC members. Others are members of the Association of Independent Consumer Credit Counseling Agencies (AICCCA).
5. Until recently, this source of funding was not always disclosed to borrowers. In 1997, the NFCC reached an agreement with the Federal Trade Commission (FTC) to make such disclosures a matter of policy.
6. This question applies equally to credit counselors who rely primarily on fees charged to consumers.
7. Another third of borrowers receive financial education or household budget counseling.
8. See Ausubel and Dawsey (2002) and White (1998).
9. Good summaries of consumer bankruptcy law are found in Li (2001) and Mester (2002). Significant changes to U.S. bankruptcy law were enacted in 2005 (see page 48).
10. Exempt property is typically determined by state law. It may include some portion of equity in the borrower's home, automobiles, household goods and clothing, and tools used for one's trade.
11. See Flynn, Burke, and Bakewell (2002).
12. See Lander (1999; 2004).
13. There is no direct test for this, but the Visa study (discussed later) is suggestive.
14. These borrowers had an average total indebtedness of $51,000 including mortgages, medical debt, and tax liens.
15. The statistics on debt management plans are from the articles by David Lander and statistics provided by the NFCC. The statistics on Chapter 13 plans are from the report by the Congressional Budget Office and Braucher (1993); Norberg (1999); and Whitford (1994).
16. See the Bermant (2005). These amounts do not include filing fees.
17. But when asked, "What was the last straw?" borrowers cited collection tactics four times as often as any other factor.
18. The samples were selected to exhibit comparable distributions of credit scores.
19. Borrowers who received counseling were identified from the files of five NFCC member counseling organizations.
20. Not all of these survive—there are currently about 870 active nonprofit credit counseling organizations.
21. This number is derived from data contained in Permanent Subcommittee on Investigations (2004).
22. By way of contrast, the average set-up fee among NFCC organizations is $25, and the average monthly maintenance fee is $15.
23. While it is difficult to measure the frequency of such practices, a number of examples can be found in the report of the Permanent Subcommittee on

Investigations (2004), the testimony of Howard Beales of the FTC (2003), and the report by Loonin and Plunkett (2003).

24. See the March 30, 2005, Federal Trade Commission press release.
25. A similar pattern is observed when comparing the 1992 and 2001 editions of the Survey of Consumer Finances (SCF). According to the SCF, the number of families with bankcards increased by 19 million. The share of families 60 or more days late on a debt payment increased from 6 to 7 percent. Taking into account the increase in households over this period, it appears that about 1.9 million more families were having trouble paying their debts in 2001 than in 1992.
26. Another factor was the declining market share of NFCC members—the figure includes only debt management plans administered by those organizations.
27. See Cowen and Kawecki (2004) for a review state and federal regulation of credit counselors. The Federal Trade Commission can sue counseling organizations that engage in unfair or deceptive trade practices, but its jurisdiction does not include nonprofit organizations. That means the FTC must also convince a court that these institutions are "organized to carry on business for its own profit or that of its members."
28. This may be due in part to antitrust concerns. In 1994, several independent credit counseling organizations sued Discover Card and NFCC, alleging an illegal restraint of trade, because Discover would make fair share payments only to NFCC members. The suit was eventually settled. See Fickenscher (1997).
29. See Punch (2003) and Permanent Subcommittee on Investigations (2004).
30. See Loonin and Plunkett (2003) and Adler (2001).
31. See the 1999 press release by the Consumer Federation of America. It also documents the decline in fair share contribution ratios among a number of large banks.
32. For examples, see Permanent Subcommittee on Investigations (2004), Breitkopf (2004), and Simpson (2004).
33. Public Law No. 109–8. For a summary, see the January–March 2005 issue of the Federal Reserve Bank of Philadelphia's *Banking Legislation and Policy*.
34. See *Zimmerman v. Cambridge Credit Counseling Corp.*, 409 F.3d 473 (1st Cir. 2005). A key test, according to the decision, is whether the organization is generating income for itself or others.
35. See Everson (2003), the March 2005 press releases from the Federal Trade Commission, and the report of the Permanent Subcommittee on Investigations (2004).

References

Adler, Jane. 2001. "Merger Mania Hits Credit Counseling." *Credit Card Management* 13 (January): 48–54.

Ausubel, Lawrence M., and Amanda Dawsey. 2002. "Informal Bankruptcy." Mimeo, University of North Carolina, Greensboro.

Beales, Howard. 2003. Prepared Statement of the Federal Trade Commission, in *Non-Profit Credit Counseling Organizations*, Hearings before the Subcommittee on Oversight of the House Committee on Ways and Means, 108th Congress, 1st Session (November 20).

Bermant, Gordon. 2005. "Bankruptcy by the Numbers: Trends in Chapter 13 Disbursements." *American Bankruptcy Institute Journal* 24 (February): 20, 53.

Braucher, Jean. 1993. "Lawyers and Consumer Bankruptcy: One Code, Many Cultures." *American Bankruptcy Law Journal* 67 (Fall): 501–83.

Breitkopf, David. 2004. "Credit Advice Agencies Adjusting to New Scrutiny." *American Banker* 169 (May 14).

California Department of Corporations. 2003. *Study of the Consumer Credit Counseling Industry and Recommendations to the Legislature Regarding the Establishment of Fees for Debt Management Plans and Debt Settlement Plans*. Sacramento, CA: California Department of Corporations.

Congressional Budget Office. 2000. *Personal Bankruptcy: A Literature Review*. Washington, DC: U.S. Congressional Budget Office.

Consumer Federation of America. 1999. "Large Banks Increase Charges to Americans in Credit Counseling." CFA Press Release, July 28.

Cowen, Debra and Debra Kawecki. 2004. "Credit Counseling Organizations." Internal Revenue Service CPE-2004-1.

Elliehausen, Gregory, E. Christopher Lundquist, and Michael Staten. 2003. "The Impact of Credit Counseling on Subsequent Borrower Credit Usage and Payment Behavior." Mimeo, Georgetown University, Credit Research Center.

Everson, Mark. 2003. Prepared Statement of the IRS Commissioner, in *Non-Profit Credit Counseling Organizations*, Hearings before the Subcommittee on Oversight of the House Committee on Ways and Means, 108th Congress, 1st Session (November 20).

Federal Trade Commission. 1997. "FTC Staff Works with Credit Counseling Agencies to Insure Disclosure of Counselors' Dual Role of Assisting Both Consumers and Creditors," FTC Press Release (March 17).

———. 2005. "FTC Settles with AmeriDebt: Company to Shut Down." FTC Press Release (March 21).

———. 2005. "Debt Services Operations Settle FTC Charges." FTC Press Release (March 30).

Fickenscher, Lisa. 1997. "Discover's Parent Settles Suit by 13 Independent Credit Counselors." *American Banker* 162 (July 18).

Flynn, Ed, Gordon Burke, and Karen Bakewell. 2002. "Bankruptcy by the Numbers: A Tale of Two Chapters, Part I." *American Bankruptcy Institute Journal* 21 (July/August): 20–26.

Furletti, Mark. 2003. "Consumer Credit Counseling: Credit Card Issuers' Perspectives." Federal Reserve Bank of Philadelphia Payment Cards Center Discussion Paper.

Hall, Perry B. 1968. *Family Credit Counseling—An Emerging Community Service*. New York: Family Service Association of America.

Kabot Schiller, Margery. 1976. "Family Credit Counseling: An Emerging Community Service Revisited." *Journal of Consumer Affairs* 10 (June): 97–100.

Lander, David A. 1999. "A Snapshot of Two Systems that Are Trying to Help People in Financial Trouble." *American Bankruptcy Institute Law Review* 7 (Spring): 161–91.

———. 2002. "Recent Developments in Consumer Debt Counseling Agencies: The Need for Reform." *American Bankruptcy Institute Journal* 21 (February): 14–19.

———. 2003. "Is Credit Counseling Charitable?" Mimeo, ABA Section of Taxation Committee on Exempt Organizations.

———. 2004. "One Lawyer's Look at the Debt Counseling Industry." Mimeo, Thompson Coburn, LLP.

Li, Wenli. 2001. "To Forgive or Not To Forgive: An Analysis of U.S. Consumer Bankruptcy Choices." Federal Reserve Bank of Richmond *Economic Quarterly* 87 (Spring): 1–22.

Loonin, Deanne, and Travis Plunkett. 2003. *Credit Counseling in Crisis: The Impact on Consumers of Funding Cuts, Higher Fees and Aggressive New Market Entrants*. Washington, DC: Consumer Federation of America.

Loonin, Deanne, and Heather Packard. 2004. *Credit Counseling in Crisis Update: Poor Compliance and Weak Enforcement Undermine Laws Governing Credit Counseling Agencies*. Boston: National Consumer Law Center.

Mester, Loretta. 2002. "Is the Personal Bankruptcy System Bankrupt?" Federal Reserve Bank of Philadelphia *Business Review* First Quarter: 31–44.

Norberg, Scott F. 1999. "Consumer Bankruptcy's New Clothes: An Empirical Study of Discharge and Debt Collection in Chapter 13." *American Bankruptcy Law Institute Law Review* 7 (Winter): 415–63.

Permanent Subcommittee on Investigations. 2004. *Profiteering in a Non-Profit Industry: Abusive Practices in Credit Counseling*. Senate Committee on Homeland Security and Government Affairs. 109th Congress, 1st Session (March).

Punch, Linda. 2003. "Regulating the Counselors." *Credit Card Management* 16 (August): 36–38.

"Pushed Off the Financial Cliff." 2001. *Consumer Reports* 66 (July): 20–25.

"Relief for the Wage-Earning Debtor: Chapter XIII, or Private Debt Adjustment." 1960. In *Consumer Credit Symposium: Developments in the Law. Northwestern University Law Review* 55: 372–88.

Simpson, Burney. 2004. "The Crisis in Credit Counseling." *Credit Card Management* 17 (February): 40–44.

Sniderman Milstein, Abbey, and Bruce C. Ratner. 1981. "Consumer Credit Counseling Service: A Consumer-Oriented View." *New York University Law Review* 56 (November/December): 978–98.

Spurgeon, Ralph E. 1995. "Are They Worth It? Credit Counseling Agencies." *Credit World* (March/April): 26–27.

Stanley, Anne. 2001. "A Panel Discussion on Dynamics in the Consumer Credit Counseling Service Industry." Federal Reserve Bank of Philadelphia Payment Cards Center Discussion Paper.

U.S. Bureau of the Census. *Statistical Abstract of the United States*. Washington, D.C.: U.S. Government Printing Office, various years.

Visa. 1999. *Credit Counseling Debt Management Plan Analysis*. San Francisco: Visa, USA.

White, Michele J. 1998. "Why Don't More Households File for Bankruptcy?" *Journal of Law, Economics and Organization* 14 (October): 205–31.

Whitford, William C. 1994. "The Ideal of Individualized Justice: Consumer Bankruptcy as Consumer Protection, and Consumer Protection in Consumer Bankruptcy." *American Bankruptcy Law Journal* 68 (Fall): 397–417.

Williams, Winton E. 1998. *Games Creditors Play*. Durham, NC: Carolina Academic Press.

CHAPTER 4

CONSUMPTION, DEBT, AND PORTFOLIO CHOICE: TESTING THE EFFECTS OF BANKRUPTCY LAW

Andreas Lehnert and Dean Maki

Introduction

In the United States, consumer bankruptcy (Chapter 7 and Chapter 13) is designed to provide debtors a fresh start. Broadly speaking, after a household successfully files a bankruptcy petition, its unsecured debts are erased, but it must forfeit any assets above an exemption level determined by law. Laws regulating bankruptcy are a complex mix of state and federal rules. While the specific legal details are beyond the scope of this essay, in general, state laws set the exemption levels above which households forfeit assets; these range from exemptions as low as $75 to more than $100,000 (or, indeed, potentially unlimited levels).[1]

U.S.-style consumer bankruptcy laws, combined with unsecured debt, provide households with a crude form of insurance. Households can lower their buffer-stock savings secure in the knowledge that they can tap a line of unsecured debt. If they suffer a severe, persistent, income shock they can default on their debts while still keeping some assets to use as a buffer stock.[2] In the absence of other forms of insurance, households would be less willing to use unsecured debt in states with less generous bankruptcy laws, although lenders would be more willing to extend unsecured debt in such states. Further, a household with relatively large debts would cut consumption more in response to an income shock in less generous states.

At the same time, though, Chapter 7 bankruptcy laws distort households' portfolio choices. Households that file for bankruptcy are better off if they have assets right up to the exemption level set in law. Thus, it is in households' interest to simultaneously hold low-return liquid assets even while they have a significant amount of high-interest debt. Morrison (1999) and Bertaut (2001) have documented the existence of this anomaly using the Survey of Consumer Finances. Telyukova (2006) calibrates a model of liquidity shocks in a model with cash and credit goods in which households carry both low-return liquid assets and high-cost unsecured debts.

Finally, all else equal, households will be more likely to declare bankruptcy in states with more generous exemptions. Of course, all else may not be equal, as lenders may react to prevailing bankruptcy laws by restricting credit to borrowers living in states with generous laws; so the net effect of bankruptcy law on bankruptcy rates may go in either direction.

To test these effects, we collected data on state personal bankruptcy exemptions and other state-level information from 1984 to 1999. We matched these data with household-level responses from the Consumer Expenditure Survey (CE) over the same period. The CE contains detailed information about households' consumption, along with some information about their geographic location, demographic characteristics, finances, income, occupation, employment, assets, and debts. We use the CE's portfolio information to test whether households in generous bankruptcy law states are more likely to simultaneously hold low-return liquid assets and high-interest unsecured debt. We refer to this practice as *borrowing to save.*

The CE interviews the same household once per quarter for five quarters; the first interview is excluded from the public use microdata, but all other interviews are available. Thus it is possible to construct a short panel for each household, testing how consumption growth responds to shocks of various types.[3]

Our main findings are as follows: (1) bankruptcy rates are higher in states with more generous exemptions; (2) households are more likely to borrow to save in states with more generous exemptions; and (3) there is a U-shaped relationship between consumption insurance and bankruptcy exemptions.

While this essay mainly studies the broader effects of bankruptcy law, many other essays have directly studied the bankruptcy decision itself.[4] Fay, Hurst, and White (2002) argue that the bankruptcy decision is heavily influenced by the financial benefit of filing.[5] White (1998) finds that at least 15 percent of households would benefit financially from declaring bankruptcy. She argues that the option cost of filing is substantial enough to prevent many households from declaring bankruptcy.

Olney (1999) studies the effect of bankruptcy law on households' consumption decisions during the Great Depression in the United States. She compares consumption's sensitivity to income shocks before and after a major bankruptcy law reform in the early 1930s. She finds that households cut consumption more in response to income shocks under the less generous bankruptcy regime. Thus she concludes that punitive bankruptcy laws contributed to the consumption collapse of the early 1930s.

In October 2005 the U.S. government enacted the Bankruptcy Abuse Prevention and Consumer Protection Act, a comprehensive set of changes to the national bankruptcy code. The law, in part, imposed a means test for debtors to have access to Chapter 7 bankruptcy; in effect, debtors deemed to have sufficient means to repay part of their obligations are steered toward filing under Chapter 13 of the bankruptcy code, which specifies a repayment plan. In addition, the law for the first time imposed national limits on the amount of home equity that filers could protect from creditors.

The law's ultimate effects remain unclear. Predictably, households rushed to file ahead of the enactment of the new rules. In the months since then, bankruptcy filing rates have fallen to less than half their average rate in the years prior to the reform. However, it is too soon to determine whether this drop is permanent.

From the point of view of the analysis in this essay, the major effect of the new law is to significantly raise the fixed cost of filing for bankruptcy and, in certain cases, to limit the generosity of an individual state's exemption. However, borrowers still have access to relief from their creditors, and this relief continues to vary across states. Thus, much of the analysis in this essay will remain relevant.

The plan of this essay is as follows. We first provide a theoretical framework for our analysis. Next we describe our data sources and the construction of the bankruptcy law database and generosity measures. We then present our results. The final section concludes the findings of this study. A companion appendix, available upon request, provides complete documentation on data construction, coding of bankruptcy laws, and an exhaustive set of robustness tests.

The Effect of Bankruptcy Exemptions

In this section we discuss the effect of bankruptcy exemptions on equilibrium borrowing, bankruptcy filings, portfolio choice, and consumption smoothing. In addition, we present our empirical identification strategies to test for these effects.

Consumer bankruptcy laws define an *exemption level* for a household's assets. In a Chapter 7 bankruptcy, the household's unsecured debts are, in essence, erased. At the same time, creditors seize all of the household's assets above the exemption threshold. (In practice, laws are more complicated than this, with separate exemptions for different types of asset; we discuss this in greater detail later.)

Theoretically, larger bankruptcy exemptions can either increase or decrease bankruptcy rates. By making default more attractive, exemptions increase the probability that any given borrower will file for bankruptcy. On the other hand, lenders may demand higher interest rates or restrict credit in other ways in reaction to expected defaults. Such restrictions could lead to a decrease in bankruptcy filings. The empirically interesting question is whether exemptions have any measurable correlation with filings, and the direction and magnitude of this effect.

Households that intend to file for bankruptcy should hold a gross portfolio that maximizes their post-bankruptcy welfare. For example, a household living in a state with a \$10,000 exemption level that had \$8,000 in assets should borrow an extra \$2,000 in unsecured debt before filing for bankruptcy. We refer to this behavior as "borrowing to save." Unsecured debts typically carry high interest rates while liquid assets typically pay low returns; so borrowing to save is costly. Indeed, bankruptcy laws are one of these few rational reasons for this behavior. (See Telyukova [2006] for a model without bankruptcy law in which households also rationally borrow to save.)

Finally, consumer bankruptcy laws combined with unsecured debt can provide a crude form of insurance. Households could use their credit cards to buffer consumption when faced with a bad income shock. If the income shock persists, the household will approach its borrowing limit. At a certain point, debt repayment would require an unacceptable drop in consumption, so the household instead files for bankruptcy, discharging its debt at the cost of limited future borrowing opportunities. (This is precisely the model used by Chatterjee et al. 2003 and others.) However, the relationship between the insurance value of bankruptcy exemptions and their generosity is not monotone. If large exemptions make unsecured borrowing extremely expensive, households will be unable to use unsecured debt to buffer consumption in the first place. On the other hand, as Carroll and others have emphasized, if exemptions are too low, households will be unwilling to risk the severe consumption penalties associated with default to borrow even small amounts.

Thus, theory predicts that there should be a relationship between exemption levels and the sensitivity of consumption growth to income shocks. Further, this sensitivity ought to depend on the amount of unsecured debt a household has, relative to its permanent income. The stock of household debt represents the results both of the household's optimal consumption plan and the shocks the household has experienced. The propensity and ability of households to borrow may very well (as we discussed) depend on the prevailing bankruptcy exemption. Nonetheless, comparing how two similar high-debt households, one facing low exemptions and the other facing high exemptions, alter consumption in the face of similar income shocks will identify the insurance role of bankruptcy exemptions if the laws are not correlated with the income shocks.

As we have discussed, the phenomena we test in this essay do not have monotone relationships with bankruptcy exemptions. However, in order to determine whether current bankruptcy exemptions are socially suboptimal, policy makers need estimates of the marginal effects of bankruptcy laws on bankruptcy rates, portfolio distortions, and consumption insurance. These are precisely the estimates we provide in this essay.

Data

Overview

To test the implications of our model, we will use three different datasets. The first comprises annual state-level bankruptcy rates and our measures of each state's Chapter 7 bankruptcy asset exemptions from 1984 to 1999. We refer to this database as the *bankruptcy law database*.

The second and third datasets are nested subsets of the Consumer Expenditure Survey (CE). The CE interviews a rotating panel of households five times with the interviews spaced three months apart; however, responses to the first interview are not part of the public use micro dataset for privacy reasons. For about 80 percent of observations, we know the household's state of residence, and thus can match these households with the prevailing bankruptcy law that they face.

Our second database, which we refer to as the *portfolio database*, comprises those households in the CE with valid responses to the CE's questions about portfolios. At the fifth interview, participants are asked about their holdings of financial assets and about their unsecured debts outstanding. We are particularly interested in holdings of liquid assets, defined as transaction accounts plus savings accounts, which typically pay a low return because of their liquidity. We are also interested in the quantity of unsecured debt outstanding, for which lenders charge a spread over the low-risk liquid return paid on liquid assets.

Our final database, the *insurance database*, comprises those households in the portfolio database for whom we have valid income and consumption measures at the second and fifth interviews. Thus the insurance database exploits the short panel nature of the CE.

Bankruptcy Law

Coding bankruptcy laws is a necessarily complex procedure, reflecting the complexities of the laws themselves. The most crucial distinction in the law is between homeowners and renters. Homeowners have access to each state's *homestead exemption*, the exemption applied to equity in a home used as a primary residence. Homestead exemptions vary considerably, from zero in Delaware and Maryland, to explicitly unlimited in Florida, Texas, and a few other states. (Minnesota capped its homestead exemption in 1993, and Iowa's homestead exemption is effectively unlimited; in addition, in our sample period, Oklahoma, South Dakota, and Kansas had unlimited exemptions.) Renters, by contrast, have access only to a state's *personal exemptions*, which are not only significantly lower, on average, than homestead exemptions, but are also often complex and asset-specific. Homeowners may claim both the local homestead exemption and the personal exemption.

States also differ in their treatment of married filers: Some allow doubling of exemptions, some take no notice of a filer's marital status, and others make special provisions for married filers. More detail on the construction of the bankruptcy law exemptions is contained in the companion appendix to this essay (available upon request).

Exemption Quartiles

As we are probably measuring bankruptcy law with error, we create *exemption quartiles* to use as our primary regressors. Moreover, even if we measured bankruptcy law perfectly, there is still the issue of how to classify states with unlimited homestead exemptions. Here, they are simply assigned to the top quartile.

We created two classes of quartiles: the *U.S. quartiles* and the *CE quartiles*. The *U.S. quartiles* treat all 51 states equally over the entire sample period. Thus in constructing the quartile ranks for married homeowners (for example), we first deflated the nominal exemptions set by law for married homeowners in all states and all years and then divided the resulting 816 state-year combinations into four groups of 204 state-years each.

By contrast, *CE quartiles* are based on households in the CE. We matched each married homeowner (for example) to the real prevailing bankruptcy exemption available to it. We then produced quartiles from this sample. Because the CE suppresses the state identifiers of all households from about eight states (for privacy reasons), it is possible that the CE is not a representative sample of the distribution of national bankruptcy law. (The number of states for which location information is available in the CE changes over time, and depends on the CE's strategy for maintaining privacy.) In the companion appendix to this essay (available upon request), we demonstrate that the distribution of states in the CE quartiles closely approximate the U.S. quartiles. We also show that the quartiles do not generally favor one part of our sample over another; that is, the nominal bankruptcy exemptions changed often enough to prevent variation over time from being driven entirely by the deflator.

Results

Testing the Effect of Law on Bankruptcy Rates

Model and Tests

We begin by showing that our constructed quartile variables are correlated with observed aggregate bankruptcy rates. Our household-level data do not contain information on the household's bankruptcy experience; so for this exercise we use only aggregate, state-level variables. As a result, any model specification will have a tenuous link to theory. We present here only the results from a static model with fixed effects for each state and year in our sample. Sample statistics are shown in table 4.1.[6]

We model an individual i living in state s and year t as having a probability π_i of declaring ($p_i = 1$) or not declaring ($p_i = 0$) Chapter 7 bankruptcy. We do not observe the *individual's* bankruptcy decision, p_i, only the aggregate result of all individuals' decisions in a particular state-year combination, $P_{s,t}$. Moreover, we do not know, in a given state-year, how bankruptcy filers split by housing tenure (i.e., owning vs. renting one's residence) and marital status. Thus, one can envision two separate procedures: testing the effect of the U.S. quartiles for renters and for owners *separately* or *jointly*. We test the joint effect of U.S. quartiles; results testing the separate effects show a similar pattern to those presented here.

One potential problem with any joint test of the effect of bankruptcy law provisions for different types of filers is that states' quartile ranks do not differ significantly by marital status. This makes identifying the effect of marriage provisions in the law difficult. Table 4.2 shows the distribution of states across married homeowner quartiles conditional on states' single homeowner quartile rank and renter rank. As the table shows, there is little variation between the single and married homeowner quartiles, but there is significant variation between the quartiles for married homeowners and single renters. Indeed, there appears at first glance to be

Table 4.1 State-level sample means

	U.S. Quartile Rank			
Variable	*Bot*	*3rd*	*2nd*	*Top*
	Married Homeowners			
Exemption	24,580	40,648	91,779	212,703
	(4,471)	(7,802)	(20,222)	(90,140)
Chapter 7 rate	0.22	0.18	0.22	0.23
	(0.11)	(0.11)	(0.11)	(0.12)
	Single Renters			
Exemption	5,201	8,676	12,928	23,696
	(1,258)	(1,089)	(1,583)	(9,113)
Chapter 7 rate	0.23	0.17	0.22	0.23
	(0.10)	(0.11)	(0.12)	(0.12)

Note: Table 4.1 gives sample means and standard deviations from a sample of 51 states over the 16 years 1984–1999, conditional on the state's exemption quartile. States switch quartiles across years, so that any one state's data may be present in the results for many different quartiles. Statistics for exemptions are taken among states with finite exemptions only.

Table 4.2 Relation of U.S. quartiles

Married Homeowners	*Single Homeowners*			
	Bottom	*3rd*	*2nd*	*Top*
Bottom	189	15	0	0
3rd	15	169	20	0
2nd	0	12	170	21
Top	0	8	13	184
Married Homeowners	*Single Renters*			
	Bottom	*3rd*	*2nd*	*Top*
Bottom	105	60	38	1
3rd	40	85	51	28
2nd	13	38	60	92
Top	46	25	52	82

Note: Table 4.2 gives the number of state-year combinations in each of the indicated categories.

no relationship between the two quartile rankings. Further, studies of bankruptcy filers show that a plurality of Chapter 7 filers are married homeowners, followed by single renters. Thus, we use the quartile dummies for married homeowners and single renters.

Given that our data are a series of individual decisions aggregated within states, we use a grouped version of a limited dependent estimator. We use a logistic model specification for ease of computation:

$$\log\left(\frac{P_{s,t}}{N_{s,t} - P_{s,t}}\right) = b^{Top}\delta^{Top}_{s,t} + b^{2nd}\delta^{2nd}_{s,t} + b^{3rd}\delta^{3rd}_{s,t} + \mathbf{X}_{s,t} \cdot \mathrm{B} + \epsilon_{s,t}.$$

Here $N_{s,t}$ is the total population in state s and year t; the variables $\delta_{i,s,t}$ are indicator variables set to unity if state s in year t is in bankruptcy exemption quartile i; and $\mathbf{X}_{s,t}$ is a vector of other explanatory variables, which contains a full set of state and year dummy variables. The weights associated with each observation, denoted. $\omega_{s,t}$, are $(N_{s,t} - P_{s,t})P_{s,t}/N_{s,t}$. Note that $\omega_{s,t}$ is the inverse of the large-sample variance of $\epsilon_{s,t}$.

Table 4.3 displays coefficient estimates and robust standard errors for the joint regression, which includes quartile rank dummies for married homeowners and single renters.

Notice that bankruptcy laws are correlated with bankruptcy rates: the largest coefficient is associated with the top quartile for married homeowners, the largest group of Chapter 7 filers. Further, the coefficient estimates generally become smaller as one moves down exemption quartiles.

Policy Experiment

With the coefficient estimates from table 4.3, we can determine the effect of a policy experiment where homestead exemptions are capped so that all states currently in the top three quartiles are forced to have exemptions equal to those of the bottom quartile of married homeowners, but personal exemptions are untouched.

Note that while the 2005 reform act limited some filers' access to homestead exemptions, the rules are more complex than the policy experiment conducted here. Our policy experiment is stylized, and is mainly intended to demonstrate the relative importance of bankruptcy law in our empirical results.

In 1999, there were 885,571 total Chapter 7 bankruptcy filings. Under the change described earlier, we predict that there would instead have been only 724,003 filings, a decrease of 161,584 filings or more than 18 percent.

However, if instead of tightening their bankruptcy laws, states were instead to loosen them, so that all states moved to the top quartile of married homeowner exemptions, the effects would be relatively larger. In that case, we predict that there would have been approximately 250,000 more Chapter 7 bankruptcy filings, an increase of 29 percent. The effect of loosening exemptions is larger in part because of the pattern of bankruptcy filings across quartiles. The bottom quartile of states actually had the second-highest number of bankruptcy filings; these are the states that would be most affected by an increase in bankruptcy exemptions.

Comparison to Other Studies

A few other essays have examined the link between bankruptcy exemptions and bankruptcy rates, including Mulligan (2001) and Hynes (1998).[7] Hynes (1998) (Chapter 2) uses panel data from 1980 to 1998 on states to estimate linear probability

Table 4.3 Joint effect of homeowner and renter exemptions

Explanatory variable	*Coefficient Estimate*	*Robust Std. Err.*
Married homeowner quartiles		
Top	0.4941	0.0793
2nd	0.3257	0.0673
3rd	0.1128	0.0286
Single renter quartiles		
Top	0.1020	0.0463
2nd	0.0798	0.0447
3rd	0.0895	0.0349
F(*State*)	691.43	
F(*Year*)	161.49	
Observations	816	

Note: Table 4.3 gives coefficient estimates and robust standard errors from a weighted least squares regression of Chapter 7 bankruptcy rates on the U.S. quartile dummies for married homeowners and single renters (the two largest groups of bankruptcy filers). *F*(*Variable*) gives *F*-test statistic of hypothesis that all *variable* dummies are jointly equal to zero.

and grouped probit models of bankruptcy rates with a variety of measures of the generosity of state-level bankruptcy laws. He finds that being in the top quartile of states is associated with a higher filing rate; however, his results are of smaller magnitude than ours, and are sensitive to specification, whereas our results are both economically and statistically significant and robust to changes in specification. The main differences in our results appear to be in the effect of the personal (renter) exemptions, where measurement problems (as we discussed) are greatest. In addition, White (1987) and Nelson (2000) examine the effect of the 1978 Bankruptcy Reform Act on household bankruptcy filings. We find that a plausible bankruptcy reform measure (although, we emphasize, not the one enacted in 2005) would lower Chapter 7 filings more than 18 percent.

Further, the result provides some assurance that we are actually measuring bankruptcy law fairly well, despite the inherent difficulties in coding the laws. For these empirical results, we cannot use the household-level datasets that we constructed, because they do not contain information on households' bankruptcy decisions. Instead, we must use the purely state-level database that we constructed.

Testing the Portfolio Choice Effects of Bankruptcy Law

As shown earlier, bankruptcy law encourages households to simultaneously hold low-return liquid assets and high-interest unsecured debt. In this section we present evidence that households living in states with higher bankruptcy exemptions are more likely to engage in this behavior.

One of our primary sources for bankruptcy law is the attorney's handbook by Williamson (published annually); see, for example, Williamson (1999). These books explicitly recommend that bankruptcy lawyers advise their clients to convert as many of their assets as possible into exempt forms before filing for bankruptcy, a practice known as "negative estate planning." Thus, one can take our results here as evidence that negative estate planning is more common in states with more generous bankruptcy laws.

Definitions and Empirical Specification

Our general strategy is to divide households by housing tenure (owners and renters) and estimate probit regressions of whether a household borrows to save on bankruptcy law variables and a full set of controls. We estimate these models using the portfolio database described earlier.

We first determine whether a given household is, in fact, "borrowing to save." The CE asks about the balance on checking and savings accounts, as well as for unsecured debt. For each household, we generate an indicator variable, set to one if (1) both liquid assets and unsecured debt exceed a threshold level and, (2) liquid assets exceed 3 percent of gross income. We vary the threshold in thousand-dollar increments, from $2,000 to $5,000. Sample statistics from the dataset are available upon request.

In addition to bankruptcy law, we included indicator variables for whether the household head was married, had a high school diploma, a college degree, or was a minority (as of the fifth interview). We also included a full set of indicators for the nine different family types recorded by the CE; indicators for the month of the fifth interview (to pick up seasonal effects); and indicators for the year of the fifth interview. We also included the level and the log of real total family income before taxes, the number of family members, the number of earners, the average age of the household head and spouse, and age squared. For brevity, coefficient estimates for these control variables are not presented.

As bankruptcy law variables we used both the CE and the U.S. quartiles described in an earlier section. In addition, some specifications include a full set of state fixed effects; identification in these specifications comes only from states that switch exemption quartiles over the time period.

Results

In table 4.4 we display selected results for regressions using the $2,000 threshold for renters and the $5,000 threshold for homeowners. (Extensive robustness tests, including results for all combinations of thresholds, show similar patterns.) The tables show results from eight regressions: specifications estimated separately for homeowners and renters, both with and without a full set of state fixed effects and using either the U.S. or CE quartiles.

We find strong evidence that homeowners in the top quartile of bankruptcy generosity are more likely to borrow to save than homeowners in the bottom quartile of bankruptcy generosity (controlling for a number of characteristics). We estimate that homeowners living in states in the top quartile of bankruptcy exemptions are between 1 and 4.5 percent more likely to borrow to save than homeowners living in states in the

Table 4.4 Selected results from the borrowing to save model

	Probability Derivatives $\partial F/\partial x$			
	Renters: $2,000 Threshold			
	Quartile			
	CE		*U.S.*	
Top	0.0054	0.0020	0.0078	0.0173
	(0.0046)	(0.0137)	(0.0041)	(0.0147)
2nd	0.0000	0.0051	−0.0049	0.0084
	(0.0045)	(0.0118)	(0.0049)	(0.0128)
3rd	−0.0032	−0.0032	−0.0004	0.0045
	(0.0044)	(0.0097)	(0.0046)	(0.0110)
	Homeowners: $5,000 Threshold			
Top	0.0092	0.0448	0.0073	0.0273
	(0.0078)	(0.0176)	(0.0079)	(0.0160)
2nd	0.0080	0.0292	0.0063	0.0222
	(0.0044)	(0.0144)	(0.0043)	(0.0133)
3rd	0.0052	0.0207	0.0016	0.0115
	(0.0047)	(0.0092)	(0.0046)	(0.0093)
State dummies	No	Yes	No	Yes

Note: Table 4.4 gives probability derivatives from a profit regression of *BORRSAVE* (with a cutoff of $2,000 for renters and $5,000 for owners) on a set of control variables (results not shown here); and bankruptcy exemption quartiles. CE quartiles are formed from the CE sample while U.S. quartiles are formed from the U.S. states over the sample period (see section 3 for details). Some state dummy variables predict failure perfectly; all such states are dropped for regressions using state-fixed effects. For regressions without state-fixed effects, standard errors are corrected for clustering; robust, cluster-adjusted, standard errors are in parentheses.

bottom quartile (the excluded category). Compare these effects to the overall rate of borrowing to save among homeowners for the full sample: among homeowners at the $5,000 threshold the incidence is 7.5 percent. Thus the effects are substantively large.

By contrast, we find very weak evidence of this effect among renters. Renters living in states in the top quartile of bankruptcy exemptions are at most 1.7 percent more likely to borrow to save than renters living in states in the bottom quartile; at the higher thresholds the effect vanishes, suggesting that renters, who are poorer on average than homeowners, are doing their borrowing to save (if any) at a lower level. The sample incidence of borrowing to save among renters at the $2,000 threshold is about 9 percent.

Testing the Insurance Role of Bankruptcy Law

The theory developed earlier also predicts the possibility of *Olney effects*, the increased sensitivity of consumption to income shocks in tight bankruptcy states.

In states with low Chapter 7 exemptions, lenders are more willing to extend credit, which some households use to bring forward consumption. As a result, *ex ante* they are better off, but at the cost of servicing a large *ex post* debt burden. Almost mechanically, such a result requires households to cut consumption more in response to shocks. Note that our theory only raises the *possibility* that these effects would appear in equilibrium; it is by no means certain.

Definitions and Measurement Issues

Our general strategy is to use the CE's short-panel nature to test for the presence of Olney effects. Because the CE reports each household's total family income as it enters the survey and at its final interview, we can construct each household's income growth over the duration of the CE. We can combine this with the CE's excellent consumption information to construct a consumption growth measure over the same time period. We examine the correlation of consumption and income growth for different types of household; large correlations we take to mean less consumption insurance and small correlations we take to mean more consumption insurance.

For this test, we use the insurance dataset described earlier. Essentially, the insurance dataset comprises those observations from the portfolio dataset for which we have valid second and fifth interviews.

Based on the CE's portfolio information, we can split households on the basis of their outstanding debt on the eve of entering the CE. One complication with this strategy is that we do not know whether a household has zero debt because it is thrifty or is credit constrained. Unlike the Survey of Consumer Finances, the CE does not ask whether a participant has been turned down for credit, or is discouraged from borrowing. Thus we will treat the approximately 37 percent of the sample that report having no debt at the second interview differently than those that report having some debt.

We define consumption as real expenditures on nondurables, excluding expenditures on educational services, health services, charitable contributions, and any housing-related expenditures, including rent, equivalent rent, and imputed rents. The major components of this consumption measure are food (both at home and out), clothing, footwear, alcohol, and tobacco. This is the same consumption measure used by Parker (1999), but is slightly broader than the measure used by Souleles (1999).

Before we can analyze the effect of debt on consumption, we have to determine which households have an unusually high debt burden at the second interview. We constructed four separate indicators of high debt, based on two different *absolute* dollar thresholds, the ratio of debt to *actual* income, and the ratio of debt to *potential* income. We formed potential income by regressing log income on a variety of explanatory variables with a restricted data set that excluded those households who were too sick to work or involuntarily unemployed; we estimated the model's coefficients separately for homeowners and renters. The full specification and parameter estimates are in a separate appendix, available upon request.

We use $3,000 and $6,000 as our two absolute dollar thresholds. These are about the 75th and 87th percentiles of real debt holdings. For the thresholds based on actual or potential income, we labeled all households with debt-to-income ratios greater than the median (among households with positive debt) as being "high debt."

Table 4.5 displays sample means for a variety of variables in each realization of the debt indicator. One arresting observation is that households with zero debt have the fastest income growth (marked as $\Delta\log(y)$ in the tables); at the same time, they have the lowest level of income, homeownership rate, and are least likely to be married or to have a high school or college degree. Thus we conclude that zero-debt households are in general relatively poor and high-risk. However, we shall also argue that the group of zero-debt households conceals heterogeneity, with some of the households being relatively wealthy.

Note also that households with high debt in the sense of a high absolute *level* of debt are different from households with high debt in the sense of a high *ratio* of debt to income. These differences are robust to changes in the threshold level of debt, and to whether actual or potential income is used. Households with high

Table 4.5 Sample means by debt status for the insurance model

		Threshold		*Debt-to-Income*	
	Zero debt (1)	*Low* (2)	*High* (3)	*Low* (4)	*High* (5)
Income	31.69	41.72	50.05	44.56	46.03
	(23.29)	(23.09)	(22.61)	(23.50)	(22.98)
Debt		1.09	9.52	1.00	8.42
		(0.84)	(10.11)	(0.89)	(9.75)
Assets	8.05	8.34	6.00	9.07	5.60
	(16.44)	(14.86)	(11.26)	(15.43)	(10.92)
Age	45.68	43.61	41.54	43.40	42.05
	(14.05)	(12.82)	(11.08)	(12.39)	(11.86)
$\Delta\log(y)$	0.07	0.04	0.04	0.04	0.04
	(0.67)	(0.57)	(0.53)	(0.56)	(0.54)
			Percent		
Own home	52.01	68.50	73.68	74.22	67.22
Married	49.84	60.84	69.44	67.09	61.98
Black	18.54	11.19	9.00	8.74	11.76
H.S.	51.29	58.74	60.87	58.68	60.62
College	17.47	23.78	27.66	27.34	23.55
Top quart.	23.77	24.60	26.94	24.42	26.79
Bot. quart.	24.47	25.76	25.31	25.34	25.79
N	5,937	5,552	4,176	4,865	4,863

Note: Table 4.5 gives sample statistics from the insurance model database for households with no debt (column 1), households with debt between \$1 and \$3,000 (column 2), households with more than \$3,000 in debt (column 3), households with debt to potential income ratios greater than zero but below the median (column 4), and households with potential income ratios greater than the median (column 5). See the text for definition of potential income. All dollars figures are in thousands and deflated to 1996.

levels of debt appear to have higher permanent incomes than households with high *ratios* of debt to income. Under the level criterion, high-debt households are more likely to own their homes, have college degrees, and be married; under the ratio criterion these differences are exactly reversed. In addition, while high-debt households under the level criterion have much higher incomes than their low-debt counterparts, high-debt households under the ratio criterion have only slightly higher incomes. This fact reassures us that the ratio criterion is not driven by households with extraordinarily low incomes.

We can address the nature of zero-debt households, and the differences between households satisfying our various high-debt criteria, by plotting the empirical distribution of income for each group. Figures 4.1 and 4.2 give the distributions of real incomes among those with zero debt, low debt, and high debt for two definitions of "high debt": one based on a dollar threshold and one based on a ratio to potential income. Three striking facts emerge from these figures. (1) The group of zero-debt households does appear to contain a wide variety of household types. The income distribution of zero-debt households is more or less flat among incomes from \$18,000 to \$75,000. (2) Using a dollar threshold produces two sets of households with dissimilar incomes; high-debt households clearly have higher incomes. (3) By contrast, dividing households based on the ratio of debt to potential income produces two sets of households with similar incomes.

Considering these facts, we use a ratio measure to classify households as high debt or low debt. To avoid misclassifying households with temporarily low income, we use the ratio of debt to potential income as our measure.

Figure 4.1 Income by debt status (absolute threshold of \$3,000)

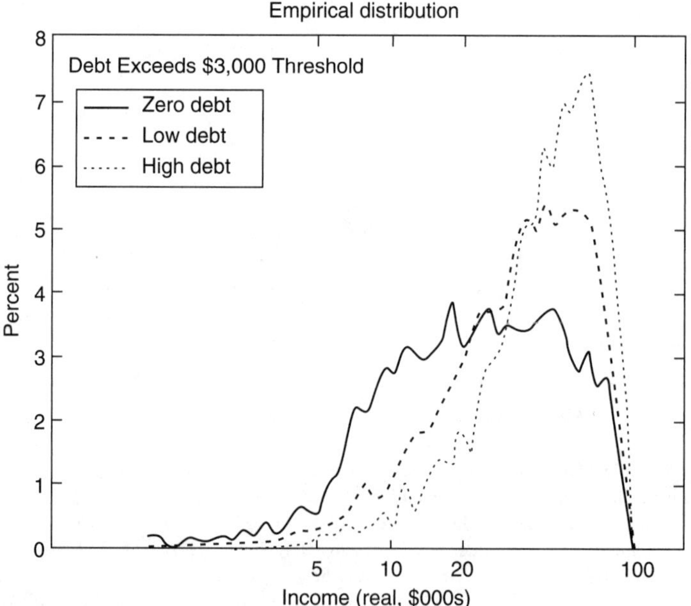

Figure 4.2 Income by debt status (debt/potential income)

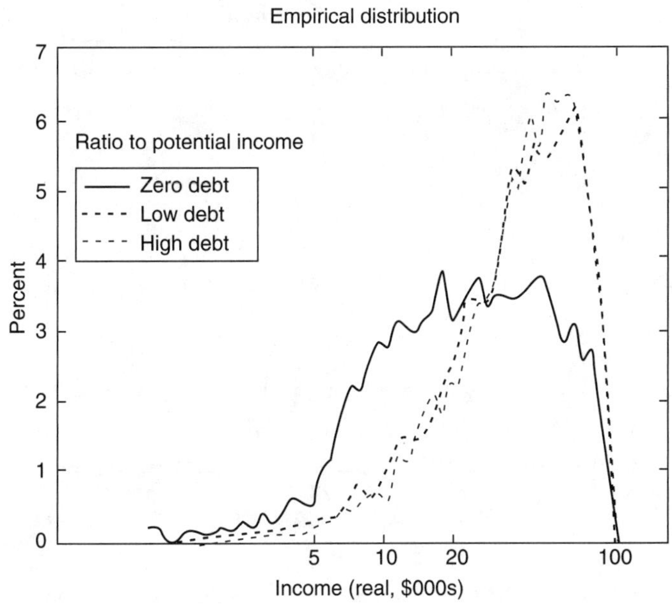

Empirical Test

We wish to test whether high-debt households' consumption in tight bankruptcy states is more sensitive to changes in income than high-debt households' consumption in generous bankruptcy states. As a preliminary step, we display the empirical distributions of income and consumption changes in figure 4.3. The income shocks have the unusual feature that they are either quite small (tightly centered around zero) or quite large, with income increasing or decreasing by more than a factor of five in about 2 percent of cases (marked with the grey dots in the figure). These large changes reflect households that experienced or recovered from a devastating income shock, for example, unemployment or illness, or misreported their income at one interview. Notice that the distribution of consumption assumes a more conventional shape, not showing the extreme points that income shocks do.

As an initial trial of the hypothesis, we can simply calculate the average log difference in consumption for every combination of debt status and bankruptcy exemption quartile (table 4.6).

In our analysis we want to measure the treatment effect of tight bankruptcy law on high-debt households. Clearly, households' access to credit and desire to borrow will in turn depend on the local bankruptcy law. Thus the road to debt will be different in different states; however, the reaction of consumption to an income shock ought to allow us to measure the effect of bankruptcy law. Because consumption's reaction to income shocks may depend on state-specific effects, we also include a full set of state-level indicators.

Figure 4.3 Consumption and income shock distributions

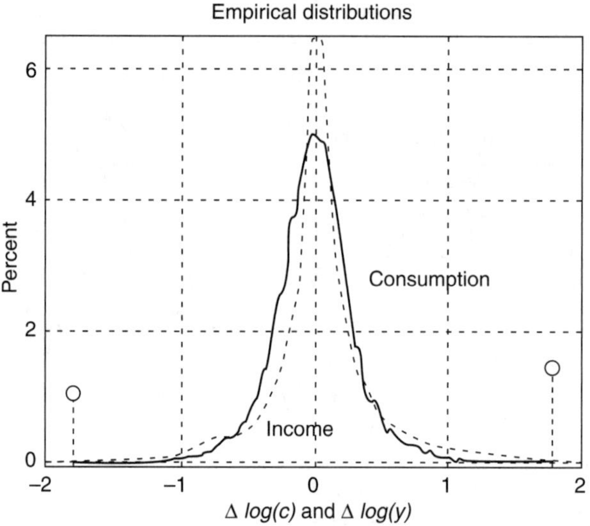

Table 4.6 Δlog(c) by debt and bankruptcy exemption

		Asset Exemption Quartile			
		Bottom	*3rd*	*2nd*	*Top*
			Homeowners		
Debt status					
Zero	$d = 0$	0.0140	−0.0128	−0.0093	−0.0111
		(0.2948)	(0.3010)	(0.2845)	(0.3049)
Low	$d/\hat{y} \leqslant 6.4\%$	−0.0021	−0.0084	−0.0203	−0.0034
		(0.2596)	(0.2705)	(0.2691)	(0.2890)
High	$d/\hat{y} > 6.4\%$	−0.0125	−0.0116	−0.0089	−0.0225
		(0.2634)	(0.2775)	(0.2702)	(0.2631)
			Renters		
Debt status					
Zero	$d = 0$	0.0055	0.0149	0.0076	0.0244
		(0.3153)	(0.3404)	(0.3086)	(0.3278)
Low	$d/\hat{y} \leqslant 6.4\%$	−0.0035	−0.0062	−0.0409	0.0019
		(0.2874)	(0.3064)	(0.2951)	(0.2995)
High	$d/\hat{y} > 6.4\%$	−0.0096	−0.0101	0.0012	0.0030
		(0.2875)	(0.2768)	(0.2801)	(0.3063)

Note: Table 4.6 gives means and standard deviations (in parentheses) for the log difference in nondurable consumption from the second to the fifth interviews of the CE depending on (1) the household's debt status and (2) the quartile bankruptcy exemption rank of the state-year in which the household resides. The median ratio of debt to potential income among households with any debt is 6.4 percent.

We thus estimate the parameters for the following regression equation for each of the three debt groups that we have defined (zero debt, low debt, and high debt):

$$\Delta\log(c_i) = \delta_i^{Top}\left[b^{Top} + \gamma^{Top}\Delta\log(y_i)\right] + \delta_i^{2nd}\left[b^{2nd} + \gamma^{2nd}\Delta\log(y_i)\right] + \delta_i^{3rd}\left[b^{3rd} + \gamma^{3rd}\Delta\log(y_i)\right] + \delta_i^{Bottom}\left[b^{Bottom} + \gamma^{Bottom}\Delta\log(y_i)\right] + \mathbf{X}_i \cdot \mathbf{B} + \epsilon_i. \quad (2)$$

We are most interested in how the consumption of a high-debt household reacts to income shocks relative to the consumption reaction of a low-debt household. If we did not split the samples by bankruptcy exemption quartiles (so that $\delta_i^{Top} = \ldots = \delta_i^{Bottom} = 1$) the reaction of households to income shocks would be captured by $\hat{\gamma}$. However, we are splitting our sample into high- and low-debt portions and by bankruptcy exemption quartile. Thus we will be comparing $\widehat{\gamma^{Bottom}}$ estimated among low-debt households to $\widehat{\gamma^{Top}}$, also estimated among low-debt households.

Results

The regression results are presented in table 4.7. Among low-debt households there is a clear U-shaped relationship between bankruptcy exemption and the correlation of consumption growth to income growth. Increasing personal exemptions leads to better insurance for renters, while increasing total exemptions (personal plus homestead) leads to worse insurance for homeowners. Among high-debt households, these results are almost repeated, except for the group of high-debt renters living in states with generous personal bankruptcy exemptions.

First, consider only high-debt homeowners: their log consumption growth responds at a rate of 0.0426 to their log income growth in generous bankruptcy states; at the same time, consumption growth responds only at a rate of 0.0037 in tight bankruptcy states, which is not statistically different from zero. Thus consumption growth is actually *less* sensitive to income growth in tight bankruptcy states than in loose bankruptcy states. The pattern is the same for low-debt homeowners, so that the difference between high- and low-debt households' response to income growth does not vary across states by bankruptcy generosity.

For renters the results are more complex; perversely, *low*-debt households feel the effects of income shocks more keenly in tight bankruptcy states. For high-debt households, the average consumption response to income growth is lower in the top two quartiles than in the bottom two quartiles, but the high sensitivity in the top quartile is still evidence against an Olney effect. Relatively low-debt renters thus appear to be the single group that exhibits a clear form of the Olney effect, although an argument can be made that high-debt renters also appear to suffer from a form of Olney effect.

Table 4.7 Test for Olney effects

	Owners			*Renters*		
	Zero-Debt	*Low-Debt*	*High-Debt*	*Zero-Debt*	*Low-Debt*	*High-Debt*
γ^{Top}	0.0358	0.0507	0.0426	−0.0087	0.0101	0.0417
	(0.0222)	(0.0183)	(0.0188)	(0.0207)	(0.0255)	(0.0223)
γ^{2nd}	0.0646	0.0463	0.0181	−0.0060	0.0279	0.0025
	(0.0163)	(0.0195)	(0.0278)	(0.0171)	(0.0364)	(0.0322)
γ^{3rd}	0.0234	0.0349	0.0218	0.0768	0.0326	0.0309
	(0.0135)	(0.0170)	(0.0207)	(0.0199)	(0.0289)	(0.0321)
γ^{Bottom}	0.0598	0.0127	0.0037	0.0028	0.0703	0.0468
	(0.0198)	(0.0160)	(0.0209)	(0.0220)	(0.0236)	(0.0217)
b^{Top}	−0.1489	−0.1522	−0.0758	−0.0462	0.3851	−0.0993
	(0.1103)	(0.1021)	(0.1192)	(0.1098)	(0.1462)	(0.1230)
b^{2nd}	−0.1594	−0.1501	−0.0822	−0.0743	0.3695	−0.0966
	(0.1052)	(0.0988)	(0.1159)	(0.1064)	(0.1425)	(0.1235)
b^{3rd}	−0.1023	−0.1177	−0.1247	−0.0728	0.4725	−0.1189
	(0.0996)	(0.0947)	(0.1132)	(0.1088)	(0.1459)	(0.1293)
b^{Bottom}	−0.0660	−0.1118	−0.1291	−0.1004	0.5262	−0.1019
	(0.1040)	(0.0975)	(0.1152)	(0.1180)	(0.1554)	(0.1401)
F(State)	2.05	1.23	2.50	3.76	3.07	2.12
Prob >F	(0.0001)	0.1471	(0.0000)	(0.0000)	(0.0000)	(0.0001)
Observations	3,088	3,611	3,269	2,849	1,254	1,594

Note: Table 4.7 gives selected regression coefficients and robust standard errors from estimating equation (2) under the indicated subsets of the data. The dependent variable in all cases is log consumption growth; the γ parameters give the coefficient on log income growth interacted with bankruptcy generosity quartile, the b parameters give the intercepts (the constant is suppressed). Here low debt is defined as having positive debt, but below the median debt to potential income ratio in the sample. Households with debt to potential income ratios above the median among those households with positive debt are classed as high debt. Only those households with exactly zero unsecured debt are classed as zero debt.

Permanent vs. Transitory Shocks to Income

Our model and data are very close to those used by Dynarski and Gruber (1997); they also used the log difference of consumption over the CE's short panel as their dependent variable, and they were also interested in the effect of income growth on consumption growth. Reaction to that study, including Moffit and Burtless (1997), pointed out that Dynarski and Gruber were not able to satisfactorily distinguish between transitory shocks to income (which ought to be smoothed away) and permanent shocks (for which insurance schemes would be less likely to compensate households). Indeed, much of the work in applied consumption concentrates precisely on this issue.[8] Furthermore, there can be no doubt that income is misreported in the CE, prompting the usual measurement error problems in our estimate of its effect.

However, in order to overturn our results, one would have to argue that the mix of permanent and transitory income shocks and the measurement error of income are somehow correlated with the quartile exemption rank of the state-year in which the household lives. Remember that our regressions all include a complete set of state and year fixed effects; so identification of the differential effect of bankruptcy law comes purely from a state's ranking relative to all other states in a given year. One may be able to make a case that permanent shocks to income are more common in a given year or in a given state or even in a given state in a given year (e.g., in Texas in 1987); nonetheless, so long as one is willing to accept that these effects are uncorrelated with bankruptcy exemption ranks, our estimates of the *relative magnitudes* of γ parameters will remain valid. The *absolute magnitudes* are probably attenuated by measurement error, but, again, this is unlikely to be correlated with bankruptcy law generosity.

Conclusion

In this Chapter we analyzed the relationships among bankruptcy law, bankruptcy rates, portfolio choice, and consumption. We used state-level and household-level data to test the effect of bankruptcy law variations. In particular we tested three propositions of interest to policy makers: (1) whether loose bankruptcy laws lead to increased bankruptcy rates, (2) what effect bankruptcy laws have on household portfolios, and (3) whether bankruptcy law provides an appreciable form of insurance to households.

We find that generous bankruptcy laws indeed lead to increased state-level bankruptcy rates and that they also discourage households from using their low-return liquid assets to pay off their high interest unsecured debt bills. We find some evidence that for renters, generous bankruptcy laws do appear to protect household consumption from income shocks. For homeowners, though, the opposite seems to hold true, with generous bankruptcy laws actually making consumption more sensitive to income.

Our results shed light on the differential effects of bankruptcy law on homeowners and renters. If states severely restricted their homestead exemptions, our results suggest that Chapter 7 filings would decrease, the incidence of borrowing to save would fall, and homeowners' consumption would be less sensitive to income shocks. At the same time, if states liberalized their personal exemptions (the exemptions that affect renters directly), our evidence suggests that bankruptcy filings and borrowing to save would increase only slightly, while renters' consumption would be less sensitive to income shocks.

Further, our study attempts to discern an effect of unsecured debt on consumption. Although much work obviously remains to be done in this area, our results can be taken as evidence that high levels of debt do not, by themselves, threaten households' consumption.

Notes

An earlier version of this paper circulated under the title The Great American Debtor. The views expressed in this essay are ours alone and do not necessarily reflect those of the Board of Governors or its staff or Barclays Capital. We thank Daniel [illegible], Karen

Dynan, Ronel Elul, Gary Engelhardt, David Laibson, Nick Souleles, Robert Townsend, and seminar participants at the Federal Reserve Board, the NBER Summer Institute, the meetings of the Society of Economic Dynamics in Costa Rica, Syracuse University, and the Seventh Annual Meeting of CEMLA in Guatemala. We received excellent research assistance from Sigurd Lund, Richard Sauoma, and Marcin Stawarcz. Any remaining errors are our own responsibility.

Board of Governors of the Federal Reserve System, Washington DC, 20551. Andreas.Lehnert@frb.gov.

Barclays Capital, New York.

1. As we discuss later, in 2005 the federal government enacted a major national reform of U.S. bankruptcy laws. For information on consumer bankruptcy laws outside the United States, see Alexopoulous and Domowitz (1998) and Ziegel (1997). For an analysis of the political economy of state bankruptcy laws, as well as a history of U.S. bankruptcy legislation, see Posner, Hynes, and Malani (2002).
2. Carroll (1992) argues that households face a small but real probability of earning zero non-capital income for an entire year; in such a setting bankruptcy law becomes essential if households are to borrow any amount at all.
3. Dynarski and Gruber (1997) also use the CE's short panel to test for consumption smoothing.
4. See Gross and Souleles (1998); Edelberg (2002); and Dawsey and Ausubel (2001).
5. See also Domowitz and Sartain (1999) and Elul and Subramanian (1999).
6. We have estimated dynamic versions of this model, using the dynamic panel models of Arellano and Bond (1991) and Bond (2002). The long-run effects of bankruptcy law were very similar to those presented here. We also estimated versions of this model that included myriad covariates, including state Chapter 13 bankruptcy rates, unemployment, income growth, house price growth, poverty rates, and nonlinear and lagged versions of these covariates. Again, the effects of interest were largely unchanged.
7. Mulligan (2001) uses a cross-section of states in 1993 and controls for socioeconomic and other legal variables (such as wage garnishment) that do not change much over time, but that do have powerful effects on bankruptcy rates. Because we have constructed a panel of states, we can work, in essence, with first-differences by state and ignore such factors.
8. See Gourinchas and Parker (2002); Stephens (2001); Banks, Blundell, and Brugiavini (2001); and Blundell, Pistaferri, and Preston (2002).

References

Alexopoulos, M., and I. Domowitz. 1998. "Personal Liabilities and Bankruptcy Reform: An International Perspective." *International Finance 1*(1): 127–59.

Arellano, M., and S. Bond. 1991. "Some Tests of Specification for Panel Data: Monte Carlo Evidence and an Application to Employment Equation." *Review of Economic Studies 58*(2): 277–97.

Banks, J., R. Blundell, and A. Brugiavini. 2001. "Risk Pooling, Precautionary Saving and Consumption Growth." *Review of Economic Studies 68*(4): 757–79.

Bertaut, C.C., and M. Haliassos. 2001. "Debt Revolvers for Self-Control." Manuscript, Federal Reserve Board, Washington, D.C.

Blundell, R., L. Pistaferri, and I. Preston. 2002. "Partial Insurance, Information, and Consumption Dynamics." Manuscript, Department of Economics, Stanford University, Palo Alto CA.

Bond, S. 2002. "Dynamic Panel Data Models: A Guide to Micro Data Methods and Practice." Centre for Microdata Methods and Practice Working Paper CWP09/02, The Institute for Fiscal Studies and the Department of Economics, University College, London.

Carroll, C.D. 1992. "Buffer Stock Saving: Some Macroeconomic Evidence." *Brookings Papers on Economic Activity 1992*(2): 61–156.

Chatterjee, S., D. Corbae, M. Nakajima, and J.-V. Rios-Rull. 2003. "A Quantitative Theory of Unsecured Consumer Credit with Risk of Default." Manuscript, Department of Economics, University of Pennsylvania, Philadelphia, PA.

Dawsey, A.E., and L.M. Ausubel. 2001. "Informal Bankruptcy." Manuscript, Department of Economics, University of Maryland, College Park MD.

Domowitz, I., and R.L. Sartain. 1999. "Determinants of the Consumer Bankruptcy Decision." *Journal of Finance 54*(1): 403–20.

Dynarski, S. and J. Gruber. 1997. "Can Families Smooth Variable Earnings?" *Brookings Papers on Economic Activity 1997*(1): 229–84.

Edelberg, W. 2002, December. "Risk-Based Pricing of Interest Rates in Consumer Loan Markets." Department of Economics, University of Chicago, Chicago IL.

Elul, R., and N. Subramanian. 1999. "Forum-Shopping and Personal Bankruptcy." Brown University Working Paper #99-1.

Fay, S., E. Hurst, and M. White. 2002. "The Household Bankruptcy Decision." *American Economic Review 92*(3): 706–18.

Gourinchas, P.-O., and J.A. Parker. 2002. "Consumption over the Life Cycle." *Econometrica 70*(1): 47–89.

Gropp, R., J.K. Scholz, and M.J. White. 1997. "Personal Bankruptcy and Credit Supply and Demand." *Quarterly Journal of Economics 112*(1): 217–51.

Gross, D.B., and N.S. Souleles. 1998. "Explaining the Increase in Bankruptcy and Delinquency: Stigma versus Risk-Composition." The Wharton School, University of Pennsylvania.

Hynes, R. 1998. *Three Essays on Exemptions and Consumer Bankruptcy*. Ph.D. thesis, University of Pennsylvania.

Moffit, R.A., and G. Burtless. 1997. "Can Families Smooth Variable Earnings?" Comments and discussion. *Brookings Papers on Economic Activity 1997*(1): 285–303.

Morrison, A.K.M. 1999. *The Economics of Consumer Debt: Two Essays*. Ph.D. thesis, University of Chicago.

Mulligan, J.V. 2001 (May). "The Impact of State Exemptions on Personal Bankruptcy Filings." M.A. thesis, Virginia Polytechnical Institute.

Nelson, J.P. 2000. "Consumer Bankruptcies and the Bankruptcy Reform Act: A Time-Series Intervention Analysis, 1960–1997." *Journal of Financial Services Research* 17(4): 181–200.

Olney, M.L. 1999. "Avoiding Default: The Role of Credit in the Consumption Collapse of the 1930s." *Quarterly Journal of Economics 114*(1): 319–35.

Parker, J.A. 1999. "The Reaction of Household Consumption to Predictable Changes in Social Security Taxes." *American Economic Review* 89(4): 959–73.

Posner, E.A., R. Hynes, and A. Malani. 2002. "The Political Economy of Property Exemption Laws." John M. Olin Law & Economics Working Paper (2d Series) 136, The University of Chicago Law School.

Souleles, N. 1999. "The Response of Household Consumption to Income Tax Refunds." *American Economic Review* 89(4): 947–58.

Stephens, Jr., M. 2001. "The Long-Run Consumption Effects of Earnings Shocks." *Review of Economics and Statistics* 83(1): 28–36.

Telyukova, I. 2006. "Household Need for Liquidity and the Credit Card Debt Puzzle." Manuscript, Department of Economics, University of California San Diego.

White, M. 1998 (March). "Why Don't More Households File for Bankruptcy." Department of Economics Working Paper 98-03, University of Michigan.

White, M.J. 1987. "Personal Bankruptcy under the 1978 Bankruptcy Code: An Economic Analysis." 63(1): 1–57.

Williamson, J.H. 1999. "The Attorney's Handbook on Consumer Bankruptcy and Chapter 13." Lakewood, CO: Argyle Publishing Company.

Ziegel, J.S. 1997. "Canadian Perspectives on the Challenges of Consumer Bankruptcies." *Journal of Consumer Policy* 20(2): 199–221.

PART III

HOUSEHOLD USE OF PERSONAL CREDIT

CHAPTER 5

COLLATERAL AND SORTING: AN EMPIRICAL INVESTIGATION OF THE MARKET FOR HELOCs

Shubhasis Dey and Lucia Dunn

Introduction

Collateral has always played an important role in commercial lending and in the real estate market. With the emerging importance of home equity lending, secured credit is also gaining ground in the consumer credit market via the rapid growth of Home Equity Lines of Credit (HELOCs). An examination of the HELOC market raises many questions about interest rates and the role of collateral. The dispersion of interest rates in the secured credit market depends primarily on how collateral helps to sort borrowers according to their riskiness. Theoretical studies have predicted different roles for collateral in the sorting equilibria of the secured credit market. The two major explanations of the collateral-risk connection are (a) the *sorting-by-observed-risk paradigm* whereby observably riskier borrowers must pledge more collateral than less risky borrowers; and (b) the *sorting-by-private-information paradigm* whereby low-risk borrowers signal their superior risk-type by pledging more collateral than their high-risk counterparts. Here we empirically investigate these two opposing hypotheses that have not previously been tested in the market for collateralized HELOCs.

The equity in the home forms the collateral against which a borrower takes out a HELOC. While a borrower does not have the option to choose the amount of home equity to pledge at the point of the HELOC application, he or she is, however, allowed to choose the amount of credit line to take out for the amount of equity pledged. We use the Loan-to-Value (LTV) ratio, which measures the amount of HELOC taken out per dollar of collateral put in, to examine the collateral-based sorting mechanism in the HELOC market. If the relationship between the LTV and the interest rate is positive, then this would imply that banks are interpreting a higher-LTV consumer to be of higher risk and, therefore, are charging them a higher interest rate. This would suggest that the *sorting-by-private-information paradigm* is in operation in the market. A negative relationship would support the *sorting-by-observed-risk paradigm*. The results of our empirical investigation favor the *sorting-by-private-information paradigm*.

Background and Previous Literature

Although issues concerning the use of collateral have been explored in a variety of settings in the previous literature on the credit market, much of the theoretical work has focused on commercial loans. This earlier work includes Barro (1976), Jensen and Meckling (1976), Scott (1977), Smith and Warner (1979), and Stulz and Johnson (1985). An explanation for the secured lending arrangement that was not specifically addressed in this earlier literature is the sorting role of collateral in *asymmetrically informed* environments. In the banking community the use of collateral has generally been associated with observably riskier borrowers (Morsman, 1986). This is often referred to as the *sorting-by-observed-risk paradigm*. Consistent with this view, Swary and Udell (1988) provide a motivation for the use of collateral by suggesting that secured debt may be useful in enforcing optimal firm closure (or bankruptcy). Boot, Thakor, and Udell (1991) consider a model where the borrower's risk-type is observable to the lender, while the borrower's action is privately known, and derive sufficient conditions under which observably riskier borrowers pledge more collateral in equilibrium. Boot and Thakor (1994), using a model of multi-period loan contracts, have also found evidence in favor of this paradigm.

Another strand of the theoretical literature in the commercial loan market has focused on information about risk known only to borrowers, leading to a paradigm known as the *sorting-by-private-information paradigm*. Chan and Kanatas (1985) and Bester (1985) have found that low-risk borrowers pledge more collateral than high-risk borrowers because collateral-associated costs produce different marginal rates of substitution between collateral and interest rates. Bester incorporated collateral as screening mechanism in the Stiglitz and Weiss (1981) credit rationing model and has shown that rationing then becomes unnecessary. Besanko and Thakor (1987a) find that lenders are at an informational disadvantage with respect to borrower default probabilities, and in equilibrium low-risk borrowers in commercial loan markets pledge more collateral than their high-risk counterparts. In other research Besanko and Thakor (1987b) find a similar negative relationship between collateral and borrower risk under loan contracting with a multidimensional pricing menu. Chan and Thakor (1987) have examined the form of the optimal secured loan contract assuming the existence of both adverse selection and moral hazard. Igawa and Kanatas (1990), assuming that moral hazard exists due to the use of collateral, show that the optimal secured loan contract for higher-quality borrowers involves over-collateralization, whereas self-financing and unsecured credit are chosen by the intermediate and lowest-quality borrowers respectively.

Empirical studies of the collateral-risk relationship based on bank files and survey data in the market for commercial loans include that of Orgler (1970), Hester (1979), and Berger and Udell (1990), who find that riskier borrowers pledge more collateral. Berger and Udell (1995) further find that collateral use decreases significantly with the length of the firm's relationship with the bank, a fact that was theoretically explained in an earlier study by Boot and Thakor (1994).

More recent theoretical work on the use of collateral in commercial lending has been put forward in a context of symmetric information with entrepreneurs' overoptimistic evaluation of their project (de Meza and Southey, 1996) or costly state verification (Bester, 1994). Moreover, issues of collateral have also been extensively researched in markets where secured lending is predominant, such as the real estate and automobile markets.

In this chapter we empirically investigate the relationship between the value of collateral and credit risk within the market for HELOCs. The econometric model that we propose estimates the HELOC rate of interest as a function of the endogenous choice variable, the LTV ratio. It has been argued in a recent study by Agarwal et al. (2005) that utilization of lines of credit is correlated with borrower risk. Moreover, the collateral-based sorting literature postulates that the value of the collateral is crucially related to the risk-type of the borrower. Therefore, our econometric model should account for the fact that a borrower of a given risk-type can simultaneously choose the LTV ratio and how much of the HELOC to utilize when banks choose the rate of interest. Our empirical work supports a positive association between the LTV ratio and the rate of interest that banks charge, implying that a higher value of collateral pledged relative to the credit line taken is associated with a lower risk, as opposed to the opposite relationship usually found for commercial loans.

Data

The dataset used in this study consists of a pooled sample from the 1995, 1998, and 2001 rounds of the U.S. *Surveys of Consumer Finances* (SCF).[1] We have selected 9,105 households who have positive equity in their homes. Among them, 1,054 households have a HELOC and 585 households carried positive HELOC debts. Letting D^H and r_H denote the observed HELOC debt and interest rate respectively, there are two types of sample members:

Type I: $D^H = r_H = 0$.

Type II: $D^H > 0$ and $r_H > 0$.

The descriptive statistics for HELOC debtors and HELOC non-debtors in this dataset are presented in the appendix.

An Econometric Model

We consider the following variables in our model:

Definitions of Variables

W_i—Wealth of household i	t_i—Income tax rate; $0 < t_i < 1$
s_i^H—Probability of default on HELOC	δ_i—Discount factor; $0 < \delta_i < 1$
τ_i—Fixed cost of HELOC, $\tau_i > 0$	α_i—Rate of repayment; $0 < \alpha_i < 1$

The market for HELOCs that we deal with is realistically assumed to have the following institutional background. HELOCs are secured lines of credit. In the event of a default on HELOCs, households lose their financial wealth and the equity in their homes. Hence defaulting households can only retain wealth of amount $\gamma_{Hi} W_i$, where $0 < \gamma_{Hi} < 1$.

Following Dey (2005), the household i's discounted expected lifetime utility from optimally carrying $D_i^{H\star}$ amount of HELOC debt is as follows:

$$V_i^{H\star} = V_i^H(W_i, \tau_i, s_i^H, \gamma_{Hi}, t_i, r_{Hi}, \alpha_i, \delta_i, D_i^{H\star}).$$

Hence for household i we have, $D_i^{H\star} = h(W_i, \tau_i, s_i^H, \gamma_{Hi}, t_i, r_{Hi}, \alpha_i, \delta_i)$.

Counterparts from the Data

We use the following empirical quantities (see table 5.1 here) to represent the variables of the model:

Utility Function Curvature Factors C_i: a vector including dummies capturing household's expressed attitude toward risk.[2]

Wealth Factors W_i: a vector including the equity in the home, financial assets, other nonfinancial assets, and household size.

Risk Factors R_i: a vector including a dummy variable based on the incidence of delinquency, employment dummies, household income, financial assets, and the repayment rate α_i.

Tax Factors T_i: a vector including a dummy variable that determines whether household i itemizes income tax deductions or not, and household income.

Discount Factors S_i: a vector including age, sex, ethnicity, marital status, and education level.

Loan-to-Value LTV_i: the HELOC credit limit divided by the amount of home equity pledged.

Since the fixed costs[3] of obtaining HELOCs (τ_i) have no variation across households, they go into the constant term of the optimal HELOC debt equation. Moreover, the fraction of assets retained during default on HELOC debt (γ_{Hi}) can be captured by other nonfinancial assets and the household size. The probability of default on HELOC debt (s_i^H) is considered to be a function of the indicators of household's risk-type (R_i). The discount factor δ_i is captured by the vector S_i. The vector T_i captures the income tax rates t_i. Hence we have

$$s_i^H = \alpha_0 + \alpha_1' R_i + \varepsilon_{1i},$$
$$t_i = \alpha_2 + \alpha_3' T_i + \varepsilon_{2i} \text{ and}$$
$$\delta_i = \varphi_i' S_i + \eta_i.$$

In order to determine the rate at which to lend, banks take the LTV ratio (given by LTV_i) as a signal of the amount of loan supplied per dollar of collateral, use R_i as a key signal of the risk-type, and utilize some variables in S_i to capture households' discount factors. Hence, using a vector containing LTV_i, R_i, and the observed indicators of household's discount factor (all the variables in S_i except the educational level) we can come up with the following structural-form equation determining the interest rate prevailing in the HELOC market:[4]

$$r_{Hi} = \gamma LTV_i + \beta_1' X_{1i} + v_{1i} \tag{1}$$

where X_{1i} is a vector of exogenous variables.

The choice of the amount of HELOC to take out per dollar of the home equity pledged depends on some indicators of household's risk-type (R_i), measures of the curvature of the utility function (C_i), and the value of home equity.[5] The dummies capturing household's attitude toward risk (making up C_i) are not part of the banks' information set and hence are not present in X_{1i}. Moreover, we know that HELOC utilization rates and households' risk-types should be correlated (see Agarwal et al., 2006). Hence, it is argued that households who borrow on HELOCs belong to a different risk-class than those who do not. Moreover, following the collateral-based sorting literature, we model this difference in risk between the HELOC debtors and non-debtors by two different LTV equations. Hence for HELOC debtors we have the following equation explaining their choice of LTV:

$$LTV_i = \beta_2' X_{2i} + v_{2i}. \tag{2}$$

However, for HELOC non-debtors we have the following:

$$LTV_i = \beta_3' X_{2i} + v_{3i}. \tag{3}$$

Substituting for s_i^H, t_i, δ_i, τ_i, γ_{Hi}, and r_{Hi} into D_i^{H*}; using LTV_i, C_i, α_i, and W_i, we have a reduced-form equation for D_i^{H*},

$$D_i^{H*} = \delta' Z_i - v_i \tag{4}$$

where Z_i is a vector of all the exogenous variables of our econometric model. The incidence of HELOC borrowing has implications for household's risk-type.[6] Consequently, the act of HELOC borrowing is likely to affect household's choice of LTV and hence the choice of HELOC interest rates charged by the banks. This implies that LTV_i in equation (1) is an endogenous variable.

We should note that lines of credit are sometimes used by consumers as insurance against uninsured or uninsurable wealth shocks. Therefore, some HELOC borrowers may be found to borrow, not when the LTV and interest rates are negotiated, but when the wealth shocks have been realized. For these HELOC borrowers, the incidence of borrowing and the consequent variation in riskiness will not be reflected in their choice of LTV and the interest rate charged by the banks. However, due to the predominant use of HELOCs as a mode to refinance and consolidate existing debt and because of the upfront costs of taking out these lines, most HELOC borrowings are likely to occur right during the time their terms are negotiated.

Therefore, let us consider the following endogenous switching regression model:

$$\left.\begin{aligned} r_{Hi} &= \gamma LTV_i + \beta_1' X_{1i} + v_{1i} \\ LTV_i &= \beta_2' X_{2i} + v_{2i} \end{aligned}\right\} \qquad \text{if } D_i^{H*} > 0$$

$$\left.\begin{aligned} &r_{Hi} \text{ unobserved} \\ <V_i = \beta_3' X_{2i} + v_{3i} \end{aligned}\right\} \qquad \text{if } D_i^{H*} = 0$$

where v_{1i}, v_{2i}, v_{3i}, and v_i follow multivariate normal with zero means, variances σ_1^2 σ_2^2, σ_3^2, and 1, respectively, and with covariances σ_{12}, σ_{23}, σ_{13}, σ_{1v}, σ_{2v}, and σ_{3v}. If X_{2i} contains at least one variable that is not included in X_{1i}, then all the parameters of the model are identified. Since the measures of the curvature of the utility function (C_i) are part of the variables explaining household's choice of LTV and are not part of the banks' information set, we have the variables sufficient for identifying all the parameters of the model.[7] In order to correct for the endogeneity present in the HELOC interest rate equation, our two-stage estimation procedure uses an estimate of the LTV, $\widehat{LTV}_i$, as an instrument.

We use a two-stage probit method as described in Lee, Maddala, and Trost (1980) to estimate our econometric model. This two-step procedure yields consistent estimates of all our parameters.

Let us define a dummy variable, I_i, such that

$$\begin{aligned} I_i &= 1 \text{ if household } i \text{ carries positive HELOC debt (i.e. if } D_i^{H*} > 0) \\ &= 0 \text{ otherwise.} \end{aligned}$$

Let us assume that there are N_1 observations for which $I_i = 1$ and N_2 observations for which $I_i = 0$, so that the total sample size is $N = N_1 + N_2$. We then define

$$\phi_i = \phi(\delta' Z_i) \text{ and}$$

$$\Phi_i = \Phi(\delta' Z_i),$$

where $i = 1, 2. \ldots .N$; ϕ is the standard normal density, and Φ is the cumulative normal.

Since

$$E(v_{2i} \mid I_i = 1) = -\sigma_{2v}\frac{\phi_i}{\Phi_i},$$

we can write equation (2) for the HELOC debtors as

$$LTV_i = \beta_2' X_{2i} - \sigma_{2v}\frac{\phi_i}{\Phi_i} + \mu_{2i}$$

where $E(\mu_{2i}) = 0$.

For HELOC non-debtors the LTV equation can be written as

$$LTV_i = \beta_3{}'X_{2i} + \sigma_{3v}\frac{\phi_i}{1 - \Phi_i} + \mu_{3i}$$

where $E(\mu_{3i}) = 0$.

We first estimate δ by probit maximum likelihood (i.e., we get $\hat{\delta}$). Then we estimate

$$LTV_i = \beta_2{}'X_{2i} - \sigma_{2v}\frac{\hat{\phi}_i}{\hat{\Phi}_i} + \overline{\mu_{2i}}$$

by ordinary least squares. Here $\hat{\phi}_i$ and $\hat{\Phi}_i$ are ϕ_i and Φ_i with $\hat{\delta}$ substituted for δ.

We similarly estimate the reduced-form parameters in equation (3) using

$$LTV_i = \beta_3{}'X_{2i} + \sigma_{3v}\frac{\hat{\phi}_i}{1 - \hat{\Phi}_i} + \overline{\mu_{3i}}$$

The structural HELOC interest rate equation is given by

$$r_{Hi} = \gamma LTV_i + \beta_1{}'X_{1i} + v_{1i}.$$

Since

$$E(v_{1i} | I_i = 1) = -\sigma_{1v}\frac{\phi_i}{\Phi_i},$$

we can write equation (1) as

$$r_{Hi} = \gamma LTV_i + \beta_1{}'X_{1i} - \sigma_{1v}\frac{\phi_i}{\Phi_i} + \mu_{1i}$$

where $E(\mu_{1i}) = 0$.

We estimate

$$r_{Hi} = \gamma L\hat{T}V_i + \beta_1{}'X_{1i} - \sigma_{1v}\frac{\hat{\phi}_i}{\hat{\Phi}_i} + \overline{\mu_{1i}}$$

by ordinary least squares, where $L\hat{T}V_i = \hat{\beta}_2{}'X_{2i} - \hat{\sigma}_{2v}\frac{\hat{\phi}_i}{\hat{\Phi}_i}$.

Since all the second-stage estimations use estimated variables as regressors, the asymptotic covariance matrices of the second-stage ordinary least squares estimators require corrections. See Lee et al. (1980) for the derivations of the asymptotic covariance matrices of two-stage probit estimators.

Empirical Results

Table 5.1 presents the probit results explaining the decision to carry HELOC debt. We find that the amount of equity in the home and the size of the household positively influence the household to borrow on HELOCs. Those households who itemize income tax deductions are also more likely to hold HELOC debt, undoubtedly due to the savings from tax deductibility of HELOC interest payments. A higher level of financial and nonfinancial assets as well as higher income weaken households' tendency to borrow on HELOCs. Lack of employment and higher degrees of risk aversion also reduce the tendency to carry HELOC debt.

Table 5.2 presents results of the second stage of the two-stage analysis of the choice of LTV among HELOC debtors. We find that among those with HELOC debt, self-employed households and households with high financial assets take out high-LTV HELOCs. Controlling for the observed indicators of risk-type, the higher the household's home equity, the lower will be the LTV chosen for the HELOCs. Moreover, the coefficient of LAMBDA is significant. Hence, we find that the incidence of HELOC indebtedness is indeed relevant for the choice of LTV among HELOC debtors.

Table 5.3 shows the choice of LTV among HELOC non-debtors using a two-stage probit analysis. We find that among households with no HELOC debt, those with high income and financial assets are more likely to take out high-LTV HELOCs. Controlling for the risk- type of the household, we again find that the higher the household's home equity, the lower the LTV chosen for the HELOCs.

Finally, table 5.4 presents the two-stage probit results of the variables that explain the rate of interest prevailing in the HELOC market. Most important among these results is the positive relationship between the LTV and the rate of interest being charged. This implies that banks are interpreting a high-LTV household to be of high risk and, therefore, are charging them a higher interest rate. This positive relationship is evidence that the *sorting-by-private-information paradigm* is in operation in the market for HELOCs.

Summary and Conclusions

This chapter has addressed the use of collateral in the HELOC market. We have explored the role that collateral plays in sorting borrowers according to risk-types, which helps to explain the observed spread of HELOC rates of interest. The equity in the home is the value against which a borrower takes out a HELOC. We use the Loan-to-Value (LTV) ratio, a choice variable for the potential HELOC borrower, to capture the amount of HELOC taken out per dollar of home equity pledged. It has been shown in previous research that the utilization rates of lines of credit are correlated with borrower risk-types. The collateral-based sorting literature tells us that borrower risk-types should in turn determine the LTV ratio and the rates charged by the banks for the credit extended. We, therefore, use an endogenous switching regression model, with HELOC utilization representing the switch in risk-type and the consequent switch in LTV. The

Table 5.1 A Household's decision to carry HELOC debt[a]

Variables	*Explanation*	*Probit Coefficients*	*Standard Errors*
Constant		−1.8497***	0.2535
Lhomequity	Logarithm of equity in home[b]	0.1566***	0.0258
Lfinassets	Logarithm of financial assets	−0.0306**	0.0119
Lotherassets	Logarithm of other nonfinancial assets	−0.1071***	0.0216
Household size	Size of household	0.0495***	0.0186
High-risktaker[c]	1—Above average risk-taker 0—Otherwise	0.0787	0.0483
Not-risktaker	1—Not a risk-taker 0—Otherwise	−0.192***	0.0646
Delinquency	1—Behind in payments by two months or more 0—Otherwise	−0.1805	0.1613
Log income	Logarithm of income	−0.0615***	0.016
Tax	1—Itemize income tax deductions 0—Otherwise	0.3978***	0.0628
Repayment rate	The rate of repayment[d]	0.1057	0.0884
Age	Age of the household head	−0.0001	0.0023
Sex	1—Female 0—Otherwise	0.0963	0.1016
Married	1—Married 0—Otherwise	0.2379***	0.0903
Ethnicity	1—Nonwhite 0—Otherwise	−0.1465	0.0729
Not working	1—Not working 0—Otherwise	−0.2961***	0.1094
Retired	1—Retired 0—Otherwise	−0.3421***	0.0805
Self-employed	1—Working and self-employed 0—Otherwise	−0.037	0.0549
Education	Years of schooling of the household head	0.0285***	0.0102

Note: *** Significant at 1 percent; ** significant at 5 percent; * significant at 10 percent.

[a] HELOC rate is the maximum interest rate charged among different HELOCs taken out by the household.

[b] Home equity = value of the house—all outstanding mortgages excluding HELOC.

[c] Household's risk-tolerance on a 1 to 4 scale.

[d] Fraction of HELOC and mortgage debt repaid.

Table 5.2 HELOC debtor's choice of loan-to-value ratio

	Second Stage Regression	
Variables	*Coefficients*	*Standard Errors*
Constant	2.36297***	0.76561
High-risktaker	0.14203	0.10043
Not-risktaker	0.1635	0.15857
Not working	0.06514	0.27893
Retired	−0.1707	0.1889
Self-employed	0.18596*	0.1086
Lfinassets	0.10668***	0.02903
Log income	0.04767	0.03878
Lhomequity	−0.42677***	0.0561
Delinquency	−0.05693	0.38029
Repayment rate	−0.3102	0.7088
LAMBDA[a]	0.73756***	0.26545

Note: *** Significant at 1 percent; ** significant at 5 percent; * significant at 10 percent; $N = 585$.

[a] LAMBDA $= \frac{\hat{\phi}_i}{\hat{\Phi}_i}$.

Table 5.3 HELOC non-debtor's choice of loan-to-value ratio

	Second Stage Regression	
Variables	*Coefficients*	*Standard Errors*
Constant	0.03232	0.02722
High-risktaker	0.00428	0.00685
Not-risktaker	−0.00397	0.00814
Not working	−0.0003975	0.01282
Retired	−0.01276	0.0095
Self-employed	0.00611	0.00752
Lfinassets	0.00487***	0.00141
Log income	0.00492**	0.00241
Lhomequity	−0.00981***	0.00298
Delinquency	−0.02316	0.01862
Repayment rate	0.00593	0.01854
LAMBDA[a]	0.01589	0.05671

Note: *** Significant at 1 percent; ** significant at 5 percent; * significant at 10 percent; $N = 8520$.

[a] LAMBDA $= \frac{\hat{\phi}_i}{1 - \hat{\Phi}_i}$.

Table 5.4 A Bank's choice of HELOC interest rate

	Second Stage Regression	
Variables	*Coefficients*	*Standard Errors*
Constant	11.66759***	1.34486
Repayment rate	3.6597**	1.44632
Delinquency	−0.25665	0.77639
Age	0.00225	0.0104
Sex	0.41309	0.48375
Married	0.15274	0.42744
Ethnicity	0.55992*	0.33274
Log income	0.05861	0.07766
Lfinassets	−0.23253***	0.05165
Not working	0.62576	0.56633
Retired	0.54721	0.42448
Self-employed	0.18537	0.21246
LTV	1.00664***	0.27047
LAMBDA[a]	−0.95003	0.65366

Note: *** Significant at 1 percent; ** significant at 5 percent; * significant at 10 percent; $N = 585$.

[a] LAMBDA $= \frac{\hat{\phi}_i}{\hat{\Phi}_i}$.

HELOC rate of interest is then formulated as a function of the endogenous choice variable, the LTV ratio. We estimate this model using data from the U.S. *Survey of Consumer Finances*.

In the secured commercial loan market, where the sorting by collateral phenomenon has primarily been studied, researchers have typically found the *sorting-by-observed-risk paradigm* to be dominant. This implies that larger collateral is associated with borrowers who are perceived to be of higher risk to the banks. However, in the market for HELOCs, we find that relatively low-risk borrowers signal their superior risk-types by taking out low-LTV HELOCs and thereby receive lower interest rates. Our finding thus supports the *sorting-by-private-information paradigm* in the HELOC market.

The HELOC market is currently growing faster than the credit card market in the United States due to the prevailing lower interest rates and tax deductible of interest payments. An understanding of the pricing mechanism of this market and how the pricing is related to credit utilization is important for a clearer insight into consumer credit behavior. As the demand for HELOCs grows, identifying the risk profiles of the consumers taking out these lines of credit will be essential for banks and policy makers. This chapter hopefully provides one step in that direction.

Notes

Shubhasis Dey, Senior Economic Analyst, Bank of Canada, Ottawa, Canada Lucia Dunn, Professor of Economics, Ohio State University, Columbus, Ohio.

1. All variables are converted to 2001 dollars.
2. A four-category survey question capturing the respondent's risk-aversion parameter.
3. These involve upfront costs, such as, appraisal fees, closing costs, and annual fees.
4. HELOC interest rates are usually variable rates that are tied to the prime rate. Since the prime rate does not have any cross-sectional variation, it can only be represented by the constant term in the HELOC rate equation.
5. While considering the risk of putting the equity in the home for borrowing purposes, three factors are thought to be important—probability of winning or losing the gamble (R_i), willingness to gamble (C_i), and the value of the gamble itself (the equity in the home).
6. It is as if the act of borrowing on a HELOC worsens the odds of winning the gamble.
7. The appendix provides a complete list of variables included in an individual credit report.

References

Agarwal, S., B.W. Ambrose, and C. Liu. 2006. "Credit Quality and Credit Commitment." *Journal of Money, Credit and Banking* 38(1): 1–22.

Barro, R.J. 1976. "The Loan Market, Collateral and Rates of Interest." *Journal of Money, Credit and Banking* 8(4): 439–56.

Berger, A.N., and G.F. Udell. 1990. "Collateral, Loan Quality, and Bank Risk." *Journal of Monetary Economics* 25(1): 21–42.

———. 1995. "Relationship Lending and Lines of Credit in Small Firm Finance." *Journal of Business* 68(3): 351–81.

Besanko, D., and A.V. Thakor. 1987a. "Collateral and Rationing: Sorting Equilibria in Monopolistic and Competitive Credit Markets." *International Economic Review* 28(3): 671–89.

———. 1987b. "Competitive Equilibrium in the Credit Market under Asymmetric Information." *Journal of Economic Theory* 42(1): 167–82.

Bester, H. 1985. "Screening vs. Rationing in Credit Markets with Imperfect Information." *American Economic Review* 75(4): 850–55.

———. 1994. "The Role of Collateral in a Model of Debt Renegotiation." *Journal of Money, Credit and Banking* 26(1): 72–86.

Boot, A.W.A., and A.V. Thakor. 1994. "Moral Hazard and Secured Lending in an Infinitely Repeated Market Game." *International Economic Review* 35(4): 899–920.

Boot, A.W.A., A.V. Thakor, and G.F. Udell. 1991. "Secured Lending and Default Risk: Equilibrium Analysis, Policy Implications and Empirical Results." *Economic Journal* 101(406): 458–72.

Chan, Y. and A.V. Thakor. 1987. "Collateral and Competitive Equilibrium with Moral Hazard and Private Information." *Journal of Finance* 42(2): 345–63.

Chan, Y., and G. Kanatas. 1985. "Asymmetric Valuations and the Role of Collateral in Loan Agreements." *Journal of Money, Credit and Banking* 17(1): 84–95.

de Meza, D., and C. Southey. 1996. "The Borrower's Curse: Optimism, Finance and Entrepreneurship." *Economic Journal* 106(435): 375–86.

Dey, S. 2005. "Lines of Credit and Consumption Smoothing: The Choice between Credit Cards and Home Equity Lines of Credit." Bank of Canada Working Paper, No. 2005–18.

Hester, D.D. 1979. "Customer Relationships and Terms of Loans: Evidence from a Pilot Survey: A Note." *Journal of Money Credit and Banking* 11(3): 349–57.

Igawa, K. and G. Kanatas. 1990. "Asymmetric Information, Collateral, and Moral Hazard." *Journal of Financial and Quantitative Analysis* 25(4): 469–90.

Jensen, M.C., and W.H. Meckling. 1976. "Theory of the Firm: Managerial Behavior, Agency Costs and Capital Structure." *Journal of Financial Economics* 3(4): 305–60.

Lee, L., G.S. Maddala, and R.P. Trost. 1980. "Asymptotic Covariance Matrices of Two-Stage Probit and Two-Stage Tobit Methods for Simultaneous Equations Models with Selectivity." *Econometrica* 48(2): 491–503.

Morsman, E., Jr. 1986. "Commercial Loan Structuring." *Journal of Commercial Bank Lending* 68: 2–20.

Orgler, Y.E. 1970. "A Credit Scoring Model for Commercial Loans." *Journal of Money, Credit and Banking* 2(4): 435–45.

Scott, J.H., Jr. 1977. "Bankruptcy, Secured Debt and Optimal Capital Structure." *Journal of Finance* 32(1): 1–19.

Smith, C.W., Jr., and J.B. Warner. 1979. "Bankruptcy, Secured Debt and Optimal Capital Structure: Comment." *Journal of Finance* 34(1): 247–51.

Stiglitz, J.E., and A. Weiss. 1981. "Credit Rationing in Markets with Imperfect Information." *American Economic Review* 71(3): 393–410.

Stulz, R.M., and H. Johnson. 1985. "An Analysis of Secured Debt." *Journal of Financial Economics* 14(4): 501–21.

Swary, I., and G.F. Udell. 1988. "Information Production and the Secured Line of Credit." Working Paper, New York University, New York, NY.

CHAPTER 6

ASYMMETRIC INFORMATION AND THE AUTOMOBILE LOAN MARKET*

Sumit Agarwal, Brent W. Ambrose, and Souphala Chomsisengphet

Introduction

Information revelation can occur through a variety of mechanisms. For example, corporate finance research has established that a firm's dividend policies provide investors with information about future growth prospects.[1] In addition, research on residential mortgages indicates that borrowers reveal their expected tenure through their choice of mortgage contracts.[2] As a result, lenders offer a menu of mortgage interest rate and point combinations in an effort to learn about borrower potential mobility.[3] Similarly, lenders may anticipate how consumer debt will perform by observing the consumption choices that are being financed. With the proliferation of risk-based pricing in credit markets, lender's ability to further differentiate between borrower credit risks, based on consumer choice of goods, offers lenders a potentially important source to enhance profitability, as well as the potential to extend credit to a wider range of borrowers.[4]

In this study, we use a unique dataset of individual automobile loans to assess whether borrower consumption choice reveals information about future loan performance. For most Americans, the automobile is the second largest asset purchased (after housing), and as Grinblatt, Keloharju, and Ikaheimo (2004) observe, automobiles are highly visible consumption goods in which interpersonal effects clearly influence purchase decisions. Furthermore, in a study of the automotive leasing market, Mannering, Winston, and Starkey (2002) report that individual characteristics (e.g., income, education, etc.) impact consumer choice among methods for acquiring vehicles (either through leasing, financing, or cash purchase). As a result, the auto loan market provides an interesting laboratory for studying whether consumers reveal information about their expected performance on financial contracts through the type of product they purchase.

Insurers have long recognized that automobile makes and models appeal to different clienteles, and that these clienteles have heterogeneous risk profiles and accident rates. As a result, insurers routinely price automotive insurance based on car make and model. For example, insurance premiums on Volvos are not necessarily lower than premiums on BMWs due to any discernable difference in car safety, but rather result from the clientele that purchase these cars. That is, the typical Volvo driver may be less aggressive, and thus less prone to accidents, on average, than the typical BMW driver. Given that individual risk behavior is revealed in the automobile insurance market, a natural question arises as to whether consumption decisions also reveal individual financial (or credit) risk behavior. In other words, does the type of automobile purchased reveal information about the consumer's propensity to prepay or default on the loan that finances that purchase?

To answer this question, we adopt a competing-risks framework to analyze auto loan prepayment and default risks using a large sample of individual automobile loans. To the best of our knowledge, Heitfield and Sabarwal (2004) conduct the only other study of default and prepayment for automobile loans. Unlike Heitfield and Sabarwal (2004), who use performance data from sub-prime auto loan *pools* underlying asset backed securities, we use conventional (non-sub-prime) individual auto loan *level* data that provides individual loan and borrower characteristics (e.g., borrower income and credit risk score) and individual automobile characteristics (e.g., auto make, model, and year).

Our results can be summarized as follows. First, we find that factors that traditionally predict automobile default and prepayment continue to perform as expected. Specifically, we find that (1) a decline in borrower credit risk lowers the likelihood of default and raises the probability of prepayment; (2) an increase in the loan-to-value ratio increases the risk of default and lowers the likelihood of prepayment; (3) an increase in borrower income increases the probability of prepayment, whereas an increase in local area unemployment increases the risk of default; (4) a decrease in the market interest rate increases both the probability of prepayment and default. Finally, we also find that vehicle manufacturer location (America, Europe, and Japan) significantly impacts both the prepayment and default behavior of borrowers, and increases the model explanatory power by 52 percent. In an extended model, we also find significant dispersion in prepayment and default rates across the specific automobile manufacturers.

These results provide evidence that the type of automobile purchased reveals the consumer's propensity to prepay or default on the loan used to finance that purchase. Since knowledge of the type of automobile purchased is available to the lender at the point of origination, our results suggest that lenders could utilize this information in risk-based pricing by moving away from the standard "house-rate" loan pricing for auto loans. Risk-based pricing could not only help the bank achieve a lower capital allocation, but also provide credit access to higher-risk borrowers.

The remainder of this chapter is structured as follows. A brief discussion of the auto loan market is presented first. The next section describes the data, which is followed by the section that provides the methodology for empirical estimation. The subsequent section describes the regression results for the prepayment and default model for auto loans. The next section discusses the results in light of recent studies of the changes in vehicle manufacturer market share. The final section offers concluding remarks.

The Market for Auto Loans

According to Aizcorbe, Kennickell, and Moore (2003), automobiles are the most commonly held nonfinancial asset. For example, in 2001, over 84 percent of American households owned an automobile.[5] In contrast, approximately 68 percent of American households owned their primary residence.[6] Furthermore, loans related to automobile purchases are one of the most common forms of household borrowing (Aizcorbe and Starr-McCluer 1997; Aizcorbe, Starr, and Hickman, 2003). Consistent with the high penetration of automobile ownership among households and the average automobile purchase price, Dasgupta, Siddarth, and Silva-Risso (2003) note that the vast majority of auto purchases are financed. In fact, Aizcorbe, Starr, and Hickman (2003) report that in 2001 over 80 percent of new vehicle transactions were financed or leased. As a result, given the size of the U.S. automotive market, it is not surprising that automobile credit represents a sizeable portion of the fixed-income market. For example, in 2002, debt outstanding on automobile loans was over $700 billion, and a growing percentage of this debt is held in "asset backed securities."

Financing for automobile purchases comes from three primary sources: dealer financing, leasing, and third-party loans. Based on a sample of auto sales in Southern California between September 1999 and October 2000, Dasgupta, Siddarth, and Silva-Risso (2003) report that 24 percent of the transactions were leased, 35 percent of the sales were dealer-financed, and the remaining 40 percent of the cash transactions were most likely financed from third-party lenders (credit unions or banks). Furthermore, using a national sample of 654 households that purchased new vehicles, Mannering, Winston, and Starkey (2002) find that 51.6 percent financed, 28.1 percent paid cash, and 20.3 percent leased. Based on these surveys, clearly third-party financing represents a sizable portion of the automobile credit market.

One of the key features of the third-party auto loan market is the standard practice of using a "house rate" for pricing loans, such that all qualified borrowers with similar risk characteristics pay the same rate at any given point in time. In other words, prospective borrowers secure a loan before they contract to buy. The lender simply underwrites the loan based on the borrower's credit score and required downpayment.[7] With the loan commitment in hand, the borrower then shops for a particular vehicle. As a result, these lenders do not incorporate information about the purchase decision into the loan pricing.

In contrast, before lenders originate a mortgage, typically they have information on the underlying asset as well as the borrower's personal characteristics. Thus, information about the underlying asset often plays a role in determining the mortgage contract rate. For example, lenders know that a borrower who seeks a loan above the government-sponsored enterprise "conforming loan limit" is almost certainly purchasing a high-valued asset, while a borrower who requests an FHA-insured mortgage is likely purchasing a lower-valued home. Since standard mortgage-pricing models show that the volatility of the underlying property value is important in determining the probability of mortgage termination, borrowers originating mortgages on properties with higher volatilities pay higher contract rates.[8]

Extending this analogy to the auto loan market, if third-party lenders required information about the car being purchased prior to approving the loan, then they could price that into the loan. Currently, this is not the practice. Thus, our study suggests an avenue for lenders to potentially increase auto loan profitability by utilizing the information about the car being purchased when they set their loan terms.

Data

The data comes primarily from a large financial institution that originates *direct* automobile loans.[9] Our data consists of 6,996 loans originated for purchase of new and used automobiles. The loans have fixed interest rates and are originated with four- or five-year maturities. We observe the performance of these loans from January 1998 through March 2003, providing a monthly record for each loan until it either prepays, defaults, pays in full at maturity, or is still current as of the last month of the observation period (right censored). We classify a loan as prepaid if, prior to maturity, the borrower pays off a loan having a balance greater than $3,000.[10] Following standard industry practice, we classify a loan as being in default when the payment is 60 days past due.[11] We removed loans from the analysis if (1) they originated after March 2002, (2) they were made to lender employees, and (3) the automobile was stolen or fraud was suspected. Using our default and prepayment definitions, we find that 1,216 loans had prepaid (17.4 percent), 251 loans had defaulted (3.6 percent), and 5,529 loans were still active as of the last date of the study period.

Loan characteristics include automobile value, automobile age, loan amount, loan-to-value (LTV), monthly payments, contract rate, time of origination (year and month), as well as payoff year and month in the cases of prepayment and default. We also have access to the automobile model, make, and year. Borrower characteristics include credit score (FICO score), monthly disposable income, and borrower age. The majority of the loans originated in eight northeast states.

Since the purpose of our study is to determine whether the type of vehicle reveals information about future loan performance, we classify the cars by manufacturer headquarter location (i.e., American, Japanese, or European). Although this is a crude initial classification of the auto market, classification of automobiles along this basic dimension follows the prevailing consumer sentiment of the automotive market. Obviously, this classification system no longer matches the global automotive manufacturing landscape. For example, BMW has manufacturing plants at 23 sites in 15 countries; Chrysler (one of the Big Three U.S. manufacturers) merged with the German firm Daimler-Benz in 1998 to form DaimlerChrysler, and General Motors

(GM) is the largest shareholder of South Korean manufacturer, Daewoo. However, most consumers still perceive the foreign/domestic classification when referring to automobiles. For example, the Toyota Camry is generally referred to as a Japanese car even though it is manufactured in Georgetown, Kentucky, and Chrysler products are still perceived as American even though Chrysler is a unit of DaimlerChrysler.

Following standard practice, we differentiate cars by their make and model. Automotive make refers to the car manufacturer (e.g., BMW, Toyota, Ford, etc.), model defines the particular car (e.g., BMW 325, Toyota Camry, etc.), and vintage denotes the model year.[12]

Table 6.1 presents the sample descriptive statistics and also reports a series of pair-wise t-statistics testing the null hypothesis that the sample means are equal across manufacturer location. At this basic classification level, we find significant differences. For example, given the concentration of European manufacturers in the U.S. luxury-auto segment, we find that the average price for European cars ($27,269) is significantly greater than the average cost for American or Japanese cars ($19,441 and $21,149, respectively). Consistent with this pricing pattern, we also observe that European cars have higher loan amounts. Since lenders offer a "house rate" for automotive loans, we note that no significant difference exists in loan interest-rate spreads at origination.[13]

Table 6.1 also reports borrower characteristics. For example, on average, borrowers who purchased American cars were older (45 years versus 41 and 38 for European and Japanese buyers, respectively), borrowed more relative to the purchase price (80 percent versus 65 percent and 76 percent for European and Japanese buyers, respectively), and had higher credit scores (720 versus 715 and 708 for European and Japanese buyers, respectively). We also see that European car purchasers had higher monthly incomes on average ($4,625) than either American ($4,024) or Japanese ($4,114) buyers.

Table 6.2 shows the sample distribution by loan outcome and manufacturer location. We note that differences appear in loan performance based on automotive type. For example, 19.9 percent of the loans on European cars were prepaid versus 18.1 percent of loans on American cars and 15.5 percent of loans on Japanese cars. Also interesting is that European and Japanese car loans have lower default rate (2.9 percent) than American car loans (4.7 percent). In the next section, we present a more formal analysis of loan performance.

Methodology

Following the standard practice in mortgage performance analysis, we estimate a competing-risks model of auto loan prepayment and default. The competing-risks framework has the advantage of explicitly recognizing the mutually exclusive nature of prepayment and default. That is, if the borrower exercises the prepayment option then this necessarily means that the borrower is unable to exercise the option to default and vice versa. In the mortgage literature, recent studies such as Deng et al. (2000), Ambrose and Sanders (2005), and Calhoun and Deng (2002) use this competing-risks framework, while Heitfield and Sabarwal (2004) employ the same method in analyzing pool-level auto loan data.[14] As with Gross and

Table 6.1 Descriptive statistics—means and standard deviations

Cars Make	*Price*	*Loan Amt.*	*Mth. Pymt.*	*Rate Spread*	*Income*	*Credit Score*	*LTV*	*Unemp.*	*Owner Age*	*Frequency*
American cars (U.S.)	$19,441	$15,765	$324	0.95	$4,024	720	80%	4.36	45	2780
Std	$4,637	$3,338	$615	0.56	$2,022	61	17%	1.04	14	
Japanese cars (JP)	$21,149	$16,347	$323	0.97	$4,114	708	76%	4.15	38	2873
Std	$4,929	$3,087	$535	0.58	$2,109	62	17%	1.05	12	
European cars (EU)	$27,269	$17,708	$353	0.96	$4,625	715	65%	4.14	41	1343
Std	$7,483	$4,215	$676	0.57	$2,196	61	17%	1.06	12	
All cars	$21,597	$16,177	$329	0.96	$4,173	714	74%	4.23	41	6996
Std	$6,091	$3,445	$596	0.57	$2,102	61	17%	1.06	13	
T-test U.S.-JP	−13.41*	−6.81*	0.03	−1.31	−1.63	7.12*	8.84*	7.57*	21.10*	
T-test U.S.-EU	−41.17*	−16.03*	−1.38	−0.04	−8.69*	2.44**	26.55*	6.28*	9.56*	
T-test JP-EU	−31.57*	−11.80*	−1.54	1.00	−7.24*	−3.29**	19.57*	0.23	−7.50*	

Note: * significant at the 1 percent level, ** significant at the 5 percent level, *** significant at the 10 percent level.

Table 6.2 Auto loans by outcome

	American	*Percentage*	*Japanese*	*Percentage*	*European*	*Percentage*	*Total*	*Percentage*
Good accounts	2146	77.19	2346	81.66	1037	77.22	5529	79.03
Default	130	4.68	82	2.85	39	2.90	251	3.59
Prepayment	504	18.13	445	15.49	267	19.88	1216	17.38
Total	2780	100	2873	100	1343	100	6996	100

Souleles (2002) and Heitfield and Sabarwal (2004), we use the discrete outcome interpretation of duration models as presented by Shumway (2001).

In the competing-risks framework, we first recognize that during our observation period a borrower prepays, defaults, or else remains current through the end of the time period of study (censored). We define T_j (j = 1,2,3) as the latent duration for each loan to terminate by prepaying, defaulting, or being censored, and the observed duration, τ, is the minimum of the T_j.

Conditional on a set of explanatory variables, x_j, that include personal risk characteristics, market conditions at the time of origination, and characteristics of the consumption choice, the probability density function (*pdf*) and cumulative density function (*cdf*) for T_j are

$$f_i(T_j|x_j;\theta_j) = h_j(T_j|x_j;\theta_j)\exp(-I_j(r_j|x_j;\theta_j)) \tag{1}$$

$$F_j(T_j|x_j;\theta_j) = 1-\exp(-I_j(r_j|x_j;\theta_j)) \tag{2}$$

where I_j is the integrated hazard for outcome j:

$$I_j(T_j|x_j;\theta) = \int_0^{T_j} h_j(s|x_j;\theta_j)ds, \tag{3}$$

r_j is an integer variable taking values in the set {1,2,3} representing the possible loan outcomes, and h_j is the hazard function.

The joint distribution of the duration and outcome is

$$f(\tau,j|x;\theta) = h_j(\tau|x_j;\theta_j)\exp(-I_0(\tau|x;\theta)) \tag{4}$$

where $x = (x_1,x_2,x_3)$, $\theta = (\theta_1, \theta_2, \theta_3)$ and $I_0 = \Sigma\ I_j$ is the aggregated integrated hazard. Thus, the conditional probability of an outcome is

$$\Pr(j|\tau,x;\theta) = \frac{h_j(\tau|x_j;\theta)}{\sum_{j=1}^{3} h_j(\tau|x;\theta)}. \tag{5}$$

In order to simplify estimation, we specify a separate exponential hazard function for each outcome

$$h_j(\tau_j|x_j;\theta_j) = \exp(x'_j\beta_j). \tag{6}$$

and estimate (5) in a multinomial logit framework.

Since our purpose is to determine the information content of borrower consumption decisions on loan performance, we follow Gross and Souleles (2002) and separate x_j into components representing borrower risk characteristics, economic conditions, and consumption characteristics. Specifically, we assume that

$$x'_j\beta_j = \beta_0\tau_t + \beta_1 age_{jt} + \beta_2 risk_{jt} + \beta_3 econ_{jt} + \beta_4 car_{jt} \tag{7}$$

where τ_t represents a series of dummy variables corresponding to calendar quarters that allows for shifts over time in the propensity to default or prepay; age_{jt} is a third order polynomial in loan age that allows for nonparametric variation in the prepayment and default hazard; $risk_{jt}$ represents a set of borrower characteristics, including credit score, that reflect the lender's underwriting criteria; $econ_{jt}$ is a set of variables capturing changes in local economic condition, and car_{jt} is a set of variables identifying information concerning the type of car purchased.

In equation (7), the combination of the age variables (age_{jt}) and the risk measures ($risk_{jt}$) account for borrower risk in the auto loans. As Gross and Souleles (2002) point out, "age_{jt} allow for duration dependence in the baseline hazard" while the initial risk characteristic ($risk_{j0}$) "allows this hazard to shift across accounts that start the sample period with different risk characteristics."[15]

To establish a baseline to judge the importance of product information on loan performance, we first estimate a restricted model of prepayment and default with only age_{jt} and τ_t:

$$x'_j\beta_j = \beta_0\tau_t + \beta_1 age_{jt}. \tag{8}$$

Since age_{jt} represents a third-order polynomial, the corresponding prepayment and default hazards are nonparametric. By incorporating the quarterly time dummy variables, we are able to determine whether the baseline hazards of prepayment and default have shifted over time.

Next, we extend the analysis to include borrower risk characteristics and local economic conditions:

$$x'_j\beta_j = \beta_0\tau_t + \beta_1 age_{it} + \beta_2 risk_{jt} + \beta_3 econ_{jt}. \tag{9}$$

Equation (9) represents the traditional loan performance specification and is extensively used in the analysis of mortgage and credit card performance. We then extend this model to the full specification described in (7) that includes information about the asset securing the loan. By comparing the model log-likelihood ratio statistics, we can determine the marginal impact of incorporating consumer consumption information in evaluating the likelihood of loan default or prepayment.

In modeling the termination probability of auto loans, we incorporate a set of explanatory variables that capture the financial incentives associated with prepayment. For example, to approximate the value of the borrower's prepayment option, we follow the standard approach followed in the mortgage literature, as outlined in Deng, Quigley, and Van Order (2000), and estimate the prepayment option as

$$PPOPTION_{j,t} = \frac{V_{j,t} - V^{\star}_{j,t}}{V_{j,t}} \tag{10}$$

where $V_{j,t}$ is the market value of loan j at time t (i.e., the present value of the remaining payments at the current market rate), and $V^{\star}_{j,t}$ is the book value of loan j at time t (i.e., the present value of the remaining payments at the contract interest rate). We calculate $V_{j,t}$ by assuming that the current market rate at time t is the average auto loan interest rate in month t as reported in the Informa interest rate survey. Since consumers are more likely to prepay following a decline in the prevailing interest rate relative to the original contract rate, a positive value for *PPOPTION* is indicative of an "in-the-money" prepayment option. In order to account for any nonlinearity in the prepayment option, we also include the square of *PPOPTION*.

To determine the impact of differences in auto depreciation rates on loan termination probabilities, we estimated the depreciation schedule for each auto manufacturer based on the five-year blue-book values reported by the National Automobile Dealers Association (www.nada.com). For example, to determine the average expected depreciation for Subaru vehicles, we collected the estimated market value during the fall of 2003 for the base-level Forrester, Impresa, and Legacy models beginning with the 1998 model year through the 2002 model year. This provides a rough estimate of the yearly change in value for a base-level model experiencing an average driving pattern. For each model, we calculate the yearly depreciation experienced by the baseline car and then average the expected depreciation by manufacturer. Unfortunately, given the heterogeneous nature of the models from year to year, we are unable to match all models to a set of used car values. Thus, we assume that all models within each manufacturer follow a similar depreciation schedule. Obviously, our valuation algorithm is only an approximation since individual cars will vary based on the idiosyncratic driving habits of the borrowers.

Based on these estimated changes in value, we construct monthly loan-to-value ratios (*CLTV*). We expect *CLTV* to be positively related to default since higher depreciation in auto values, holding other things constant, serves to increase the loan-to-value ratio. Given the significant depreciation in auto values upon purchase, many borrowers have an auto loan balance greater than the current car value. Thus, including *CLTV* allows for a direct test for the link between auto quality and credit performance. That is, if an auto manufacturer produces a disproportional number of low-quality cars, then the secondary market value for the manufacturer's cars will reflect this lower quality. We also include the square of *CLTV* to control for any nonlinearity.

In addition to changes in the auto value relative to the debt burden, we also capture changes in borrower credit constraints via the time-varying borrower credit score (*FICO*). Borrower credit history is one of the key determinants of auto loan approval. Thus, we expect the *FICO* score to be negatively related to default, implying that borrowers with lower current *FICO* scores are more likely to default on their auto loans. We also include the square of *FICO* to capture any nonlinearity present in borrower credit scores.

Local economic conditions may also impact borrower loan termination decisions. For example, borrowers who lose their jobs are more likely to default due to inability to continue the loan payments. We use the county unemployment rate (*UnempRate*), updated monthly, as a proxy for local economic conditions. Finally, we include a series of dummy variables that denote the borrower's location (state) to control for unobserved heterogeneity in local economic conditions.

As discussed earlier, the set of variables included in *car* represents information about the purchase decision that is available to the lender at the time of loan origination, but is not utilized in the underwriting decision. By incorporating this set of information into the model, we can ascertain whether data about the consumption decision contains predictive value concerning the performance of debt. Although rather obvious, we also include the auto purchase price in the performance model. Since the lender provides the loan commitment prior to the purchase decision, the lender does not know the actual purchase price. We also include the square of the purchase price to control for any nonlinear effects. Next, we incorporate a dummy variable that is set equal to one if the purchase price is above the average purchase price for that car manufacturer. This variable is designed to flag borrowers who are purchasing higher-valued cars relative to other cars sold in that brand. Finally, in separate models we include a series of dummy variables that control for either the type of auto manufacturer (American, Japanese, or European) or specific auto manufacturer (e.g., BMW, GM, Toyota, etc.).

Results

As outlined earlier, we first estimate the baseline survival function of the cumulative likelihood of automobile loans surviving (i.e., not prepaying or defaulting) by manufacturer location. Figures 6.1 and 6.2 present the baseline survival curves for prepayment and default by manufacturer location (America, Japan, or Europe), respectively. Figures 6.3 and 6.4 present the baseline survival curves for, prepayment and default by vehicle make (Benz, VW, Chevy, Dodge, Honda, Toyota), respectively. While over 20 different automobile makes are in our dataset, we present only the results for select automobile makes.

Considering prepayment first, figures 6.1 and 6.3 show clearly that at any given age, European automobiles (Benz and VW) have a lower survival rate than either American or Japanese, and the prepayment survival rates for American and Japanese automobiles are statistically indifferent. This implies that at a given age, the prepayment rate of European automobiles is higher than that of American and Japanese, and American and Japanese automobiles have relatively the same prepayment rates.

Figure 6.1 Prepayment probability of European (EU), Japanese (JP), and American (US) automobiles

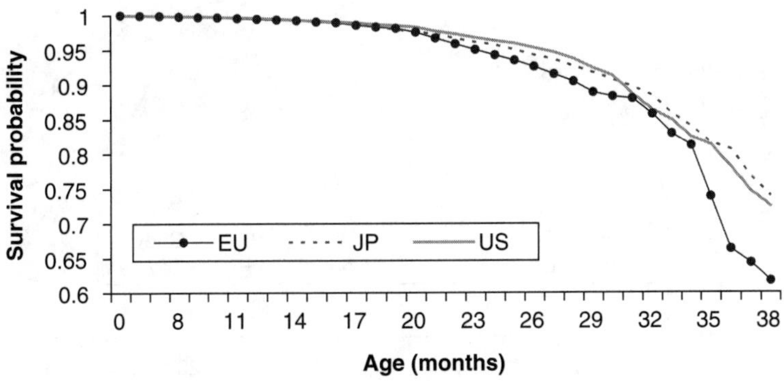

Figure 6.2 Default probability of European (EU), Japanese (JP), and American (US) automobiles

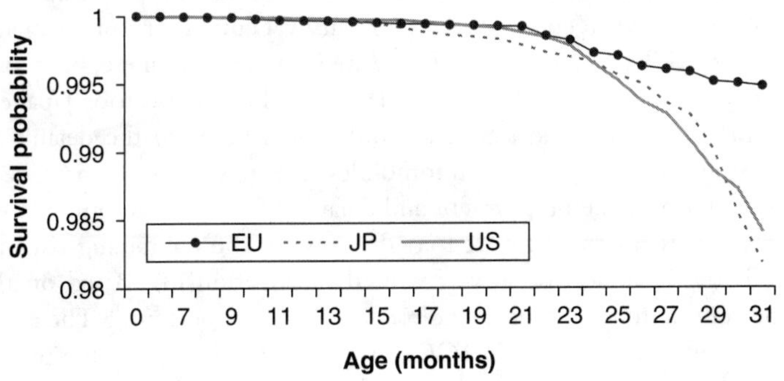

Figure 6.3 Prepayment probability of select automobile makes

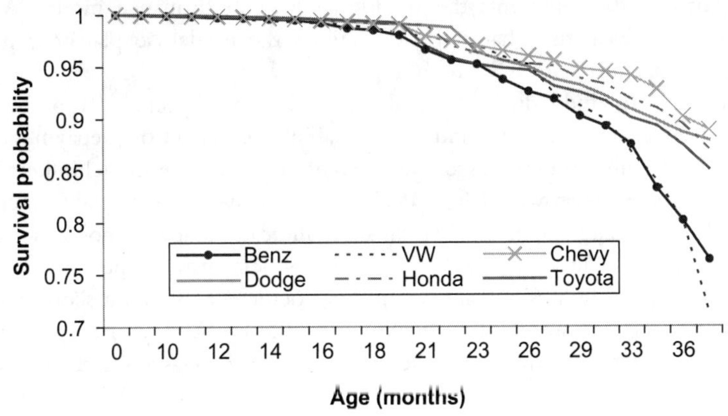

Figure 6.4 Default probability of select automobile makes

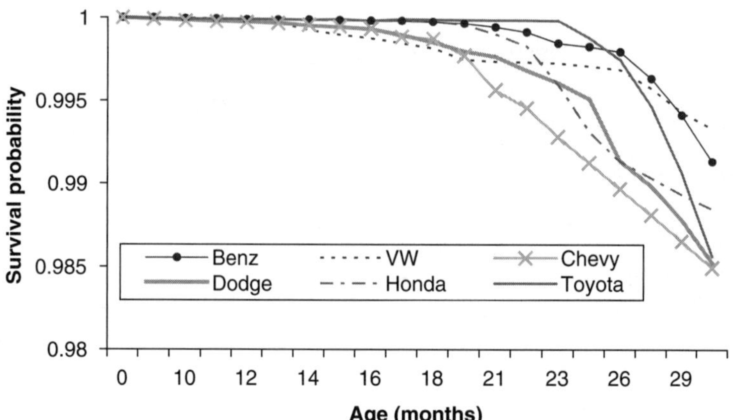

Figures 6.2 and 6.4 show the baseline default survival curves. Unlike the baseline prepayment survival curves, the default survival curves for European automobiles are higher (Benz and VW) than American and Japanese, implying that European cars have lower default risk relative to the American or Japanese cars. Once again, we do not find significant differences between the default survival rates for American and Japanese automobiles. Next, we present a more formal analysis to determine the prepayment and default behavior of automobile types.

Table 6.3 presents the estimated coefficients for the competing-risks models. Model 1 is the baseline case as represented in equation (8). Based on the log-likelihood statistic for this model, the pseudo R^2 is 8.2 percent.[16] The statistically significant coefficients for *AGE*, *AGE2*, and *AGE3* indicate that the prepayment and default hazards follow a distinctly nonlinear pattern. Each subsequent model reflects the inclusion of a new set of explanatory variables.

Model 2 corresponds to equation (9) and represents the introduction of borrower risk characteristics and local economic conditions into the specification. Again, this model represents the traditional loan performance model. Adding borrower and local risk characteristics doubles the model's explanatory power, raising the pseudo R^2 from 8.2 to 16.6 percent.

Turning to the individual risk variables, we find the expected relation between current borrower credit score and the probability of default or prepayment. The negative and significant credit score coefficient on the default model indicates that the likelihood of borrower default declines as borrower credit quality increases. Examining the marginal effect of credit score indicates that a 20-point increase in borrower credit quality reduces the likelihood of default by 9.9 percent.[17] On the prepayment side, the positive and significant coefficient for credit score indicates that a 20-point increase in credit quality raises the probability of prepayment by 3.3 percent. These marginal effects clearly demonstrate the asymmetric response to changes in borrower credit quality on auto loan performance. We also find that

Table 6.3 Competing Risks Models

	Model 1		*Model 2*		*Model 3*		*Model 4*	
Variable	*Default*	*Prepayment*	*Default*	*Prepayment*	*Default*	*Prepayment*	*Default*	*Prepayment*
Intercept	−7.194300	−2.910700	−10.330200	−12.129600	−10.757800	−12.650300	−10.984600	−12.863500
	−11.79	−11.19	−3.62	−5.81	−3.75	−6.02	−3.75	−6.09
Monthly income$_{t0}$			−0.000400	0.000010	−0.000380	0.000020	−0.000390	0.000020
			−3.81	2.00	−3.62	3.28	−3.61	2.00
Monthly income$_{t0\ (sq)}$			0.000000	0.000000	0.000000	0.000000	0.000000	0.000000
			3.86	−0.70	3.68	−0.83	−3.55	−0.79
Credit score$_{t-6}$			−0.032400	0.022500	−0.032100	0.022900	−0.029400	0.023100
			−3.76	3.82	−3.75	3.88	−3.41	3.91
Credit score$_{t-6(sq)}$			0.000040	−0.000020	0.000040	−0.000020	0.000040	−0.000020
			0.57	−4.71	5.69	−4.70	5.67	−4.69
Unemployment$_{t-6}$			0.136600	−0.084500	0.136800	−0.087300	0.109800	−0.088500
			1.85	−2.20	2.14	−2.27	1.95	−2.30
CLTV$_{t-6}$			5.129400	−9.708600	5.136400	−9.649800	4.765600	−9.672500
			2.78	−11.41	2.76	−11.34	2.62	−11.36
CLTV$_{t-6(sq)}$			3.142500	−9.849800	3.119800	−9.793600	2.762100	−9.828800
			1.60	−10.92	1.58	−10.86	1.44	−10.90
Payment$_{t-6}$			0.000191	0.000299	0.000192	0.000294	0.000193	0.000294
			2.25	6.23	3.00	6.13	2.12	6.13
Car value$_{t0}$			0.000046	0.000013	0.000092	0.000053	0.000134	0.000040
			2.19	1.70	2.19	3.12	2.63	2.11

Continued

Table 6.3 Continued

	Model 1		*Model 2*		*Model 3*		*Model 4*	
Variable	*Default*	*Prepayment*	*Default*	*Prepayment*	*Default*	*Prepayment*	*Default*	*Prepayment*
Car value$_{t0(sq)}$			0.000000	0.000000	0.000000	0.000000	0.000000	0.000000
			−1.14	−0.02	−1.47	−2.13	−2.05	−1.47
PPOption$_{t-6}$			0.407300	0.587300	0.368000	0.606200	0.346600	0.612100
			3.06	3.57	2.75	3.68	2.52	3.71
PPOption$_{t-6(sq)}$			0.009750	0.188500	0.019400	0.192500	0.021500	0.194300
			0.68	3.58	1.36	3.65	1.43	3.68
Owner age			−0.091900	−0.042800	−0.093500	−0.045200	−0.091400	−0.044600
			−3.85	−4.56	−3.88	−4.81	−3.70	−4.69
Owner age^2			0.000929	0.000398	0.000941	0.000411	0.000937	0.000415
			3.48	3.90	3.51	4.03	3.39	4.03
Loan age	−0.182300	0.161600	−0.109900	0.197700	−0.108300	0.197600	−0.098200	0.197400
	−2.45	4.42	−3.29	5.33	−1.30	5.33	−1.18	5.32
Loan age^2	0.006320	−0.009430	0.003220	−0.010100	0.003130	−0.010100	0.002750	−0.010100
	2.26	−6.01	2.90	− 6.39	1.00	−6.39	0.89	−6.39
Loan age^3	−0.000075	−0.000150	−0.000047	−0.000140	−0.000046	−0.000140	−0.000042	−0.000140
	−2.34	−7.14	−1.31	−6.67	−1.28	−6.67	−1.17	−6.67
Buick dummy							−1.733700	−0.069800
							−1.00	−0.42
Cadillac dummy							−0.549700	0.379300
							−2.48	2.62
Chevy dummy							−0.150100	−0.328000
							−0.52	−3.52

Chrysler dummy	−0.936900	0.473700
	−0.90	2.68
Dodge dummy	1.045200	−0.358100
	3.74	−3.36
Geo dummy	−1.115200	1.178300
	−0.91	1.14
GM dummy	−0.442000	0.263900
	−0.88	2.07
Lincoln dummy	0.591700	0.111200
	4.01	0.74
Oldsmobile dummy	0.813400	0.210100
	2.24	1.14
Plymouth dummy	0.046600	0.427800
	1.76	2.39
Pontiac dummy	0.527400	0.377500
	2.38	2.52
Saturn dummy	1.814300	−0.204200
	3.87	−0.85
Audi dummy	−1.489800	0.218300
	−1.95	3.05
BMW dummy	−0.247100	0.106400
	−2.20	2.07
Jaguar dummy	−0.862600	0.396700
	−1.44	2.50

Continued

Table 6.3 Continued

	Model 1		*Model 2*		*Model 3*		*Model 4*	
Variable	*Default*	*Prepayment*	*Default*	*Prepayment*	*Default*	*Prepayment*	*Default*	*Prepayment*
Benz dummy							0.194300	0.021900
							2.16	3.07
Saab dummy							−0.721300	0.225600
							−3.08	1.52
Wolkswagen dummy							0.012400	0.024600
							0.04	0.21
Accura dummy							0.071900	−0.084200
							0.21	−2.69
Honda dummy							−0.004120	−0.092600
							−2.35	−1.97
Infinity dummy							−0.214800	0.342100
							−1.89	2.24
Isuzu dummy							1.105700	−0.173300
							3.15	−0.80
Lexus dummy							−0.270200	0.444600
							−2.42	2.94
Mazda dummy							0.333600	0.077600
							2.09	0.50
Mitsubishi dummy							0.226300	0.302900
							1.94	2.27

Nissan dummy							0.4359	0.1295
							2.01	1.31
Subaru dummy							−1.8415	0.0183
							−4.24	0.10
European auto dummy					−0.148100	−0.231600		
					−3.71	−4.06		
Japan auto dummy					−0.262600	−0.323000		
					−2.28	−2.92		
Above avg. car dummy					0.345900	0.094300	0.533400	−0.054200
					2.00	1.48	2.68	−0.76
Used car dummy	0.213500	0.008340	0.154100	0.040900	0.114000	0.042900	0.165600	0.034500
	1.92	0.20	1.36	0.98	0.99	1.00	1.40	0.79
CT dummy	0.320800	−0.494400	−0.366100	−0.536300	−0.359300	−0.540000	−0.315800	−0.550100
	1.96	−7.86	−2.08	−8.21	−2.04	−8.27	−1.77	−8.39
FL dummy	−1.138400	−0.093300	−1.991100	0.020200	−1.347700	−0.001480	−1.897400	−0.021900
	−1.03	−0.49	−1.53	0.11	−1.12	−0.01	−2.03	−0.11
ME dummy	−2.717600	−0.165800	−2.493900	−0.124500	−2.516300	−0.146300	−2.402200	−0.157200
	−2.70	− 1.47	−2.46	−1.07	−2.48	−1.26	−2.35	−1.35
NH dummy	−1.678000	−0.000070	−1.518500	−0.047600	−1.518000	−0.062700	−1.603900	−0.064500
	−3.29	0.00	−2.94	−0.53	−2.94	−0.70	−3.07	−0.71
NJ dummy	−0.945200	−0.379900	−0.996400	−0.314200	−1.006900	−0.317300	−1.080200	−0.323100
	−3.91	−5.43	−3.92	−4.01	−3.96	−4.04	−4.18	−4.10
NY dummy	−0.039300	−0.499800	0.275700	−0.366100	0.260200	−0.388700	0.234000	−0.394800
	−0.30	−9.70	1.51	−4.61	1.43	−4.88	1.24	−4.94
PA dummy	−1.384400	−0.338900	−0.939600	−0.238900	−0.962600	− 0.236700	−0.860700	−0.251500
	−1.38	−1.48	−0.92	−1.02	−0.94	−1.01	−0.84	−1.07

Continued

Table 6.3 Continued

	Model 1		*Model 2*		*Model 3*		*Model 4*	
Variable	*Default*	*Prepayment*	*Default*	*Prepayment*	*Default*	*Prepayment*	*Default*	*Prepayment*
RI dummy	0.564700	−0.193800	0.460400	−0.105100	0.462100	−0.103300	0.452800	−0.089900
	2.57	−1.76	1.97	−0.90	1.97	−0.89	1.87	−0.77
Q399 dummy	−1.120600	−0.031700	−0.777500	−0.044200	−0.773500	−0.045300	−0.749500	−0.039500
	−3.10	−0.35	−2.12	−0.48	−2.11	−0.49	−2.04	−0.42
Q499 dummy	−1.093300	−0.260400	−0.883200	−0.335700	−0.873900	−0.337500	−0.839500	−0.334600
	−3.21	−2.72	−2.56	−3.40	−2.53	−3.42	−2.43	−3.39
Q100 dummy	0.531200	0.007800	0.234200	−0.013500	−0.231300	−0.011200	−0.221200	−0.010200
	2.11	0.09	0.91	−0.16	−0.89	−0.13	−0.85	−0.12
Q200 dummy	0.277000	−0.180800	0.107200	−0.178300	0.103900	−0.172800	0.104400	−0.172400
	1.26	−1.99	0.46	−1.88	0.45	−1.82	0.45	−1.82
Q300 dummy	0.114500	−0.087900	0.376700	−0.024400	0.374000	−0.016600	0.353800	−0.017400
	0.57	−1.01	1.68	−0.26	1.66	−0.18	1.57	−0.19
Q400 dummy	0.403500	0.989700	0.114100	1.065300	0.108500	1.074100	0.093200	1.072900
	1.73	17.15	0.44	15.13	0.41	15.21	0.36	15.20
Q101 dummy	−0.192300	0.049300	0.341600	0.134100	0.333200	0.142500	0.351100	0.141200
	−0.84	0.55	1.27	1.28	1.23	1.35	1.29	1.34
Q201 dummy	−0.220400	−0.159600	0.228800	−0.077100	0.221100	−0.068300	0.214200	−0.072000
	−0.94	−1.60	0.84	−0.69	0.81	−0.61	0.79	−0.64
Pseudo- R^2	0.08		0.16		0.23		0.26	
Number of observations	290685/6996		290685/6996		290685/6996		290685/6996	

Note: The table provides the coefficient values and the t-statistics (below the coefficient value).

borrower income has the expected impact on prepayment and default. The significantly negative coefficient for monthly income in the default model suggests that borrowers with higher incomes at loan origination are less likely to default. Conversely, higher-income borrowers are more likely to pay off their loan prior to maturity.

The impact of the current loan-to-value ratio also follows the anticipated pattern. The positive and significant coefficient in the default model indicates that the probability of default increases as the loan-to-value ratio increases. Since these loans are positive amortizing loans, an increase in the current loan-to-value implies that the underlying asset (the car) value has declined. On the prepayment side, the significantly negative coefficient suggests the opposite effect. That is, a decline in the asset's value reduces the likelihood of prepayment.

The coefficients for the variable measuring the borrower's incentive to prepay are significant and have the expected signs. Recall that the variable *PPOPTION* captures the borrower's financial incentive to prepay as reflected in the relative difference between the current market loan rate and the contract interest rate. Since positive values of *PPOPTION* indicate that the borrower's prepayment option is "in-the-money," the significantly positive coefficient for *PPOPTION* in the prepayment model indicates that borrowers are more likely to pay off their auto loan when interest rates decline. Not surprisingly, we find that *PPOTION* is significant in the default model, suggesting that current interest rates have a considerable impact on the borrower's default decision.

Finally, we note that the local unemployment rate is significantly positive in the default model. We use the unemployment rate as a proxy for local economic conditions, with higher unemployment rates implying worsening economic conditions. Thus, the positive coefficient in the default model implies that during periods of greater economic uncertainty, the probability of auto loan default increases; however, we note that the coefficient for unemployment is not significant in the prepayment model.

Model 3 represents our first attempt to include information beyond the traditional risk factors associated with loan performance. In Model 3 we include two dummy variables denoting whether a European or Japanese automobile secures the loan. We find that including these dummy variables in the loan performance model increases the pseudo R^2 by 28.5 percent (from 16.6 to 23.2 percent), supporting our hypothesis that the consumer consumption decision provides information about the performance of the debt securing the car. The marginal effects indicate that loans secured by European and Japanese cars are 50 percent and 56 percent, respectively, less likely to default than loans secured by American cars. We also find that loans on European cars are 18.8 percent less likely to prepay than loans secured by American cars, while loans on Japanese cars are 11.7 percent less likely to prepay than loans secured by American cars. From a risk-reward trade-off standpoint, the results suggest that loans to borrowers who purchase Japanese cars have the lowest default risk, while loans to borrowers of European cars have the lowest prepayment risk (most likely to be carried to maturity). We note that the variables controlling for the car purchase price are not significant in the prepayment or default models.

As a final test of the information value related to the consumption decision, we incorporate a series of dummy variables for each auto manufacturer (Toyota is the base case) in Model 4. We find that incorporating greater specificity about the type of car purchased provides only marginal improvement in assessing the probability of a loan prepaying or defaulting. We note that the pseudo R^2 for Model 4 increases only 10.8 percent (from 23.1 to 25.9 percent). However, the individual coefficients reveal that significant dispersion exists in the performance of auto loans after controlling for manufacturer. For example, we see that loans on Saturns have default hazards that are 22 times higher than the default hazard of Toyotas. Furthermore, the individual responses show that the hazards are not monolithic. For example, although the results from Model 3 indicate that loans on U.S. cars have significantly higher default rates, incorporating individual manufacturer control variables shows that five of the American auto manufacturers have significantly higher default hazards than Toyota, while one has significantly lower default hazards. In addition, we find significant variation within the foreign vehicle segment. For example, the model coefficients indicate that loans on Mazdas are six times more likely to default than loans on Toyotas.

The results clearly show that significant variation exists in the default hazard rates on auto loans across manufacturer, even after controlling for the usual factors considered by lenders at the time of loan origination. Furthermore, since this information is available to the lender at the point of origination, our results suggest that lenders could utilize this information in risk-based pricing by moving away from the standard "house-rate" loan pricing for auto loans.

Implications for U.S. Auto Manufacturers

Our results on auto loan performance combined with recent empirical work on automotive brand loyalty suggest a bleak future for U.S. auto manufacturers. For example, Train and Winston (2004) find that U.S. automakers lost significant market share to European and Japanese automakers between 1990 and 2000 and that this loss in market share is partly due to declining consumer brand loyalty toward U.S. automakers. Train and Winston's (2004) analysis suggests that the primary reason for this shift in consumer demand is the perception that U.S. automakers no longer provide a sufficient price/quality trade-off. As a result, U.S. automakers have increasingly relied on price reductions and financing incentives to retain market shares.

If we assume that the auto loan performance observed from our sample represents the general market, then the empirical results reported in this study question the American automotive manufacturers' reliance on financing incentives to retain market share. Our results indicate that loans on American cars have default rates that are approximately 50 percent greater than loans on European or Japanese cars. All else being equal, this finding suggests that loans secured by American cars should have significantly higher interest rates to compensate for the higher default risk. Thus, to compensate for the low credit risk premium earned on their loan portfolios (as a result of low- or zero-interest rate financing incentives), American automobile manufacturers must price their products above the equilibrium quality adjusted clearing price. This finding implies that cash purchasers of American cars are, in effect, subsidizing the poor credit performance of buyers who finance the purchase of American cars. As a result, we should observe a greater percentage of cash buyers opting for European or Japanese cars where the product price does not incorporate the expected losses on the loan pool. Mannering, Winston, and Starkey (2002) present evidence consistent with this prediction. In their study of the automobile leasing market, Mannering et al. (2002) find that consumers who pay cash are more likely to acquire a Japanese vehicle.

Conclusions

This chapter uses a unique dataset of individual automobile loan performance to assess whether borrower consumption choice reveals information about future loan performance. Automobiles are a highly visible consumption good and are directly marketed to appeal to targeted demographic groups. Insurers have long recognized that automobile makes and models appeal to different clienteles, and that these clienteles have heterogeneous risk profiles and accident rates. Given that individual risk-behavior self-selection is evident in the automobile market, a natural question arises: Does this self-selection also reveal information about the consumer's propensity to prepay or default on the automotive loan?

We use a unique dataset consisting of 6,996 new and used automobile loans originated by a large financial institution between January 1998 and March 2002. The loans are fixed-rate notes and have four- and five-year maturities. We observe the performance of these loans from January 1998 through March 2003, creating a monthly record denoting whether the loans are paid-in-full, prepaid, defaulted, or still current at the end of the sample period. In addition to the loan performance, we observe a number of loan characteristics including the automobile value and age at origination, loan amount, and automotive make, model, and year. We also observe a number of borrower characteristics including credit score, income, and age.

Our results show that the factors that traditionally predict default and prepayment continue to perform as expected. Specifically, we find that (1) a decline in borrower credit risk lowers the probability of default and raises the probability of prepayment; (2) an increase in the loan-to-value increases the probability of default and lowers the probability of prepayment; (3) an increase in borrower income increases the probability of prepayment, whereas an increase in local area unemployment increases the probability of default, and (4) a decrease in the market interest rate increases both the probability of prepayment and default. We also find that automobile manufacturing location (America, Europe, and Japan) significantly impacts both the prepayment and default behavior of borrowers; including the location dummies increased the pseudo-R^2 by 28 percent. Finally, we control for individual automobile-make dummies and find them to be significant drivers of default and prepayment.

Our results provide evidence that the type of automobile a consumer purchases reveals information about the consumer's propensity to prepay or default on the loan used to finance that purchase. Since the information on the type of automobile purchased is available to the lender at the point of origination, we suggest that lenders could use this information by moving away from the standard "house-rate" loan pricing for auto loans. Instead, lenders could profitably pursue risk-based pricing based on the type of car the borrower purchases.

Notes

* The authors would like to thank Michael Carhill, Erik Heitfield, Bert Higgins, Brad Jordan, Larry Mielnicki, Jim Papadonis, Kenneth Train, and Clifford Winston for helpful comments. We are grateful to Diana Andrade, Ron Kwolek, and Greg Pownell for excellent research assistance. The views expressed in this research are those of the authors and do not represent the policies or positions of the Office of the Comptroller of the Currency, of any offices, agencies, or instrumentalities of the U.S. Government, or of the Bank of America.

1. See Miller and Rock (1985) for a discussion of dividend policy as a mechanism for managers to signal the value of the firm.
2. For example, Brueckner and Follain (1988) and Quigley (1987) discuss the tradeoffs between mortgage contract terms and expected tenure.
3. See Stanton and Wallace (1998) and LeRoy (1996) for a discussion of the mortgage menu problem and the implications concerning asymmetric information about borrower expected mobility.
4. Edelberg (2003) provides empirical evidence that the greater use of risk-based pricing during the 1990s has resulted in an increase in the level of credit access for high-risk borrowers.
5. Automobile ownership statistics are fairly stable across various demographic characteristics such as income, age, race, employment, net worth, and homeownership.
6. U.S. homeownership data is reported in "Census Bureau Reports on Residential Vacancies and Homeownership" available at http://www.census.gov/hhes/www/housing/hvs/.
7. For example, a borrower with an acceptable credit score may be offered a loan up to $20,000 conditional on making a 5 percent downpayment. Thus, if the borrower purchases an $18,000 car, the lender provides a $17,100 loan.
8. In an empirical analysis of house-price volatility, Ambrose, Buttimer, and Thibodeau (2001) show that house-price volatility displays a U-shaped pattern when ranked by house value.
9. Automobile loans can be classified into two broad categories, "direct" and "indirect." Direct loans are issued directly to the borrower, and indirect loans are issued through the dealer. In case of indirect loans, the financial institution contracts with the automobile dealership to provide loans at fixed interest rates. However, they have to compete with automobile finance companies that can provide the loan at a much cheaper rate, even if they have to bear a loss on the loan. For example, a GM finance company could take a loss on the financing of a GM automobile if GM profits on the automobile sale. Hence, financial institutions usually cannot compete in the market for indirect automobile loans. As a result, our study focuses only on direct automobile loans.
10. Our results are robust to alternative definitions of prepayment (e.g., early payoffs greater than $2,000 or $4,000) and default (90 days past due).
11. Since financial institutions try to repossess automobiles once accounts are 60 days past due, our definition is consistent with practice.

12. Dasgupta, Siddarth, and Silva-Risso (2003) and Train and Winston (2004) use this breakdown.
13. The interest-rate spread is defined as the loan annual percentage rate (APR) at origination less the corresponding one-year Treasury rate.
14. Competing-risks models are well developed in the labor economics literature. For example, see Mealli and Pudney (1996), Burdett, Kiefer, and Sharma (1985), Narendranathan and Stewart (1993), and Flinn and Heckman (1982).
15. Gross and Souleles (2002: 330).
16. The pseudo R^2 is calculated from the ratio of the model log-likelihood statistic to the restricted model log-likelihood statistic, where the restricted model is a model with only an intercept term.
17. The marginal effect is calculated as $e^{\beta} - 1$.

References

Aizcorbe, A., A.B. Kennickell, and K.B. Moore. 2003. "Recent Changes in U.S. Family Finances: Evidence from the 1998 and 2001 Survey Consumer Finances." *Federal Reserve Bulletin* January, 1–32.

Aizcorbe, A., and M. Starr-McCluer. 1997. "Vehicle Ownership, Vehicle Acquisitions and the Growth of Auto Leasing: Evidence from Consumer Surveys." Working Paper, Federal Reserve Board.

Aizcorbe, A., M. Starr-McCluer, and J.T. Hickman. 2003. "The Replacement Demand for Motor Vehicles: Evidence from the Survey of Consumer Finance." Working Paper, Federal Reserve Board.

Ambrose, B.W., and A. Sanders. 2005. "Legal Restrictions in Personal Loan Markets." *Journal of Real Estate Finance and Economics* 30(2): 133–52.

Ambrose, B.W., R.J. Buttimer, Jr., and T. Thibodeau. 2001 "A New Spin on the Jumbo/Conforming Loan Rate Differential." *Journal of Real Estate Finance and Economics* 23(3): 309–35.

Brueckner, J., and J. Follain. 1988. "The Rise and Fall of the Arm—An Econometric-Analysis of Mortgage Choice." *Review of Economics and Statistics* 70(1): 93–102.

Burdett, K., N. Kiefer, and S. Sharma. 1985. "Layoffs and Duration Dependence in a Model of Turnover." *Journal of Econometrics* 28: 51–70.

Calhoun, C.A., and Y. Deng. 2002. "A Dynamic Analysis of Fixed- and Adjustable-Rate Mortgage Termination." *Journal of Real Estate Finance and Economics* 24(1): 9–33.

Dasgupta, S., S. Siddarth, and J. Silva-Risso. 2003. "Lease or Buy?: A Structural Model of the Vehicle Acquisition Decision." University of Southern California, working paper.

Deng, Y., J.M. Quigley, and R. Van Order. 2000. "Mortgage Terminations, Heterogeneity and the Exercise of Mortgage Options." *Econometrica* 68(2): 275–307.

Edelberg, W. 2003. "Risk-Based Pricing of Interest Rates in Consumer Loan Markets." University of Chicago, working paper.

Flinn, C.J., and J.J. Heckman. 1982. "Models for the Analysis of Labor Force Dynamics." *Advances in Econometrics* 1: 35–95.

Grinblatt, M., M. Keloharju, and S. Ikaheimo. 2004. "Interpersonal Effects in Consumption: Evidence from the Automobile Purchases of Neighbors." NBER working paper #10226.

Gross, D.B., and N.S. Souleles. 2002. "An Empirical Analysis of Personal Bankruptcy and Delinquency." *Review of Financial Studies* 15(1): 319–47.

Heitfield, E. and T. Sabarwal. 2004. "What Drives Default and Prepayment on Subprime Auto Loans?" *Journal of Real Estate Finance and Economics*. 29(4): 457–77.

Leroy, S. 1996. "Mortgage Valuation under Optimal Prepayment." *Review of Financial Studies* 9(3): 817–44.

Mannering, F., C. Winston, and W. Starkey. 2002. "An Exploratory Analysis of Automobile Leasing by US Households." *Journal of Urban Economics* 52: 154–76.

Mealli, F., and S. Pudney. 1996. "Occupational Pensions and Job Mobility in Britain: Estimation of a Random-Effects Competing Risks Model." *Journal of Applied Econometrics* 11: 293–320.

Miller, M., and K. Rock. 1985. "Dividend Policy under Asymmetric Information." *Journal of Finance* 40(4): 1031–51.

Narendranathan, W., and M.B. Steward. 1993. "Modeling the Probability of Leaving Unemployment: Competing Risks Models with Flexible Base-Line Hazards." *Applied Statistics* 42: 63–83.

Quigley, J. 1987. "Interest-Rate Variations, Mortgage Prepayments and Household Mobility." *Review of Economics and Statistics* 69(4): 636–43.

Stanton R., and N. Wallace. 1998. "Mortgage Choice: What's the Point?" *Real Estate Economics* 26(2): 173–205.

Shumway, T. 2001. "Forecasting Bankruptcy More Accurately: A Simple Hazard Model." *Journal of Business* 101–24.

Train, K., and C. Winston. 2004. "Vehicle Choice Behavior and the Declining Market Share of U.S. Automakers." Working Paper, University of California, Berkeley.

CHAPTER 7

INTRODUCTORY CREDIT CARD OFFERS AND BALANCE SWITCHING BEHAVIOR OF CARDHOLDERS

Tufan Ekici, Lucia Dunn, and Tae Hyung Kim

Introduction

American consumers carry over $800 billion in unpaid credit card balances.[1] With several thousand banks issuing credit cards today, the effort to lure these cardholders has become increasingly competitive. One of the most common business practices in this industry is the use of the introductory offer with a "teaser" interest rate below the going market rate for a fixed period of time. Frequently the low-rate offers will be connected to a transfer of balances from another account. The phenomenon of introductory rates and balance switching has become very important in this industry, and it has been estimated that around 5 billion direct solicitations go out annually, almost 4 solicitations per month per American household.[2] This aggressive marketing behavior by banks is credited with increasing competition in the credit card market and the drop in average interest rates that occurred throughout the 1990s. In principle, a strategic consumer can avoid paying high interest rates by taking advantage of these offers. However, not all consumers revolving on credit cards are taking these introductory offers, and it is important to understand the behavior involved in this decision.

There has been relatively little work on the introductory offers and balance switching, primarily because of the difficulty of obtaining data on these phenomena. Here we will utilize a new set of nonproprietary survey data taken from a large sample of credit cardholders, which directly addresses these issues. Respondents in this survey were asked a series of questions on their credit card usage, including whether they were currently subject to an introductory annual percentage interest rate (APR), and if so, was this connected to a switch of balances.

This chapter is organized as follows. We review the relevant literature in the next section. Next, we discuss theoretical considerations. The succeeding section introduces the data source and provides some descriptive statistics of the variables of interest. Econometric methodology and the results are explained in the sections that follow. Finally, we present our summary and conclusions.

Background and Previous Research

While there has been little work on the actual topic of switching credit card balances, a number of researchers have examined the related issue of high credit card interest rates. Ausubel (1991) was one of the first to carry out an empirical study of this market, finding high profits and high and sticky interest rates in spite of a seemingly competitive structure in the industry. He speculated that search/switching costs and a type of irrational consumer behavior might be involved in these paradoxical outcomes. Countering this reasoning, Brito and Hartley (1995) argued theoretically that the aspect of the liquidity service of credit cards saves consumers the opportunity cost of holding money for payment and makes it rational for them to hold balances even in the face of the high interest rates. Mester (1994), Stavins (1996), and Park (1997) also addressed the issue referring to information problems, high interest elasticities for defaulters, and the open-ended nature of credit card loans, respectively, all of which create high risks for banks. The work of Gross and Souleles (2002) examines the issue further by estimating the long-run interest elasticity of credit card debt.

Consumer search in the credit card market, which could ultimately lead to a lower APR, has been another strand of research. Calem and Mester (1995), using 1989 *SCF* data, find that consumers with high balances are discouraged from searching because of their high likelihood of rejection. Using the 1998 *Survey of Consumer Finance* data, Crook (2002) finds, however, that this discouragement to search no longer exists. Kerr and Dunn (2005) and Kim, Dunn, and Mumy (2005) come to a similar conclusion with different methodologies. All of this work takes into account the risk category of the consumer since interest rates reflect the riskiness of borrowers for banks. The finding that in recent years factors which might signal risk—such as high balances—no longer inhibit search is probably linked to the large number of credit card solicitations that come in consumers' mail, since they have greatly reduced their search costs.

Lack of data has resulted in relatively little previous research dealing with the actual phenomenon of credit card balance switching in response to solicitations. There are three previous studies that have dealt directly with the topic, as well as one that has dealt with a related issue. Ausubel (1999) used a bank client base in an experiment to generate proprietary data for studying adverse selection in the credit card market. He found that adverse selection exists in that riskier consumers were more likely to engage in balance switching. The work of Kim (2000) analyzed the balance-switching phenomenon with a smaller subset of the sample used here and a different methodology from that employed in this essay. The current research will thus build upon Kim's work. Frank (2001) examined balance switching in a survey of around 200 credit cardholders and found that balance and interest rate were the most important determinants in the switching decision. Agarwal et al. (2005) also conducted a market experiment in collaboration with a large U.S. bank to examine consumer preferences in the trade-off between interest rates and annual fees. Again, this work is based on proprietary data. In the current research, we use what is to our knowledge the only large, nonproprietary survey data set that has direct information on balance switching.

Theoretical Considerations

The decision to switch balances could be modeled as a sequential process. In this analysis we assume that each cardholder in our sample has received at least one introductory offer. This is reasonable given that the 5 billion annual offers issued by U.S. credit card banks represents more than 19 offers for every man, woman, and child in the country. The agent first decides whether or not to accept the offer. Once the intro-rate card has been selected, the agent then has the option of transferring some of his or her existing balances from other cards to the new card. This process is repeated when a new offer is received. We analyze the acceptance/switch decision first with simple independent probit models. Then we use a probit sample selection model with a selection equation for accepting the intro card and then another probit equation for the balance-switching decision.

Variables Influencing the Decisions

Interest Rate Factors

An agent should accept an intro offer if the terms of the offer are better than the terms on the existing card minus any transactions cost, which would largely be nuisance value in this case. We assume that the offered APR relative to the current APR is the most important aspect of the acceptance and switching decision.[3] Therefore, an agent should accept the current offer if the current APR minus the APR on the intro offer is sufficiently large to offset any nuisance value involved in a switch. The difference between the current APR and the intro offer APR will be denoted as *APR Difference*. Hence we have:

Accept offer if *APR Difference* > nuisance value of the switch.[4]

Since we do not have survey data on the intro APR of the respondents who do not have an introductory offer, nor on the non-intro APR for respondents who have taken the intro offer, we impute both an intro and a non-intro APR for the relevant groups. The details of the imputation are presented in appendix B.

Risk Type

Risk type of the cardholder is another important aspect in considering introductory offers, and we control for this in our model. We expect it to affect the terms of the offer from the bank,[5] and it may also affect the cardholder's response to the offer. Our measure of risk type is based on a separation of the sample into three groups. In ascending order of risk, they are as follows: (1) convenience users (i.e., nonrevolvers), (2) those who carry a balance and have no default history, (3) those who carry a balance and have a positive default history. Thus our risk measure is as follows:

> *Risk Level.* A set of three variables that captures the three risk levels as noted earlier, with Risk Level 1 being the lowest risk type and Risk Level 3 being the highest risk type.

Table 7.1, based on a sample of 9,950 respondents from our survey data, gives relevant statistics for these three risk groups. It shows that Group 1 customers, the lowest risk group, are less likely to own an intro-rate card than other two groups. This is expected since convenience users would be less likely to be interested in intro rates. Group 1 is also the least profitable group for banks and thus may be offered less attractive terms. Conditional on having an intro-rate card, the interest rate is the lowest among Group 2 customers—the group that banks will be most interested in attracting. We see that Group 3, the high-risk revolvers, are also very likely to accept an intro offer even though banks are more likely to offer inferior terms to this group. We expect Group 3 will also be likely to transfer balances.

Card Use Factors

The acceptance of an intro offer and the decision to switch should be affected by several additional considerations involving card usage. These include the amount of the current balance and utilization rate of the cardholder. A consumer who has larger balances and is close to the credit limit may be more likely to accept an intro offer and transfer balances, as it will lessen his or her financial constraints. On the other hand, these consumers may feel overextended and be wary of accepting additional credit, and we will check for these factors in our empirical results. These variables cannot, of course, be identified precisely unless one has information at the time of the offer. Since our dataset observes households after they have accepted the offers, we cannot identify if, for example, high balances were accumulated before or after the offer has been accepted. However, if we assume that card usage habits tend to persist, then there are several observed variables that could be

Table 7.1 Characteristics of the cardholder sample by ascending risk type

	Convenience Users—Risk Level 1	*Carry Balance/No Default History—Risk Level 2*	*Carry Balance/ Positive Default History—Risk Level 3*
Number of observations	2680	6320	950
(Percentage of sample)	(27%)	(63.5%)	(9.5%)
Percentage of group having an intro card	8.3%	13.3%	12.9%
Average APR conditional on having an intro card	11.9%	8.1%	11.2%

thought of as proxies for the consumer's past credit card usage habits. They are as follows:

Balance-to-Income. The ratio of monthly credit card balances to monthly household income. This variable captures the debt burden of the households.

Utilization Rate. The ratio of credit card balance to total credit limit. This variable captures the extent of the constraint on available liquidity.

Maxedout. A dummy variable indicator of whether the charging limit on any of the credit cards has been reached. This variable captures both the debt burden and the degree of liquidity constraint of the household.[6]

The Accept and Switch Equations

Taking the factors discussed earlier into account, we represent both the acceptance and the switching decisions as follows:

Decision = f (*APR Difference, Risk Level, Balance-to-Income, Utilization Rate, Maxedout,* X_i),

where X_i is a vector of socioeconomic control variables including *Log(Income), Age, Education, Household Size,* and *Homeownership.*

DATA

The Survey

The data used in this research come from a household survey that was conducted each month by the Ohio State University Center for Survey Research in the state of Ohio between November 1996 and April 2002. The *Ohio Economic Survey (OES)* includes extensive information on respondents' credit card use as well as other socioeconomic characteristics. Some of the credit card questions are unique to this survey and unavailable in other publicly available datasets. More detail on the survey including the exact wording of the questions used here can be found in appendix A.

The major questions of interest are (1) whether the main credit card used by the respondent is an intro-rate offer card, and if so, (2) whether the respondent has switched any balances to that card.[7] We also know the APR on this main card used by the household. These questions were asked in the *OES* beginning July 1999. For the entire sample (N = 10,785), 88 percent of the sample did not have an intro offer on their credit card, and for those who had an intro offer, 40 percent of the respondents had indeed switched some balances from another card to this new card. Our goal here is to identify the factors that led to the decision to switch balances.

Descriptive Statistics

Table 7.2 below shows the definitions and the means of the variables used in the estimation. The sample is then separated into three distinct groups as follows: (1) non-intro rate card users (*N* = 9,409), (2) intro-rate card users who switched balances

Table 7.2 Variable definitions and sample means

Variable	*Definition*	*Mean (Standard Deviation)*
APR	Annual percentage rate	14.3 (5.5)
Log(income)	Log of annual household income	10.73 (0.71)
Income	Annual household income	\$57,161 (38,412)
Balance	Total amount owed on all cards after the most recent payment	\$2,652 (5,500)
Maxed cards	Number of credit cards at charging limit	0.20 (0.78)
Maxedout	Dummy for being at charging limit on any credit cards (At Limit = 1; Not at Limit = 0)	11% (0.32)
Default—used to determine risk type	Variable for a missing minimum required payment in the last six months	11% (0.31)
Utilization rate	Ratio of balance to credit limit	0.20 (0.27)
Balance-to-income	Ratio of balance to household income/12	0.82 (2.9)
Age	Age of the respondent	45.7 (14.4)
Homeownership	Dummy for homeownership (Own = 1; Rent = 0)	83% (0.37)
Education	Highest degree attained by the respondent	13.5 (1.94)
Household size	Sum of the number of adults and the children in the household	2.71 (1.46)

(N = *507*), and (3) intro-rate card users who did not switch any balances (N = *781*). The differences between these three groups are also displayed in table 7.3.

Econometric Methodology

In this section we employ several econometric techniques to analyze the intro-rate offers and balance-switching behavior of consumers. We assume that each cardholder in our sample has received at least one introductory offer. The intro-rate offers and balance switching can be represented as follows. Consumers will accept an intro offer if the utility derived from having an intro-rate card

Table 7.3 Comparisons of means by different groups

	Non-Intro	*Intro/Switch*	*Intro/No-Switch*
APR	15.1	5.6	11.7
Log(Income)	10.7	10.8	10.5
Income	$57,777	$60,478	$47,294
Balance	$2,597	$5,308	$1,607
Maxed cards	0.20	0.11	0.26
Maxedout	11%	8%	16%
Default	11%	10%	15%
Utilization rate	20%	24%	20%
Balance-to-monthly income	81%	132%	58%
Balance-to-annual income	7%	11%	5%
Age	45.9	41.8	44.7
Homeownership	83%	84%	74%
Education	13.6	13.9	13.0
Household size	2.7	3.1	2.7

through the lower APR and balance transfer possibility is greater than the utility from not having an intro card. Therefore the acceptance of an intro-rate offer by the ith consumer can be modeled by using the latent variable $I_i^{\star} = V_{I,i}(W_{1i}, \lambda_i) - V_{NI,i}(W_{1i}, \lambda_i')$ where $V_{I,i}$ and $V_{NI,i}$ denote the utility derived from having an intro-rate card and non-intro rate card, respectively. The utilities depend both on individual specific characteristics (W) and the terms of the offers (λ). Writing the utilities as a linear approximation of the individual specific characteristics, the differences between the terms of the offers, and a normal error term, the determinants of the probability of having an intro-rate card can then be analyzed with the following probit equation:

$$I_i^{\star} = \alpha_1 W_{1i} + \alpha_2(\lambda_i - \lambda_i') + \varepsilon_{1i}$$

where individual i has an intro rate card if $I_i^{\star} > 0$ and does not if $I_i^{\star} \leqslant 0$, and the following are observed in the data,

$$Intro_i = 1 \text{ when } I_i^{\star} > 0$$

$$Intro_i = 0 \text{ otherwise}$$

The balance-switching phenomenon can also be represented in a similar fashion. Consumers will transfer balances to the new card if the utility of transferring balances is greater than the utility of not transferring. Thus the switching behavior of the ith consumer can be represented by the following probit equation:

$$S_i^{\star} = \beta_1 W_{2i} + \varepsilon_{2i}$$

where W_2 includes the personal specific credit and socioeconomic characteristics as well as the intro APR. Therefore,

$Switch_i = 1$ when $S_i^* > 0$
$Switch_i = 0$ otherwise

Taking Selection Bias into Account:

There is an issue of selection bias in this model. In our data we only observe balance switching if the consumer indeed has an introductory rate offer, that is, we observe $Switch_i$ if and only if $Intro_i = 1$. Thus we do not know whether those without an intro offer would have switched any balances had they had an intro offer. Therefore, we estimate a probit model of balance switching taking selection into account. The index function and the outcome equation are the same as before. We make the additional assumption that $(\varepsilon_{1i},\varepsilon_{2i}) \sim iidN(0,\tilde{V})$ and $\tilde{V} = \begin{bmatrix} 1 & \tilde{\rho} \\ \tilde{\rho} & 1 \end{bmatrix}$. The model is estimated by full information maximum likelihood, and the results are presented in table 7.5.

Results

Independent Probit Results: Decision to Hold Intro Offer Card

Table 7.4 column (1) shows that, as expected, the probability of having an intro-rate credit card is positively related to the APR difference between the current and offered card. The probability of having an intro card goes up with increasing risk type. However, it is *not* found to be significantly related to having reached the borrowing limit, or being maxed out, on at least one card. On the contrary, the probability of having an intro card goes down as consumer utilization rate increases. This could reflect a self-policing mechanism among consumers who are concerned that they may be overextended on credit. The probability is positively related to household size, which is reasonable since a larger family may increase credit needs. Finally, the probability of holding an intro card is negatively related to household income, education, and age. These results are in line with the position of industry critics who argue that more upscale consumers are less likely to be tempted by the "teaser rates" offered by credit card companies. Also, homeowners have home equity to draw on via HELOCs and, therefore, may be less interested in intro-rate credit cards.

Independent Probit Results: Decision to Switch Balances

Column (2) of table 7.4 above shows the results for estimating the probability of switching balances for the intro-rate cardholders.

Similar to our results for having an intro card, we find that a greater difference between the current and intro-offer APR will increase the probability of switching a balance. A higher balance to income also is found to increase the probability of switching balances. A respondent who has maxed out one or more of his credit cards

Table 7.4 Coefficients from probit estimation of column (1): intro-rate cardholding decision and column (2): balance switching conditional on having an intro-rate card

Variable	*Column (1) Coefficient (Standard Error)*	*Column (2) Coefficient (Standard Error)*
APR difference	0.025***	0.083***
	(0.005)	(0.008)
Risk level 2	0.292***	0.899***
	(0.054)	(0.169)
Risk level 3	0.234***	0.357
	(0.08)	(0.232)
Balance-to income	0.0016	0.244***
	(0.007)	(0.067)
Utilization rate	−0.313***	−0.087
	(0.093)	(0.262)
Maxedout	0.058	−0.759***
	(0.068)	(0.177)
Log(income)	−0.127***	0.537***
	(0.033)	(0.088)
Age	−0.0057***	−0.016***
	(0.002)	(0.004)
Education	−0.023**	0.116***
	(0.012)	(0.028)
Household size	0.042***	0.034
	(0.015)	(0.036)
Homeownership	−0.099*	0.388***
	(0.034)	(0.136)
Number of observations	7,300	892
Log likelihood	−2649.1652	−424.68327

Note: *** significant at 1 percent level or better; ** significant at 5 percent level or better; * significant at 10 percent level or better.

is actually found to be less likely to switch balances. This may again reflect a self-policing mechanism and will be discussed further later. Higher-risk level consumers are somewhat more likely to switch balances. Switching probability goes up with income and education, which may reflect logistical sophistication about switching.

Results Taking Selection Bias into Account

For the switching regression model, we use the same set of explanatory variables used earlier. This fit is identified because *age* is not in the main equation for switching a balance. The results are presented in table 7.5.

Table 7.5 Coefficients for probit sample selection model

	Variable	*Coefficient (robust standard error)*
Selection equation for accepting an intro card	APR difference	0.025***
		(0.005)
	Risk level 2	0.293***
		(0.054)
	Risk level 3	0.245***
		(0.08)
	Balance-to-income	0.004
		(0.007)
	Utilization rate	−0.324***
		(0.093)
	Maxedout	0.060
		(0.067)
	Log(income)	−0.124***
		(0.032)
	Age	−0.006***
		(0.001)
	Education	−0.023**
		(0.012)
	Household size	0.038**
		(0.015)
	Homeownership	−0.095*
		(0.052)
Main equation for switching a balance	APRDIFF	0.015**
		(0.007)
	Risk level 2	0.116
		(0.104)
	Risk level 3	−0.065
		(0.121)
	Balance-to-income	0.131***
		(0.039)
	Utilization rate	0.189
		(0.154)
	Maxedout	−0.37***
		(0.10)
	Log(income)	0.360***
		(0.054)
	Education	0.711***
		(0.018)
	Household size	−0.016
		(0.021)
	Homeownership	0.224***
		(0.07)
Number of observations	Censored	6,402
	Uncensored	892
Wald test of independent equations ($\rho = 0$)		$\chi^2_{(1)} = 58.26$
Log likelihood		−3,059.931

Note: ***significant at 1 percent level or better; **significant at 5 percent level or better; *significant at 10 percent level or better.

The results for the decision to hold an intro-rate card are qualitatively similar to those reported in table 7.4 for the independent probit fit. The likelihood of having an intro card increases with the APR difference and risk type of the consumer and decreases with utilization rate, income, age, education, and homeownership.

The results from the main balance-switching equation show that the major behavioral factors involved with a switch work as expected. A greater APR difference increases the likelihood of a switch. Higher balance to income induces more switching. Risk level, however, is not found to influence a balance switch once selection is taken into account. Being maxed out on at least one credit card again is shown to have a negative impact on the likelihood of a switch. This is probably related to stress factors for the consumer that cannot be identified explicitly from our existing data. We interpret this again to be a reflection of the same self-policing mechanisms that we feel may be causing the likelihood of accepting an intro card to go down with utilization rate. That is, overextended consumers may be trying to reign in their spending on credit. The results for socioeconomic variables are qualitatively similar to the independent probit fit for switching probability. Once a consumer has an intro-offer card, he or she is more likely to switch as income and education go up. This is probably related to the sophistication level needed to handle the details of a switch. Owning a home makes a consumer more likely to switch a balance. This indicates that availability of HELOC credit has not significantly impacted consumers' credit card balance-switching behavior.

Summary and Conclusions

This chapter has examined the phenomena of accepting introductory credit card offer and switching balances. In recent years, the typical American household has received on average four credit card solicitation offers per month in the mail. The acceptance of intro offers and balance switches that have resulted from this have become a major feature in the credit history of U.S. consumers. There has been relatively little research on these phenomena despite its importance in increasing competition among banks and in lowering average credit card interest rates. This has been primarily due to the lack of nonproprietary data on intro offers. Here we have used a switching regression model to examine a new and unique source of household data on intro offers and balance switching, and our results provide insights into factors that are affecting household's credit card management.

Most consistently, we find that the difference between a cardholder's existing APR on the card he/she uses most often and the intro-offer APR is a key factor in both the decision to accept an intro-offer card and to switch a balance. It is well recognized that credit card interest rates on average began to fall in the mid-1990s. Our result here is, therefore, noteworthy because it demonstrates one mechanism by which the increased competitive environment for credit card banks has worked to lower interest rates for consumers.

Our results also show that riskier consumers are more likely to have an intro-rate card, but risk class is not significant in the decision to switch a balance. It is noteworthy that there appear to be some self-policing mechanisms at work in our data because a higher utilization rate discourages accepting an intro offer, and being maxed out on at least one card discourages a balance switch among holders of intro-offer cards. This suggests that factors are at work that hold overextended credit card users in check, which should be welcome news for the industry.

Older, more educated, and high-income households are less likely to accept the teaser-rate cards offered by banks, as has been suggested by critics of the industry. However, once a household has accepted such an offer, more educated and high-income consumers are more likely to switch a balance. This probably reflects the degree of logistical sophistication required to accomplish a balance switch. Finally, there is some tendency for homeowners to hold fewer intro cards than non-homeowners. A logical explanation would be that the home equity line of credit alternative is more attractive for these consumers. However, once a homeowner holds an intro card, they are actually more likely to switch balances. Therefore, home equity credit does not appear to discourage consumers from engaging in the balance-switching phenomenon. This is consistent with data available from the *Survey of Consumer Finances*, which shows that many holders of the lower-cost home equity lines of credit do not actually use them and continue to hold conventional credit card balances.[8]

According to industry sources, introductory offers and balance switching have become a way of life for many credit cardholders. Clearly many questions about the motivations behind these behaviors remain. While the present research provides some clues in this direction, new and better data sources will ultimately be the key to a full understanding of these phenomena.

Appendix A: Background of the *OES* and Wording of the Questions

The data for this research were collected in a monthly household telephone survey administered by the Ohio State University Center for Survey Research beginning in November of 1996 using the latest technology available in the survey area. A simple random sample was taken each month, and the monthly sample size was at least 500 adult household members. The Random-Digit-Dialing method of sample selection was used to select a statewide sample. To account for possible nonresponse error, the results are weighted to take into account the number of telephone lines in each household and to adjust for variations in the sample from the population related to gender, age, racial background, education, and presence of children.

Respondents were encouraged to consult their most recent credit card statements in order to facilitate the recall of the credit card information. This could include terminating the current phone call with the scheduling of a callback when the respondent has all the information together to answer the questions. To ensure the highest data quality, a number of steps were undertaken. There was third-party monitoring of the interview process. There were extensive checks for internal consistency in the responses, including the use of filtering algorithms. The sample characteristics for the Ohio sample are very close to characteristics of the national sample used for the *Survey of Consumer Finances (SCF)* in the same time period.[9]

Most of the following questions have been asked in OES since the beginning of the survey. However, some questions, including the balance-switching questions, began later in the survey period. The starting month for these questions is indicated in parentheses.

Questionaire

1. The following set of questions ask about your use of credit cards. When we say credit cards in these questions, we do not include any debit cards that you may have, which merely subtract funds from a bank account. Do you have any credit cards?
2. How many credit cards do you have?
3. According to your most recent statements, approximately what did the total charges and/or cash advances amount to for the last month for all your credit cards together?
4. Have you or will you pay off all of the last month's charges and/or cash advances on your most recent statements or did you or will you carry some of them over?
5. Approximately how much of the total amount of your last month's charges and/or cash advances on your most recent statements have you or will you pay off?
6. Right now, approximately what is the total amount you owe on all your credit cards after your most recent payments?
7. Now think of the minimum required payments you need to make on all your credit card statements this last month. Approximately what was the total amount you were required to pay in minimum monthly payments last month on all your credit cards taken together? *(Beginning August 1997).*
8. Considering all the credit card accounts that you have, approximately what is your total line of credit or credit limit?
9. How many, if any, credit cards have you currently reached your charging limit on? *(Beginning February 1998).*
10. In the past six months, how many times did you not pay off at least the minimum amount due on any of your credit cards?
11. Now, I would like to ask you to think about the one credit card your household uses the most often. What is the interest rate that your credit card issuer will charge you for carrying a balance on that card? *(Beginning December 1998).*
12. Is that percent rate an introductory rate which will be increased after the introductory period is over? *(Beginning June 1999).*
13. Have you switched any balances from another credit card to that introductory rate card? *(Beginning June 1999).*

Appendix B: Imputation of APR

We do not observe the intro APR for the respondents who do not have an intro-rate card, and we do not observe the non-intro APR for those who have an intro-rate card. Since the difference between the offers is considered to be one of the most important factors in accepting an offer, we impute the missing APR for each group in order to calculate the difference between intro and non-intro APRs. The imputation is as follows.

We first divide the sample into two groups according to the type of the credit card (intro vs. non-intro). We then estimate the following equation by OLS for each group.

$$APR_i = \alpha_0 + \alpha_1 X_i + \varepsilon_i \text{ (for intro-rate cardholders)}$$

$$APR_i = \beta_0 + \beta_1 X_i + \varepsilon_i \text{ (for non-intro- rate cardholders)}$$

where X_i includes number of times the respondent missed paying the required minimum payment in the last six months, ratio of minimum required payment to household income, utilization ratio, number of cards charging limit has been reached on, log of household income, age, education, homeownership, and the number of children in the household.

We use the estimated coefficients to impute the missing APR within each group. Therefore, the imputed intro APR for non-intro-rate cardholders will be $APR_i = \hat{\alpha}_0 + \hat{\alpha}_1 X_i$ and the non-intro APR for the intro-rate cardholders will be $APR_i = \hat{\beta}_0 + \hat{\beta}_1 X_i$. Once we obtain both types of APR in each group, we combine the groups and calculate the difference between non-intro and intro rates as

$$APR\ Difference = \text{(non-intro APR)} - \text{(intro APR)}$$

After these calculations we find that, for convenience users, the mean intro APR is larger than the non-intro offer APR. For other risk types, the intro rate is smaller than the non-intro-offer APR. This is consistent with our intuition that banks try to target balance carriers with their intro offers because convenience users are the least likely to be profitable for banks.

Notes

1. Figures from the Nilson Report, *Wall Street Journal*, March 25, 2006, p. B1.
2. Federal Reserve Board's 2001 *Annual Report.*
3. Reward features may also play some role in a consumer's decision to switch, but we do not address these features since this survey did not take data on rewards.
4. We should note that for "convenience users" (who pay their balances in full every month and hence do not accumulate any interest charges), the APR may not be relevant Hence the above proposition does not necessarily apply in the case of convenience users.
5. It may be the case that when banks evaluate the relative risk and profitability of customers, they will not offer a low APR to convenience users since they are less profitable.
6. Note that the questions on *the number of cards a consumer has maxed out on*, as well as *the number of missed payments in the last six months*, are unique and not available in other publicly available datasets.
7. These survey questions referred to the card that the household uses most often.
8. See Dey and Dunn (2005) for a discussion of this phenomenon.
9. For comparison of *OES* and *SCF* the readers are referred to Dunn et al. (2004).

References

Agarwal, Sumit, Souphala Chomsisengphet, Chunlin Liu, and Nicholas S. Souleles. 2005. "Do Consumers Choose the Right Credit Contracts?" *Center for Financial Studies* Working Paper No. 2005/32, November.

Ausubel, Lawrence M. 1991. "The Failure of Competition in the Credit Card Market." *The American Economic Review* (March) 81 (1): 50–81.

———. 1999. "Adverse Selection in the Credit Card Market." Working Paper, Department of Economics, University of Maryland, June.

Brito, Dagobert L., and Peter R. Hartley. 1995. "Consumer Rationality and Credit Cards." *Journal of Political Economy* 103 (21): 400–33.

Calem, Paul S., and Loretta J. Mester. 1995. "Consumer Behavior and the Stickiness of Credit Card Interest Rates." *American Economic Review* (December). 85 (5): 1327–36.

Crook, Jonathan N. 2002. "Adverse Selection and Search in the US Bank Credit Card Market." University of Edinburgh Credit Research Center Working Paper No. 01/1, March.

Dey, Shubhasis, and Lucia Dunn. 2004. "Choice of Lines of Credit: The Choice between Credit Cards and Home Equity Lines of Credit." Ohio State University Working Paper 04–05, October.

Dunn, Lucia F., Tufan Ekici, Paul J. Lavrakas, and Jeffrey A. Stec. 2004. "An Index to Track Credit Card Debt and Predict Consumption." Ohio State University Economics Working Paper No. 04–04.

Frank, David. 2001. "To Switch or not to Switch: An Examination of Consumer Behavior in the Credit Card Industry." *Issues in Political Economy, Undergraduate Student Research in Economics* (July) 10.

Gross, David B. and Nicholas S. Souleles. 2002. "An Empirical Analysis of Personal Bankruptcy and Delinquency," *Review of Financial Studies* (Spring) 15 (1): 319–47.

Kerr, Sougata, and Lucia Dunn. 2002. "Consumer Search in the Changing Credit Card Market." Ohio State University Department of Economics Working Paper No. 02–03, September.

Kim, TaeHyung. 2000. "An Investigation of the U.S. Credit Market Using Original Survey Data." Ph.D. Dissertation, Ohio State University.

Kim, TaeHyung, Lucia F. Dunn, and Gene E. Mumy. 2005. "Bank Price Competition and Asymmetric Consumer Responses to Credit Card Interest Rates." *Economic Inquiry* 43 (April): 344–53.

Mester, Loretta J. 1994. "Why are Credit Card Rates Sticky?" *Economic Theory* 4: 505–30.

Min, Insik, and Jong-Ho Kim. 2003. "Modeling Credit Card Borrowing: A Comparison of Type 1 and Type 2 Tobit Approaches." *Southern Economic Journal* (July) 70 (1): 128–43.

Park, Sangkyun. 1997. "Effects Of Price Competition in the Credit Card Industry," *EconomicLetters* 57: 79–85.

Stavins, Joanna. 1996. "Can Demand Elasticities Explain Sticky Credit Card Rates?" *New England Economic Review* (July/August): 43–54.

CHAPTER 8

AN EXPLORATION OF USAGE OF PERSONAL CREDIT CARDS BY SMALL BUSINESSES

Grace Kim

Introduction

Small businesses generally represented 99.9 percent of the 25.8 million employer and nonemployer businesses in the United States in 2005. These businesses, officially defined as an independent business having fewer than 500 employees, also accounted for 99.7 percent of employer businesses and nearly half of the total U.S. private payroll and generated 60–80 percent of net new jobs annually over the last decade. In their ownership of 6.5 million businesses in 2002, women business owners generated nearly $1 trillion in revenues, accounted for nearly $200 billion in payroll, and employed as many as 7.1 million workers.[1] Figures also suggest that their numbers are growing at a faster rate than primarily men-owned businesses. Thus, the survival and performance of women-owned small businesses is of concern to policy makers and researchers.

A critical element impacting these businesses is lack of start-up capital. As the largest suppliers of debt to small businesses, commercial banks account for more than 80 percent of lending in the credit-line market and generally more than 50 percent in other markets, such as commercial mortgages and vehicle, equipment, and other loans to small businesses (U.S. Small Business Administration). Furthermore, banks are increasingly targeting women-owned businesses in marketing their loan portfolio activity. Yet, these businesses still face greater constraints than men-owned businesses in their financing and are seen as more reliant on informal sources of capital, including own personal finances.

Much of the small business financing literature focuses on the difficulties that women-owned businesses face in obtaining formal sources of capital and their sources of informal financing. However, generally no attention has been paid to difficulties they may also experience with regard to informal finance. Using micro-level data, this study focuses on the use of personal credit by women small business owners to address their reliance on informal finance.

The analysis examines to what extent personal finances play a role in the financing of the women-owned small businesses. The incidence and extent of personal finance usage for business purposes is not as different from men-owned businesses as might be expected. Explanatory factors are examined. Results indicate that similar ownership and business characteristics primarily determine the usage of personal credit by both groups of businesses.

This chapter is structured as follows: An overview of the relevant literature is followed by a description of the data, which is then followed by a discussion of the empirical methodology in the succeeding section. Findings are discussed in the next section. The final section concludes with implications.

Literature Review

Small Business Financing Mix

The majority of small business personal and business financing mix studies look at capital structure (Romano et al. 2000), internal versus external finance (Bhattacharya and Ravikumar 2001), household debt structure (Haynes and Avery 1996), bankruptcy (Berkowitz and White 2002), and comparisons among small businesses, primarily between family and nonfamily businesses (Yilmazer and Schrank 2006). Marital status is also considered in understanding the impact of family small business finances on household financing choices (Haynes and Avery 1996).

However, Haynes et al. (1999) find that where personal and business financing mix, the flow of funds from household to business and usage of personal financing by the small business is more frequent. Ang et al. (1995) explore the degree of separation between personal commitments and business and find high incidence of personal collateral for small business loans. Personal commitments often are substitutes for business collateral (Avery et al. 1998). However, none of these studies examine the use of personal credit by women-owned small businesses, partly due to the lack of sufficient micro-level data and partly due to the focus on their access to formal business credit.

Women-Owned Small Business Financing

A vast literature finds that women-owned small businesses generally face more difficulties than men-owned small businesses in obtaining credit from financial institutions, the implication also being that they then cannot obtain funds from the capital market. More specifically these businesses are more likely to face rejection in their credit applications and obtain smaller amounts of funding than men-owned small businesses, but factors other than gender may explain these differences. Buttner and Rosen (1989), among others, do not find evidence of gender discrimination by loan officers. Rather the business owners' own perceptions of discrimination (Fabowale et al. 1995; Orhan 2001) and of the banking relationship (McKechnie et al. 1998) may be important. Owner characteristics such as experience

(Verheul and Thurik 2001), age (Coleman 2002), and education (Fay and Williams 1993), as well as business characteristics such as major activity (Verheul and Theurik 2001) and size (Coleman 2002), also may influence the differential credit market outcomes. Furthermore, their choices and different sources of funding (Carter and Rosa 1998) may result in different credit constraints for women-owned small businesses. Thus, Haynes and Haynes (1999), among other studies, find that such small businesses tend to have higher probabilities of borrowing from their social network of relatives and friends than obtaining lines of credit from commercial banks. Coleman and Carsky (1996) indicate that women-owned businesses may pursue different business strategies that may result in small funding needs that may be satisfied by personal finances and not require formal business credit. However, the majority of these studies do not address the issue of their informal financing difficulties. Among the few, Carter and Kolvereid (1997) find that women's constrained work situation in turn reduces their personal savings levels that women-owned businesses may depend upon. Thus, reduced employment opportunities in turn may reduce self-employment ventures. This exploratory study integrates the findings from the small business household/business financing mix studies and the small business financing studies with regard to ownership gender to determine how reliant women-owned businesses indeed are on a particular source of informal financing, personal credit card debt.

Data

The majority of small business studies that examine the mix of financing use the Survey of Consumer Finances (SCF), which offers information on household balance sheets and some information about businesses owned and managed by the household. Their focus is on understanding how small business ownership impacts the household. Thus, few examine the Survey of Small Business Finance (SSBF), which offers unique data on small business balance sheets and information about personal finances. The SSBF is more appropriate here to avoid entangling separate motivations in the usage of personal finance by households and businesses. This study's focus is on the small business use of personal finance.[2]

The 1998 SSBF was conducted during 1999–2000 and is the population of for-profit, nonfinancial, nonfarm, nonsubsidiary small businesses that had fewer than 500 employees and were in operation as of year-end 1998. The random sample was drawn from the Dun's Market Identifier file as of 1999 and is generally representative of the U.S. small business population, except where larger small businesses and minority-owned small businesses were oversampled to ensure adequate numbers of observations in the data set (Bitler et al. 2001). Another limitation of the SSBF is that the lack of information about household financing prevents the study of the flow of business funds to the entrepreneurial household. However, these data constraints do not change the findings of the focus of this study on the usage of personal credit by businesses.

As the most recently available data set of the Federal Reserve Board of Governor's periodic surveys of financing of small businesses, the 1998 SSBF includes 3,561 firms. Of these, more than one-third are primarily owned by women, nearly two-thirds are primarily owned by men, and fewer than 1 percent are equally owned by women and men. Primarily owned here means greater than 50 percent concentration of ownership, while equally owned means an equal 50–50 division of concentration of ownership between women and men owners. Thus, 796 are primarily women-owned, 2,618 are primarily men-owned, and 147 are equally owned small businesses.

Methodology

A magnitude measure of the relative mix of personal and business credit cards usage suggests that there is no statistically significant difference between women and men in their relative usage. However, this may be the result of men-owned businesses having higher average monthly charges than women-owned businesses with respect to both personal credit cards and business credit cards, though not much larger.

Statistically significant differences between women-owned small businesses and men-owned small businesses in their usage of personal and business credit cards are also found elsewhere. Women-owned businesses are more likely to have used an owner's personal credit card, while men-owned businesses are more likely to have used a business credit card. Thus, 46.1 percent of women-owned businesses used a personal credit card, while only 32.0 percent used a business credit card. Likewise, 42.4 percent of men-owned businesses used a personal credit card, and a nearly similar percentage used a business credit card. Higher percentages of both women-owned and men-owned businesses paid their business credit card balance in full than their owner's personal credit card balance in full. Despite charging more on average each month, male-owned businesses were more likely than women-owned businesses to have paid their balances in full on both types of card. Finally, where balances were not paid in full, men-owned businesses had higher average remaining balances on an owner's personal credit card, though this result is insignificant, than on a business credit card The higher balances can be attributable to the higher monthly charges. In sum, women-owned businesses have a slightly higher incidence of personal credit card usage, while men-owned businesses have somewhat greater magnitude of such usage.

Since business credit cards for small businesses are typically secured with an owner's personal assets, the use of personal business credit cards implies difficulties with even the use of business credit cards. Thus, the use of personal business credit card is reflective of overall difficulties with obtaining more formal types of credit, such as credit lines, for the small business.

These differences are noted in table 8.1. Thus, a pooled regression with gender as a dummy variable will only confirm that gender is a factor in the relative reliance of small businesses on personal credit. Also, where no statistically significant differences are found, no further interpretation can be made with such a pooled regression. Rather multivariate regressions are conducted separately for the women-owned small businesses and the men-owned small businesses to determine whether similar factors can influence their financing mix, in particular their use of an owner's personal credit card.[3] This approach offers a more sophisticated interpretation into how they differ, rather than merely whether they differ.

Table 8.1 Summary mean statistics for credit card usage by small businesses

Credit Card Usage	*Coded (Categorical or Scale Variable)*	*All (N = 3561)*	*Women (N = 796)*	*Men (N = 2618)*	*Equality Tests*[a]
Personal credit card					
Used owner's personal credit card	yes = 1 no = 0 (categorical)	43.3%	46.1%	42.4%	3.337*
Average monthly charge	dollars (scale)	$1981.01 (6223.850)	$1176.47 (3248.577)	$2442.76 (6997.732)	3.949*** (270.020)
Paid balance in full	yes = 1 no = 0 (categorical)	74.4%	66.5%	76.9%	15.180***
Remaining balance on card	dollars (scale)	$5477.71 (11202.272)	$4366.43 (10758.203)	$6094.98 (11559.877)	−1.429 (1209.530)
Business credit card					
Used business credit card (growth from previous fiscal year)	yes = 1 no = 0 (categorical)	39.9%	32.0%	42.1%	25.366***
Average monthly charge	dollars (scale)	$4137.25 (16700.897)	$2119.04 (5189.353)	$4724.07 (18753.915)	−3.995*** (652.018)

Continued

Table 8.1 Continued

Credit Card Usage	*Coded (Categorical or Scale Variable)*	*All (N = 3561)*	*Women (N = 796)*	*Men (N = 2618)*	*Equality Tests*[a]
Paid balance in full	yes = 1 no = 0 (categorical)	87.4%	82.4%	89.1%	8.233***
Remaining balance on card	dollars (scale)	$5831.28 (14273.094)	$2975.73 (3695.145)	$7086.21 (17062.273)	−2.488** (1652.100)
Relative mix(personal/business)					
Average monthly charge (personal charge/business charge)	percentage (scale)	2.71×100 = 271% (8.22748)	3.02×100 = 302% (9.08530)	2.52×100 = 252% (7.60729)	0.529 (0.94605)

Note: Standard deviation is reported in parentheses for scale variables.

[a] Pearson Chi-Square statistic reported for two-sided tests of equality of proportions for categorical variables.

T-statistic with s.e. of difference in parentheses reported for two-sided tests of equality of means for scale variables (accounts for Levene's test for equality of variances).

* 10 percent significance level, ** 5 percent significance level, *** 1 percent significance level.

Table 8.2 offers a summary of the descriptive statistics of the independent variables used in the regressions to explain the usage of personal credit cards. Generally, women owners were less educated (only 43.1 percent had at least a college degree compared to 54.6 percent of men), had fewer years of business experience (15.1 years compared to 20.5 years), and were more likely to be a member of a racial minority (17.6 percent compared to 13.2 percent) than men owners of small businesses. At the same time, interestingly, women were slightly more likely to be involved in the business as a manager and had higher ownership concentrations than men.

Similarly, differences in business characteristics between these two groups of owners were also statistically significant. Women-owned small businesses were less likely to be incorporated (41.7 percent compared to 55.9 percent), younger (11.7 years compared to 15.4 years) and smaller (12.8 non-owned employees compared to 26.8 non-owned employees) than their men-owned counterparts. Likewise, women-owned businesses concentrated their sales more locally or regionally (87.1 percent compared to 82.4 percent) and were more likely to be in the service industries (83.5 percent compared to 71.6 percent). At the same time, they were less likely to have a close relationship with their financial institution, in terms of their usage of complementary transaction services.

Regressions of the measure of use of personal credit are reported in table 8.3 for women-owned small businesses and for men-owned small businesses, respectively. Logit regression analysis is used in the determination of incidence of personal credit card use. Ordinary Least Squares (OLS) multivariate regression analysis is utilized in the separate regressions of magnitude of personal credit card use.

The reduced-form specification for both types of regression analysis is as follows:

$$Y = \beta_0 + \beta_i X_i + \gamma_j Z_j + \varepsilon,$$

where Y represents business usage of owner's personal credit card, X_i represents the i owner characteristics together with respective regression coefficients β_i, and Z_j represents the j business characteristics together with respective regression coefficients γ_j. Specifically, X_i indicates independent owner characteristic variables (owner education, owner experience, ownership share percentage, owner rather than employee as manager, minority owner, and court judgments against owner). In addition, Z_j indicates independent small business characteristic variables (organization type, age of firm, size of firm, type of business activity, primary area of sales, and relationship with financial institution). In turn, β_0 represents the constant term, and ε indicates the error term.

Empirical Findings

Generally, similar factors for both women-owned and men-owned businesses were found to explain the usage of an owner's personal credit card by small businesses. Although women-owned and men-owned businesses differed in whether they used such a card in their small business financing and to what extent they used

Table 8.2 Summary mean statistics for independent variables

Independent Variables	*Coded (Categorical or Scale Variable)*	*All (N = 3561)*	*Women (N = 796)*	*Men (N = 2618)*	*Equality Tests*[a]
Owner characteristics					
Owner education	at least college degree = 1	52.2%	43.1%	54.6%	32.055***
	otherwise = 0				
Owner experience	years	19.2	15.1	20.5	−11.996***
		(11.791)	(10.693)	(11.865)	(0.444)
Ownership share	percentage	80.4%	84.2%	80.9%	3.155***
(Principal owner's share)		(27.252)	(24.922)	(27.580)	(1.035)
Owner/manager	owner is manager = 1	89.6%	91.5%	89.0%	3.800*
	other is manager = 0				
Minority owner	yes = 1	14.3%	17.6%	13.2%	9.201***
(Primarily owned by minority)	otherwise = 0				
Judgments against owner	yes = 1	3.9%	3.5%	4.0%	0.327
	otherwise = 0				
Business Characteristics					
Organization type	incorporated = 1	53.9%	41.7%	55.9%	45.410***
	otherwise = 0				
Age of firm	years	14.4	11.7	15.4	−8.125***
		(12.109)	(10.655)	(12.538)	(0.450)
Size of firm	number of employees	23.5	12.8	26.8	−6.516***
		(53.318)	(39.284)	(56.771)	(1.780)
Type of business activity	service = 1	74.5%	83.5%	71.6%	44.936***
(SIC code)	otherwise = 0				
Primary area of sales	local or regional = 1	83.5%	87.1%	82.4%	9.172**
(local, regional, nation, international)	otherwise = 0				
Relationship with financial institution	use of transaction services = 1	46.9%	43.5%	47.7%	4.164**
	no = 0				

Note: Standard deviation is reported in parentheses for scale variables.

[a]Pearson Chi-Square statistic reported for two-sided tests of equality of proportions for categorical variables.

T-statistic with s.e. of difference in parentheses reported for two-sided tests of equality of means for scale variables (accounts for Levene's test of equality of variances).

* 10 percent significance level, ** 5 percent significance level, *** 1 percent significance level.

Table 8.3 Regression results for women-owned businesses and for men-owned businesses

	Regression Results **WOMEN-Owned Businesses**			*Regression Results* **MEN-Owned Businesses**		
	Dependent Variables (Owner's Personal Credit Card Usage)					
	Used Personal Credit Card (Logit)[a]		*Average Monthly Charge (OLS)*[b]	*Used Personal Credit Card (Logit)*[a]		*Average Monthly Charge (OLS)*[b]
Independent Variables	β	$Exp(\beta)$`		β	$Exp(\beta)$	
Constant	0.100	1.105	1.298★★★	0.611★★	1.842	1.678★★★
	(0.034)		(4.006)	(4.162)		(2.698)
Owner characteristics						
Owner education	0.730★★★	2.076	1.284	0.416★★★	1.517	0.520
	(22.339)		(−0.038)	(23.748)		(1.275)
Owner experience	−0.004	0.996	−0.031	−0.002	1.002	−0.050
	(0.173)		(−0.386)	(0.159)		(1.264)
Ownership share	−0.004	0.996	−1.265★★	−0.010★★★	0.990	−0.088★★★
(Primary owner's share)	(1.008)		(−3.375)	(31.912)		(−2.603)
Owner/manager	0.549★	1.731	0.212★★★	0.380★	1.462	0.200★
	(3.634)		(4.120)	(7.653)		(1.673)
Minority owner	0.040	1.041	0.016	0.029	0.971	0.172
(Primarily owned by minority)	(0.041)		(0.300)	(0.058)		(0.296)
Judgments against owner	0.321	1.378	0.014	0.487★★	1.627	0.022
	(0.642)		(0.265)	(5.667)		(0.730)
Business characteristics						
Organization type	−0.428★★	0.651	1.479★	−0.209★★	0.812	1.624★★
(Incorporated)	(5.399)		(−1.450)	(5.017)		(0.725)
Age of business	−0.007	1.007	−1.110	−0.001	1.001	−0.063★
	(0.532)		(0.324)	(0.019)		(1.861)

Continued

Table 8.3 Continued

	Regression Results **WOMEN-Owned Businesses**			*Regression Results* **MEN-Owned Businesses**		
	Dependent Variables (Owner's Personal Credit Card Usage)					
	Used Personal Credit Card (Logit)[a]		*Average Monthly Charge (OLS)*[b]	*Used Personal Credit Card (Logit)*[a]		*Average Monthly Charge (OLS)*[b]
Independent Variables	β	*Exp*(β)`		β	*Exp*(β)	
Age of business[2]	0.009	1.004	0.077	0.035	1.341	0.152
	(0.466)		(0.026)	(0.094)		(0.721)
Size of business	−0.004	0.847	−0.008	−0.002**	1.002	−0.152***
	(2.497)		(0.147)	(5.049)		(4.463)
Type of business activity	−0.166	0.742	0.548	0.075	1.078	1.202
(Service industry or not)	(0.626)		(0.005)	(0.644)		(1.255)
Primary area of sales	0.299	0.641	−0.072*	0.271**	0.762	−0.003
(Regional or not)	(1.750)		(−1.395)	(6.029)		(−0.089)
Relationship with financial institution	−0.445***	1.105	0.043	−0.305***	0.737	−1.672**
	(8.236)		(0.819)	(13.070)		(−2.005)
R^2	0.084 (Nagelkerke)		0.310 (Adjusted)	0.060 (Nagelkerke)		0.223(Adjusted)
χ^2-*Value*	51.638***		Not applicable	120.433***		Not Applicable
F-Value	Not applicable		3.147***	Not Applicable		4.791***
N	796		367	2618		1109

Note: * 10 percent significance level, ** 5 percent significance level, *** 1 percent significance level.
[a] Wald statistics reported in parentheses for logit regression.
[b] T-statistics reported in parentheses for OLS regression.

such a card, they were influenced by similar owner characteristics and business characteristics.

With large Chi-square statistics for tests of model fit, the logit regression models for both the women-owned businesses and men-owned businesses appear sufficient to explain the incidence of use of an owner's personal credit card by businesses. Additional Hosmer-Lomeshow tests, with significance levels of 0.941 and 0.216, respectively, confirmed the models' goodness of fit, with levels much larger than 0.05. The models also offered better than chance predictive capabilities; thus the model was correct 62.3 percent of the time in predicting that a women-owned small business would actually use an owner's personal credit card and correct 69.0 percent of the time in determining whether a women-owned business would not use an owner's personal credit card. Likewise, the logit model was correct 63.3 percent of the time in predicting that a men-owned small business would be observed using a personal credit card and correct 82.0 percent of the time in predicting whether such a business would not use the card.

The Exp(β)s are reported along with the β regression coefficients, since the Exp(β) indicates how the log-odds that increase the use of an owner's personal credit card change as an independent variable changes by a unit. The β coefficients by themselves do not indicate the degree of impact that an independent variable has on the likelihood of the small business' using an owner's personal credit card, and only the signs have any meaning. Thus a positive sign can be interpreted to increase the likelihood, while a negative sign can be interpreted to decrease the likelihood for purposes of understanding the influence of the independent variables.

Owner characteristics appear to be less significant than business characteristics for the usage of personal credit by both groups of businesses. Having at least a college degree increased the probability that both groups used a personal credit card. This result is expected, since education may be correlated with personal finance and business finance knowledge. This result might be extended to the type of training and skills acquired (Brush 1992).[4] Though not significant, owner experience reduced the likelihood of both women-owned and men-owned businesses using a personal credit card. Shaw, Carter, and Brierton (2001) find that women-owned businesses have less of a credit history to reflect their creditworthiness. Thus, years of experience would be expected to enhance the performance and survival of a small business and thus enhance its creditworthiness to less informed investors and thus reduce the need of the business to rely on personal finance, including the owner's personal credit card. Likewise, the owners' involvement as managers of the business rather than using a paid manager or employee also positively affected both groups' use of a personal credit card. This may be the result of less interest in ceding control of the firm to outside management and thus more reliance on internal financing and personal finances. Mukhtar (2002) indeed finds that women have a managerial style that involves less delegation than that of men's. For male-owned businesses, greater ownership share of the primary owner decreased the likelihood that the male-owned business would use a personal credit card for the financing purposes of the business. The same reasoning as that for owner management control applies here.

Though not significant, minority ownership had the expected positive sign, since such owners have been found typically to experience more severe external credit constraints (Coleman 2005; Blanchflower et al. 2003; Cavalluzzo et al. 2003, for example) and thus would be expected to use personal finance as a substitute. Finally, judgment against the primary owner increased the likelihood of use of a personal credit card by a men-owned small business. Such court orders or lawsuits requiring payment or other action by the primary owner might result in more severe credit constraints for the business and thus require greater use of personal credit. On the other hand, the business might wish to devolve from association with such a primary owner's creditworthiness and thus be less reliant on such credit.

Incorporation has been found to lower the risk of closure (Boden and Headd 2002). An incorporated business was thus found to be less likely to use a personal credit card; their financial transparency also would enhance their creditworthiness and reduce the need for such financing. Though not significant, age of the business would indicate its viability and thus also enhance its creditworthiness and also produce the similar negative sign for use of a personal credit card. Squaring the age of business accounts for a possible nonlinear relationship between age and usage of personal credit, particularly a change in financing behavior from the business nascent stage to its exit stage. However, this variable was not found be statistically significant. A larger employee base, as a measure of the size of the business, was found to be significant in decreasing the usage of a personal credit card by men-owned businesses; the greater demands for funding to meet payroll, for example, might require a larger financing amount than a personal credit card could perhaps provide. This confirms previous findings about age and credit constraints (Coleman 2002).

Type of business activity was surprisingly not found to be significant; those small businesses in a relatively less capital-intensive industry that requires less start-up financing were generally found to be more likely to rely on a personal credit card than those in the non-service-oriented industry. Concentration of sales may reflect founding attitudes toward growth (Cliff 1998). As expected, those businesses with sales that were concentrated locally or regionally rather than nationally or abroad had smaller expansion requirements and thus less demand for financing, and could thus be expected to depend more on a personal credit card.

The expected sign of the relationship with the financial institution was ambiguous, since it was measured in terms of a transaction-based relationship. On the one hand, such a relationship would not necessarily enhance the lender's information production about the creditworthiness of the small business; such use would not necessarily reduce usage of a personal credit card. On the other hand, to the extent that such services were complementary, such as the processing of credit card receipts, such a relationship would increase the likelihood of business use of an owner's personal credit card. Interestingly, the relationship reduced the likelihood of use by both women-owned and men-owned businesses.

Though not large, the adjusted R^2s, 0.310 and 0.223, for the Ordinary Least Squares (OLS) regressions for both women-owned businesses and men-owned businesses, respectively, are comparable to other small business studies using micro-level data.[5] Furthermore, the significant F values indicate goodness of fit with regard to the models. Relatively similar factors again affect both groups of businesses in their magnitude of personal credit card usage, specifically their average monthly charge. The primary owner's share of ownership concentration and involvement as a manager were both important for women- and men-owned businesses alike, as was organizational structure, in terms of incorporation.

However, size of business, and a transactions-based relationship were also influential in the average monthly charge of men-owned businesses. Age of the business increased the size of the charge, where a personal credit card was used. At the same time, a regional or local concentration of sales reduced the magnitude of usage of an owner's personal credit card by women-owned businesses. Signs otherwise are generally consistent with those found for incidence of usage.

Conclusion

This study finds that women-owned small businesses are not that different from men-owned businesses in their usage of a particular informal financing source, the owner's personal credit card. Though they were more likely to use such a card, women-owned businesses did not charge as much as men-owned businesses. The results suggest that researchers must consider disaggregating the informal credit market to understand to what extent women-owned businesses also experience difficulties in this market.

Similar factors also appear to affect the overall personal credit card usage by both women-owned businesses and men-owned business, though some differences arise between incidence of use and magnitude of use. The findings indicate that ownership education is more important than ownership experience in the use of personal credit by small businesses. Concern about delegation of firm management also may drive women-owned businesses and men-owned businesses alike to use the owner's personal credit card. Minority ownership surprisingly does not appear to be as important for usage of this particular source of informal finance.

Incorporation and primary area of sales appear to be more important than age of the business and type of business activity in the use of personal credit by small businesses. A transactions-based relationship also appears to be influential, but the results are not definitive. The results also suggest that a closer look at the sources of financing narrows the differences found between women-owned small businesses and men-owned small businesses, in terms of their financing experiences.

Some limitations of this study derive from data considerations. For example, costs associated with using the personal credit card that might impact differential usage are not available. Size of the credit limit on the card that would influence the average monthly charge is also missing from the data. Furthermore, the credit card issuer's perspective cannot be directly obtained and must be inferred. However, because the study is heavily focused on the demand for credit card usage by small businesses, it avoids some entanglement with supply-side issues.

Future research may more clearly distinguish the extent to which personal credit is a substitute and a complement to business credit for the small business owner, in the manner that Avery et al. (1998) have with personal collateral and business collateral. Another avenue may be to extend this study by considering differences in usage of the personal credit card between minority-owned businesses, another documented group of credit-constrained businesses, and non-minority-owned businesses.

Finally, the results also imply that the rise in household debt may be partially attributable to small business ownership growth and usage of personal credit cards. Thus, credit concerns of small businesses eventually may translate to household credit concerns.

Notes

1. All statistics are drawn from the U.S. Small Business Administration Office of Advocacy.
2. With regard to small business financing, Avery et al. (1998) is one of the few studies to use both datasets.
3. A similar approach is taken by Kim (2006) in a study on the access of small businesses to credit based on ownership gender, including those businesses that are equally owned by women and men.
4. Thus, Astebro and Bernhardt (2003) interestingly find that self-selection by business owners leads to highly qualified owners, with high levels of human capital and wealth, choosing to use informal market sources of funding rather than commercial bank loans.
5. The regressions were weighted where White's tests indicated the presence of heteroscedasticity.

References

Ang, J.S., J.W. Lin, and F. Tyler. 1995. "Evidence on the Lack of Separation between Business and Personal Risks among Small Businesses." *Journal of Small Business Finance* 4: 197–210.

Astebro, Thomas, and Irwin Bernhardt. 2003. "Start-Up Financing, Owner Characteristics, and Survival." *Journal of Economics and Business* 55: 303–19.

Avery, Robert B., Raphael W. Bostic, and Katherine A. Samolyk. 1998. "The Role of Personal Wealth in Small Business Finance." *Journal of Banking & Finance* 22: 1019–61.

Berkowitz, Jeremy, and Michelle J. White. 2002. "Bankruptcy and Small Firms' Access to Credit." NBER Working Paper No.w9010 (June).

Bhattacharya, Utpal, and B. Ravikumar. 2001. "Capital Markets and the Evolution of Family Businesses." *Journal of Business* 74(2): 187–219.

Blanchflower, David G., Phillip B. Levine, and David J. Zimmerman. 2003. "Discrimination in the Small-Business Credit Market." *Review of Economics and Statistics* 85(4): 930–43.

Boden, Richard J., and Brian Headd. 2002. "Race and Gender Differences in Business Ownership and Business Turnover." *Business Economics* 61–72.

Brush, Candida. 1992. "Research on Women Business Owners: Past Trends, a New Perspective, and Future Directions." *Entrepreneurship Theory and Practice* 16: 5–30.

Buttner, E. Holly, and Benson Rosen. 1989. "Funding New Business Ventures: Are Decision Makers Biased against Women Entrepreneurs?" *Journal of Business Venturing* 4: 249–61.

Carter, Nancy, and L. Kolvereid. 1997. "Women Starting New Businesses: The Experience in Norway and the US." *OECD Conference on Women Entrepreneurs in SMEs* (April): Paris.

Carter, Sara, and Peter Rosa. 1998. "The Financing of Male- and Female-Owned Businesses." *Entrepreneurship & Regional Development* 10: 225–41.

Cavalluzzo, Ken, Linda Cavalluzzo, and John D. Wolken. 2002. "Competition, Small Business Financing, and Discrimination: Evidence from a New Survey." *The Journal of Business* 75(4): 641–79.

Cliff, Jennifer. 1998. "Does One Size Fit All? Exploring the Relationship between Attitudes towards Growth, Gender, and Business Size." *Journal of Business Venturing* 13: 523–42.

Coleman, Susan. 2002. "Constraints Faced by Women Small Business Owners: Evidence from the Data." *Journal of Developmental Entrepreneurship* 7(2): 151–74.

———. 2005. "Is There a Liquidity Crisis for Small, Black-Owned Firms?" *Journal of Developmental Entrepreneurship* (April) 10(1): 29–47.

Coleman, Susan, and Mary Carsky. 1996. "Financing Small Business: Strategies Employed by Women Entrepreneurs." *The Journal of Applied Management and Entrepreneurship* 3(1): 28–42.

Fabowale, Lola, Barbara Orser, and Allan Riding. 1995. "Gender, Structural Factors, and Credit Terms between Canadian Small Businesses and Financial Institutions." *Entrepreneurship Theory and Practice* 19(4): 41–65.

Fay, Michael, and Lesley Williams. 1993. "Gender Bias and the Availability of Business Loans." *Journal of Business Venturing* 8: 363–76.

Haynes, George W., and Rosemary J. Avery. 1996. "Family BUSINEsses: Can the Family and the Business Finances Be Separated? Preliminary Results." *Entrepreneurial and Small Business Finance* 5(1): 61–74.

Haynes, George W., and Deborah C. Haynes. 1999. "The Debt Structure of Small Businesses Owned by Women in 1987 and 1993." *Journal of Small Business Management* (April): 1–19.

Haynes, George W., Rosemary Walker, Barbara R. Rowe, and Gong-Soog Hong. 1999. "The Intermingling of Business and Family Finances in Family-Owned Businesses." *Family Business Review* XII(3): 225–39.

Kim, Grace. 2006. "Do Equally Owned Businesses Have Equal Access to Credit?" *Small Business Economics* 27(4): 369–86.

McKechnie, Sally A., Christine T. Ennew, and Lauren H. Read. 1998. "The Nature of the Banking Relationship: A Comparison of the Experiences of Male and Female Small Business Owners." *International Small Business Journal* 16(3): 39–55.

Mukhtar, Syeda-Masooda. 2002. "Differences in Male and Female Management Characteristics: A Study of Owner-Manager Businesses." *Small Business Economics* 18(4): 289–311.

Orhan, Muriel. 2001. "Women Business Owners in France: The Issue of Financing Discrimination." *Journal of Small Business Management* 39(1): 95–102.

Romano, Claudio A., George A. Tanewski, and Kosmas X. Smyrnios. 2000. "Capital Structure Decision Making: A Model for Family Business." *Journal of Business Venturing* 16: 285–310.

Shaw, E., S. Carter, and J. Brierton. 2001. *Unequal Entrepreneurs: Why Female Enterprise Is an Uphill Business*. London: The Industrial Society.

Verheul, Ingrid, and Roy Thurik. 2001. "Start-Up Capital: Does Gender Matter?" *Small Business Economics* 16(4): 329–345.

Yilmazer, Tansel, and Holly Schrank. 2006. "Financial Intermingling in Small Family Businesses." *Journal of Business Venturing* 21(5): 726–51.

CHAPTER 9

DEBIT CARDS: THE NEW, OLD WAY TO PAY

Marc Anthony Fusaro

Debit cards have seen explosive growth over the last decade. Debit cards are now used for more transactions than credit cards. Debit cards are moving into new purchase types such as fast food. The young used debit cards more often than the old; but this should not be surprising since most new technology is more heavily used by the young. Debit cards are more heavily used in smaller transactions while credit cards are more heavily used for larger purchases, as is noted in research by Beth Klee (2004). This should not be surprising since people are more likely to borrow for larger purchases or durable goods. Finally, income is a factor in the use of debit cards. In this case, the relationship is not monotonic. Debit use rises with income to a point. Eventually, as income rises, consumers use credit cards more often (Borzekowski and Kiser 2006).

Despite the hype with debit cards, they are not as new as they appear. They are built on old technology. Consider the slow spread of technologies such as HDTV. Content providers do not want to invest in the broadcasting technology if customers do not have HD TV sets. And consumers do not want to buy expensive HD sets if there are no shows that are broadcast in HD. This chicken and egg problem was circumvented in the case of debit cards by using old technology.

The addition of the option to use debit cards adds little to consumers' payment choices. To consumers, they are simply the newest way to access funds in a checking account. A recent study of consumer choice between debit cards and credit cards is discussed later. This study recognizes that the primary difference between a debit card and a credit card is the option to engage in long-term borrowing when using a credit card. Debit, on the other hand, limits the user to cash on hand. Paying with cash or a check accomplishes the same goal. Debit cards allow better tracking of purchases. This was impossible when consumers paid with cash or even with checks. The evidence shows that some consumers use debit cards, rather than credit cards, because debit cards help control their spending.

One new development due to debit cards is the fierce competition among debit card networks. This competition takes place in a complicated environment, a two-sided network. The economics of two-sided networks and some of the issues surrounding the competition between the two types of debit cards is discussed in the following section.

This chapter contains a summary of some recent and ongoing work concerning debit cards. In the first section, titled "Industrial Organization, Networks and Debit Cards," competition between the two types of debit card networks is examined. In the second section, titled "Consumer Demand for Debit Cards," evidence is developed to support the notion that many people use debit cards to restrain their spending.

Industrial Organization, Networks, and Debit Cards

The competition between credit cards and debit cards is muted because the same companies—Visa and MasterCard—are the major players in both industries. Within the debit industry, passions are stirred in the struggle between the following two types of debit: PIN-based and Signature-based. Oddly the fireworks fly not between the network operators but between the merchants and the banks. The economics of a network industry are more complicated than that of a normal industry. The debit card industry is a two-sided network, the economics of which are only beginning to be understood. This section summarizes the market and issues addressed in some ongoing debit card research (Fusaro 2005).

The Debit Industry

Debit cards evolved from two older electronic services, the credit card and the ATM. Credit cards are accepted by many merchants worldwide. Consumers sign a receipt to authorize the transfer of money. Visa and MasterCard brand credit cards and process the transactions.[1] Visa is organized as a joint venture owned by the members of the banking industry. MasterCard was a similar organization but is now a public company. With credit cards, a bank issues a Visa or MC branded card, which accesses a line of credit provided by the bank. As early as the 1980s, some innovative banks realized that they could pay for card purchases directly out of a checking account rather than from a line of credit. Thus, the early debit cards were born before the term debit card was coined and before Visa and MasterCard developed a separate "debit" product. Currently, the Visa Check Card leads the debit market. MasterCard offers the Debit MasterCard. Transactions are processed by technology and infrastructure parallel to that of credit cards. Transactions using these cards are authorized when the customer signs a receipt. These debit card networks are called *signature* or *offline debit*. Generally, there is no charge to the cardholder; in some cases, the cardholder earns rewards for using the card. Merchants who accept credit cards were required by Visa and MasterCard to accept these debit cards. This "Honor All Cards" policy was ended as the outcome of legal action brought by merchants. Issues involving this policy are discussed later.

ATMs have been offered by banks since the late 1960s. Consumers enter a four-digit personal identification number (PIN) in order to authorize the transfer of money. The transactions are processed by electronic funds transfer (EFT) networks that historically were owned by banks, but consolidation has led to third-party processors dominating the industry. The EFT networks also offer a debit product called *PIN* or *online* debit. Retailers install key pads at cash registers so that customers can enter their PIN to authorize payment of funds. The payment is then processed through the EFT network.

Most banks issue one card that can be used as either a signature debit, PIN debit, or ATM card. In July of 2005, 55 percent of financial institutions issued Visa Check Cards; 25 percent offered Debit MasterCard; the rest did not offer debit cards.[2] Therefore, nearly all consumers have the option of using either type of debit. Merchant acceptance of PIN debit is less than for credit and signature debit—5.7 million Visa locations compared to 4.9 million PIN debit terminals in 2004 (Thompson Media 2004). Some banks (15 percent as discussed later) charge a per-transaction fee for using PIN debit. In 2005, customers made 13.5 billion signature debit transactions and 8.1 billion PIN debit transaction. PIN debit has its advantages. Many merchants offer customers the option of getting cash back with their PIN debit purchase. Consumers use this feature to avoid ATMs with high fees.

Networks

The common conception of a network is a system of interconnected nodes. Economists mean something very different when using the word "network." To industrial organization economists, a network product is one for which the value increases with the number of users. For example, a phone would be worthless if you were the only customer in the world. Who would you call? Suppose that everyone has a phone but the two phone providers are not connected. The larger provider (the larger network) provides more value because there is a higher likelihood that the intended call recipients are on that network. In this situation, a monopoly network provides the most value to the customer. The value people place on the network increases as the number of customers using the network increases.

A debit card network is a more intricate kind of network, a two-sided network. Two-sided networks serve two distinct types of customers, using the network to interact with each other. The value that users attach to the network product increases not with the number of users of their own type, but with the number of users of the other type. For example, in a payment card network the two users are card holders and merchants. Customers are not directly affected by the number of other customers using the same type of card; but they do value a card that many merchants accept. And merchants do not care how many other merchants use the card (except for competitive reasons) but do care how many of their customers have the card.

One truism in economics is that everything is simple when there is a buyer paying a price for a product to a seller; but strange things happen when you add more parties to the transaction. One example of this maxim is the way we buy healthcare. The consumer does not pay, the payer does not consume, and the seller tries to please one side or the other. The economics of the two-sided network is similarly complex. Merchants derive a benefit of network membership (more customers) and pay a price for network membership. If the benefit is worth the price, then they will join the network. Consumers face a similar problem. They benefit from using the card (convenience) and face a cost of using the card. If the benefit outweighs the cost, then they will use the card. The network provider, in this case, the bank, has a more complicated decision. They face costs of serving merchants and costs of serving customers. They also charge a price to merchants and to customers. In a normal market, the seller must set price above cost to earn a profit. But in a two-sided network, the sum of these revenues must exceed the sum of the costs. This condition leaves open the possibility that they could charge one side of the market below the cost of serving that side of the market if the loss is compensated by the other side of the market. In the debit card industry, it is precisely the case that merchants subsidize customers. This is a fundamental insight of Baxter (1983).

Recently, economists have shown interest in studying two-sided markets (Rochet and Tirole 2003; Rochet 2003; Wilko and Tieman 2003; Chakravorti and Roson 2004). Among these, one in particular is worth noting. Bolt and Tieman note that if demand for the card is very elastic on one side of the market and not very elastic on the other side, then the side with low elasticity will see high prices while the side with high elasticity will see low prices. In other words, merchants and customers are competing with each other over who will bear the cost of the network. The group that wants it more will pay more while the other group pays less (or nothing). This is exactly what happens in the payment card industry, especially for signature debit, where merchants pay a high price and customers generally pay nothing or get money back.

The Issues

Competition between PIN and signature networks plays out less between the network providers themselves (e.g., Visa versus First Data), and more between the merchants and the banks. Merchants are network users and prefer the PIN debit network because the PIN network charges the merchant less. Banks are a part of the network structure that issues both PIN and signature cards, but earn greater revenue from signature transactions. Merchants, led by Wal-Mart, sued MasterCard and Visa over the Honor All Cards Rule, a clause in the contract between the card association and the merchant. The rule states that merchants who accept Visa cards must accept all Visa credit and debit cards. The case was settled much to the advantage of the merchants. Merchants also sued the card associations seeking removal of the No-Surcharge Rule, which is discussed later.

The issue in the case of the Honor All Cards rule is tying. Tying was also the issue in the Microsoft case concerning Internet Explorer. To see why tying is important in the card industry, consider the distinction between network membership and network use. In order for a network transaction to occur, several conditions must be met. First, the merchant and the consumer must belong to the same network or networks (i.e., the merchant must accept the card and the customer must carry the card). If either the merchant or the customer belong to only one network then they will use that network. Or if they both belong to multiple networks (called multi-homing) but have only one network in common, they will have to use the common network. In this industry, multi-homing is common on both sides. On the customer side, 68 percent of cards issued at the top eight banks are dual signature/PIN cards (they access both networks meaning that the consumer multi-homes [*Card Industry Directory*]). On the merchant side, some merchants are members of only the PIN debit market. More merchants join the signature debit network but not a PIN network. Many merchants, especially large retailers, multi-home accepting Visa, MasterCard, and PIN cards.

With multi-homing common on both sides of the market, the typical transaction is one where the merchant and the customers have both PIN and signature networks in common. When this is the case, either network could be used and the customer chooses the network. Merchants could discontinue the acceptance of a particular card, as Wal-Mart did of MasterCards briefly. When the Honor All Cards Rule was in effect, debit card acceptance was tied to credit card acceptance. In other words, this entailed discontinuing acceptance of both signature debit and credit cards. Merchants certainly do not want to stop accepting credit cards. Even though the Honor All Cards Rule has been discontinued, this is quite a drastic step since some customers prefer one type of card. Indeed there has been no drop-off in signature debit acceptance since the repeal of the Honor All Cards Rule.

If customers choose which network is used, how the banks or merchants influence that decision is the subject of the second controversy, the No-Surcharge Rule. Banks have substantial influence over which card consumers choose. Many banks charge customers a fee for using their PIN debit card. Fees for using signature debit cards are rare. In the years 2001 through 2005, the percentage of banks and credit unions that charged customers a fee for using PIN debit were 8.6 percent, 11.1 percent, 3.8 percent, 16.9 percent, and 15.2 percent, respectively. Fees for signature debit are very rare accounting for only 1.12 percent and 1.09 percent of banks and credit unions in the years 2004 and 2005, respectively (author's calculations are based on data provided by Moebs $ervices). These numbers show that some banks push customers toward signature debit through fees. In addition, often bank employees actively encourage customers to use signature debit instead of PIN debit. The author of this chapter has heard employees of numerous banks counsel customers to use signature debit instead of PIN debit.

Merchants have less ability to influence the decisions of customers. It appears that small business owners can channel their customers toward a preferred payment method with polite requests. Large corporate retailers, however, have no such option. Merchants, in general, seem to have little ability to charge their customers for using signature debit. The No-Surcharge Rule precludes merchants from charging a higher price for card transactions. In theory, nothing prevents them from offering a discount for preferred payment methods. In practice, this is not always an option. For instance, consider the retail grocery industry. Due to a complicated network of state and federal laws and Visa and MasterCard regulations, the store would have to post two prices for each item in the store. Stores with few goods do just this. Some gas stations offer a cash discount. Merchants with only three products (regular, mid-grade, and premium) can easily offer a cash discount. Much is unknown about the consumer response to these strategies. If a merchant charges more for a signature card payment, will customers switch cards or will they switch merchants? If a merchant charges less for a cash payment, will customers use cash or will they switch merchants? Do customers view a card surcharge the same as a cash discount? Answers to these questions are unknown at this point.

In an attempt to analyze this two-sided market (the payment card) in isolation of other products such as the items being purchased, economists modeling these markets have assumed that the item sales are unaffected by the market. This assumption violates three principles. First, it is well known that consumers purchase more when they have credit cards. Second, the following section discusses why some consumers use debit cards specifically to restrict their purchases. Third, consumers might prefer merchants who accept cards. This third principle is incorporated into the model that addresses these issues (Fusaro 2007).

Consumer Demand for Debit Cards

Recent research looked at a consumer's choice to use debit. Certainly many consumers have switched from cash and checks to debit cards. This is a natural consequence of technological development. The more interesting topic, and the subject of the research (Fusaro 2007), is consumers' choice between credit and debit cards.

The Puzzle

Debit cards have experienced impressive growth in the last decade. According to the EFT Data Book, debit card transactions grew by over 20 percent per year from 1998 to 2004 while credit cards grew at an annual rate of 10 percent. On the strength of this growth, debit cards are now used for more transactions than credit cards.

The dominance of debit cards comes despite the apparent benefits of credit. When a consumer pays for a purchase with a debit card the money is withdrawn almost immediately. A consumer who uses a credit card at the point of sale will be billed for that and other purchases within a month and has more time to pay the bill. The consumer benefits from this float. The credit card user can select from a menu of cards that offer the user a kickback for every purchase. These kickbacks come in the form of cash, airline miles, charitable donations, and many others. These rewards until recently were rare for debit cards, but are quickly becoming common. Some banks charge the customer for each debit card purchase (15 percent in July 2005 [author's calculation]).

Why do so many people use debit cards when credit cards appear to be more appealing? The rapid growth in debit card use mentioned earlier has come largely at the expense of paper checks and cash. But this begs the question, why would anyone use cash or a check to pay for a purchase when credit cards are accepted? At its root, the puzzle is why people pay out of liquid funds when they could just as easily charge the purchase and be billed later. One explanation is that some people spend in excess of income when paying with credit. In this situation, debit is used to restrain spending.

The Theory

One explanation for debit card use is that some people lack self-control and need a mechanism to restrain their spending. Is it irrational behavior to purchase that which is not affordable? Not necessarily. Budgeting is a time-consuming process that involves tracking expenses, forecasting demand for various goods and planning. Prices vary across retail outlets and time. A consumer who finds a high price can potentially get a lower price by waiting for a sale or by visiting another store. As consumers postpone their purchase in search of low prices or purchase more when prices are low, they cause their expenditure to vary from month to month. Thus, even a rigid, well-disciplined consumer will have variation in expenditure, which makes budgeting difficult.

In this environment, consumers who desire a balanced budget have three basic options. First, they could expend effort in a planning process that involves forecasting needs, tracking expenses, and reviewing results. Some consumers are better at this than others. Second, consumers can restrict themselves to only spending what money is available; when the money is gone, expenditure waits until the next paycheck. Using a debit card is one way of accomplishing this. Third, they could do no budgeting, use no restraining debit cards, and just estimate what is affordable. They spend what they think they can afford. If it works, this is the easiest of the three.

Both credit and debit cards have their advantages. The credit card has float, flexibility, and rewards. The debit card has the advantage of keeping its user out of debt. Customers who calculate their budget should not need the debit card to keep them out of debt. Those who choose not to budget have two options, they could use a debit card or they could use a credit card and estimate what is affordable. If they use credit, they might overestimate or they might underestimate; the reality is that people who overestimate their spending potential do so persistently and accumulate high credit card balances. The problem is that people do not know whether they will overestimate. When customers weigh credit versus debit they are considering the sure benefits of credit against debit's ability to keep them out of debt which they might not need. Many people choose the sure benefits of credit over the potential benefits of debit. As indicated earlier, some of these credit users will be able to properly manage their finances without a budget or a debit card to restrain spending. But others, when given a credit card, will start to accumulate high balances. Once that happens—once the potential benefit of debit is a sure benefit—they value debit's spending restraint much more than they had before. Many, after accumulating high credit card balances, switch to debit to restrain their spending.

This is a bit unexpected. Credit card users, those who continue to use credit cards, will tend to have lower, if any, credit card balances than those who switch to debit. While it may have been unexpected, it should now be obvious: those who can handle the temptation of credit cards—those not carrying balances—would have lower balances than those who could not handle credit cards and switch to debit cards—those with high balances.

The Evidence

The research (Fusaro 2007) tests this theory and the results support the view that debit card users are the irresponsible ones—those who could not handle credit. One feature that distinguishes this theory from other explanations for debit card use is the higher credit card balances of the debit users. In principle, this should be easy to verify. But in practice, the credit-card-only banks issue a majority of the credit cards. Therefore, it is difficult to find information on a customer's bank account and credit card—on both debit and credit activity. But all is not lost; much can be learned by analyzing bank account records in isolation.

The theory is that debit users are more likely to have outstanding credit card balances than credit card users. Looking at a sample of checking accounts confirms that this is the case.[3] Specifically, people paying down a high credit card balance are likely to make round payments and/or identical payments month after month. Whereas, people using the card for convenience and then paying the balance monthly are very unlikely to make round or identical payments. The checking account records confirm that those who use debit cards are more likely to make round payments and identical payments than those not using debit cards. This confirms that people who primarily use a debit card for purchases are more likely to be paying down credit card balances than those who primarily make payments using a credit card.

The second feature of the spending control motive for using debit cards is that some people can live within their means without much effort and others budget to stay within their means. But others (those using debit cards to restrain spending) cannot control their spending. We all know these people. We call them impulse purchasers or recreational shoppers. These people see something they like and they have to buy it. In contrast, the others are much more disciplined. Disciplined shoppers are likely to go back to the same merchants; whereas the less-disciplined debit card users are more likely to purchase wherever and whenever something catches their fancy. We cannot verify this using card purchases because we do not see the locations of credit card purchases. But if we look at cash purchases we can learn something. Naturally, we cannot track cash purchases but we can track ATM withdrawals. And if people withdraw money near the location at which it is spent, then this is a useful statistic. The evidence suggests that debit card users have a greater variety of ATM withdrawal locations than do credit card users, indicating that they are less-disciplined spenders.

The final piece of evidence that debit cards are used for self-control comes from people's cash holding. Using a debit card is one method of restraining oneself from overspending. Another method is to carry less cash. If they withdraw small amounts from the ATM they will have to return more frequently. In contrast, people with no self-control problems can save time and fees by withdrawing large sums of money and returning less often. This is in fact the case. The evidence shows that consumers who use debit cards are also more likely to make smaller ATM withdrawals more often than non-debit users.

The Numbers

Economists often distrust what people say preferring to watch what they do. This is why many economists discount surveys in favor of observing behavior. The previous discussion is an example of learning something by watching people's checking account behavior. When trying to learn the "what" this research style works very well. (What do they do? What will they do if conditions change?) However, when trying to learn about the "why" it is much harder to get a complete answer from simply observing behavior. While the evidence presented in the previous paragraphs makes great strides in deducing motives by observing behavior, it begs the question, why do you not just ask them why they use a debit card? The Federal Reserve did just that.

The results of the Federal Reserve survey are reported in a working paper written by Borzekowski, Kiser, and Ahmed (2006). At first glance, the results of the survey do not give much support for the theory that people use debit cards to restrain their spending. Survey respondents are asked whether they use a debit card. If they do, they are asked why they use the debit card. Their answers were recorded verbatim. Only 5.8 percent of debit card users made reference to spending restraint as a motive for using the debit card. However, upon further examination, the results of this survey are much more friendly to the spending restraint motive.

For a moment, return to the big picture. The survey focused on cash, checks, debit cards, and credit cards. A debit card is one form of payment that restrains spending because it limits one to funds in a checking account. A check also limits one to checking account funds and cash limits one to the funds that have been withdrawn from a checking account. Thus cash, check, and debit cards could all be tools of spending restraint. A credit card in contrast does not limit the user to liquid funds.

In using this survey, we hope to learn the source of consumers' preferences for debit over credit but several of the survey respondents expressed their preference for debit over cash or check. For instance, if a consumer answers "Because debit cards allow me to track my purchases," they are obviously not talking about debit's advantage over credit since credit and debit both allow tracking of expenses. For the present purposes, the informative responses are those who expressed their preferences for debit over credit. The survey reveals the number of respondents reporting spending restraint as a motive for using debit, the number reporting that they choose debit over credit, and the number who do not report their alternative to debit. When all these factors are considered, 23.5 percent of debit users who reveal their preference for debit over credit report doing so for reasons of controlling spending. Not all debit users are motivated by spending-control considerations. But a significant number of debit users are motivated as such—too many for researchers, businesses, or the government to ignore the phenomenon.

Conclusion

Debit cards are the hottest thing in consumer payments. They are in more wallets; their merchant acceptance is spreading; they are quickly becoming the most used payment instrument. Debit cards are the wave of the future. But just how different are they?

In the first section of this chapter, the competition among debit card providing networks was addressed. Before debit cards, there was some competition between credit card networks. But this competition was rarely as intense as rising to seemingly continuous lawsuits. The market structure of paper check clearing and other electronic networks such as Fedwire and ACH looks much more like regulated monopolies or cartels than ruthlessly competitive markets. And while standard wisdom is that competition is good for the consumer, in these two-sided networks strange things can happen. So far one type of consumer (payers) seems to be benefiting at the expense of the other type of consumer (merchants). And the competitor who does this the best (signature debit) is, so far, ahead in the competition.

The reasons why consumers like debit cards was covered in the second section of this chapter. There were two main points of this section. First, many consumers use debit cards as a tool of self-restraint. Evidence—admittedly indirect—is presented to support this conclusion. Industry insiders often wonder why we go to such lengths to prove "the obvious." But this conclusion is a bit controversial among economists. The second point, which is less explicit in this chapter, is that debit cards are not new. The technologies are new applications of old technologies. More importantly, the economics are not new. Debit cards are just the newest high-tech way of writing checks.

Notes

1. The minor players, Discover and American Express, issue their own cards in addition to processing. These companies are not bank owned. Since they do not issue debit cards they are omitted from mention.
2. Source: Author's calculations based on data provided by Moebs $ervices, Lake Bluff, IL.
3. A small depository institution in the Midwest provided the checking account information.

References

Baxter, William F. 1983. "Bank Interchange of Transactional Paper: Legal Perspectives." *Journal of Law and Economics* 26(3) (October): 541–88.

Bolt, Wilko, and Alexander F. Tieman. 2003. Pricing debit card payment services: An IO approach. IMF Working Paper no. 03/202.

Borzekowski, Ron, and Elizabeth Kiser. 2006. "The Choice at the Checkout: Quantifying Demand Across Payment Instruments." Federal Reserve Board FEDS papers #2006–17, February.

Borzekowski, Ron, Elizabeth Kiser, and Shaista Ahmed. 2006. "Consumers' Use of Debit Cards: Patterns, Preferences, and Price Response." Federal Reserve Board FEDS papers #2006–16, February.

Card Industry Directory, 18th edition, Thompson Media, Chicago, IL.

Chakravorti, Sujit and Roberto Roson. 2004. "Platform Competition in Two-Sided Markets: The Case of Payment Networks." Mimeo.

Fusaro, Marc Anthony. 2005. "Competition in Two-Sided Markets: The Wal-Mart v. Visa/MC Antitrust Struggle over Debit Cards and the Honor All Cards Rule." Mimeo.

———. 2007. "Debit vs Credit: A Model of Self-Control with Evidence From Checking Accounts." East Carolina University Department of Economics Working Paper #0613.

Klee, Beth. 2004. "How People Pay: Evidence from Grocery Store Data." Mimeo.

Rochet, Jean-Charles. 2003. "The Theory of Interchange Fees: A Synthesis of Recent Contributions." *Review of Network Economics* 2(2) June.

Rochet, Jean-Charles, and Jean Tirole. 2003. "Platform Competition in Two-Sided Markets." *Journal of European Economic Association* 1(4): 990–1029.

Thompson Media. 2004. "EFT Data Book: The Complete Guide to the ATM and POS Debit Markets, 2005 Edition." *ATM & Debit News* 4 (45) September 16.

CHAPTER 10

LINKAGES BETWEEN CONSUMER PAYMENTS AND CREDIT

Sujit Chakravorti

Introduction

Payors, those that make payments, and payees, those that receive payments, choose among various payment instruments based on their preferences toward convenience, risk, and cost. According to a recent U.S. survey, the usage of payment cards is increasing as a proportion of in-store sales while check usage continues to decrease (American Bankers Association and Dove Consulting 2005). Recently, a café in Washington, D.C. stopped accepting cash for purchases primarily because of the cost of safekeeping (National Public Radio 2006). This shift toward electronic payments is occurring because they offer greater benefits to a growing set of consumers and merchants.

There are two forms of credit associated with payments—payment credit and consumption credit. Payment credit is the credit that is extended by the receiver of payment or a third-party until the payment instrument is converted into good funds. For example, payment credit is granted by the recipient of funds when she accepts a check in exchange for goods and services. Today, greater use of real-time authorization systems along with faster clearing of payment instruments has significantly reduced payment credit risk. Consumption credit is extended by the payee or a third-party, which is separate from payment credit. For example, credit card issuers extend credit to their cardholders, which can be paid at the end of the billing cycle or over a longer time period. Cardholders choose when to pay back these loans subject to minimum payment requirements. Financial institutions also offer overdraft facilities to reduce payment defaults on checks due to non-sufficient funds and fees associated with bounced checks. While consumers bear the cost of overdraft facilities, merchants benefit from potentially fewer bounced checks. Similarly, payees can contract with third parties to reduce this risk as well.

A key issue that has received attention globally is the pricing of payment and consumption credit to consumers and merchants especially for payment cards. In the case of credit and debit cards, merchants pay a fee to their financial institutions, called acquirers, for each payment transaction. Acquirers pay interchange fees to issuers, those that issue payment cards, for each transaction. In the case of credit cards, some have argued that issuers use their revenue from interchange fees to encourage consumers to make more purchases with their credit cards instead of less costly payment instruments such as PIN-based debit cards. Defenders of the current interchange fee pricing structure argue that the fee is necessary to balance the demands of consumers and merchants. In other words, both consumers and merchants benefit from the extensions of credit.

After discussing the costs and benefits of major retail payment instruments, I review a number of regulatory and legal challenges to the payment card industry. Most of these challenges question the degree of competition and its impact on consumer and merchant welfare. Following this discussion, I review two academic models that focus on the benefits of consumption credit to consumers and merchants along with how that credit is priced.

The Retail Payment System

In this section, the cost and benefits of the main retail payment instruments to consumers and merchants are summarized. Payment instruments can be categorized into three groups: value based, account based, and credit based.[1] Value-based transactions involve a transfer of monetary value at the time of exchange. Currency is an example of a value-based instrument. Account-based instruments initiate transfers of monetary value from a payor's account at its financial institution to a payee. Checks and debit cards are examples of account-based instruments. Credit-based instruments access a line of credit to make purchases. Examples of credit-based instruments are credit and charge cards.[2]

Value-Based Instruments

Cash has several advantages over other payment instruments. First, repeated cash transactions can take place without third-party intermediation. In other words, no relationship with a financial institution is required for the payor or payee to use cash. Second, cash is widely accepted for payment by individuals, businesses, and government because no special payment infrastructure is required. Third, some consumers and merchants may prefer to have transactions that are not easily tracked.

However, cash does pose some challenges for consumers and merchants. First, while cash is the most popular for low-value transactions, consumers and merchants usually prefer other types of payment options for larger-value transactions. If cash is lost or stolen, consumers have little recourse to recover their loss. Second, cash is generally not ideal for non-face-to-face transactions.

Account-Based Transactions

In a transaction with an account-based instrument, the consumer's transactions account at a financial institution is debited the value of the transaction. Hence, account-based transactions require payors to have an existing relationship with a financial institution. These types of transactions are generally more secure than cash transactions for payors because access to a transactions account may be turned off or a stop payment can be requested to prevent unauthorized use. They also reduce cash-handling costs for merchants. While the example of a café owner refusing to accept cash is not a common strategy by merchants to reduce cash-handling costs, recently, several cash-only merchants have started to accept payment cards.[3] The shift from only accepting cash suggests that these merchants benefit from accepting noncash payment instruments.

Checks are account-based instruments that started to replace cash after the 1870s.[4] Checks paid declined in the United States from 41.9 billion in 2000 to 36.7 billion in 2003 (Federal Reserve System 2004).[5] However, checks still remain a popular means of payment for remote bill payment, although the share of electronic alternatives continues to grow in these payment segments.

Electronic account-based transactions continue to grow. An electronic alternative for certain check payments are automated clearinghouse (ACH) payments. ACH payments increased from 6.2 billion to 9.1 billion (Federal Reserve System 2004). With ACH payments, the payor's or the payee's financial institution initiates a payment via an ACH network. While developed primarily for recurring remote payments, ACH payments have also spread to other payment segments, such as point-of-sale and Internet purchases. Debit cards are account-based instruments that are primarily for point-of-sale transactions.[6] Today, debit cards are increasingly being used for remote transactions. Debit card payments increased from 8.3 billion in 2000 to 15.6 billion in 2004 (Federal Reserve System 2004). In order to accept debit cards, payors must have contracted with a debit card processor.

Account-based instruments benefit consumers and merchants in several ways. Consumers benefit from being able to readily access their transactions accounts to make point-of-sale and remote payments. They may also benefit from interest income on their funds before their payments clear and settle. Merchants benefit from lower cash-handling costs and potentially greater sales from selling to consumers who may not have sufficient cash in their wallets. Financial institutions benefit from interest income on idle funds in transactions accounts, possible fee income from account holders, and interchange fees if debit cards are used by account holders.

Credit-Based Transactions

Credit and charge cards are examples of credit-based instruments because credit is being extended to the payor. These types of payments increased from 15.6 billion to 19.0 billion from 2000 to 2003 in the United States (Federal Reserve System 2004). Credit and charge card transactions are similar to debit card transactions, except that payors do not access a demand deposit account at financial institutions but instead establish credit lines that are accessed when making purchases. Consumers often receive incentives to use their credit cards such as dispute resolution services, frequent-use awards, and interest-free short-term loans if no balances are carried between billing periods. Credit cards also provide various security features and limit consumer liability in the event of fraudulent use. Merchants also benefit from selling to consumers that do not have cash in their wallets or funds in their transactions accounts.

The Linkages between Payment and Credit

As mentioned before, there are two forms of credit associated with payment mechanisms. First, there is payment credit where payees extend credit to payors until they are able to convert payments into good funds. Second, there is consumption credit where credit is granted by the payee or a third party to the payor to make purchases that will be paid back at a later date.[7]

Payment Credit

Technological advances in processing consumer payments along with third parties willing to guarantee payments for a fee have significantly reduced payment credit risk to payees. Greater transference of payment credit risk to third parties has partly contributed to greater investment in risk-reducing infrastructure such as real-time authorization systems and monitoring of irregular spending patterns by card issuers.

Unlike most other forms of payments, currency has extremely low settlement risk—the risk that the payee is unable to convert the payment into good funds. The risk of counterfeit is the settlement risk of cash. Counterfeit risk is very small. The level of counterfeit U.S. notes worldwide is between 0.01 to 0.02 percent (U.S. Department of State, Bureau of International Information Programs 2003). However, as we discussed, because of security concerns by both consumers and merchants, noncash payment instruments are generally preferred for larger-value transactions.

In a check transaction, the payor is generally granted credit by the payee until the check is converted to good funds. While not common, payees may wait until good funds are received before delivering goods and services. Alternatively, payees may pay third parties to guarantee checks or match checking account information against a database of bad checking accounts and reject checks from accounts that show up in the database. In addition, payees may impose penalties if the check is returned for non-sufficient funds in an effort to deter bad checks.

Financial institutions earn significant revenue from non-sufficient funds fees. Chakravorti and McHugh (2002) reported that banks earned $8.1 billion from non-sufficient fund fees in 1995 while bank net losses were around $400 million for check fraud in the same year. While check usage has decreased significantly since 1995, especially those written by consumers, financial institutions still earn significant revenue from non-sufficient funds fees. Therefore, Chakravorti and McHugh suggest that financial institutions may not necessarily provide incentives to their customers not to use checks.

The payor's financial institution may extend a line of credit that is accessed if the checking account does not have sufficient funds. The extension of this type of credit often referred to as overdraft protection continues to grow. In fact, the extension of credit for payment credit essentially becomes a consumption credit loan. In other words, the payor's access to consumption credit reduces payment credit risk for the payee although the cost of such credit falls solely on the payor.

Depending on the type of ACH payment—debit or credit—payment credit may or may not exist. In an ACH debit transaction, the payee's financial institution initiates the funds transfer from the payor's institution. Similar to checks, ACH debit payments may be denied because payors do not have sufficient funds in their accounts. Similar to checks, financial institutions may impose non-sufficient funds fees and may offer overdraft protection for their consumers to avoid these fees. In an ACH credit transaction, the payor's financial institution initiates the funds transfer to the payee's financial institution. ACH credit payments are only initiated when payors have sufficient funds in their accounts or have access to overdraft facilities.[8]

Most debit and credit card transactions are authorized by the payor's financial institution, known as the issuer, before the payment is accepted thereby substantially reducing or eliminating settlement risk. Generally, if merchants follow certain procedures, card issuers guarantee payment. Clearly, merchants value these guarantees and payment card networks' set fees that incorporate this benefit.

Consumption Credit

Consumption credit can be accessed via various payment instruments. Basically, consumers using checks, debit cards, and ACH payments may access a line of credit when sufficient funds are not available to them. However, when using credit and charge cards, payors access a line of credit to make purchases. Furthermore, if the previous month's card balance has been paid in full, consumers benefit from a short-term interest-free loan unlike lines of credit associated with demand deposit accounts where interest accrues immediately. Unless the payee is issuing consumption credit, the credit risk for consumption credit generally falls on a third party. In this section, we focus on consumption credit attached to credit cards.

Prior to the introduction of general-purpose credit cards, merchants often extended credit to their consumers directly.[9] When general-purpose credit cards were introduced, many small merchants found the cost of accepting general-purpose credit cards lower than the cost of extending credit and debt collection. On the other hand, many large department stores were initially reluctant to accept general-purpose cards because they feared their own credit card programs would be adversely affected. While extension of credit by merchants is common, general-purpose credit card transaction volume dwarfs the volume of merchant-issued credit cards. However, store cards generate significant revenues and have the added benefit of increasing repeat business.

Comparing costs and benefits to use various payment instruments, Chakravorti (1997) concluded that consumers should always use their credit cards to make payment and pay off their balances in full by the due date.[10] In addition to the free short-term loan, if balances are paid in full, cardholders often enjoy frequent-use awards such as cash back or frequent flyer miles. However, some consumers are reluctant to make most of their purchases with credit cards because they fear that they may not be able to make full payment when their credit card bills are due.

Furthermore, there are certain purchases that cannot be made with credit cards although this set continues to decrease.

Like some other payment instruments, credit cards allow consumers to access long-term credit, mostly uncollateralized, at the point of sale.[11] Consumers that use this feature of credit cards are known as revolvers. Those cardholders who do not avail the credit feature are commonly referred to as convenience users. Industry estimates of U.S. convenience users range from 30 percent to 40 percent of all cardholders.[12]

Credit cards also offer several benefits to merchants. Merchants are usually paid in good funds within 48 hours of submitting the transaction to their acquirers. In a survey, 83 percent of merchants said that their sales increased and 58 percent said that their profits increased by accepting credit cards (Ernst and Young 1996). In other words, credit cards allow merchants to sell to illiquid consumers or to those paying with future income. Some industry analysts have suggested that credit card consumers may purchase more than those using other forms of payment.

Clearly, these benefits do not come without costs. Merchants pay their financial institutions a percentage of the sales price for credit card purchases known as a merchant discount fee. Merchants have successfully negotiated lower merchant discount fees since the introduction of credit cards when the merchant discount rate was 6 percent. In the next section, I discuss recent challenges to common business practices of credit card networks such as merchant pricing restrictions and setting of interchange fees.

Legal and Regulatory Challenges

Public authorities around the world are considering or have considered the following questions. First, should consumers that use their credit cards pay more for goods and services than those who do not access a line of credit? Second, should merchants pay a third party a portion of the cost of extending credit to their customers? Third, should issuers offer greater incentives to consumers to use credit cards instead of other payment instruments?

A significant number of U.S. merchants along with their foreign counterparts are seeking legal and regulatory relief from what they consider "too high" payment card fees. Studies from the Food Marketing Institute (1998 and 2000) concluded that credit cards and signature-based debit cards cost significantly more than other payment products. On the other hand, Garcia Swartz, Hahn, and Layne-Farrar (2006) argued that these figures are misleading because the Food Marketing Institute surveys only considered grocers and did not correct for differences in merchant type and transaction size.

Merchant Pricing Decisions

A policy concern in various jurisdictions is the ability of merchants to charge different prices based on the type of payment instrument used.[13] In the United States, merchants cannot be prevented from offering cash discounts. While there is no federal statute banning surcharges in the United States, some states ban them.[14]

Furthermore, the card networks usually prevent merchants from imposing surcharges.

Katz (2001) suggests two potential effects of one-price policies. One-price polices are defined as policies set by law or card networks that require consumers to pay the same price regardless of the type of payment instrument used. First, one-price policies may distort the nature of competition and limit the retail price as a mechanism to provide incentives to use certain payment instruments. Second, one-price rules prevent the neutrality of interchange fees. These fees are neutral if the consumption of consumers, profits of merchants, and the ability of banks to be compensated for their costs are not affected by the level of the interchange fee.

Even in jurisdictions where merchants are able to set different prices, most merchants do not set multiple prices based on the cost associated with accepting the payment instrument. A notable departure occurred in the 1980s, when many U.S. gas stations posted a credit card price and a lower cash price.[15] However, such practices are not common in the United States today. A study on surcharging practices in the Netherlands, where merchants cannot be prevented from imposing surcharges, found that only 10 percent of merchants surcharge (Vis and Toth 2000). A similar study in Sweden, another country where payment network rules cannot prevent merchants from surcharging, found that only 5 percent of merchants impose surcharges (IMA Market Development AB 2000).[16]

Although not very common, there are examples of where merchants discount credit card purchases versus purchases made with other payment instruments. In Germany, a department store, immediately following the launch of the euro, discounted credit card purchases 20 percent over cash purchases because of the added cost of handling cash at that time (Benoit 2002). In the United States, an online merchant imposed a $3 fee to process check payments while imposing no such fee for credit card payments. These anecdotes may suggest that the benefits to at least some merchants outweigh the costs by such a margin that these merchants are willing to steer consumers to using payment cards with price incentives.

Given merchants' reluctance to price purchases made with different payment products differently when allowed to do so suggests that the removal of merchant pricing restrictions may not result in a menu of prices. However, if these restrictions are not likely to affect merchant decisions, why should they be in place? If there are merchants willing to pass these costs to those consumers that use more costly payment instruments, they should be allowed to do so.

Interchange Fees

The level and determination of the interchange fee has received attention in various parts of the world. Most investigations challenge the collective setting of interchange fees by otherwise competitors. In the United States, National Bancard Association, a third-party processor, sued Visa arguing that interchange fees should be set to zero in 1979. The court ruled in favor of Visa allowing collective setting of interchange fees.[17] Recently, a group of merchants filed a lawsuit against some of the payment networks alleging that the current method of setting interchange fees violates antitrust laws and the level of the fee is too high. Public authorities have intervened formally or persuaded payment networks to lower interchange fees in other parts of the world. In Australia, the Reserve Bank of Australia imposed regulations regarding the determination of the level of interchange fees in open-system credit card networks. The European Commission negotiated a reduction in intra-EU interchange rates.

Merchants argue that they are paying a disproportionate share of the cost of credit cards. Thus, the consumer's incentive to use less costly payment instruments may be misaligned. Furthermore, they claim that card issuers are enticing consumers with rewards to use more costly payment instruments especially when these consumers may not be availing the credit feature in the case of credit cards or are not using less costly alternatives such as PIN-based debit cards.[18]

Economic Models

Recently, several economists have investigated price structures in two-sided markets with network effects. Armstrong (2006), Caillaud and Jullien (2001), Jullien (2001), Rochet and Tirole (2003), and Schiff (2003) explore platform competition for various industries. A major contribution of this literature is that different types of end-users may not share equally in the costs of providing the good or service and this outcome may be economically efficient. Many of the results depend on the accessibility of different types of end-users to different platforms, the underlying fee structure, and their demands for services from a specific platform.

Networks providing payment services are two-sided markets. In these markets, more than one type of end-user must be convinced simultaneously.[19] In other words, payment networks have to "get both sides on board." Rochet and Tirole (2004) state that a necessary condition for a two-sided market is the failure of Coase theorem. A key observation in the market for payment services is that merchants generally charge the same price regardless of the type of payment instrument used to make the purchase. However, Rochet and Tirole argue that the failure of Coase theorem is not sufficient for a market to be two-sided. They state that a market is two-sided, if the proportion of fees paid by each type of end-user affects the total consumption of the good.

Modeling Payment and Credit

For the most part, the payment card literature ignores the credit aspect of payments. Analysis of this component is particularly important in understanding the willingness of payors and payees to use payment cards. Chakravorti and Emmons (2003) and Chakravorti and To (2007) construct models of payment cards that focus on the costs and benefits of payment to payees, payors, and financial institutions that provide credit card services. Both models emphasize the grace period for credit card users that pay off their balances in full every month. The question that both articles ask is which participant is willing to bear the cost of the interest-free short-term credit?

There are several explanations. First, merchants benefit from card acceptance and may be willing to pay for it. Merchants often offer credit at below market rates, for example, interest-free and no payments for a year. Second, those consumers that borrow may be willing to pay for those that do not borrow. Third, financial institutions may be anticipating that a significant number of consumers will revolve eventually and may be willing to subsidize them initially. These explanations may not be mutually exclusive.

Chakravorti and To (2006) construct a two-period model to investigate the following questions.[20] Why do merchants accept credit cards even though credit cards are the most costly payment instrument to process? Does the decision of a merchant to accept credit cards affect profits of other merchants? They depart from the payment card literature in the following ways. First, rather than taking a reduced-form approach where the costs and benefits of credit cards are exogenously assigned functional forms, a model is specified that endogenously yields costs and benefits to the involved parties. Second, the model uses a dynamic setting where there are intertemporal trade-offs for all of the parties involved. Using this approach, they identify an intertemporal externality that merchants impose on one another because their credit acceptance decision has little impact on their own future earnings.

They explain why merchants accept credit cards using the most restrictive possible environment—a single issuer, massless merchants, and no cost sharing by consumers either directly in the form of fees or finance charges or indirectly in the form of higher prices. Credit increases sales because both purchases and incomes vary over time and with credit cards, "credit worthy" consumers are able to purchase—all else equal, merchants prefer to make a sale today rather than tomorrow. They demonstrate that a credit card equilibrium can exist if the cost of funds is relatively low and the merchant's profit margin is sufficiently high. They also show that using the merchant discount, the issuer will be able to fully extract rents from merchants resulting from sales to consumers with no income in the first period.

Furthermore, the interaction between the merchant discount and the accessibility of credit has network effects. If the card issuer makes credit more widely available, the merchant increases its sales. This in turn allows the card issuer to increase the discount the merchant is charged. In other words, merchants are willing to pay higher merchant discounts if credit cards generate greater sales. Specifically, the card issuer is able to provide more consumers, only if it is willing to take more credit risk and is able to pass this onto merchants.

Finally, they show that there is an externality where merchants find themselves in a prisoner's dilemma situation. In equilibrium, each merchant chooses to accept credit cards. However, when all merchants accept credit cards, they are all worse off. Basically, merchants accepting credit cards in the first period are able to steal consumers from merchants in the second period. Because they consider an infinite number of merchants that have low probability of facing the same consumer in the second period, merchants individually are unable to internalize the effect of accepting payment cards on future sales. This result is dependent on the degree of market power held by the issuer, the amount of bargaining power held by merchants, and the frequency of future sales to first-period consumers.

Chakravorti and Emmons (2003) add revolving credit to a Diamond-Dybvig type model where consumers face income shocks. Consumers either receive income in one of two periods or never receive income. Issuers make fully enforceable contracts prior to the realization of income. In their model, banks and retailers provide goods and services in competitive markets. Thus, consumers as a group or certain types of consumers ultimately pay for the real resource cost of credit card services.

They derive four main results. First, a card-accepting merchant can serve the entire market charging different prices based on the payment method used, but then only liquidity-constrained customers will use credit cards. This separating equilibrium assigns the costs of credit cards to revolvers alone.

Second, if merchants charge a single goods price regardless of how consumers pay, and if there are no side payments made by banks to convenience users, then card-accepting merchants who charge a single price for all purchases will attract only liquidity-constrained consumers. Side payments are defined as additional compensation given by one participant to another to entice usage or compensate for costs incurred. For example, card issuers sometimes offer usage awards such as cash back or frequent flyer miles to their cardholders. In a competitive goods market, a card-accepting merchant must raise the goods price to cover the cost of accepting credit cards, but the higher price drives customers who can pay cash to other merchants who do not accept credit cards and hence can charge a lower single price.

Third, they show that a merchant can, under certain conditions, attract all types of consumers—convenience users and revolvers—where a single price is charged. However, card issuers must compensate convenience users for the higher goods prices that universal card usage necessitates.[21] In their model, an equilibrium in which liquid consumers use credit cards can be supported only if liquidity-constrained consumers subsidize convenience use of credit cards.

Finally, their model shows when credit card usage can benefit all participants. The key assumption in this regard is that at least a certain number of consumers face binding liquidity constraints. Intuitively, the value of consumer credit may outweigh the costliness of the payment instrument with which it is bundled. They find that side payments to convenience users in an environment where merchants charge the same price regardless of the payment instrument used is more costly for society then one where merchants charge different prices based on the underlying cost structure of the payment instruments used.

Both of these articles highlight the importance of credit to both consumers and merchants. Consumers benefit from credit because they are able to consume today instead of tomorrow and they are willing to pay to consume today. Merchants are also willing to pay for the extension of credit because they also benefit from making sales today rather than tomorrow.

Conclusion

The movement away from paper-based payment instruments toward electronic payments that access global payment networks coupled with extensions of payment and consumption credit has allowed for more efficient payment processing. However, some market participants, most notably merchants, along with public authorities around the world have been concerned about the pricing of these services. Specifically, do current payment instrument usage fees for consumers favor inefficient payment instruments? Furthermore, are merchants paying an unfair share of the cost of providing efficient payment instruments?

Recently, economists have constructed theoretical models to address these questions. The broader payments literature using a two-sided markets approach finds that prices among end-users may not be symmetric to yield economically efficient prices. However, most of these models ignore the intertemporal aspect of payment cards. In this chapter, we reviewed two models where consumption credit was considered. Both these models concluded that even if prices are skewed in one direction, all participants benefit from the extension of consumption credit. These models suggest that policymakers should pay particular attention to the structure of the market for goods and payment services.

Notes

The views expressed are those of the author and do not represent the views of the Federal Reserve Bank of Chicago or the Federal Reserve System.

1. For more discussion on this taxonomy, see Chakravorti (1997).
2. For charge card transactions, the cardholder must settle the balance at the end of each billing cycle. For credit card transactions, the cardholder has the option to pay the balance in full or make a partial payment at the end of each billing cycle.
3. Amromin and Chakravorti (2007) conduct a cross-country analysis on the impact of debit cards on cash.
4. Humphrey (2004) reports that in addition to replacing cash for consumer payments, employee disbursements, and smaller-value business purchases, checks were used until 1915 for large-value business transactions and interbank transfers.
5. Note that checks paid differ from checks written because some checks are converted to ACH payments at the point of sale or at retail lock boxes.
6. There are two types of debit card transactions—those authorized by PIN (personal identification number) and those authorized by signature. For more details, see Lubasi (2005).
7. In the large-value payment system context, Zhou (2000) differentiates between consumption and investment debt, resulting from a real resources transaction, and payment debt that is created only for payment needs.
8. However, ACH credit payments require payors or their financial institutions to know the payees' account information. While this form of payment is common in many parts of Europe, it is primarily used for wage disbursements in the United States.
9. For the history of credit cards, see Evans and Schmalensee (1999); Mandell (1990); and Nocera (1994).
10. I did not consider the costs and benefits of credit card borrowing but instead focused on the payment aspect.
11. For empirical studies of consumer decisions to use the long-term credit component, see Ausubel (1991); Brito and Hartley (1995); and Stavins (1996).
12. Some issuers have attempted to drop cardholders that pay off their bills suggesting that convenience users may not be profitable (*USBanker*, 1997).

13. For a discussion of U.S. legislative history of credit card surcharges, see Board of Governors of the Federal Reserve System (1983); Chakravorti and Shah (2003); Kitch (1990); and Lobell and Gelb (1981).
14. For more discussion on states that ban surcharging, see Levitin (2006).
15. For more details, see Barron, Staten, and Umbeck (1992).
16. However, acquirers are allowed to impose no-surcharge rules. Visa (2001, p. 36) states the following: "Swedish law permits acquiring banks to enter into contracts with their merchants under which the merchant is prevented from surcharging. Such merchant-to-acquiring bank agreements enforcing a no-surcharge rule are now commonplace in Sweden."
17. For more discussion of this case, see Ahlborn, Chang, and Evans (2001); Balto (2000); Carlton and Frankel (1995); and Evans and Schmalensee (1999: 275–81).
18. Chakravorti and Shah (2003) argue that financial institutions may have incentives to subsidize convenience users. Issuers may offer convenience users payment services below their marginal cost because such a pricing strategy improves the risk of their credit portfolios or increases market share of payment card transactions.
19. For a review of the payment card literature, see Chakravorti (2003).
20. Most models of payment networks are only one-period models and are unable to consider intertemporal effects.
21. If all markets are competitive, the costs of credit cards fall on consumers either in the form of higher prices or fees and finance charges imposed by card issuers. However, if markets are not competitive, merchants and card issuers may share in the costs. Nevertheless, consumers may still pay a portion of these costs indirectly in the form of higher prices or higher finance charges and other fees imposed by card issuers.

References

Ahlborn, Christian, Howard H. Chang, and David S. Evans. 2001. "The Problem of Interchange Fee Analysis: Case without a Cause?" *European Competition Law Review* 22 (8): 304–12.

American Bankers Association and Dove Consulting. 2005. *2005/2006 Study of Consumer Payment Preferences*. American Bankers Association and Dove Consulting.

Amromin, Gene, and Sujit Chakravorti. 2007. "Debit Card and Cash Usage: A Cross-Country Analysis." Federal Reserve Bank of Chicago Working Paper, WP 2007-04.

Armstrong, Mark. 2006. "Competition in Two-Sided Markets." *Rand Journal of Economics* 37 (3): 668–91.

Ausubel, Lawrence M. 1991. "The Failure of Competition in the Credit Card Market." *American Economic Review* 81 (1): 50–81.

Balto, David A. 2000. "The Problem of Interchange Fees: Costs without Benefits." *European Competition Law Review* 21 (4): 215–24.

Barron, John M., Michael E. Staten, and John Umbeck. 1992. "Discounts for Cash in Retail Gasoline Marketing." *Contemporary Policy Issues* 10 (January): 89–102.

Benoit, B. 2002. "Defiant C&A Reignites Debate on German Shopping Laws." *Financial Times*, January 9, 2.

Board of Governors of the Federal Reserve System. 1983. *Credit Cards in the U.S. Economy*, July 27.

Brito, Dagobert L., and Peter R. Hartley. 1995. "Consumer Rationality and Credit Cards." *Journal of Political Economy* 103 (2): 400–33.

Caillaud, B., and B. Jullien. 2003. "Chicken & Egg: Competition among Intermediation Service Providers." *RAND Journal of Economics* 24: 309–28.

Carlton, Dennis W., and Alan S. Frankel. 1995. "The Antitrust Economics of Payment Card Networks." *Antitrust Law Journal* 63 (2): 643–68.

Chakravorti, Sujit. 1997. "How Do We Pay?" Federal Reserve Bank of Dallas. *Financial Industry Issues*, First Quarter.

———. 2003. "Theory of Credit Card Networks: A Survey of the Literature." *Review of Network Economics* 2 (2): 50–68.

Chakravorti, Sujit, and Timothy McHugh. 2002. "Why Do We Use So Many Checks?" Federal Reserve Bank of Chicago *Economic Perspectives*, 3rd Quarter, 44–59.

Chakravorti, Sujit, and Alpa Shah. 2003. "Underlying Incentives in Credit Card Networks." *The Antitrust Bulletin* (Spring): 53–75.

Chakravorti, Sujit, and William R. Emmons. 2003. "Who Pays for Credit Cards?" *Journal of Consumer Affairs* 37 (2): 208–30.

Chakravorti, Sujit, and Ted To. 2007. "A Theory of Credit Cards." *International Journal of Industrial Organization* 25 (3): 583–95.

Ernst and Young. 1996. "Survey of Retail Payment Systems." *Chain Store Age*, January.

Evans, David S., and Richard L. Schmalensee. 1999. *Paying with Plastic: The Digital Revolution in Buying and Borrowing*. Cambridge, MA: The MIT Press.

Federal Reserve System. 2004. *The 2004 Federal Reserve Payments Study*, report, Washington D.C., December 15.

Food Marketing Institute. 1998. *A Retailer's Guide to Electronic Payment Systems Costs*, Washington, D.C.: Food Marketing Institute.

———. 2000. *It All Adds Up: An Activity Based Cost Study of Retail Payments*. Washington, D.C.: Food Marketing Institute.

Garcia Swartz, Daniel D., Robert W. Hahn, and Anne Layne-Farrar. 2006. "A Move Toward a Cashless Society: A Closer Look at Payment Instrument Economics." *Review of Network Economics* 5 (2): 175–98.

Humphrey, David. 2004. "Replacement of Cash by Cards in U.S. Consumer Payments." *Journal of Economics and Business* 56 (3): 211–25.

IMA Market Development AB. 2000. *Study Regarding the Effects of the Abolition of the Non-Discrimination Rule in Sweden*. IMA Market Development AB: Frodingsvagen.

Jullien, B. 2001. "Competing in Network Industries: Divide and Conquer." Mimeo, IDEI and GREMAQ, University of Toulouse.

Katz, Michael L. 2001. *Reform of Credit Card Schemes in Australia II*, Sydney, Australia: Reserve Bank of Australia.

Kitch, Edmond W. 1990. "The Framing Hypothesis: Is It Supported by Credit Card Issuer Opposition to a Surcharge on a Cash Price." *Journal of Law, Economics, and Organization* 6 (Spring): 217–33.

Levitin, Adam J. 2006. "Payment Wars: The Merchant-Bank Struggle for Control of Payment Systems." Working Paper, September 5.

Lobell, Carl D., and Joseph W. Gelb. 1981. "The Cash Discount Act." *New York Law Journal* (December): 1–4.

Lubasi, Victor. 2005. "Debit Card Competition: Signature Versus PIN." *Chicago Fed Letter*, Federal Reserve Bank of Chicago, No. 221, December.

Mandell, Lewis. 1990. *The Credit Card Industry: A History*. Boston, MA: Twayne Publishers.

National Public Radio. 2006. "Plastic Only: Café Refuses to Accept Cash." Morning Edition, October 11, transcript reprinted in Factiva.

Nocera, Joseph. 1994. *A Piece of the Action: How the Middle Class Joined the Money Class*. New York, N.Y.: Simon & Schuster.

Rochet, Jean-Charles, and Jean Tirole. 2002. "Cooperation among Competitors: Some Economics of Payment Card Associations." *Rand Journal of Economics* 33 (4): 549–70.

Rochet, Jean-Charles, and Jean Tirole. 2003. "Platform Competition in Two-Sided Markets." *Journal of European Economic Association* 1 (4): 990–1029.

———. 2004. "Two-Sided Markets: An Overview." Paper presented at *The Economics of Two-Sided Markets* conference at the University of Toulouse, January 23–24.

Schiff, Aaron. 2003. "Open and Closed Systems of Two-Sided Networks." *Information Economics and Policy* 15: 425–42.

Stavins, Joanna. 1996. "Can Demand Elasticities Explain Sticky Credit Card Rates?" Federal Reserve Bank of Boston, *New England Economic Review* (July/August): 43–54.

USBanker. 1997. "Penalizing the Convenience User," 17.

U.S. Department of State, Bureau of International Information Programs. 2003. "Fact Sheet: U.S. Secret Service on Currency Protection." Fact Sheet, Washington, DC, May 13.

Vis, E., and J. Toth. 2000. *The Abolition of the No-Discrimination Rule*. ITM Research for Competition DG: Amsterdam.

Visa International Service Association. 2001. *Credit Card Schemes in Australia: A Response to the Reserve Bank of Australia and Australian Competition and Consumer Commission Joint Study*.

Zhou, Ruilin. 2000. "Understanding Intraday Credit in Large-Value Payment Systems." Federal Reserve Bank of Chicago *Economic Perspectives*, 3rd Quarter, 29–44.

CHAPTER 11

PAYDAY LENDING: EVOLUTION, ISSUES, AND EVIDENCE

Katherine A. Samolyk

Introduction

Payday loans (also called deferred presentment loans) are small, very short-term loans extended with minimal underwriting in exchange for a postdated check. The typical payday loan is a two-week loan for an average amount in the range of $250–$300. A typical fee of $15–$20 per $100 borrowed translates into a very high annualized rate of interest (APRs of 390 percent or more). In states that do not have specific legislation that permits payday lending, usury ceilings would generally prohibit the high APRs associated with typical payday loan fees; however in some states, either the absence of usury ceilings or the existing small-loan laws have allowed payday lenders to operate. As of year-end 2006, payday stores were operating in 40 states and in the District of Columbia.

Payday loan borrowers can typically obtain cash quickly and conveniently. To get a payday loan, generally an applicant must simply be able to verify employment, the existence of a checking account in good standing, and contact information.[1] Many payday lenders use subprime credit-checking services, such as Teletrak, to make sure a prospective borrower does not have a history of bouncing checks or not paying creditors. In exchange for the advance, the borrower provides the lender with a personal check for the amount of the loan plus the finance charge, which is post dated to reflect the date the loan must be repaid (its maturity date).

On or before the loan maturity date, the borrower is supposed to redeem the check by paying off the loan. Depending on state regulations, a borrower may be able to rollover the loan by paying the stipulated fee upfront to defer the payment of the original loan plus the fee for another two-week period. For example, if someone borrows $300 by writing a postdated check for $345, that person would pay $45 in cash to extend the due date of the original $345 check for another two weeks. If loan rollovers are prohibited, a borrower who still needs funds will have to come up with the entire $345 payment that is due, whereupon he or she can write a new postdated check (for $345) to obtain the next $300 loan. This type of transaction is referred to in the industry as a consecutive transaction.

Payday loans are often called unsecured loans, but they are better thought of as quasi-secured since the lender has a claim on the customer's checking account. (The term "quasi-secured" refers to the fact that although a checking account is a financial asset; a claim on an empty account may not have value.) Having a check written on a borrower's account makes it more likely that the lender will receive payment. If the borrower does not repay or renew the loan, the lender can deposit the check for collection. If the check is honored, the lender has been made whole. If the check does not clear, the lender (as well as the customer's bank) may impose NSF fees or other fees and the lender can begin collections procedures. All of these considerations encourage a customer to remain in good standing and, therefore, represent an important part of a payday lender's loss mitigation strategy.[2] Some payday lenders substitute an agreement allowing them to automatically debit a borrower's checking account for the postdated check.[3]

Payday lenders are often classified as alternative financial service (AFS) providers—which are "companies [that provide] basic retail financial services to the unbanked and underbanked consumer."[4] The AFS sector includes check cashers, pawn shops, rent-to-own businesses, and payday lenders, which are distinct from what are referred as "mainstream" financial institutions (commercial banks, thrifts, finance companies, brokerage firms, and mutual funds). Industry estimates for 2006 place the dollar volume of storefront payday loan originations at around $42 billion, extended to as many as 15 million customers from more than 24,000 storefront locations (up from only several hundred in the early 1990s).[5]

Clearly, many consumers are using these small, short-term consumer loans as a source of funds. For a credit-constrained individual, a payday loan can be a cheaper way of coping with a temporary cash flow imbalance than relying on fee-based overdraft protection or simply not making payments.[6] However, available data generally indicate that a sizable subset of payday loan customers borrow more than infrequently and/or rollover their loans, paying additional fees for each loan.[7] Concerns voiced by consumer advocates reflect the high cost of chronic payday loan use and suspicions that the industry's inherent business model depends on repeat customers.[8] Payday lenders say that they cannot charge less and still cover their operating costs and loan losses.

It is generally recognized that making small loans is inherently more expensive than making large loans because there are fixed costs to screening, underwriting, servicing, and monitoring a loan, particularly for borrowers who are hard to evaluate.[9] It is also recognized that one must charge higher rates on loans to more-risky borrowers since they are more likely not to pay you back. But how much higher? Thus, important questions for the payday lending debate are whether the operating costs and loan losses associated with making these loans justify the price and whether repeat use is a critical part of the business model.

To put the price in perspective, it is useful to do some arithmetic. If a two-week $300 loan having a fee of $45 is renewed for a seventh time (14 weeks later), the payday lender will have received fees of $315 while the borrower will still owe the entire face value of the original check (the original loan balance plus the original fee). If this loan is renewed for an entire year and then repaid, the lender will have received $1,170 in fees for having advanced $300 to the borrower for one year; a cash flow that translates into an annualized percentage rate (APR) of interest of 390 percent.[10] The very short loan maturity and the rapid accumulation of fee income explain why loan renewals are viewed as an important dimension of payday lending profitability.

This chapter describes the evolution of the payday lending industry, focusing on what is now referred to as the "traditional" payday lending business model of extending small, very short-term, deferred-presentment loans through storefront locations.[11] We then discuss issues that frame the debate about payday lending and empirical evidence about the provision and the use of payday loans. Because of the types of information that are available, more has been written about the use of payday loans than about industry costs, profitability, and performance. We summarize our own research studying payday store costs, profitability, and performance using data for two large monoline payday lenders along with evidence about the industry provided by others.

Evolution and Recent Trends

The provision of relatively high-cost small loans to consumers is not new. As Caldor (1999) discusses, "Credit for consumer goods is the oldest of all forms of credit, with a history stretching back to antiquity."[12] However, before the birth of modern consumer finance in the early twentieth century, household borrowing was generally conducted at "the subterranean levels of society, where for those who needed to go beyond family and friends, the likely options were retailers, pawnbrokers, and illegal moneylenders, or 'loan sharks.'"[13] Moreover, which households sought financial assistance from which sources of credit depended a great deal on the borrower's economic standing and social class; and patterns of gender, race, and ethnicity played an important role in the system. Illegal lenders of the late nineteenth century included wage assignment lenders (similar to payday lenders), which as Caldor notes "charged the highest rates because their loans were the smallest."[14]

The emergence of institutionalized consumer finance came with the passage of state small-loan laws during the 1920s and 1930s. These laws allowed lenders to legally charge rates on small consumer loans that exceeded usury ceilings and permitted the emergence of the modern finance company industry. Finance companies, now viewed as mainstream nonbank credit providers, evolved from illegal lenders of the late 1800s that made small higher-priced loans to working-class individuals.[15] But, according to Caldor (1999), wage assignment lenders fought legislation to legalize the small-loan business because "they had no hoped that legislators would ever legalize the rates they charged."[16]

The Emergence of Modern Payday Lending

A century after the wage assignment lenders of the late 1800s, the United States has witnessed a significant growth in the provision of financial services to consumers of modest means outside of the financial mainstream. A substantial segment of the emerging AFS sector provides modest amounts of credit to financially-strapped borrowers at a relatively high price in the form of pawn lending, rent-to-own agreements, auto-title loans, sale-leaseback loans, tax anticipation loans, and payday loans.[17]

Deferred presentment lending—payday lending in its modern form—emerged in the early 1990s when check-cashing firms realized they could earn additional fee income by advancing funds to their customers in exchange for postdated checks to tide them over until payday—hence the name.[18] Given the small and very short-term nature of the advances, the effective APRs on these loans exceeded the maximums allowed by state small-loan laws and usury ceilings; thus the loans were illegal in most states. Fox (1998) noted: "By labeling the transaction as check cashing instead of lending, companies sought to avoid credit laws."[19] Subsequently, "Litigation by Attorney Generals and private class action lawsuits have produced court decisions and settlements confirming that payday loans are subject to usury limits, small-loan caps, and other credit protection laws."[20] Pressure from the check-cashing industry led some states to enact enabling legislation that permitted payday lending. In some states, by defining the transaction as "deferred presentment" with an associated fee not to be considered interest for purposes of state usury laws, lenders were able to circumvent local usury ceilings. Other states permitted payday loans if the fee was the same as that allowed for the cashing of a check.[21] By 1998, 19 states had specific laws permitting payday lending, and 13 states allowed payday lending under their existing small-loan laws or in the absence of usury ceilings. In the remaining 18 states, existing small-loan laws or usury ceilings and the absence of explicit enabling legislation prohibited payday lending.[22]

Interestingly, the early debates about payday lending sound a lot like current debates about the fee-based overdraft protection programs that depository institutions offer to account holders. Early payday loan providers argued that the deferred-presentment transaction was equivalent to cashing the check as long as the fee charged did not exceed the fee that they would have charged to cash the check immediately. Today, fee-based overdraft protection is argued to be a payment service because the per-transaction fee charged for an NSF item that is paid by an institution is often the same as what the institution would charge on an NSF transaction that is not paid.; but the customer receives the convenience of having the item paid.

Because of its roots, payday lending during the first part of the 1990s tended to be viewed as a component of the check-cashing business rather than a distinct industry.[23] As Caskey (2005) discusses, it is hard to trace the growth and performance of the early industry because firms making payday loans did not advertise as offering "payday loans" in phone books and states did not regulate payday lending per se. According to available estimates, there were probably only several hundred payday stores in the United States in the early 1990s.[24] As payday lending grew and states began to permit and regulate the industry, estimates of industry scale in some states could be pieced together from data collected by state agencies.[25]

Stand-alone monoline payday loan stores emerged rather quickly. Check Into Cash opened its first payday store in 1993 and it expanded to 34 outlets in 15 states by 1998; it now operates 1,200 outlets in 30 states. Check N Go, which opened its first store in 1994, grew to 400 stores by 1998, and now operates more than 13,000 stores in 30 states. By far the largest payday lending firm at this time is Advance America, a monoline firm, which opened its first store in 1997 and now operates more than 2,600 stores in 36 states. The emergence of the very large monoline payday advance firms is an interesting phenomenon since these firms depend solely on payday loans for their profitability. Their product focus has been viewed as a benefit in lowering loss rates; however, monoline firms acknowledge that their lack of product diversification makes them more vulnerable to the fortunes of the industry, including regulatory and litigation risks.[26] The emergence of the monoline firms led to the establishment of a national trade organization, the Community Financial Services Association (CFSA), whose membership is estimated to represent more than half of the industry's storefronts. Previously, the National Check Cashers Association (the NaCCA), the trade group that represented the check-cashing industry, was the main advocate for payday lending.[27]

In 2004, two monoline payday loan companies became publicly traded (Advance America and QC Holdings Inc).[28] Company acquisitions have also facilitated industry consolidation and entry by AFS firms interested in providing payday loans.[29] With the emergence of large publicly traded payday lenders, industry data and analysis became more widely available through public disclosures and research undertaken by investment banking firms. Reports by Stephens Inc. (an investment banking firm that helps finance the industry) for 2001 placed the total number of stores at around 10,000, with half of them also operating as check cashers and roughly 44 percent being controlled by large multistate firms that operated more than 200 stores. Stephens Inc. (2006) estimated that the number of payday loan stores (not firms) had risen to 21,500 by year-end 2004.

The growth of the payday loan industry reflects in part the growing number of states that were permitting payday lending. Moreover, in states where usury ceilings prohibited payday lenders from making loans directly, payday lenders formed partnerships with banks.[30] Both the National Bank Act and the Federal Deposit Insurance Act permit banks to charge customers in other states the loan interest rates permitted in the banks' home state; in this sense banks are allowed to "export their interest rates." Payday loan companies have tended to partner with banks located in South Dakota or Delaware (states that have no usury ceilings) because banks in these states can make loans having the high APRs that are effective on payday loans. Under these partnership arrangements (referred to as operations under the bank model), the payday lending firm is said to act as the "agent" of the bank while the bank is said to be making the loan subject to the higher usury ceiling of the bank's home state. States where payday lending has occurred through bank partnerships became known as bank-model states, in contrast to the direct-lending model that tends to be used where payday lending is permitted by state laws.

Consumer groups strongly objected to payday lender-bank partnerships in states where these partnerships allowed state consumer protection regulations to be circumvented. These groups argued that the partnerships amount to little more than "charter renting" by payday lending firms, allowing payday lenders to operate in states that have chosen not to permit payday lending.[31] It is important to emphasize that this objection reflects the use of the bank-payday lender partnerships to get around state laws. As we discuss later, some banks make payday-type loans directly to deposit customers (subject to the laws of the states where the customers are located), and some banks play an important role in funding payday lenders through the issuance of lines of credit and other loans.[32] Both of these latter types of activities facilitate the extension of payday loans in states where they are permitted.

The growth of payday lending in the United State is cited as evidence of consumers' demand for the product. Thus before we discuss the current state of the payday industry and the evidence about the business model, it is useful to think about the emergence of payday lending in the context of broader changes in consumer credit markets during the past several decades. Deregulation, innovations in data processing, and advances in risk management have altered the types of loans available to households, how these loans are marketed, who can get credit, and who ultimately funds it. Credit services provided to consumers are much more automated and standardized than in the past. Mortgage credit is increasingly brokered, originated, serviced, and funded by different parties, and scale economies in providing consumer credit—particularly credit cards—have shifted to favoring large institutions. Innovations in data collection have allowed the widespread application of credit-scoring models to loan marketing, underwriting, and pricing—allowing lenders to offer a wider array of loan products to a broad array of customers. At the higher end of the risk spectrum, the ability to implement risk-based pricing has greatly expanded the credit products available to more marginal—that is, sub-prime—borrowers.

Meanwhile in the modern world of consumer finance, lenders are under greater competitive pressure to ensure that the products and services they offer are profitable on the margin and contribute to the bottom line.[33] Full-service financial institutions increasingly view profitability on a fee-per-service basis or in terms of the overall package of services that a customer will use. Thus, the nature of relationship lending in consumer credit markets has changed from face-to-face knowledge to data on credit and payment histories and prospects for the use of multiple banking services. Because of the more limited basket of services used by customers of modest means, the provision of services to this segment has become more fee based; and the cost savings associated with automation and standardization have been critical in determining the types of products that are offered. In this context, payday lending is often viewed as emerging to fill a void as banks have shifted away from extending small closed-end personal loans to extending open-ended unsecured and mortgage-secured credit.[34] More generally, the growth of the alternative financial sector has been viewed as reflecting an increasing bifurcation in the provision of financial services to individuals having different levels of income and wealth.[35] And this is not just a U.S. phenomenon. Alternative financial services providers and products have their parallels in other countries including Canada, Britain, and Australia.[36]

Recent Regulatory and Industry Trends

The payday loan industry has matured far beyond its early roots in check cashing to an industry making billions of dollars in loans to millions of customers. In the absence of bank-model lending, the industry's operation in a state generally reflect the state's laws that permit payday lending. Thus, one cannot characterize the industry without describing the regulatory environment. Just as there is no federal usury law, there are no federal laws that explicitly regulate payday lending in the United States. Payday lenders are required to comply with federal consumer protection laws that apply to credit extensions, including the Truth in Lending Act (TILA), the Equal Credit Opportunity Act (ECOA), and the Fair Debt Collections Act.[37] Recently, because of concerns that military personnel are vulnerable to repeat use of high-cost loans, there has been federal legislation that broadly limits the APRs on loans to military personnel nationwide to no more than 36 percent.[38] Concerns about payday lending were an impetus for this legislation.

In the absence of explicit federal legislation, payday lending continues to be regulated at the state level. Enabling regulation can cover many aspects of payday lending arrangements, including maximum fees, loan amounts, minimum or maximum terms to maturity, rollovers, frequency of use, legal recourse in the event of default, and reporting requirements. The passage of explicit enabling legislation is viewed positively by the industry because the legislation generally establishes limits on fees and other loan terms at levels that allow payday lenders to operate their standard business model (storefronts making traditional payday loans) profitability.[39] Explicit enabling legislation also reduces regulatory risks for payday loan firms operating in the states with such legislation. Thus, not surprisingly, the CFSA favors enabling legislation and has a model bill for which it lobbies.[40]

As noted earlier, payday lending stores operated in 40 states and the District of Columbus at year-end 2006. However, payday lenders have been forced to cease payday lending operations in most states where state laws do not permit payday lending. Although bank-model payday lending is not illegal, bank regulatory agencies have issued strict supervisory guidance to address the risks associated with this type of third-party lending—risks that include safety and soundness risks; consumer and compliance risks; and legal and reputational risks.[41] In Georgia and North Carolina, legal arguments were raised about the nature of bank-payday lender partnerships in which the agent (the payday lender) retains most of the fee income. The argument is basically that the small share of fee income earned by the bank indicates that the payday lending firm—not the out-of-state bank—has the primary economic and financial interest in the loans and thus the loans do not constitute lending activity by the out-of-state bank.[42] Currently, there are no banks that partner with payday lending firms to extend payday loans under the bank model. States do have to contend with other attempts by payday lenders to do business in states that do not permit payday lending.[43] However, industry analysts increasingly view enabling legislation as a prerequisite for payday lending in a state, now that bank-model lending has ceased.[44]

Although a few states have recently raised loan fee maximums and lending limits, the more common regulatory trend has been to tighten limits on fees, rollovers, and customer usage. According to a quarterly Securities and Exchange Commission (SEC) filing submitted by Advance America in 2006: "In 2005, bills that severely restrict or effectively prohibit payday cash advances were introduced in 26 states. In addition, two states have sunset provisions in their payday cash advance laws that require renewal of the laws by the state legislatures at periodic intervals."[45] In some states (including Florida, Indiana, Illinois, and Michigan), lenders are supposed to report borrower activity to statewide reporting agencies to allow the monitoring of customer use.[46] In New Mexico, new regulations that were scheduled to become effective in September 2006 not only limited renewals to a maximum of two, but also stipulate that after two renewals, customers will "have sole discretion to enter into a free and longer payment plan" for a minimum of 130 days, with no additional fees.[47] Perhaps the most dramatic legislation is the law due to take effect in Oregon in mid-2007: it caps the APR on payday loans at 36 percent—the same limit as stipulated by the federal legislation affecting loans to military personnel.[48]

Variations in states regulations, local economic and demographic conditions, and other factors affecting the local payday loan industry manifest themselves in differences in payday store activity across states. For a number of years, Stephens Inc. conjectured that market saturation in a state "could" occur when store concentration reached one store per 5,000 residents.[49] But Stephens Inc. estimates for 2005 projected that a number of southern states had gone beyond this hypothetical saturation point (see table 11.1).

At the aggregate level, the payday loan industry continues to be viewed as fragmented, referring to the fact that such a large share of stores are operated by small, locally operated businesses. According to Stephens Inc. (2007), 15 major payday loan companies controlled 45 percent (around 10,800 stores) of the estimated 24,200 stores operating in 2006. Payday loan industry fragmentation reflects the relative ease of entry into the business, since the operation of a payday loan store requires a fairly modest amount of financial capital. Store operators are supposed to obtain licenses from their local state regulator but can operate fairly easily without them.[50] We have not been able to find estimates of the size of the unlicensed payday loan industry.

Researchers have speculated about how both very large and very small payday firms can operate profitably. Similar to arguments made about the viability of community banks, smaller mom-and-pop shops may be able to operate profitably because of the local nature of the lending activity, which allows the owners to identify good locations and an attractive customer base. Mann and Hawkins (2006) observe that larger providers often find it more advantageous to grow by acquiring small shops rather than by opening new stores of their own.[51] But it also could be the case that small lenders can charge more or engage in practices that violate regulations.

Assessments of recent industry trends underscore the important role that regulations play in the payday loan business. Regulatory pressures are seen as a factor driving current industry consolidation because larger payday operators are viewed as better able to withstand regulatory changes that are lowering fees or limiting usage.[52] Slower growth in the number of payday loan stores during 2005 and 2006 has been attributed to changes in state regulations, the discontinuation of partnerships with banks, and a shift in the focus of the largest firms to loss-mitigation strategies.[53] Compared with previous years, payday loan activity flattened out in 2005 and loss rates edged up. Store closures in former bank-model states had a negative effect on lending, and lower fee limits negatively affected revenues because

Table 11.1 Payday store outlets by state

	2003		*2004*		*2005*	
	Number of Stores	*Population Per Store*	*Number of Stores*	*Population Per Store*	*Number of Stores*	*Population Per Store*
Alabama	858	5,246	1085	4,175	1165	3,912
Alaska			25	26,217	21	31,603
Arizona	521	10,712	673	8,535	735	8,081
Arkansas	63	43,265	209	13,170	209	13,297
California	1950	18,197	2134	16,820	2445	14,778
Colorado	424	10,733	619	7,434	578	8,071
Connecticut						
Delaware	30	27,250	52	15,969	73	11,555
DC	21	26,828	37	14,960	45	12,234
Florida	1081	15,744	1092	15,931	1217	14,618
Georgia	111	78,241	17	519,375	17	533,681
Hawaii			3	420,947	3	425,065
Idaho	42	32,532	206	6,763	222	6,437
Illinois	620	20,409	707	17,983	734	17,389
Indiana	315	19,669	480	12,995	540	11,615
Iowa	186	15,828	216	3,678	244	12,157
Kansas	202	13,483	213	12,843	340	8,073
Kentucky	550	7,487	660	6,282	701	5,954
Louisiana	770	5,839	882	5,120	1009	4,483
Maine			6	219,542	6	220,251
Maryland						
Massachusetts						
Michigan	167	60,359	347	29,143	370	27,354
Minnesota	62	81,603	63	80,968	55	93,324
Mississippi	935	3,082	1005	2,889	1095	2,668
Missouri	1000	5,704	1194	4,820	1230	4,716
Montana	98	9,363	107	8,662	106	8,827
Nebraska	135	12,884	159	10,989	184	9,559
Nevada	300	7,471	331	7,054	413	5,847
New Hampshire	20	64,384	20	64,975	25	52,398
New Jersey						
New Mexico	300	6,249	374	5,089	254	7,592
New York						
North Carolina	170	49,454	370	23,084		
North Dakota	60	10,564	66	9,612	77	8,269
Ohio	1140	10,031	1195	9,589	1371	8,362
Oklahoma	358	9,809	395	8,920	401	8,848
Oregon	41	86,819	297	12,103	359	10,142
Pennsylvania	74	167,101	236	52,569	270	46,036
Rhode Island	5	215,233	13	83,126	13	82,784
South Carolina	900	4,608	1023	4,104	1069	3,980
South Dakota	92	8,308	91	8,471	90	8,621

Continued

Table 11.1 Continued

	2003		2004		2005	
	Number of Stores	*Population Per Store*	*Number of Stores*	*Population Per Store*	*Number of Stores*	*Population Per Store*
Tennessee	1200	4,868	1272	4,639	1325	4,500
Texas	1090	20,292	1475	15,247	1500	15,240
Utah	300	7,838	336	7,110	350	7,056
Vermont						
Virginia	579	12,757	679	10,986	748	10,117
Washington	515	11,906	595	10,427	714	8,806
West Virginia			11	165,032	11	165,169
Wisconsin	342	16,001	399	13,807	446	12,413
Wyoming	52	9,639	74	6,845	74	6,882
Totals	17679		21443		22854	

Source: Stephens Inc. (2006) and U.S. Census Bureau data.

they reduced the fee dollars generated per loan. Payday lending firms and industry analysts clearly view limits on repeat customer business as reducing industry profitability and increasing loss rates. The poorer performance of large monoline firms in 2005 (compared with their more-diversified multiline counterparts) has been attributed to their greater exposure to changes in regulatory factors limiting their primary activity—payday lending. But, although the industry cites loan losses as a rationale for charging fees that range from 15 to 20 percent of loan volume, large lenders report that only 2–6 percent of payday loans are not repaid.[54]

Other Sources of Payday Loans

Before turning to issues and evidence about the payday lending business model, we should note that there are other sources of payday loans besides nonbank payday lenders operating in storefront locations. Internet payday lenders are thought to be a rapidly growing source of loans, but it is difficult to measure their activity.[55] Stephens Inc. (2007) estimated that Internet payday lenders advanced as much as $5.7 billion in loans during 2006. Mann and Hawkins (2006) found that Internet payday loan fees have tended to be lower, in the range of $10 per $100 borrowed, but websites tend to contain little information about who is making the loan.[56] Nonbank Internet providers are supposed to comply with state regulations when they make loans to individuals in a particular state, but the growth of online payday lending presents enforcement challenges.[57] States have had some success in prosecuting larger Internet providers for violating local statutes,[58] but the fact that the Internet allows payday lenders to reach out to customers virtually anywhere makes enforcement difficult.

Although depository institutions currently do not partner with nonbank payday lenders, at this time at least two large national banks offer payday-type advances as a checking account feature to customers that have direct deposit.[59] The advances offered by both of these banks are somewhat cheaper than the payday loans offered by storefront providers. The prerequisite of direct deposit reduces the risk of nonpayment relative to that faced by storefront providers, but it also limits who can use the product. As we discuss more later, researchers have argued that banks inherently have the infrastructure to be able to provide small-denomination advances on future deposits.[60]

Issues and Evidence about Payday Lending

Consumer advocates are concerned with the high price of repeated use of payday loans and payday loan extensions to individuals with longer-term financial imbalances who are unlikely to be able to repay the loans (and thus will have to renew them or incur the costs of default). Critics also object to practices that are potentially misleading or deceptive that can precipitate or perpetuate chronic payday loan use. These concerns reflect the fact that the fees translate into very high APRs, and that because of the very short period a borrower is given to repay, "the biweekly interest obligation can lead to permanent cash annuity for the lender."[61]

Some contend that it is difficult for many payday customers to evaluate the true cost of their borrowing. Mann and Hawkins (2006) discuss cognitive failures and behavioral considerations that can explain observed behavior.[62] They note that it is not all that easy to compare the price of alternatives, since to do so customers will have to estimate a variety of costs. Moreover they argue, "There is every reason to think that typical decision making problems. . . . and the optimism bias will cause the consumer to give inadequate weight to the risks that the transaction will turn out poorly."[63] In other words, going into the transaction, a borrower finds it hard to process future outcomes and costs and finds it easy to discount the future relative to the immediate benefit of getting cash. Ex post, when faced with the prospect of coming up with full payment of the loan and fee in two weeks or paying an additional fee to extend the loan, many cash-constrained individuals understandably end up renewing their loans.

Industry critics contend that whereas payday lenders claim that the product is intended for occasional use, the industry in fact makes its money by exploiting the behavior that encourages frequent use. For example, Skillern (2002) argues that "the short-term of the loan is used as a mechanism to increases repeat transactions, since borrowers often cannot repay the loan at the end of the time period."[64] Some accuse payday lenders of targeting vulnerable populations—such as military families—who can least afford the high price and have few alternatives.[65]

In response, the payday loan industry cites the growth in payday loan use as evidence of a need for the product. The industry benefits from the perception that banks are becoming more fee driven and less consumer friendly, particularly to individuals of modest means.[66] Payday lenders argue that the payday loans are intended for occasional use and can be a cheaper alternative to other costs associated with not being able to pay bills (late payment fees, bounced check or overdraft protection fees, and service disruptions). The industry also argues that the fees and terms of payday loans are justified by the fixed costs of making small, very short-term loans in convenient storefront locations and by high losses on payday loans. Finally a prominent argument for permitting payday lending is that without it, cash-strapped people will be forced to choose among worse alternatives.[67]

To evaluate these claims, researchers have turned to data collected by some state governments, surveys sponsored by the payday loan industry, and publicly available information (such as data for large payday firms and data compiled about store locations). But few states have sponsored the more detailed data collection efforts necessary to examine the determinants of customer use or industry performance, and the data collected in industry-sponsored surveys are not available to the public.[68] In 2004, a Canadian trade group representing AFS providers commissioned a study to examine the costs and profitability of firms that make payday loans in Canada.[69] To our knowledge, there has been no comparable study for the U.S. industry. In 2005, the FDIC obtained proprietary store-level data from two large monoline payday lenders, including detailed information on fees, loan volume, customer activity, costs, and revenues for a sample of 300 of each firm's stores.[70] In discussing empirical evidence about payday lending, we summarize what we have found out thus far using the data for these large monoline lenders.

Who Uses Payday Loans, How Much and Why?

More is known about who uses payday loans and how often than about the circumstances that borrowers are facing when they choose to take out payday loans. Surveys sponsored by the CFSA have tended to yield a fairly consistent profile of payday loan customers.[71] According to these surveys, payday borrowers are more likely to be women, to be younger, to have children under 18, and to rent rather than own their homes. Less has been reported about the racial and ethnic composition of payday loan customers. However, one of the industry-sponsored surveys indicated that blacks were overrepresented in the payday population.[72] Consistent with the prerequisites that payday borrowers have jobs and bank accounts, their mean income and mean level of educational attainment are neither exceptionally low nor exceptionally high. According to Cypress Research Group (2004), less than one-third (31%) of surveyed borrowers had incomes below \$25,000 (compared to 30% of U.S. households); while more than half (52%) had income in the \$25,000–\$50,000 range (compared to 29% of U.S. households).[73] Researchers using data on payday borrower characteristics collected by some states have profiled customers as being somewhat poorer. Chessin (2005) finds that individuals earning less than \$2,500 per month made up 63 percent of Colorado borrowers and that, in terms of occupation, 54 percent were laborers or office workers.[74] A critical feature of payday borrowers is their financial situation. Elliehausen and Lawrence (2001) report that of the 57 percent of respondents that held bank credit cards, only 25 percent reported that they almost always paid their balance in full (compared to 49 percent of the broader U.S. population of bank card holders); and 27 percent of their respondents had monthly debt service to income ratios of 20 percent or more (compared to 10 percent of the broader population).[75]

The available data on customer frequency of use also yield fairly consistent information. Elliehausen and Laurence (2001) find that close to half of payday advance customers reported more than 6 advances during the preceding 12 months and 23 percent had 14 or more. Iota Data Corporation (2002) reports that more than half of respondents said their most recent advance was a renewal of an existing loan. As summarized in Caskey (2005), the data collected by state governments indicate that a majority of customers have used the product more than 6 times a year and roughly a fourth had 14 or more loans during the year. Our data for large monoline firms have yielded similar evidence about customer frequency of use and loan renewals.[76] However, as Caskey (2005) quantifies, annual data will tend to understate customers' true frequency of use, since these data truncate the use by customers who were already using the product before the beginning of the year and by customers who began to use the product toward the end of the year and continued borrowing during the next year. Using data from state audits of payday lenders in Colorado, Chessin (2005) finds that the typical Colorado borrower was a 36-year-old single woman making $2,370 a month; she borrowed $300 or less nine times a year from the same payday shop; and the typical finance charge associated with this borrowing was $477.16. Moreover, since payday borrowers can take out loans from more than one store ("borrowing from Peter to pay Paul"), borrowing from a particular store will understate the overall incidence of repeated borrowing. Elliehausen and Lawrence (2001) found that 47 percent of their survey respondents had used more than one payday advance company during the previous 12 month period.

By construction, more frequent users will account for a disproportionate share of payday loan activity over any given period of time. As Skillern (2002) reports for North Carolina, roughly half of borrowers had more than 6 payday loans per year, but these borrowers accounted for more than 80 percent of total loans advanced, and 22 percent of borrowers had more than 12 loans in the year—but these borrowers accounted for more than half of the loans made by the industry. Using the data for Colorado, Chessin (2005) finds that payday customers who borrow 12 or more times a year constituted a third of payday loan borrowers, but these customers accounted for 65 percent of total loan volume.[77]

As to why a payday loan is chosen, most respondents to industry-sponsored surveys report convenience of use as the main reason. But these survey questionnaires are not designed to get at the more fundamental issues of whether the funds were used in a cost-effective manner and whether the nature of the expense justified the high price.[78] The lack of good information about the financial situation that borrowers face and about the nature of the expenses that cause people to take out payday loans is a critical limitation to having a meaningful payday loan debate. Although the industry argues that people take out payday loans in emergencies; its advertisements tend to market the loans as an easy source of quick cash. And although anecdotal stories abound that illustrate how people started using payday loans, there is little systematic information about payday customers' financial situations and behavioral choices.

Another limitation of the available evidence about payday loan use is its focus on univariate statistics (customer profiles) rather than on multivariate analysis that relate how use is related to customer characteristics. One exception is Stegmen and Faris (2003), who used the detailed data from the 2001 North Carolina Financial

Services Survey of low-income households to analyze the likelihood of using payday loans and the frequency of use. Controlling for other factors, they find that blacks were more likely to borrow than whites; people with less than a high school education were less likely to borrow than people with more education; and older people were less likely to borrow than younger individuals.[79]

Store Location Choice

A less direct way of examining who uses payday loans is to look at where firms choose to locate their stores. As with many retail businesses, store location is important to payday lenders.[80] Given the short-term, high-frequency nature of the business, choosing store locations to maximize customer traffic is an obvious consideration for payday lenders (much as it is for fast food restaurants). Graves (2003) cites industry analysis indicating that store locations tend to be chosen to serve specific geographic neighborhoods, but also observes that stores often tend to cluster in a given commercial corridor "similar to automobile dealerships or furniture stores." This pattern would allow a borrower to pay off one payday loan by taking out another from a different store.[81]

Given payday lending's roots in the check-cashing business, one would expect that in the industry's early years, stores would have tended to be located in lower-income urban areas. Check cashers tend to be used by poorer individuals, who do not have bank accounts or who operate in "cash economies" (neighborhoods where personal checks or other means of payment are less accepted than cash).[82] But having a job and a bank account are prerequisites for obtaining payday loans; thus payday lenders will tend to serve a somewhat different clientele than check cashers. Over time, one would expect to observe store growth occurring in moderate- and middle-income neighborhoods where people have jobs but may not have high enough incomes to build a cushion of precautionary savings for unexpected expenses. We have not found research that has studied geographic patterns in payday store growth over time, but anecdotal stories report store growth in suburban areas. Our store-level data for the two monoline lenders indicate that a disproportionate share of newer stores were located in rural areas.[83]

Researchers have compared the locations of payday stores with those of bank branches to explore conjectures that payday lenders serve markets that are underserved by banks. Graves (2003) concludes that in Chicago and New Orleans, payday lenders tended to be located in poorer neighborhoods and in neighborhoods having larger minority populations than bank branches. Using data for Colorado, DeYoung and Phillips (2006) find that the presence of more commercial bank branches was associated with higher, not lower, payday loan prices; a finding they interpret as suggesting that bank branches are a complement to payday loan stores (borrowers must have a bank account). Neither result is inconsistent with conjectures that banks do not tend to provide small, short-term loans to financially strapped individuals.

Researchers have also used data on store locations to examine conjectures that payday lenders target certain populations. The evidence of these studies suggests that payday lenders tend to locate in poorer areas with higher minority populations and that they tend to be disproportionately represented near military bases.

Tempkin and Sawyer (2002) report finding "definitive evidence that alternative financial services are disproportionately located in minority and poor neighborhoods."[84] King et al. (2005) find that payday stores in North Carolina are disproportionately located in black neighborhoods, controlling for neighborhood income and other neighborhood characteristics. Graves and Peterson (2005) document the high density of payday lenders around military bases, and Oron (2005) reports evidence about the concentration of payday lenders in black neighborhoods and near military bases in the state of Washington.

Because we have data for only two firms, we are not able to conduct a geographic analysis of payday lender locations in specific geographic markets. However, we have examined the types of neighborhoods where each of our two multistate monoline firms has chosen to locate stores in the metropolitan areas where they operate.[85] In terms of neighborhood characteristics (measured relative to those of the broader metro area), we found that stores were more likely to be located in neighborhoods having lower rates of homeownership, lower median housing values, more elderly people, and more single-headed households with children. Stores tended to be located in neighborhoods where the population was moderately educated (not very low or very high educational attainment) and that tended to be moderate or middle (as opposed to low or upper) income.[86] Regarding market characteristics, we found that our firms tended to locate more stores in metropolitan areas that had lower median income or larger populations.

The Payday Loan Product

Although the traditional payday loan product tends to have fees in the $15–$20 range and a maturity of around 14–16 days, relatively little is known about the dynamics of payday loan markets in determining these contract features. Loan terms do reflect the enabling legislation that has helped to shape the industry, but as noted earlier, state legislation has tended to legalize established payday loan contract features. An obvious question is why there does not appear to be much price competition in payday loan markets, particularly if the business is so profitable. DeYoung and Phillips (2006) examined the dynamics of payday loan pricing in Colorado between 2000 and 2005 and found that payday loan fees gravitated toward the fee limit set by enabling legislation in 2000. They interpret this as evidence of focal point pricing, where firms use the legally established fee limit as the focal point in setting prices and then compete on other margins.[87] In Flannery and Samolyk (2005), we reported pricing patterns for two monoline lenders that are consistent with focal point pricing; stores by and large charged the maximum fee allowed in the states where they were located. Empirical evidence described later helps to explain this phenomenon; we find that within the range of payday loan fees charged by our two large monoline lenders, store profits varied dollar for dollar with the fee charged.

Payday Lender Costs and Profitability

Although financial data have become available for large publicly traded payday loan firms, there are too few publicly traded firms to statistically analyze the determinants of payday lender performance. Ernst and Young (2004) examined the cost structure of the Canadian payday loan industry, using data collected in a voluntary survey of 19 firms.[88] This study suggests significant economies of scale at the firm level, reporting higher unit costs for smaller payday lending firms. More controversially, Ernst and Young (2004) report notably higher costs associated with first-time customers compared with repeat customers. This study estimates that the "costs associated with serving new customers accounted for over 85 percent of the total costs across the industry" even though on average "payday lenders provide 15 repeat or rollover loans for each first-time loan they provide."[89]

Stegman and Faris (2003) used firm-level data collected by the Office of the Commissioner of Banks in North Carolina to study the profitability of licensed payday lenders operating in North Carolina in 2000. They used cross-sectional regressions to examine how profitability is related to firm size (measured by the firm's number of stores) and average store activity (including the number of customers per store, and the share of customer that borrowed at least monthly). Their results indicate that profits per store were positively related to the number of stores controlled by a firm, a result suggesting scale economies at the firm level. They also find that both the number of customers and the percentage of customers who borrowed as least monthly were positive and significantly related to profit per store. They interpret the relationship of frequent borrowers to profits as evidence that "the financial performance of the payday loan industry, at least in North Carolina, is significantly enhanced by the successful conversion of more and more occasional users into chronic borrowers" (p. 8). Although it may be true that repeat customers are more profitable, one would expect both the number of borrowers and borrower frequency of use to be positively related to profits since they are positively related to a firm's overall loan activity.

Because of the nature of the information we obtained from our monoline lenders, the primary focus of our research has been to study the costs and profitability associated with operating payday loan storefronts. In Flannery and Samolyk (2007), our focus was on understanding the importance of scale for payday store performance and on quantifying the magnitude of scale economies associated with providing payday loans at the store level. We emphasized that store age is an important determinant of store performance.[90] Loan volume increases with store age, while operating costs remain relatively fixed; costs on a per-loan basis are lower and profits per loan are higher for older stores. Thus, although some may try to cite a single point estimate of the dollar costs of making a payday loan, our research shows that unit costs vary substantially with loan output and, therefore, costs cannot be considered independent of the scale of a store's operations. Summary statistics for mature stores (stores that have operated for more than four years) suggest that they are quite profitable (see table 11.2). The typical mature store made around 8,800 loans and served 1,100 customers. Losses accounted for 21 percent of store expenses but only $6 per loan—and well below the mean fee per loan of $44 (the average loan amount was $228). Even after netting out sizable general and administrative expenses incurred at the firm level, we found that the average profit per loan for a typical mature store was around $11.[91] The average cost of originating payday loans for these stores largely reflect the relatively fixed

Table 11.2 Age profile of store performance data for monoline payday loan stores (annual store data from two monoline payday lending firms for 2002–2004)

	New Stores (In Operation Less than One Year)	*Young Stores (In Operation for One to Four Years)*	*Mature Stores (In Operation for More than Four Years)*
Selected performance data (sample means)			
1. Years in operations	0.4	2.3	6.1
2. $ Fee per $100 Borrowed	14.32	16.77	18.30
3. Average loan size ($)	255.33	257.72	227.54
4. Total advances (number)	960	5,668	8,743
5. Total advances (dollars)	254,034	1,532,979	2,059,654
6. # Customers	237	787	1113
7. Total revenues	33,870	252,918	348,950
8. Total operating costs	72,384	177,298	193,605
9. Store operating income	−38,514	75,620	155,345
10. General and administrative expenses	52,825	55,626	50,890
11. Interest expenses	1,521	2,294	2,536
12. FTE employees (number)	1.86	2.35	2.67
Costs and revenues on a per loan basis (sample means)			
13. Total revenues	32.99	45.94	43.82
14. Total operating costs	144.44	36.10	25.10
15. Wages and salaries	37.13	12.48	9.56
16. Rent, maintenance, utilities, local taxes	31.81	6.94	4.38
17. Advertising	20.19	1.88	1.43
18. Loan losses	7.54	8.88	5.72
19. Late loan collection expenses	0.16	0.29	0.30
20. Other store expenses NEC	47.60	5.64	3.71
21. Store operating income	−111.45	9.84	18.73
22. General and administrative expenses	204.87	12.36	7.12
23. Interest expenses	5.00	0.48	0.35
24. Store profits: operating income less G & A and interest expenses	−321.32	−3.01	11.26

Source: Flannery and Samolyk (2005).

costs of operating the storefront and the sizeable general and administrative expenses associated with running the firm. Funding costs for these small loans on a per-loan basis are obviously negligible.

We also estimated straightforward cost and profit functions to explore how changes in the volume of lending were related to changes in operating costs, loan losses, and store profits. Our results indicated significant cost economies associated with extending more credit (making more loans or larger loans), which translated into greater store profits. However, we also found that repeat business (serving fewer customers for a given loan volume) was associated with lower operating costs and lower default losses; and for young stores, more repeat business translated into greater profitability.[92] We interpret our findings to indicate substantial scale economics at the store level, which are consistent with a business model driven by high volume to generate fee income. However, the fact that repeat business lowers costs and lowers losses is important; lenders need to be repaid and repeat customers are paying customers.

Because loan activity is the key driver of payday store performance, we have also used our payday store data to study how neighborhood characteristics are related to a store's overall volume of loan activity and the frequency of customer use.[93] Preliminary results indicate that overall loan activity for urban stores was inversely related to homeownership rates and to the shares of the neighborhood population having very low education or very high educational attainment. The overall volume of store lending was also positively related to the neighborhood's population. With regard to frequency of customer use, we found fewer relationships to neighborhood demographics, but more evidence of an inverse relationship to income.

Alternatives to the Current Payday Loan Product

The growth and profitability of the payday lending industry raises the question of why mainstream lenders are not offering alternatives to payday lending. Numerous researchers have argued that many banks in fact do offer an alternative in the form of fee-based overdraft protection programs that cover NSF transactions up to several hundred dollars for fees in the \$20–\$35 range per transaction.[94] One can construct scenarios where a payday loan is cheaper than the per-item fees that would accrue with several overdraft transactions; but the converse is also true.

Mann and Hawkins (2006) argue that payday loans have an advantage relative to fee-based overdraft protection programs in that the transaction is relatively straightforward, "with a price that is simple for customers to understand. The overdraft product, by contrast, is much harder for customers to price, if only because it so often will be difficult for them to predict when they are issuing checks that will bounce." They believe that banks will not offer payday-type loans unless they are permitted to charge sufficiently high rates and contend that low-rate programs having APRs in the 12–20 percent range are generally not profitable. Hence a critical obstacle to providing payday loan alternative appears to be the "stigma" of making such high-priced loans.

Still, the profitability of extending short-term credit to cash-strapped customers and the interest of depository institutions in doing so is unclear. Bair (2005) discusses several business models that banks might use to profitably offer alternatives to payday loans. She argues that depository institutions have the prerequisite infrastructure and are better positioned to mitigate losses (by virtue of preexisting deposit relationships—particularly automatic deductions for repayment) than nonbank payday lenders. Bair also notes that banks have the product diversification to offer small-denomination loans at lower costs, but acknowledges that the profitability of fee-based overdraft protection may deter banks from offering alternatives to payday-type loans.

While banks are making some moves into the area, credit unions currently appear to be doing more than banks to provide alternatives to payday loans.[95] A program implemented by the North Carolina State Employees' Credit Union is a widely cited model of an alternative to payday loans. The program includes a short-term loan (up $500) having an APR of 12 percent, which requires borrowers to repay via direct deposit of their paychecks. Another feature of the program is that customers must put 5 percent of loan proceeds in a savings account. Some state governments are working with lenders to develop alternatives to payday loans and some efforts may involve subsidizing loans by covering some losses.[96] Although Mann and Hawkins (2006) seem to believe that these types of programs generally will not be profitable, clearly more research is needed to assess what works and what does not.

Some believe that the best way to promote a better alternative to payday lending in its current incarnation is by effecting change within the payday loan industry itself. Mann and Hawkins (2006) view greater participation by large payday lending firms as a means of reducing abuses, since large firms "have much more to lose from noncompliance" with state laws and regulations.[97]

Conclusion

The AFS sector represents a rapidly growing provider of financial services to people of modest means or having impaired credit histories. The evolution of credit and transaction technologies has clearly affected the provision of financial services to low- and moderate-income individuals. But there are differing views on how. Some argue that the post-World War II world of intermediation through mainstream institutions is evolving to mirror an "increasingly bifurcated economy" in which there are a "diminishing number of traditional financial services options for the un- and underbanked consumer."[98] Others view the emergence of the AFS sector as broadening access to financial services. In either scenario, an important issue for financially vulnerable people is the cost of access to financial services.

Payday lending, considered to be the fastest growing segment of the AFS sector, provides relatively high-cost loans to customers who tend to use the product more than six times a year. But although the growing use of payday loans is cited as evidence of the need for the product, we would argue that there is too little information about why people take out payday loans to evaluate their use. Evidence about the profitability and costs of the business model suggests incentives to solicit and encourage repeat business: This contrasts with the industry's claim that the loans are intended for infrequent use. Renewing customers are paying customers, as evidenced by the small share of payday loans that are not repaid and the effects of limits on customer use on loan loss rates. Thus, the payday loan represents an example of a credit transaction that may be more profitable when someone has little chance of paying off the loan as stipulated (i.e., in two weeks). The incentives to encourage customer use would seem to be particularly strong for monoline lenders that have no other product to offer customers. Although this assessment may seem provocative, it is mirrored by industry analysts who discuss the importance of repeat business for industry profits.[99] In the meantime, it will be interesting to observe the success of recent legislation to constrain excessive use and the effects of more occasional use on the industry's viability. Large firms are viewed as having the scale economies and profit margins to remain profitable in the face of tighter limits on fees and customer use. But payday firms also seem to be adept at finding ways around regulatory limits that encroach on their profitability.

Prospects for depository institutions to provide alternatives to payday loans are uncertain. One advantage that depository institutions have over payday lenders is that banks offer a wide array of services and thus could offer payday-type loans an ancillary product, with less dependence on income generated by frequent use. Another advantage is the potential for banks to help customers transition into cheaper, more mainstream credit products and savings vehicles that allow customers to build a financial buffer. Whether these potential advantages can be translated into a reality represents a challenge for policy makers.

Notes

The views stated here are those of the author and do not reflect those of the FDIC or its Board. However, I want to thank the FDIC and its Board for supporting unbiased research about a controversial topic. I also want to thank J. Aislinn Bohren for her excellent assistance with the payday loan research summarized here, which I conducted with Mark Flannery. Any errors in this paper are my own.

1. See Caskey (2003, 2005) for more detailed descriptions of payday loan practices.
2. Caskey (2005) presents a thorough discussion of loss mitigation strategies in the payday lending industry.
3. Barr (2004); Caskey (2005).
4. Roth Capital Partners, LLC (2006), p. 2. Also see various publications from the Center for Financial Services Innovation at www.cfsinnovation.com.
5. See Stephens Inc. (2007) and Snarr (2002).
6. Mainstream services, such as fee-based overdraft protection coverage, can translate into very high APRs.
7. See Caskey (2005) for a summary.
8. For example, see Skillern (2002) and Stegman and Faris (2003).
9. This point is well understood in the extensive literature that analyzes small business lending going back at least as far as Benston (1963).
10. For shorter-term loans, the effective APRs become higher.
11. Caskey (2005) refers to nonbank storefront as the "traditional" model.
12. Caldor (1999: 17).
13. Caldor (1999: 19).
14. Caldor (1999: 133).

15. For a discussion, see Elliehausen and Lawrence (2001).
16. Caldor (1999: 133).
17. For a discussion, see Caskey (1997) and Caskey (2005).
18. Mann and Hawkins (2006) present an interesting description of how the practice developed as described by an industry participant. See also Fox (1998) and Chessin (2005).
19. Fox (1998: 2).
20. Fox (1998: 2). Also see the Baterate.com article, "Officials Call Payday Financing Loan Sharking" by *Stephen Rothman*.
21. According to Caskey (2005), in 30 states there are currently no limits on the fees that check-cashing offices (CCOs) can charge.
22. Fox (1998) provides a summary of the state regulations that governed payday lending in 1998.
23. For example, see Dove Consulting (2000).
24. See Snarr (2002).
25. Caskey (2005) and others discuss these data.
26. For example, see the Securities and Exchange Commission (SEC) 10-Q report for Advance America Cash Advance Centers, Inc. for the quarterly period ended June 30, 2006; pp. 43–46.
27. See http://www.fisca.org/history.htm.
28. The SEC Form S-1 Registration Statement for the initial public offering of stock for both firms is available at www.sec.gov/Archives/edgar/data/.
29. For example, CompuCredit, a publicly traded subprime lender, entered the payday lending business by acquiring three companies (over 500 stores) in 2005.
30. Fox (1998); Mann and Hawkins (2006); and others discuss these partnerships. Business details of the arrangements involving publicly traded payday lenders are discussed in financial reports submitted to the SEC.
31. Fox et al. (2001) summarizes objections raised by consumer advocates.
32. According to Mann and Hawkins (2006), Wells Fargo has provided funding for Advance America and Cash America, JPMorgan Chase has provided funds for Cash America and for ACE Cash Express, and Bank of America and Wachovia have provided a syndicated credit line to Advance America. Also, JPMorgan and Bank of America both own more than 1 percent of Cash America.
33. See, e.g., Elliehausen and Laurence (2001) and Caskey (2002). According to the check-cashing industry's own description of its history, "The growth of the industry was stimulated, in part, by the passage of the Bank Deregulation Act of 1980, which removed deposit rate ceilings and led to explicit pricing for bank deposit services." http://www.fisca.org/history.htm (viewed October 2006).
34. According to Advance America's 2004 S-1 filing with the SEC,

    The payday cash advance services industry has grown steadily since the early 1990s in response to a shortage of available short-term consumer credit alternatives from traditional banking institutions. The rapid increase in the charges associated with having insufficient funds in one's bank account, as well as other late/penalty fees charged by financial institutions and merchants, have also helped increase customer demand for payday cash advances. . . . We believe many banks and other traditional financial institutions have reduced or eliminated their provision of small-denomination, short-term consumer loans, in part due to the costs associated with originating these loans. Advance America form S-1 Registration Statement under the Securities Act of 1933 as filed August 13, 2004; p. 5, available at http://yahoo.brand.edgar-online.com

35. For example, see Roth Capital Partners, LLC (2006).
36. Mann and Hawkins (2006) discuss payday lending in these countries.
37. In 2000, the Federal Reserve decided that payday lenders, even though not considered banks under state laws, are subject to the Truth in Lending Act, enforced under Regulation Z. Lenders are, therefore, required to fully disclose all costs and details of loans to customers, including what fees amount to as annual percentage rates (Mahon 2004).
38. The Talent-Nelson amendment to the John Warner National Defense Authorization Act for Fiscal Year 2007.
39. For example, state fee limits have tended to establish fees in the \$15–\$20 range per \$100 borrowed. Elliehausen and Lawrence (2001); Fox and Mierzwinski (2000, 2001); and Mann and Hawkins (2006) summarize regulations affecting payday lending.
40. According to Mann and Hawkins (2006), the CFSA "has supported a model bill in numerous state legislatures in recent years and has had noted success in obtaining adoption: the CFSA Web site claims adoption in 25 states" (p. 24). Also see Chessin (2005).
41. By 2003, the Office of the Comptroller of the Currency and the Office of Thrift Supervision (OTS) had decided that the risks associated with bank-payday lender partnership were unacceptable and called on federally chartered institutions to end the practice (Mahon 2004). In early 2005, the FDIC issued revised guidance encouraging banks to limit loans to customers who had been using the payday loan product for more than three of the previous twelve months. By early 2006, FDIC-supervised banks had discontinued their partnerships with payday lenders.
42. See Harnick (2006).
43. For example, in September 2006, the Pennsylvania Department of Banking filed suit against Advance America to prohibit Advance America from selling people what the payday firm calls a "choice line of credit." This product allows people to borrow up to \$500 at an annual interest rate of 5.98 percent plus a monthly "participation fee" of \$150 (Advance America, Cash Advance Centers, Inc., SEC Form 10-Q filing for the three months and nine months ended September 30, 2006: 24.). Also see "State Files Suit Against Payday Lender," by Patricia Sabatini, *Pittsburgh Post-Gazette*, October 28, 2006.
44. Before the end of bank-model lending, payday lenders developed an alternative installment loan product, which was a three-month loan with fees that translated into APRs in the range of 200–300 percent. For examples, see the annual reports for 2005 submitted to the SEC by CompuCredit and Advance America. The installment loan product constrains a borrower to pay a high APR for three months, rather than for just two weeks.
45. Form 10-Q filing submitted by Advance America to the SEC on November 9, 2006, p. 44.
46. According to Jefferies and Company Inc. (2006), a database system (where lenders enter their account information to permit the monitoring of a customer's overall borrowing over some period of time) typically leads to lower loan volumes over time and a spike in near-term credit losses.
47. Quoted from the New Mexico state government website *www.rld.state.nm.us* (viewed December 2006).
48. Kirchhoff (2006).
49. The authors of the report acknowledge that this is a crude proxy for saturation.
50. For discussions of licensing considerations, see Mann and Hawkins (2006) and Graves and Peterson (2005).

51. See Mann and Hawkins (2006) for a discussion. Analogous behavior is observed in the banking industry, where large institutions have expanded by acquiring community banks (sometime denovo banks) that have identified a local lending niche.
52. See Jeffries and Company Inc. (2006).
53. Stephens Inc. (2007).
54. Stephens Inc. (2006).
55. See Morgan Keegan and Co., Inc. (2006).
56. Mann and Hawkins (2006); see note 49.
57. For example, see Fox et al. (2005) and Mann and Hawkins (2006).
58. For example, in 2006 Quik Pay of Utah settled with the attorney general of Colorado for violating Colorado payday lending statues.
59. Wells Fargo offers a "Direct Deposit Advance" in $20 increments to accounts in good standing that qualify by having recurring electronic deposits of $100 or more from an employer or outside agency. The finance charge is $2 for every $20 borrowed or 10 percent of the funds advance. Advance and finance charges are supposed to be repaid by an incoming direct deposit within 35 days. U.S. Bank also offers similar payday-type advances to direct depositors. These products are offered if permitted by state laws where a customer resides.
60. For example, see Bair (2005); Caskey (2002).
61. Mann and Hawkins (2006), Abstract.
62. These types of decisions are receiving increased attention from behavioral economists who study intertemporal behavior—particularly financial decisions.
63. Mann and Hawkins (2006), pp 34–35.
64. Skillern (2002), p. 7.
65. For example, see Graves and Peterson (2005) and King et al. (2005).
66. For example, see Graves (2003) and Mann and Hawkins (2006).
67. Mann and Hawkins (2006) discuss this point extensively.
68. Stegman and Faris (2003) discuss data collected for the North Carolina Commissioner and Caskey (2005) discusses data collected by the State of Wisconsin.
69. The Canadian payday store data are proprietary.
70. See Flannery and Samolyk (2005, 2007) for more information.
71. Elliehausen and Laurence (2001); Iota (2002); and Cypress Research Group (2004).
72. See Cypress Research Group (2004). Using data for lower income households, Stegman and Faris (2003) found that in North Carolina, blacks were more likely to be payday borrowers; but Hispanics were not.
73. The remaining 17% of respondents had incomes of $50,000 or more (compared to 41 % of U.S. households).
74. Also see Caskey (2005), who discusses data collected from payday stores by the State of Wisconsin.
75. Also see Iota Data Corporation (2002).
76. Flannery and Samolyk (2005).
77. Note that the Colorado data included information on how many loans a customer had taken out during the previous 12 months.
78. Cypress Research group (2004) does include a question about the reason for payday loan use.
79. The authors did not expect to find a significant relationship between income and payday loan use because they are using data from a survey of low-income households, thus there is less variation in income for the sample compared to the broader population.

80. For example, Advance America stated in its 2005 Annual Report to the SEC: "We believe that the principal competitive factors in the payday cash advance services industry are location, customer service, convenience, speed and confidentiality" Advance American (2006), p. 12. http://yahoo.brand.edgar-online.com/.
81. Using the data for Colorado, Chessin (2005) found that customers do get around renewal limits by switching between different lenders, using the funds from one to pay off another.
82. For a discussion of the unbanked, see Caskey (1997).
83. Because we have information on the age and zip code location of the stores in our sample, we plan to use these data to study expansion patterns for our two firms.
84. Tempkin and Sawyer (2002), p. 3.
85. We identified all of the metropolitan statistical areas (MSAs) where a firm had a presence (i.e., operates any stores) and compared the economic and demographic characteristics of the zip codes where the firm operates stores with the characteristics of zip codes where it did not (Flannery and Samolyk 2006).
86. We also find that stores tended to be located in relatively more populated zip codes. These factors may reflect zoning requirements in locations where retail stores generally operate. Graves (2003) discusses this issue. We consider these results preliminary and plan to do more research examining store location choice.
87. They also discuss evidence suggesting exploitative relationship pricing; prices were lower for initial loans than for refinanced loans, particularly when there was less local competition.
88. As noted earlier, this study was commission by the trade-group equivalent of the Community Financial Services Association (CFSA) for the payday loan industry in Canada.
89. See Ernst and Young (2004), p. 34 and p. 36.
90. Store expansion rates are viewed by analysts as a major factor affecting a firm's performance since new stores tend to generate higher losses.
91. This measure of profit per loan is net of all expenses except income taxes paid by the firm.
92. We find strong effects of loan volume and loan size on profits. However for young stores, serving more customers (for a given loan volume) actually lowers profits.
93. We examined how loan and customer activity are related to the demographic characteristics of the neighborhood where the stores are located (Flannery and Samolyk, 2006).
94. See Bair (2005) and Caskey (2005).
95. Kirchhoff (2006).
96. For example, the Pennsylvania State Treasury Department has been working with the Pennsylvania Credit Union Association to develop a short-term loan program as a lower-cost alternative to payday loans.
97. Mann and Hawkins (2006), p. 69. Some industry analysts believe that smaller payday lenders are more reliant on repeat business to cover their costs and hence are more likely to target vulnerable borrowers such as the military (see, e.g., Morgan Keegan and Co., Inc., 2006).
98. Roth Capital Partners, LLC (2006), p. 2.
99. For example, see Roth Capital Partners, LLC (2006) and Jefferies and Company Inc. (2006).

References

Bair, Sheila. 2005. "Low-Cost Payday Loans: Opportunities and Obstacles." Anne Casey Foundation. June 2005 at www.aecf.org.

Barr, Michael S. 2004. "Banking the Poor." *Yale Journal on Regulation*. 21: 121–237.

Benston, George. 1964. "Commercial Bank Discrimination Against Small Loans: An Empirical Study." *Journal of Finance* 19 (4): 361–42.

Caldor, Lendol. 1999. *Financing the American Dream: A Cultural History of Consumer Credit.* Princeton, NJ: Princeton University Press.

Caskey, John P. 1997. "Lower Income Americans, Higher Cost Financial Services." Filene Research Institute and the Center for Credit Union Research, Madison, WI. (Monograph).

———. 2002. *The Economics of Payday Lending*. Filene Research Institute, Madison, WI. (Monograph).

———. 2005. "Fringe Banking and the Rise of Payday Lending. in Credit Markets for the Poor." Ed. Patrick Bolton and Howard Rosenthal. New York: Russell Sage Foundation, pp. 17–45.

Chessin, Paul. 2005. "Borrowing from Peter to Pay Paul: A Statistical Analysis of Colorado's Deferred Deposit Loan Act." *University of Denver Law Review* 83 (2): 387–423.

Cyprus Research Group. 2004. "Payday Advance Customer Satisfaction Survey." Cyprus Research Group, Shaker Heights, OH, March.

DeYoung, Robert, and Ronnie J. Phillips. 2006. "Strategic Pricing of Payday Loans: Evidence from Colorado, 2001–2006." Unpublished research paper.

Dove Consulting. 2000. "Survey of Non-Bank Financial Institutions. Final Report for the U.S. Department of the Treasury." www.treas.gov/press/releases/report3078.htm.

Elliehausen, Gregory, and Edward C. Lawrence. 2001. "Payday Advance Credit in America: An Analysis of Customer Demand." Monograph no. 35, Credit Research Center, Georgetown University.

Ernst and Young. 2004. "The Cost of Providing Payday Loans in Canada." Toronto, Ontario: Ernst and Young Tax Policy Services Group. October 2004.

Flannery, Mark, and Katherine Samolyk. 2005. "Payday Lending: Do the Costs Justify the Price?" FDIC Center for Financial Research Working Paper No. 2005–09.

———. 2006. "The Demographics of Payday Store Location and Customer Activity: Evidence for Two Large Firms." Unpublished research presented at the Networks Financial Institute (Indiana University) Financial Forum: Assessing Financial Literacy and Why It Matters. March 28, 2006.

———. 2007. "Scale Economies at Payday Loan Stores." Forthcoming in the Proceedings of the Federal Reserve Bank of Chicago's 43rd Annual Conference on Bank Structure and Competition (May 2007). Chicago, IL.

Fox, Jean Ann. 1998. "The Growth of Legal Loan Sharking: A Report on the Payday Loan Industry." Washington, DC: Consumer Federation of America, November.

———. 2004. "Unsafe and Unsound: Payday Lenders Hide behind FDIC Bank Charters to Peddle Usury." Washington, DC: Consumer Federation of America, March.

Fox, Jean Ann, and Edmund Mierzwinski. 2000. "Show Me the Money! A Survey of Payday Lenders and Review of Payday Lender Lobbying in State Legislatures." Washington DC: U.S. PIRG and Consumer Federation of America, February.

———. 2001. "Rent-A-Bank Payday Lending: How Banks Help Payday Lenders Evade State Consumer Protections." Washington, DC: Consumer Federation of America and the U.S. Public Interest Research Group, November.

Graves, Steven M. 2003. "Landscapes of Predation, Landscapes of Neglect: A Location Analysis of Payday Lenders and Banks." *The Professional Geographer* 55 (3): 312–34.

Graves, Steven M., and Christopher Peterson. 2005. "*Predatory Lending and the Military: The Law and Geography of 'Payday' Loans in Military Towns.*" University of Florida Law School, Working Paper, March.

Harnick, Ellen. 2006. "Georgia's Payday Loan Law: A Model for Preventing Predatory Payday Lending." Durham, NC: *Center for Responsible Lending* at www.responsiblelending.org.

Io Data Corporation. 2002. "Payday Advance Customer Research Cumulative State Research Report." Salt Lake City, UT: IO Data Corporation at http://www.cfsa.net/downloads/cumulative_state_research.pdf, September.

Jefferies and Company, Inc. 2006. "Recap of CFSA Payday Lending Conference." Consumer Finance Report., San Francisco, CA, March 9.

King, Uriah, Wei Li, Delvin Davis, and Keith Ernst. 2005. "Race Matters: The Concentration of Payday Lenders in African American Neighborhoods in North Carolina." Center for Responsible Lending, Durham, NC, March.

Kirchhoff, Sue. 2006. "Breaking the Cycle of the Payday Loan 'Trap.'" *USA Today*, September 20, 2006.

Mahon, Joe. 2004. "Banking on the Fringe." F*edgazette*, Federal Reserve Bank of Minneapolis, July.

Mann, Ronald, and J. Hawkins. 2006. "Just Until Payday." Berkeley Electronic Press Express Preprint Series. Draft Paper no. 1863, 2006. Released November 2006.

Morgan Keegan and Co Inc. 2006. "Payday Lending Update, Industry Note." March 6, 2006.

Oron, Assaf. 2005. "Easy Prey: Evidence for Race and Military Related Targeting in the Distribution of Pay-Day Loan Branches in Washington State." Department of Statistics, University of Washington. Unpublished research paper, June 2005.

Roth Capital Partners LLC. 2006. "Rentcash Inc." Equity Research Report, Toronto. July 19.

Skillern, Peter. 2002. "Small Loans, Big Bucks: An Analysis of the Payday Lending Industry in North Carolina." Durham, NC: Community Reinvestment Association of North Carolina.

Snarr, Robert W., Jr. 2002. "No Cash 'til Payday: The Payday Lending Industry." *Compliance Corner*, First Quarter, Federal Reserve Bank of Philadelphia.

Stegman, Michael A., and Robert Faris. 2003. "Payday Lending: A Business Model That Encourages Chronic Borrowing." *Economic Development Quarterly* (February) 17 (1): 8–32.

Stephens Inc. 2000. "Industry Notes: Payday Advance—The Final Innings: Standardizing the Approach." Little Rock, AR, September 22.

———. 2006. "Consumer Finance Industry Note: Recent Payday Loan Regulatory Activities." Little Rock, AR, April 21.

———. 2007. "Industry Report: Payday Loan Industry." Little Rock, AR, March 27.

Tempkin and Sawyer. 2002. "An Analysis of Alternative Financial Services Providers." FanniMae Foundation, Washington, DC.

PART IV

HOUSEHOLD USE OF MORTGAGE DEBT

CHAPTER 12

DO RENTERS MISS THE BOAT? HOMEOWNERSHIP, RENTING, AND WEALTH ACCUMULATION

C. Tsuriel Somerville, Paulina Teller,
with Michael Farrell, Yosh Kasahara, and Li Qiang

Introduction

The promotion of homeownership is an important policy of governments around the world. A variety of researchers have identified important social benefits that can justify public subsidies to promote homeownership.[1] For individuals, homeownership plays an important role in wealth accumulation. The median U.S. household has over 50 percent of their non-pension wealth in home equity and wealth levels for owners greatly exceed those of renters at all income levels.[2] However, there remains the question whether this reflects a choice in how much to save or in not owning a home, do renters miss the great wealth accumulation boat?

In this chapter we examine two different aspects of the relationship between homeownership on wealth accumulation. First, we compare the wealth homeowners can achieve by buying a home and paying down the mortgages with what a renter could amass by investing an amount equal to the downpayment and then the difference between the periodic owner and renter costs. Second, we estimate the cost to a potential buyer of delaying the purchase of a home by one year. In both cases we also examine the sensitivity of these outcomes to contemporaneous market information. What differentiates this study from others is that it uses historical data to identify the actual wealth owners and renters could achieve.

Our outcomes are quite compelling. We find that in most of the Canadian cities we study, pretax wealth of renters could exceed that of owners and in some cases by a considerable amount. Renter wealth relative to that of owners is greatest in Edmonton, Halifax, and Montreal. However, even if they were to save 100 percent of the differences in annual payments, homeowners would still amass more wealth than renters in Calgary and Toronto. To accumulate more wealth than owners, renters must be extremely disciplined, investing nearly 80 percent of the difference between the annual costs to owners and the cost to renters in a high-yield, high-risk vehicle without significant investment management costs. This requires a savings rate of over 9 percent of their gross income, well above the average rate for North America.[3] These results highlight what is perhaps the most important benefit of homeownership for individuals, that in having to make mortgage payments, which include repayment of principal, a home buyer is essentially forced to save.

The ratio of renter to owner wealth return is extremely sensitive to how much they invest on a regular basis and in what they invest. Interestingly, the marginal effect of investing in the Toronto Stock Exchange (TSE or now TSX) instead of a risk-free savings instrument, guaranteed investment certificate (GIC), is more important than going from investing 50 percent of the difference between owner and renter costs to 100 percent. Together though, they are the two most important factors, dominating the effects of prevailing interest rates, length of ownership period, and recent house price movements in their effect on renter wealth accumulation.

The second type of analysis we perform addresses the concerns of renters in rising house price markets that if they delay too long they will miss the opportunity for homeownership. We create the hypothetical case of a potential buyer and look at their wealth after one year, comparing whether they choose to delay purchase by one year and then buy or buy immediately. On average, delaying purchase had no meaningful effect on a renter's relative wealth. However, there is a risk connected to delay. In all cities those who delayed purchase had at least a 7 percent chance (2 years out of 28 in the analysis) of gaining 10 percent or more *less* than they would have if they had purchased immediately and in 1 city an almost 11 percent chance of gaining 20 percent less.

The results of the wealth analysis come with a number of important caveats. We make a number of assumptions to simplify and standardize the analysis that favors either renters or owners in the analysis. First, our analysis is pretax and homeownership is tax favored. Second, we do not adjust the wealth calculations for annual management fees for investing in equities or costs at purchase and sale. Both of these make renting appear to be more favorable. We also assume that owners will have 15 years of ownership after the mortgage is discharged, when they can save the difference between renter and owner costs. We add the present value of these savings to owner wealth. Across all scenarios this amounts to an additional 22 percent of owner wealth. However, the fundamental result that renters must be extremely disciplined, savvy investors to match owner wealth still holds. Finally, one advantage that renters have is that they can better optimize their portfolio than can owners by investing in a variety of different asset classes. However, as we have assumed they invest in the highest-yielding asset, optimizing their portfolio will lower their average wealth relative to that of owners.

Theory and Methodology

The literature on homeownership has focused primarily on determinants of tenure choice. The number of articles that tests for effects on tenure is too vast to completely address here. Studies of the role of housing in wealth tend to focus on the difference between existing owner and renter wealth (see Belsky and Prakken 2004) without studying how this occurs. There is a developed literature on the effects of homeownership on optimal portfolio choice that tends to find that households hold far too much in housing wealth.[4] One of the more recent approaches taken in the literature is to take owner-occupied real estate place as a given and see how it affects the choice of other elements of the portfolio (Flavin and Yamashita 2002). The most comparable work to ours is Hochguertel and van Soest (2001), who look at the joint investment decision for financial wealth and home equity. They find that tenure choice affects the level of financial wealth. In contrast to our work, they rely on cross-sectional analysis of fixed wealth positions; whereas the analysis we present here traces out the possible wealth accumulation path. This is the difference between observed choices and possible choices.

Our analytical approach is to measure how wealth would actually have grown for owners and renters between 1979 and 2006 in nine different Canadian metropolitan areas. Homeowners acquire home equity as they pay down their mortgages and house prices change. Renters take the money they would have used for a downpayment and invest it.[5] Each year we compare total owner's unique costs (mortgage, insurance, maintenance, and lawn care, and snow removal) with a renter's unique total costs (rent and renter's insurance).[6] The renter invests this difference when renter costs are less and the homeowner invests when the reverse holds.

We start the analysis in 1979 and look at wealth after 25 years, when the mortgage is fully amortized. After 1981, we compare wealth positions in 2006. We do this for starting years through 1996. In the analysis we limit the possible sources of variation for renters as follows: how much of the annual difference in costs renters invest (50 vs. 100 percent) and the choice of investment (higher-yielding equities—receiving the total return of the TSE—or zero-risk, low-yield GICs). For owners, we allow them to take a mortgage where the interest is fixed for one year or five years; the latter is the most common choice in Canada.[7] We assume no one moves during the analysis, and so impose a 10 percent downpayment along with the associated mortgage insurance costs.

To look at the benefits of delaying a purchase one year, we follow a similar methodology. The difference is that the wealth is evaluated after one year. For the renters, we reduce their wealth after the one-year delay by the present value of the last year of mortgage payments. For simplicity, we discount the payment they would make in the first year for 25 years using the prevailing mortgage rate.

In the United States, the tax code has historically favored homeownership. The tax treatment is not as favorable in Canada. First, there is no mortgage interest deduction for a principal residence. Second, local property taxes are also not deductible on the principal residence. Third, the one-time capital gains exemption for a principal residence is not limited. We choose to do the analysis pretax in part to avoid the larger set of assumptions about incomes and due to the need to address tax differences across provinces. While this biases the results in favor of renters, the extent of the bias is not as great as it would be with U.S. data, especially if we assume that renters invest in a registered retirement savings plan (RRSP), where contributions are tax deductible and earnings tax deferred until the funds are withdrawn.

We do not adjust the returns for management fees or transactions costs. While the latter are high for real estate, 1–3 percent at purchase and up to 5 percent at sale, they are amortized over holding periods from 10 to 25 years, lowering the annual return by as little as 0.3 percentage points. In contrast, typical management expenses for mutual funds are over 2 percent a year, which has a large effect on renter accumulation. However, for the renter who invest themselves, especially in using exchange-traded funds, through a discount broker, the costs would be much lower. The emergence of index mutual funds means the renters can have management expenses as low as 0.5 percent. Still, these costs are above those for the owner, so this assumption will bias our findings in favor of renters.

Leverage affects the wealth accumulation path of owners. Once the mortgage is paid off, their ability to accumulate wealth relative to renters increases tremendously because renter costs now significantly exceed owner costs. We assume that similar valued real estate is held for 40 years, allowing owners 15 years of accelerated wealth accumulation. To account for this we add to terminal owner wealth the present value of 15 years in rent that will accrue to owners from the date their mortgages are discharged.[8] Across all cities and scenarios this treatment raises average owner wealth from $300,400 to $367,750, an increase of 22 percent.

Data

For our analysis we use data from nine major Canadian cities that cover all major regions of the country. For each of Calgary, Edmonton, Halifax, Montreal, Ottawa, Regina, Toronto, Vancouver, and Winnipeg, we use annual time series from 1979 through 2006 for house prices, rents, operating costs (property taxes, maintenance, homeowner's and renter's insurance premiums), estimated mortgage payments, and investment returns. In the appendix we report on how we construct each series. For the total wealth accumulation analysis we have starting years from 1979 to 1996, so that the minimum holding period is 10 years, yielding 18 observations for each of 8 mortgage terms, percentage invested, and investment-type scenarios per city. For the year delay analysis we have analysis years 1979–2005 with two scenarios, by investment type, for each city.

For house prices we construct a series using the Royal LePage *Survey of Canadian House Prices*. These are created from a survey of member brokers by the national realtor Royal LePage for two-storey mid-market and bungalow single family units. The Royal LePage base data compares favorably to a repeat sales house price series for Vancouver and is much better than the Statistics Canada new house price series.[9] The LePage series also allow us to estimate a rent amount for the same house type, which we then index over time using the Statistics Canada CPI rental accommodation sub-index. In figures 12.1 and 12.2, we present real house price and rent series for the four most important Canadian cities. These figures highlight the volatility in house prices, the dramatic differences across cities in price paths, and the trend across all Canadian cities for falling real rents.

Figure 12.1 Real house prices

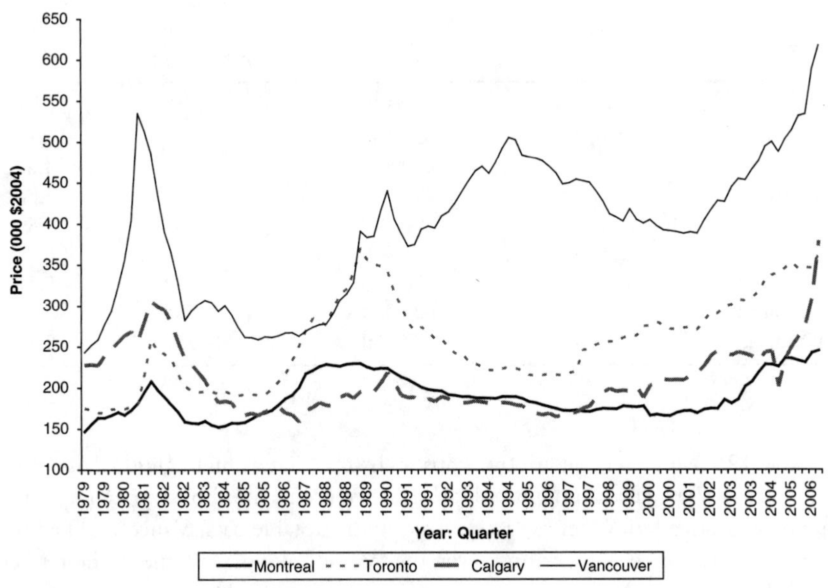

Figure 12.2 Real estimated house rents

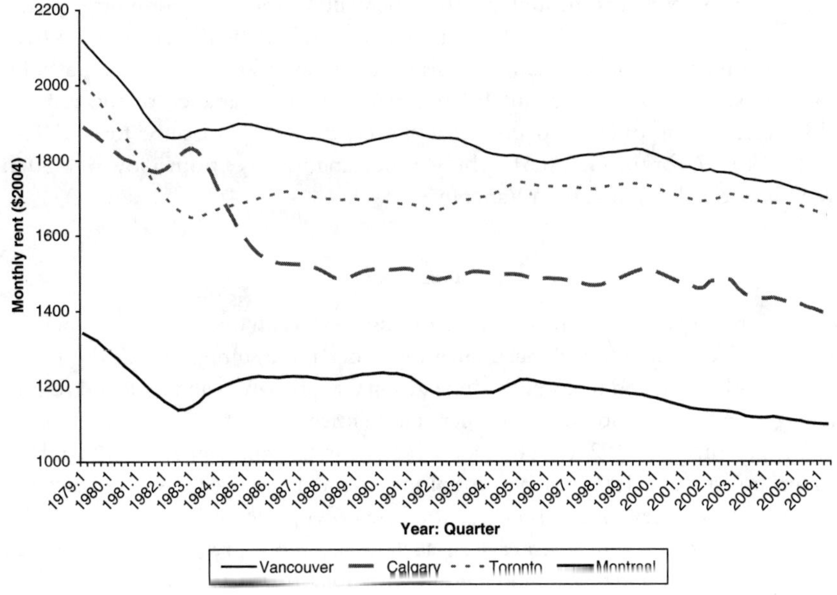

Table 12.1 Descriptive statistics

	2005 Population	*2006 House Price ($)*	*Annual House Price Appreciation (%)*	*Average Net Cap Rate (%)*
Calgary	1,060,300	395,520	5.91	6.01
Edmonton	1,016,000	325,730	4.25	4.13
Halifax	380,800	249,860	4.11	4.89
Montreal	3,635,700	228,480	5.25	4.84
Ottawa	1,148,800	294,120	5.43	4.80
Regina	199,000	181,930	4.02	6.08
Toronto	5,304,100	378,390	6.83	5.31
Vancouver	2,208,300	629,950	7.36	3.99
Winnipeg	706,900	227,170	4.75	5.49

In table 12.1 we present descriptive statistics by city. These highlight the large variation across the Canadian metropolitan areas we use in size, house price level, and net rent to price ratios (net cap rate). Among the notable data, Vancouver had the highest house price appreciation over the period, along with the highest price level. Even though Montreal is the second largest metropolitan area in Canada, its house prices are much lower than all other comparable cities. Calgary's mix of high annual price appreciation and a high average net cap rate may seem surprising, but the former is in part due to the result of extremely rapid price appreciation in 2004 through 2006 with the boom in oil prices.

The data on mortgages and the investment returns for renters are time varying but constant across cities. The average annual nominal return for the TSE investment is 13.17 percent compared with 6.86 percent for the GIC. For mortgages the average annual rate of the 1979–2006 period we study is 10.17 percent for a five-year term mortgage. The wealth analysis in this chapter is not done in a portfolio context; so we do not account for differences in the variance of the returns. However, it is instructive to note that the coefficient of variance for the TSE returns is 1.17, for the GIC 0.61, while for housing it ranges from a low of 0.50 in Winnipeg to a high of 1.46 in Vancouver.

Results

Our first results are for the ratio of renter to owner wealth over the analysis period. Table 12.2 examines wealth accumulation under the assumption that the renter invests in the TSE and receives the index capital appreciation and dividend return; averages cover scenarios where owners take either a five-year or one-year term mortgage. In table 12.2 we compare average owner and renter wealth. where renters invest either 100 or 50 percent of the annual difference between owner and renter costs and they invest 100 percent of the downpayment.

There are cities where renters can accumulate more pretax wealth than can owners. A renter in Halifax could end up with 50 percent more wealth than if she

Table 12.2 Comparing renter and owner wealth, renters invest in TSE

	Owner's Wealth ($)	*Renter's Wealth (100% Invested) ($)*	*Ratio: Renter to Owner*	*Renter's Wealth (50% Invested) ($)*	*Ratio: Renter to Owner*	*Percentage Invested for Equivalence*
Calgary	494,620	285,500	0.58	180,460	0.36	
Edmonton	345,120	493,670	1.43	288,020	0.83	63.9
Halifax	256,510	384,550	1.50	232,030	0.90	58.0
Montreal	236,570	317,560	1.34	193,740	0.82	67.3
Ottawa	318,370	338,350	1.06	208,470	0.65	92.3
Regina	209,880	247,920	1.18	154,340	0.74	79.7
Toronto	453,210	328,570	0.72	207,440	0.46	
Vancouver	644,170	651,260	1.01	394,050	0.61	98.6
Winnipeg	254,930	269,170	1.06	167,480	0.66	93.0

had purchased a house, while living in the same type of house. This requires discipline: the "Percentage Invested for Equivalence" column shows the savings rate for renters, for those cities where greater wealth is possible, that is necessary for them to approximate the wealth of owners, and on average the renter must invest 80 percent of the difference between the annual costs of renting and owning. This is analogous to savings rate of 9 percent; in comparison, the most recent Canadian savings rate was –0.4 percent.

If the renter invests both the downpayment and the annual cost savings between total renter and owner payments in a low-risk, low-return instrument, in this case the one year "Guaranteed Investment Certificate" (GIC), they cannot achieve the same wealth as homeowners. With the lower rate of return from the GIC the best they can do pretax is in Edmonton, where they can achieve 79 percent of owner wealth if they invest 100 percent of the savings.

As noted earlier, we make a number of assumptions in this analysis, which can have a substantial effect on the analysis. The most significant assumption that we make is that owners receive the present value of 15 years of the difference between estimated future renter payments and owner non-mortgage costs to reflect the period when owners have paid off their mortgage and have lower annual costs than do renters. In table 12.3 we show the effect of this assumption on the ratio of renter to owner wealth. We compare the average renter to owner wealth ratios with and without this assumption under the different investment-type and amount-saved scenarios. The assumption lowers the ratio by between 0.09 and 0.23. Without this amount, renters would still need to save approximately 67 percent of the difference between costs and invest in the TSE to achieve the same pretax wealth as owners. Even in the most favorable city for renters to accumulate wealth, Halifax, and excluding this amount, if renters invest their annual savings in a GIC they cannot match owner pretax wealth. Thus, while affecting the magnitude of the effects, this assumption does not materially change the results.

Table 12.3 Ratio of renter to owner wealth: effect of present value of future rent

	Including PV of Future Rent Savings			*Excluding PV of Future Rent Savings*		
	Average Across All Cities	*Maximum Value (Halifax)*	*Minimum Value (Calgary)*	*Average Across All Cities*	*Maximum Value (Halifax)*	*Minimum Value (Calgary)*
Invest in TSE						
Save 100%	1.10	1.50	0.56	1.33	1.78	0.69
Save 50%	0.67	0.90	0.37	0.83	1.08	0.45
Invest in GIC						
Save 100%	0.60	0.78	0.31	0.73	0.97	0.38
Save 50%	0.36	0.47	0.20	0.45	0.58	0.25

As noted in the previous section, we make a number of other assumptions to simplify and standardize the analysis. These have significant effects on the outcomes, which unlike the assumption about future owner savings; bias the results in favor of renters. To show this we use the example of Halifax with the initial purchase decision in 1979 and the most favorable scenario for renters: they invest 100 percent of their savings in the TSE and owners have a five-year mortgage, which has a renter to owner wealth ratio of 1.63. If renters must pay annual investment management expenses of 2 percent and owners must pay 5 percent commission at sale, this drops the ratio to 1.21 (if index funds were available with an expense ratio of 0.75 percent this would be 1.55). Renters unlike owners must pay capital gains; assuming they are retired and in a lower 25 percent cumulative tax bracket, this lowers the ratio to 1.03 (for the lower expenses 1.31). Posttax, whether renters can achieve wealth or not ultimately depends on their ability to be disciplined in saving 100 percent of the difference between renter and owner costs and to invest sufficiently well to achieve the TSE return, but without significant investment management expenses.[10]

Our methodology only allows renters to invest in one type of asset. For renters to achieve sufficiently high returns we require that they invest in the TSE, which on average offers a return, excluding fees, higher than for any of the housing markets, but with a standard deviation of returns that exceeds that of all cities except Calgary. An advantage that renters have over owners is that they can optimize their portfolio, so it is not so heavily weighted toward housing. In eight of the nine cities, the median optimal portfolio has 50 percent or less of an allocation to housing. The renters would be able to replicate part of this through investing in Canadian Real Estate Investment Trusts (REITs).

To test the sensitivity of the ratio of renter to owner wealth more seriously, we regress this ratio on a number of different factors for all 1,296 of the different start year-city-scenario combinations (9 cities, 8 scenarios, 18 start years). The regression

Table 12.4 Wealth accumulation determinants of the ratio of renter to owner wealth

	Reg. (1)	*Reg. (2)*	*Reg. (3)*	*Reg. (4)*	*Reg. (5)*
Invest in stocks (TSE)—dummy	0.4029\C	0.4029\C	0.4062\C	0.4064\C	0.4055\C
	(0.0169)	(0.0169)	(0.0170)	(0.0170)	(0.0170)
Mortgage has five-year term—dummy	0.1946\C	0.1946\C	0.1979\C	0.1981\C	0.1972\C
	(0.0112)	(0.0112)	(0.0111)	(0.0112)	(0.0111)
Renters invest 100% of difference between renter and owner costs—dummy	0.3214\C	0.3214\C	0.3247\C	0.3249\C	0.3240\C
	(0.0167)	(0.0167)	(0.0169)	(0.0169)	(0.0169)
Number of years of analysis		0.0353\C	0.0247\C	0.0237\C	0.0267\C
		(0.0025)	(0.0047)	(0.0053)	(0.0064)
Gross cap rate (starting year)		−0.2180\C	−0.2090\C	−0.2082\C	−0.2141\C
		(0.0130)	(0.0137)	(0.0138)	(0.0134)
House price growth rate from previous year			−0.0016	−0.0015	−0.0018
			(0.0011)	(0.0011)	(0.0011)
Mortgage rate, five year fixed (starting year)			0.0216\C	0.0261\B	
			(0.0076)	(0.0106)	
Starting year is from 1981 to 1982—dummy				−0.0368	0.1177\B
				(0.0673)	(0.0531)
Starting year is from 1991 to 1996—dummy					−0.0537
					(0.0472)
Analysis for Calgary—dummy	−0.1381	−0.0605	−0.0612	−0.0612	−0.0593
	(0.1021)	(0.0445)	(0.0434)	(0.0434)	(0.0434)
Analysis for Edmonton—dummy	0.3611\B	−0.1975\C	−0.1714\C	−0.1695\C	−0.1845\C
	(0.1469)	(0.0639)	(0.0617)	(0.0610)	(0.0621)
Analysis for Halifax—dummy	0.3839\C	0.1277\C	0.1435\C	0.1444\C	0.1376\C
	(0.1011)	(0.0439)	(0.0416)	(0.0408)	(0.0429)
Analysis for Montreal—dummy	0.3619\C	0.1556\C	0.1682\C	0.1689\C	0.1634\C
	(0.1103)	(0.0498)	(0.0480)	(0.0476)	(0.0487)
Analysis for Ottawa—dummy	0.1641\A	0.6973\C	0.6771\C	0.6753\C	0.6896\C
	(0.0956)	(0.0585)	(0.0569)	(0.0568)	(0.0569)
Analysis for Regina—dummy	0.1912\A	0.3934\C	0.3894\C	0.3887\C	0.3942\C
	(0.1112)	(0.0500)	(0.0474)	(0.0469)	(0.0487)

Continued

Table 12.4 Continued

	Reg. (1)	*Reg. (2)*	*Reg. (3)*	*Reg. (4)*	*Reg. (5)*
Analysis for Vancouver— dummy	0.1493	−0.3517\C	−0.3288\C	−0.3272\C	−0.3405\C
	(0.1098)	(0.0481)	(0.0477)	(0.0474)	(0.0474)
Analysis for Winnipeg— dummy	0.1317	0.2916\C	0.2885\C	0.2880\C	0.2923\C
	(0.1004)	(0.0455)	(0.0435)	(0.0431)	(0.0444)
Number of observations	1296	1296	1287	1287	1287
Adjusted R-sq	0.4323	0.7811	0.7916	0.7917	0.7891

Note: Standard errors are in parentheses. "A" indicates coefficient is statistically different from 0 at 10 percent level, "B" at 5 percent, and "C" at 1 percent.

results are presented in table 12.4. These regressions include dummies for each city, with Toronto as the default. The coefficients on the dummy variables are the changes in the ratio of renter to owner wealth.

Investing in the TSE over the GIC has a very large impact of approximately 40 percentage points, more important than the 32 percentage point increase from increasing the savings rate from 50 to 100 percent. The city dummies show the strong differences in returns across cities, a range of almost 100 percent from the lowest (Vancouver) to highest (Ottawa) renter wealth, and are quite sensitive to whether we control for the initial-year cap rate (regressions 2 through 5) or not (regression 1). The cap rate effect is interesting. Controlling for city fixed effects, renter wealth is higher the lower the cap rate at purchase. Recent house price movements are immaterial, but renting is comparatively better the lower the initial mortgage rate. However, the latter is relatively unimportant; a one-standard deviation increase in the five-year term fixed mortgage rate would raise the relative renter wealth by 7 percentage points (28 percentage points between the lowest and highest values).

The second part of our analysis examines the question of what does it cost renters to delay the purchase of a home for one year. In table 12.5 we present the summary results of this analysis for investing in the TSE. On average there is no benefit or cost of delay as none of the averages are statistically different from zero. It may be that the average effect is not relevant for renters who are thinking of delaying purchase, that they are more concerned with extreme losses that shut them out of the market in the future.

To test for the extremes we create dummy variables that identify the big losses or gains for delaying purchase by one year. These identify the years when the gain to renters from delay is at least 10 or 20 percent greater (*less*) than the gain to owners. These correspond to avoiding a peak or being left behind. If the main concern for renters is being left behind in a dramatic upswing, the changes are quite low; no occurrences in 4 cities and only once in the 28 years in 3 cities. However, it did occur three times in Toronto and twice in Vancouver.

Table 12.5 Effect of delaying purchase by one year (renters invest in the TSE)

			Number of Years				
City	*Renter Gain–Owner Gain ($)*	*Ratio (Renter Gain–Owner Gain) to House Price (%)*	*Renters Gain More*	*Renters Gain > than 10% of House Price*	*Renters Gain > than 20% of House Price*	*Renters Loss > than 10% of House Price*	*Renters Loss > than 20% of House Price*
Calgary	−5,450	−0.84	13	5	2	6	1
Edmonton	1,890	3.26	17	8	1	2	1
Halifax	3,000	2.82	21	2	1	2	0
Montreal	3,780	2.58	21	5	1	4	0
Ottawa	−3,860	−1.64	11	2	0	6	0
Regina	1,260	1.67	17	2	0	2	0
Toronto	1,290	0.15	14	6	2	5	3
Vancouver	220	0.02	16	6	3	6	2
Winnipeg	710	3.69	16	8	4	4	1

The figures in tables 12.5 are instructive averages, but do not highlight the sensitivity to observable factors. In table 12.6 we regress the probability of these outcomes on factors that are observable to renters at the time they decide to delay or not. We use a logit specification for the probability that renters experience a large loss, using conditional logit for those regressions with city fixed effects (dummy variables).

Table 12.6 examines the downside risk of renters delaying home purchase for one year. We look at the correlation between the probability that renters earn at least 10 percent less than owners, in regression 4 and 5 it is 20 percent less, and factors that are observable to renters at the time they decide whether to: delay their purchase or not. The higher the cap rate when renters are deciding whether to buy now or delay by a year, the greater the probability that they will experience a large loss if they delay. If prices have grown in the last year, purchasing now runs a greater chance of incurring a large loss. The mortgage rate is extremely important, with higher mortgage rates resulting in a lower probability of a loss. The effect of the past year's return on other investments is marginal.

Table 12.6 Effect of delaying purchase (probability renters gain less than owners)

Dependent Variable	*Reg. (1)* *Loss >10%*	*Reg. (2)* *Loss >10%*	*Reg. (3)* *Loss >10%*	*Reg. (4)* *Loss >20%*	*Reg. (5)* *Loss >20%*
Gross cap rate	0.3127\C	0.3149\C	0.5383\C	0.1075	0.6740\C
	(0.0818)	(0.0820)	(0.1383)	(0.1423)	(0.2452)
House price growth rate from previous year	0.1075\C	0.1081\C	0.1080\C	0.0586\C	0.0744\C
	(0.0171)	(0.0171)	(0.0179)	(0.0202)	(0.0246)
Mortgage rate	−0.3506\C	−0.3471\C	−0.4258\C	−0.1659\A	−0.3427\B
	(0.0620)	(0.0621)	(0.0764)	(0.0852)	(0.1355)
Investment return, previous year	0.0260\A	0.0221	0.0232\A	0.0476\B	0.0410
	(0.0135)	(0.0140)	(0.0138)	(0.0236)	(0.0260)
Invest in stocks (TSE)—dummy		0.2417			
		(0.3147)			
Group					
Regression type	Logit	Logit	Conditional Logit	Logit	Conditional Logit
			City Fixed Effects		City Fixed Effects
Number of observations	486	486	486	486	324
Pseudo R-sq	0.1934	0.195	0.2136	0.1015	0.1828

Note: Standard errors are in parentheses. "A" indicates coefficient is statistically different from 0 at 10 percent level, "B" at 5 percent, and "C" at 1 percent.

Conclusions

This chapter examines whether by not owning, renters miss an important opportunity for accumulating wealth. We look at the following two aspects of this question: whether this opportunity is missed over a long period, 10–25 years, and the affect on wealth caused by delaying a purchase for one year. The results are quite striking—for renters to accumulate the same amount of wealth as owners, they must be extremely diligent savers, invest in a high-yield instrument, and be fortunate to live in one of the cities where the right combination of low rents and/or low house price growth reduces the wealth that owners can accrue.

Pretax and excluding fees and transactions costs, on average renters need to save 80 percent of the savings between renter and owner costs to equalize the likely wealth over a 40-year holding period. When we change the assumptions and address some of the caveats of the results reported here the possibilities for renters become much more challenging. Even a savvy renter who can keep the transactions costs and fees for investing in equities low has very little chance of equaling the wealth of an owner after capital gains taxes are included. Our most radical assumption, which favors owners, where we add to the owner's wealth the value of the present value of the rental payments they would not have to make in the future if they continued to occupy the same home, changes the quantitative findings, but not the qualitative results.

What this analysis highlights is not that renters cannot equal owners' wealth, but rather just how important and effective homeownership is as a means of "forcing" households to save. The one advantage that renters have is that they can create a more diversified portfolio of their investments than can middle-income homeowners whose portfolios are heavily weighted to home equity. The second aspect of renter wealth accumulation that this report examines is the cost incurred by renters as a result of delaying their purchase by a year. Here the results suggest that on average renters do not lose by choosing to wait a year to purchase a unit. However, there are quite a few cities where the delay can cause the renters to experience significantly lower increase in wealth as compared to owners. The possibility of a relative loss or even a large relative loss is higher when the cap rates are high and rise with the previous year's increase in house prices.

Appendix: Data Description and Tables

House Prices—We base our estimates on Royal LePage's quarterly "Survey of Canadian House Prices."[11] We use the estimated values for the representative bungalow and standard two-storey house. For each city our estimated quarterly value is the average of the value for these two, and for price we use a weighted average (weights by number of households) across the neighborhoods and municipalities surveyed in each city. To index from the base year we use a weighted average of the quarterly growth rates to compensate for the high frequency with which survey values may be missing for an individual neighborhood or jurisdiction. We use the second-quarter values for each year as the representative value for the year.

Rents—We base our estimates on the estimated rental values for the house types and cities in Royal LePage's quarterly "Survey of Canadian House Prices" using the same approach as for prices. To index over time we use the Statistics Canada CPI Rental Accommodation series.

Property tax—Property tax data is taken from Royal LePage's "Survey of Canadian House Prices," published quarterly. Any missing tax data is extrapolated using the CPI. Property tax.

Owner's insurance—Initial levels are calculated by a phone survey of insurance rates for a typical house across the Canadian cities. We index the base-year data using the city specific Statistics Canada CPI for Homeowners' Insurance Premiums.

Renter's insurance—Initial levels are calculated by a phone survey of insurance rates for a typical house across the Canadian cities. We index the base-year data using the city specific Statistics Canada CPI for Tenant's Insurance Premiums.

Maintenance costs—Discussions with property managers for 2005 suggested that treating maintenance costs as 10 percent of rental revenues was a reasonable assumption. A phone survey of property managers across the Canadian cities produced estimates for lawn care and snow removal for a 2004 base year. These base values were then indexed using the city specific Statistics Canada All Items CPI.

Mortgage rates—Rates for five-year mortgages as listed by the Bank of Canada on the last Wednesday of June of each year.[12] We use the average rates for mortgages written by the chartered Canadian banks. The rates for one-year mortgages are calculated as this five-year rate, minus the spread between five- and one-year "listed" rates for conventional mortgages. The listed rate for conventional five-year mortgages averages 18 basis points higher than the average rate.

GIC interest rate—Average rate among chartered Canadian banks for a one-year Guaranteed Investment Certificate as posted by the Bank of Canada on the last Wednesday of June of each year.

TSE return—The sum of the average dividend yield for stocks listed on the Toronto Stock Exchange (TSE now TSX) and the percentage change in the TSE index.

Savings rate—Return on renters' security deposit. Non-checkable savings deposits rate of interest for chartered Canadian banks as posted by the Bank of Canada on the last Wednesday of June of each year.

Notes

1. See DiPasquale and Glaeser (1999); Green (2001); and Coulson, Hwang, and Imai (2003) for articles that examine the social benefits of homeownership.
2. Belsky and Prakken (2004). Canadian values are similar.
3. This assumes that in the first year of the analysis owner costs are 35 percent of income.
4. See Berkovec and Fullerton (1992) and Meyer and Wieand (1996) for endogenous housing tenure choice within the model of portfolio choice.
5. We account for a renter's half month's security deposit, on which they earn the savings rate.
6. We assume both pay for other utilities themselves and consume the same amount.
7. The vast majority of mortgages in Canada have a term of five years or less. Unless identified as an "open," prepayable mortgage, there are severe restrictions or yield

maintenance penalties on mortgage prepayment in Canada. Canadian mortgages typically have a 25-year amortization period and the interest rate is compounded semiannually.

8. To calculate this we take 2006 net rents and discount these for 15 years using the average mortgage rate over 1979–2006. This amount is further discounted to account for the date when the mortgage is actually discharged.
9. Over the period of 1979–1997 in Vancouver, the Royal LePage series and Statistics Canada New House Price Index series have correlations with a real repeat sales index of 0.95 and 0.16, respectively.
10. Effectively they must invest in exchange-traded funds through a discount or online brokerage service.
11. See http://www.royallepage.ca/CMSTemplates/GlobalNavTemplate.aspx?id=361.
12. See http://www.bankofcanada.ca/en/rates.htm.

References

Belsky, Eric and Joel Prakken. 2004. "Housing Wealth Effects: Housing's Impact on Wealth Accumulation, Wealth Distribution and Consumer Spending," Harvard University Joint Center for Housing Studies Working Paper W04-13, December.

Berkovec, James and Don Fullerton. 1992. "A General Equilibrium Model of Housing, Taxes, and Portfolio Choice." *Journal of Political Economy* 100(2): 390–429.

Coulson, N. Edward, Hwang Seok-Joon, and Susumu Imai. 2003. "The Benefits of Owner-Occupation in Neighborhoods." *Journal of Housing Research* 14(1): 21–48.

DiPasquale, Denise, and Edward L. Glaeser. 1999. "Incentives and Social Capital: Are Homeowners Better Citizens?" *Journal of Urban Economics* 45(2): 354–84.

Flavin, Marjorie, and Takashi Yamashita. 2002. "Owner Occupied Housing and the Consumption of Household Portfolio." *American Economic Review* 92(1): 345–62.

Green, Richard K. 2001. "Homeowning, Social Outcome, Tenure Choice, and U.S. Housing Policy." *Cityscape: A Journal of Policy Development and Research* 5(2): 21–29.

Hochguertel, Stefan, and Arthur van Soest. 2001. "The Relation between Financial and Housing Wealth: Evidence from Dutch Households." *Journal of Urban Economics* 49(2): 374–403.

Meyer, Richard, and Kenneth Wieand. 1996. "Risk and Return to Housing, Tenure Choice and the Value of Housing in an Asset Pricing Context." *Real Estate Economics* 24(1): 113–31.

Royal Le Page, "Survey of Canadian House Prices," quarterly, http://www.royallepage.ca/CMSTemplates/GlobalNavTemplate.aspx?id=361.

CHAPTER 13

CHOOSING BETWEEN FIXED- AND ADJUSTABLE-RATE MORTGAGES

Monica Paiella and Alberto Franco Pozzolo

Introduction

Housing is the most important asset in the portfolio of most households. It is a relatively illiquid investment, with an uncertain capital value, and it is generally highly leveraged, which makes it a potentially important channel of transmission of monetary policy. Furthermore, houses are both an asset and a consumption good.

This chapter focuses on housing finance. In recent years, in addition to the traditional fixed and adjustable rate mortgage contracts, borrowers have been given a wide variety of financing methods from which to choose. Examples include pledged savings accounts, interest-only mortgages, graduated and flexible payment mortgages, reverse annuity mortgages, renegotiable rate mortgages and numerous others. However, although there is substantial cross-country variation as to which type of mortgage contract is most common, by far the dominant two have been the standard fixed rate and the adjustable rate mortgage. In the United States, for example, most mortgage debt is at rates that are fixed for the entire duration of the contract (although prepayment options are frequent), whereas in the United Kingdom there is very little mortgage debt that is fixed for more than a few years. In the rest of Europe, despite increasing financial integration, housing credit systems have continued to be characterized by different types of contracts, with France and Germany, at one end, where over half of lending is at rates that are fixed for ten years or longer, and Finland and Portugal, at the other, where basically no loans are granted at rates that are fixed for over five years.

The specific contractual features of housing finance have important implications from a policy perspective, due to the effects that changes in interest rates may have on house price stability and on household behavior and welfare. Although there are several channels through which changes in interest rates can affect the housing market, the household sector is likely to play a key role in those countries with predominantly adjustable-rate mortgage contracts, since in this case households bear the risk of higher rates directly through their higher mortgage payments and smaller remaining income. Nevertheless, it must be said that, although a nominal fixed-rate mortgage is safe in the sense that its nominal payments are fixed, from the perspective of the borrower it is also risky because its real capital value is highly sensitive to inflation.

The purpose of this chapter is to examine the choice between the two dominant types of contract, adjustable-rate (ARMs) and fixed-rate mortgages (FRMs). The borrower's choice between mortgage contracts can be viewed as a problem in household risk management and we are interested in assessing whether households can gauge accurately their circumstances in terms of (non-mortgage-related) risk exposure and choose either an FRM or an ARM as appropriate. In this sense, our empirical setup provides a setting to test some of the predictions of Campbell and Cocco (2003), who view the choice of a mortgage contract from a normative perspective and single out the characteristics of a household that should lead it to prefer one form of mortgage over the other. In fact, in principle the relative attractiveness of a specific type of contract should depend on individual circumstances, such as the riskiness of labor income, borrowing constraints, and the probability of moving and prepaying the loan.

We conduct our empirical analysis using data on Italy, where the market for mortgages is relatively small but has been growing exceptionally fast in the past decade.[1] This makes Italy a particularly suitable setting to study housing finance. In fact, there is evidence that housing credit systems are characterized by high degrees of inertia, with the contractual features of new mortgages partly reflecting contracts and conventions established in earlier periods, when inflation, interest rate variability, and regulatory practices were very different. Contractual inertia is less likely to play a relevant role in Italian households' mortgage choice. Furthermore, the dataset that we use is representative of the whole population, whereas most of the existing studies of household mortgage choice use data that have been collected locally, or by some specific lending institution.

We find that, conditional on holding a mortgage, the ARM vs. FRM choice depends only partially on borrower characteristics. Overall, pricing variables seem to play a dominant role and the evidence suggests that in choosing the mortgage type borrowers attach a lot of weight to the initial level of repayment. Although the initial payments tend to be lower on ARMs, ceteris paribus, it seems that the premium that banks charge over their cost of funds is much higher on ARMs than on FRMs.

The rest of the chapter is organized as follows. The section that immediately follows reviews briefly the literature on the choice between FRMs and ARMs. The next one presents the data that we employ for the estimation. The succeeding section discusses the empirical setup and some empirical issues. The results are then presented and the final section concludes the chapter.

The ARM vs. FRM Choice in the Literature

The literature on the choice between FRMs and ARMs dates back at least to the first half of the 1980s, but it is still quite scant. Among the most recent theoretical contributions is Campbell and Cocco (2003), who have studied the optimal choice between ARMs and FRMs in a general framework that allows for income uncertainty, risk aversion, variability in the end-of-period value of the house, credit constraints, and FRM refinancing options. Their seminal contribution stresses that ARMs expose borrowers to income risk, while FRMs expose them to wealth risk. As such, "households with smaller houses relative to income, more stable income, lower risk aversion, more lenient treatment in bankruptcy and higher probability of moving should be the households that find ARMs more attractive."

The empirical evidence on the determinants of the choice between ARMs and FRMs is also limited. Among the most cited results are those of Dhillon et al. (1987), who estimate a standard binary choice model using a sample of about 80 borrowers from the Baton Rouge office of a national U.S. mortgage bank between January 1983 and February 1984. Their results do not match the predictions of the theoretical literature and show instead that borrower characteristics have a very weak effect on the choice between ARMs and FRMs, while price variables have a sizeable and significant role. Similar evidence is provided by Brueckner and Follain (1988), who find that the interest rate differential is the most important determinant of the choice. Besides this, they find that when market interest rates are high, borrowers tend to prefer ARMs, ceteris paribus, as if they expected some degree of mean reversion. Consistent with some of the theoretical predictions, they also report that borrowers with higher income and higher savings, and, therefore, less likely to be credit constrained in the future, have a preference for ARMs. Finally, they show that borrowers with a higher probability of moving (and prepaying the loan) have a preference for ARMs. Indeed, if the borrower knows that it will move in the near future, thus selling the home and prepaying the loan, the most appropriate contract would be the one with the lowest current interest rate.

The Data

We estimate our model using data from the Bank of Italy's Survey of Household Income and Wealth (SHIW) and consider the last five surveys covering the period 1995–2004,[2] which contain detailed and homogeneous information on housing finance. The SHIW is a representative sample of the Italian resident population. It provides detailed data on household sociodemographic characteristics, consumption, income and balance sheet items, and has plenty of information on housing tenure and finance.

After some exclusions,[3] we are left with a sample of over 28,000 observations, whose composition is reported in table 13.1. About 75 percent of households own their home and around 13 percent of homeowners have a mortgage. About half of mortgage holders have a fixed-rate loan. For the appraisal of the determinants of the choice between ARMs vs. FRMs, we focus on those mortgage holders who have purchased their home in the two years prior to the interview[4] and assume that they have obtained the loan, or recontracted the terms of an outstanding mortgage, at the time of the purchase. These households represent around 16 percent of the mortgage holders in the sample and exhibit a relatively higher share of ARM holders.

Table 13.1 Sample composition

Share of:	*1995*	*1998*	*2000*	*2002*	*2004*
Homeowners	0.718	0.751	0.762	0.767	0.753
Homeowners with home mortgage	0.173	0.120	0.118	0.117	0.143
Mortgage holders with ARM	0.462	0.547	0.533	0.512	0.538
Mortgage holders who have purchased their home in the two years before that of interview	0.114	0.189	0.175	0.119	0.153
of which: with ARM	*0.593*	*0.505*	*0.532*	*0.533*	*0.641*
Number of observations	6,078	5,346	5,844	5,606	5,579

For those mortgage holders who have purchased their home at earlier dates, there is no sufficient information to obtain reliable measures of their characteristics at the time when they acquired their home, which may have affected their financing choice (e.g., income and wealth in the years before the interview are not available).

Table 13.2 reports some summary statistics for the whole sample of households, for that of homeowners, for mortgage holders, and for several subsamples. Most of the differences in terms of socioeconomic characteristics between mortgage holders and the rest of the households in the sample are due to the fact that mortgage holders are relatively younger. So, with respect to the sample average, the head of a household with a mortgage is more likely to be a male, to be married, and is more educated. Most of the differences in terms of real asset wealth come from the fact that 25 percent of the sample consist of renters, who tend to be less wealthy than homeowners. In terms of financial wealth, mortgage holders have fewer financial assets and their liabilities are higher. The fourth column of table 13.2 reports summary statistics for the subsample of "recent" borrowers, that is, mortgage holders who have purchased their home and obtained a loan in the two years before the interview. This set, which we use for the estimation, is very similar to the sample of all borrowers.

The last two columns of table 13.2 distinguish between "recent" borrowers with an FRM and "recent" borrowers with an ARM. The head of a household with an ARM is more likely to be a male, is more educated, and is more likely to have moved away from his/her province of birth. ARM holders are wealthier, but have less financial assets. They are more likely to invest in risky assets (stocks and corporate bonds), but invest smaller amounts on average. Their liabilities are slightly higher.

Table 13.3 summarizes some characteristics of the mortgage loans held by the "recent" borrowers. ARM holders borrow larger amounts, but the differences in terms of loan-to-house value are negligible: the loan-to-value ratio is around 44 percent. Mortgage payments on ARMs are larger, but as a share of borrower's earnings, they turn out to be slightly lower (17.6 vs. 18.8 percent). The average interest rate is comparable. Under the assumption that lenders charge borrowers a rate given by the sum of their cost of funds plus a premium, this implies that

Table 13.2 Summary statistics: Household characteristics

	All	*Home-owners*	*With mortgage*	*"Recent" borrowers* *All*	*FRM*	*ARM*
Homeowners*	0.750	1	1		1	1
Mortgage holders*	—	0.134	1		1	1
ARM holders*	—	—	0.515	0.459	0	1
Age	51	52	45	41	41	40
Male head*	0.722	0.737	0.770	0.760	0.750	0.768
Married*	0.751	0.781	0.864	0.850	0.880	0.827
Household size	3.026	3.065	3.295	3.116	3.223	3.034
Less than high school*	0.592	0.565	0.404	0.394	0.462	0.342
High school diploma*	0.314	0.331	0.459	0.456	0.429	0.477
University degree*	0.094	0.104	0.137	0.150	0.109	0.181
Movers from province of birth*	0.264	0.234	0.345	0.335	0.310	0.354
Living in the North*	0.455	0.448	0.570	0.618	0.495	0.713
Living in the Center*	0.205	0.217	0.207	0.169	0.201	0.143
Living in the South and Islands*	0.341	0.335	0.223	0.214	0.304	0.143
Self-employed*	0.152	0.163	0.179	0.183	0.179	0.186
Unemployed*	0.034	0.029	0.016	0.014	0.033	0.000
Total net income	32,100	35,700	38,600	33,600	30,900	35,800
Net wealth	213,000	272,000	230,900	179,000	163,000	191,000
Home value	—	167,000	178,000	172,000	160,000	182,000
Real assets other than home	67,100	81,500	64,600	48,100	38,200	55,900
Deposits and government bonds	17,200	19,500	13,600	10,800	11,200	10,500
Other financial assets*	0.206	0.240	0.262	0.228	0.179	0.266
Other financial assets	9,200	11,100	9,100	9,400	11,900	7,400
Home-related debt*	0.142	0.180	1	1	1	1
Home-related debt	4,600	5,900	34,000	60,500	56,600	63,500
Other debt*	0.133	0.120	0.193	0.190	0.174	0.203
Other debt	832	796	1,295	1,200	1,200	1,200
No. of observations	28,449	21,333	2,866	421	184	237

Note: All refers to the entire sample. The other columns refer to homeowners, homeowners with a mortgage, households who have purchased their home and obtained a mortgage in the two years previous that of interview ("recent" borrowers), "recent" borrowers with a fixed-rate mortgage (FRM) and "recent" borrowers with an adjustable-rate mortgage (ARM) holders, respectively. * denotes a share of households. Mean values, unless specified otherwise. All monetary variables are in euros of year 2000.

Table 13.3 Summary statistics: Mortgage loan characteristics

	All	*FRM*	*ARM*
Initial loan	64,800	59,700	68,800
	(38,500)	(37,500)	(38,900)
Loan-to-value ratio	0.441	0.438	0.443
	(0.238)	(0.247)	(0.231)
Mortgage duration	14.0	13.2	14.6
	(4.9)	(5.1)	(4.7)
Interest rate	6.6%	6.6%	6.5%
	(3.3%)	(3.1%)	(3.4%)
Real interest rate	3.6%	3.6%	3.5%
	(2.8%)	(2.7%)	(2.8%)
Annual mortgage payments	5,900	5,600	6,400
	(3,300)	(3,500)	(4,900)
Mortgage payments to earnings	0.180	0.188	0.175
	(0.121)	(0.133)	(0.112)
Default-risk premium		0.196	1.250
		(2.840)	(2.699)
Share of subsidized loans	57.9%	62.3%	54.4%
No. of observations	421	184	237

Note: Mean values with standard errors in parentheses.

the premium on ARMs is higher than that on FRMs. In fact, over the sample period considered, short-term rates—the benchmark for ARMs—have been lower than long-term rates—the benchmark for FRMs. Based on this, we have computed the premium charged to mortgage holders as the difference between the mortgage rate paid by the household in the year of interview and the interest rate of one-year government bonds—if it is an ARM—or the interest rate of government bonds with a maturity as close as possible as that of the mortgage—if it is an FRM. The premium charged to ARM holders amounts to 125 basis points on average, over 100 points higher than the average premium of FRM holders.

The Empirical Framework

We consider an environment where at each date households choose whether to buy a house and ask for a loan to finance the purchase. When demanding a loan for home purchase financing, households can choose between two types of contracts, ARMs and FRMs. Conditional on buying and borrowing, we assume that the choice between mortgage contracts is a function of household characteristics and of the relative cost of the loans and estimate the following probit regression:

$$Pr(Y_{ijt} = k) = f(X_{it}, Z_{jt}),\ k = 0,1; \qquad (1)$$

where: $Y_{ijt} = 1$ if the mortgage that household i has taken at time t in the housing and credit market j is an ARM and $Y_{ijt} = 0$ if it is an FRM; X_{it} denotes the sociodemographic characteristics of the household i at time t (e.g., size, income, wealth), and Z_{jt} includes the characteristics of the mortgage products available, which may vary across credit markets j and over time (e.g., the interest rates).

We estimate equation (1) on the sample of "recent" borrowers. We, therefore, exclude all those households whose mortgage demand at time t is non-positive, which comprise renters, those who have purchased their home without needing financing, those who have inherited or just have not paid for it, and all those who are not moving and purchasing a home at t. Hence, we must allow for the possibility that our sample is "selected," so that the mortgage-type choice is not independent from the decision to buy a new house and borrow. We address this issue by estimating the model in steps as follows. First, we estimate a probit for the probability of purchasing one's home with a mortgage, and compute the Heckman correction term for the censoring of the loan demand. Then, we estimate equation (1), the probit for choosing an ARM over an FRM, augmented by the Heckman correction term. As is discussed later, identification is achieved by exclusion restrictions.

We conclude the analysis by estimating a propensity score-matching model to appraise the differences between ARMs and FRMs. A direct comparison is not feasible because we are unable to observe the characteristics of the FRM contract offered to someone who has chosen an ARM and vice versa. The differences in the terms and features of the contracts can be expected to be the most crucial determinant of the choice. Including these differences as regressors in equation (1) is however problematic, because some of the characteristics of the mortgage granted to household i may be endogenous to its choice.

The estimation of a propensity score-matching model amounts to comparing mortgages granted to households that are similar in *all* respects, except for their choice between adjustable- versus fixed-rate loans.[5] In practice, we split our sample between ARMs ("treated" observations) and FRMs ("untreated" or "control" observations), match each "treated" observation with a set of "untreated" observations (chosen so as to be as similar as possible to the "untreated" ones), and then compare the characteristics of the loans issued to the two groups. More formally, defining as Z_A a generic attribute of an ARM, as Z_F the same attribute for an FRM, and as X a set of household, credit, and housing market characteristics, this procedure amounts to estimating:

$$\alpha \equiv E\left[(Z_A) - (Z_F) \mid X\right], \tag{2}$$

where α is the relevant variable for the appraisal of the mortgage type choice.

Estimation Results

Choosing Whether to Buy and Take Out a Mortgage or Not: An Affordability Problem

As previously discussed, before estimating equation (1), we need to evaluate a binary choice model for the probability that a household has purchased its home in the two years prior the interview and has taken out a mortgage, that is, it has purchased a home, asked for a loan to finance it, and obtained it. In this instance, the control group is the entire population in the sample, as it is appropriate in relation to the type of sample selection bias that potentially affects the estimation of the model for mortgage choice.

The probability of purchasing a new home depends on a set of observable and unobservable household preference parameters and on a set of "affordability" constraints that depend in turn on household's net wealth and income, on the terms of the mortgage contract, and on the desired level of housing and of nonhousing consumption.

To estimate the model we need to find at least one variable that affects the decision to purchase one's home and ask for a mortgage, but not that regarding the type of loan. We chose the share of households renting their home and a polynomial in the average annual per-square meter rent, which varies per province and year of interview. These variables capture the development of the rental market, which matters for the household's mobility and is particularly relevant for the choice to own one's home, as opposed to renting it. We also use the number of banks where the household holds a bank account, which can be expected to be positively related to the individual's information on financial instruments. The coefficients of these variables turn out to be statistically significant in the decision to ask for a loan, but not in that regarding the choice of the type of mortgage.

Table 13.4 reports the results of the estimation of the selection equation, where the dependent variable is a dummy that takes on value 1 if the household has purchased its home and financed the purchase with a mortgage in the two years before the interview. We include year dummies because households from different surveys are pooled together and dummies for the province of residence to control for heterogeneity. Interpreting the regressor coefficients is not straightforward, as most variables affect both the demand and the supply of credit and the signs of the two effects might be different, possibly canceling each other out.

As to the variables that we use for identification, the coefficient on the share of households renting their home is negative, which is consistent with the hypotheses that the fraction of renters proxies for the efficiency of the rental market and that the more efficient the rental market the lower the likelihood to buy and borrow. Furthermore, the probability that a household has purchased its home and obtained a mortgage is concave in the rental prices and peaks past the median: the higher the rents, the more attractive the home purchase; however, if rental prices are very high, it becomes difficult for households to accumulate enough savings to afford the downpayment required for a home purchase. Finally, the coefficient on the number of banks where household members have accounts is positive, which is consistent with the hypothesis that this variable captures financial "education" and the overall familiarity with the financial instruments that are available.

Loan price considerations do seem to matter, as the probability of buying and financing the purchase with a mortgage is significantly decreasing in interest rates. Also the term spread of ten-year government bonds over one-year bills as a ratio of income is significant, which captures household's ability to endure future rate changes: the higher the term spread relative to income the lower the likelihood of

Table 13.4 Probability of holding a mortgage

	Coefficient (Standard Error)	*Marginal Effect (Standard Error)*
Share of renters (per province)	−1.41★★★	−0.01★★★
	(0.47)	(0.00)
Rent × m² (per province)	0.04★★★	2.0e-04★★★
	(0.02)	(1.0e-04)
(Rent × m²)²	−3.8e-04★★★	−1.9e-06★★★
	(1.1e-04)	(5.4e-07)
Number of banks	0.15★★★	8.0e-04★★★
	(0.04)	(2.0e-04)
Lagged mortgage rate (per province)	−0.38★★★	−2e-03★★★
	(0.02)	(2e-04)
Term spread to income	−0.01★★★	−7.5e-05★★★
	(0.00)	(1.9e-05)
House price × m² (per province)	0.20★	1.0e-03★
	(0.12)	(6.0e-04)
Age/100	−1.86	0.01
	(1.98)	(0.01)
(Age/100)²	−1.36	−0.01
	(2.11)	(0.01)
High education dummy (high school diploma or university degree)	0.12	6.0e-04
	(0.11)	(6.0e-04)
High ed. × hh. income/100,000	−0.41	−2.0e-03
	(0.27)	(1.3e-03)
Married	0.30★★★	1.2e-03★★★
	(0.09)	(3.0e-04)
Hh. size/10	−0.40	−2.0e-03
	(0.27)	(1.4e-03)
Small town (< 40,000 inhabitants)	−0.14★	−7.0e-04★
	(0.08)	(4.0e-04)
Moved from province of birth	0.10	5.0e-04
	(0.07)	(4.0e-04)
Public employee	0.10★	6.0e-04★
	(0.06)	(4.0e-04)
Self-employed	0.02	1.0e-04
	(0.07)	(4.0e-04)
Unemployed	−0.03	−1.0e-04
	(0.20)	(9.0e-04)
Hh. income/100,000	1.15★★	0.01★★
	(0.46)	(2.0e-03)
(Hh. income/100,000)²	−0.30	−1.5e-03
	(0.21)	(1.0e-03)
Lagged hh. net wealth/100,000	−0.06★★	−3.0e-04★★
	(0.02)	(1.0e-04)

Continued

Table 13.4 Continued

	Coefficient (Standard Error)	*Marginal Effect (Standard Error)*
Lagged hh. net wealth/100,000)^2	3.0e-04***	1.5e-06***
	(1.0e-04)	(4.9e-07)
Cost of housing/nondurable expenditure	1.18***	0.01***
	(0.24)	(1.1e-03)
Bank branches per 1,000 inhab (per province)	0.55	2.8e-03
	(0.72)	(3.6e-03)
Per-capita GDP/1,000 (per province)	0.02	1.0e-04
	(0.01)	(1.0e-04)
Length of civil trials days/100 (per judicial district)	−0.03	−2.0e-04
	(0.03)	(1.0e-04)
Living in the Center	4.83***	0.81***
	(0.62)	(0.13)
Living in the South	2.27***	0.07
	(0.67)	(0.06)
Constant	−0.73	
	(1.20)	
No. of observations	28,462	28,462
Pseudo R^2	0.53	
P-value test for dummies for province = 0	0.00	
P-value test for dummies for year = 0	0.00	

Note: *Number of banks* is the number of different banks where any household member has an account. *Lagged mortgage rate* refers to the average rate that banks charge households on long-term loans. *Term spread-to-income* is the ratio of the difference between the returns of ten- and one-year government bonds to nominal household income. *Lagged household net wealth* has been computed by subtracting household savings from end-of-period net wealth. *Cost of housing/nondurable expenditure* is the ratio of rent for renters or imputed rent for owners to nondurable expenditure. Standard errors in parentheses. The estimates have been corrected for clusters for provincial effects. * significant at 10 percent level; ** significant at 5 percent level; *** significant at 1 percent level.

borrowing. Furthermore, the higher the per-square meter price, the more likely that the buyer will need some finance.

The evidence regarding the other variables included in the regression is consistent with theoretical predictions and with the results of other studies on credit market participation (see, among others, Magri 2002; Fabbri and Padula 2004). In equilibrium, mortgage market participation turns out to be decreasing in the household head's age, which is consistent with the life-cycle hypothesis that the demand for credit is relatively higher for young consumers, whose earnings profiles are upward sloping. The probability of home purchasing with a mortgage is higher for married couples, to whom banks are relatively more inclined to lend, especially when they are first-time buyers. It is lower among those living in small municipalities, possibly as a result of wider intra-household informal credit in small towns. The joint significance of the provincial dummies cannot be rejected. Furthermore, the coefficients of these dummies (not shown) reveal a pattern: those households living in the central and southern provinces are less likely to finance the home purchase with a mortgage, even allowing for the positive coefficients on the area dummies (Living in the Center and Living in the South). This is indeed consistent with both lower supply, due, for example, to greater aggregate risk or contract enforcement problems, but also with lower demand, due, for example, to wider intra-household informal credit.

The probability of having purchased a home and taken out a mortgage is concave in income. It is convex in (beginning-of-period) net wealth, although the minimum is achieved at the 99th percentile of the distribution. All this is consistent with the view that, given the collateral, banks' willingness to lend depends on income, which proxies for the ability to pay regularly the installments on the mortgage: the lower the income, the lower the likelihood of being granted large amounts of credit, no matter how large one's wealth is (an income-wealth interaction term would not affect the result). On the other hand, the higher one's wealth and income, the greater the ability of paying off the house at the time of purchase, and, therefore, the lower the demand for credit. Ceteris paribus, the probability of having purchased a home and taken a mortgage is increasing in the cost of housing relative to that of nondurable consumption (measured by the ratio of rent—actual or imputed—to expenditure on nondurable goods).

Finally, the probability of asking and obtaining a mortgage is neither significantly affected by the number of bank branches in the local credit market nor by the efficiency of the legal enforcement as captured by the length of civil trials in the judicial district where the household lives.

Choosing between FRMs and ARMs: A Risk-Management Problem

Next, we estimate a binary choice model for the probability of choosing a specific mortgage type. This choice amounts essentially to one between different types of risk. A nominal FRM is a risky contract because its capital value is highly sensitive to inflation. On the other hand, the risk of an ARM comes from the short-term variability in the real payments that are required in each period. This variability matters especially if the borrower faces binding liquidity constraints. In fact, constraints bind in states of the world with low income and low house prices; in these instances, buffer-stock savings are low and home equity falls below the minimum required to obtain a second loan. The risk of an ARM is that it will require higher-interest payments in this situation causing a cut in consumption. As Campbell and Cocco (2003) point out, homeowners with expensive houses relative to their income, volatile labor income, or high risk aversion are particularly adversely affected by this type of risk.

Table 13.5 reports the results of the estimation of the probit for the probability that borrowers choose an ARM. As mentioned earlier, the model is estimated on the sample of households who have purchased their home in the two years prior the interview and have asked and obtained a loan to finance their purchase.

In the regression we control for the rate on ARMs and for the spread between fixed and adjustable rates. Since we do not observe the rates that mortgage holders would have been charged if they had chosen the alternative type of mortgage, we have predicted them by regressing the relevant mortgage rate on household and market specific characteristics, such as age, education, occupation, short-term and long-term (province-level) interest rates on bank loans.[6] FRMs are less likely when ARM rates are lower and when the fixed-adjustable interest rate spread is higher. The positive and statistically significant coefficient on the ARM rate implies that, for a given spread, an increase in short-term rates reduces the likelihood of taking on an FRM. This is consistent with the hypothesis that borrowers expect some mean reversions in market interest rates. Instead, a one percentage point increase in the imputed spread between fixed and adjustable rates raises the probability of taking out an ARM by 10 percentage points.

Average house prices have a positive statistically significant coefficient. This is consistent with the view that households choose the lowest interest rate, which is typically that on ARMs, if they are facing a relatively large expense and are, therefore, more likely to be closer to being liquidity constrained. Relative to household income, house prices have a negative effect on the probability of choosing an ARM. This suggests that households are aware that when prices are high relative to income the variability of ARM payments may pose greater risks.

Overall, individual borrower characteristics have little influence on the mortgage choice decision, which is in line with the evidence of Dhillon et al. (1987) for the United States. Notable exceptions are the household head's age and the dummy for having children, whose signs are negative. The fact that older borrowers are less likely to demand ARMs could be rationalized on the ground of lesser liquidity constraints. Households with children could be less likely to demand ARMs, because people with children tend to behave in a more risk-averse way.

Quite surprisingly, compared with the stark theoretical predictions of Campbell and Cocco (2003), the choice is also unrelated to the type of employment and to income and wealth. Holding everything else constant, the results indicate a positive relationship between the probability of taking out an ARM and the ratio of nondurable consumption-to-income, but only among those for whom such ratio is very high and for whom the benefits of low initial payments can be particularly large.

Stronger competition in the credit market, measured by the number of bank branches per thousand of inhabitants, is associated with a higher propensity to take on ARMs. Finally, the coefficients on unreported time dummies become significantly different from zero and positive starting from the year 2000, after Italy joined the European Monetary Union, consistent with the hypothesis that, expecting a more stable monetary environment, borrowers have moved further toward ARMs.

The third column of table 13.5 reports the result of a probit estimate where we control for sample selection, in order to verify whether the subsample of "recent"

Table 13.5 Probability of choosing an ARM

	Basic Specification		*Heckman Correction*	*Bank Controls*
	Coefficient (Stand. Error)	*Marginal Effect (st. err.)*	*Marginal Effect (st. err.)*	*Marginal Effect (st. err.)*
Interest rate on ARMs	0.16**	0.07***	0.08***	0.08***
	(0.07)	(0.03)	(0.03)	(0.03)
FRM-ARM spread	0.24***	0.08***	0.09***	0.08***
	(0.07)	(0.03)	(0.03)	(0.03)
Long-term yield (10 yr. gov. bonds)	0.12	0.04	0.03	0.03
	(0.08)	(0.03)	(0.03)	(0.03)
House price × m2/ (Income/100,000)	−0.10***	−0.04***	−0.04***	−0.04***
	(0.03)	(0.01)	(0.01)	(0.01)
House price × m2 (per province)	0.40***	0.16***	0.15***	0.15***
	(0.12)	(0.05)	(0.05)	(0.05)
Age	−1.67**	−0.63**	−0.72**	−0.54*
	(0.76)	(0.3)	(0.31)	(0.31)
Gender	0.14	0.06	0.06	0.02
	(0.16)	(0.06)	(0.06)	(0.06)
High education	0.08	0.04	0.04	0.03
	(0.15)	(0.06)	(0.06)	(0.06)
Married	−0.24	−0.09	−0.08	−0.09
	(0.20)	(0.08)	(0.08)	(0.08)
Children (dummy)	−0.15**	−0.06**	−0.06**	−0.05*
	(0.07)	(0.03)	(0.03)	(0.03)
No. of income recipients	−0.08	−0.04	−0.03	−0.02
	(0.11)	(0.04)	(0.04)	(0.04)
Probability of moving	1.66	0.68	0.74	0.90
	(1.72)	(0.68)	(0.67)	(0.75)
Moved from province of birth	0.06	0.02	0.02	0.02
	(0.13)	(0.05)	(0.05)	(0.05)
Public employee	0.05	0.02	0.02	0.02
	(0.14)	(0.06)	(0.06)	(0.06)
Self-employed	0.11	0.04	0.04	0.06
	(0.21)	(0.08)	(0.08)	(0.07)
Nondurable expenditure/ income	0.47	0.18	0.20	0.13
	(0.48)	(0.19)	(0.19)	(0.20)
High nondurable expenditure	0.62**	0.23***	0.22***	0.25***
	(0.27)	(0.09)	(0.09)	(0.09)
Household income/100,000	0.43	0.17	0.18	0.28
	(0.67)	(0.26)	(0.27)	(0.28)
Lagged household wealth/ 100,000	−0.01	−0.01	−0.01	−0.01
	(0.04)	(0.01)	(0.01)	(0.01)
Bank branches per 1,000 inhabitants	1.10**	0.42**	0.45**	0.47*
	(0.54)	(0.21)	(0.22)	(0.25)

Continued

Table 13.5 Continued

	Basic Specification		*Heckman Correction*	*Bank Controls*
	Coefficient (Stand. Error)	*Marginal Effect (st. err.)*	*Marginal Effect (st. err.)*	*Marginal Effect (st. err.)*
Mills ratio			0.02	
			(0.02)	
Constant	−3.62***			
	(1.4)			
No. of observations	420	420	420	420
Pseudo R^2	0.13	0.13	0.13	0.16
P-value test year dummies = 0	0.00	0.00	0.00	0.00
P-value test main bank dummies = 0				0.02

Note: Interest rate on ARMs is the rate on ARMs estimated in a first-stage regression of interest rates on borrowers' and credit market characteristics. *FRM-ARM spread* is the difference between the rate on ARMs and that on FRMs estimated in a first-stage regression of interest rates on borrowers' and credit market characteristics. *Probability of moving* is the probability that a household moves from its province of birth estimated with a probit regression on borrowers and geographical characteristics. See also note to table 13.4. The estimates have been corrected for clusters for provincial effects. * significant at 10 percent level; ** significant at 5 percent level; *** significant at 1 percent level.

borrowers, which we use for the estimation, is "selected." Our analysis of the mortgage-type decision appears to be robust to the inclusion of a Heckman correction term based on the probit of table 13.4. In fact, the additional regressor is neither significant nor does it affect the coefficients of the other variables in any noteworthy way.

Finally, the last column presents the result of a specification where a dummy for the "main bank" of the household is introduced. This should permit a better control for supply conditions, if there is a common component for all clients of the same bank. Indeed, the coefficients of the dummy variables for the major 18 banks considered are jointly significantly different from zero, although very few of them are so when considered individually. Most interestingly, the coefficients of the other variables included in the regression are virtually unchanged, confirming the overall robustness of the original specification.

Characteristics of ARMs and FRMs

As a final exercise, we have checked whether ARMs and FRMs exhibit significant differences with respect to their most important characteristics: size, interest rate, value of the house that is bought, loan-to-house value ratio, average value of the installments, maturity, and the premium charged by banks over their cost of funds. This has been done using the propensity score-matching technique described earlier, which amounts to comparing the average value of the feature under scrutiny across mortgages with the most similar characteristics, except for having an adjustable or a fixed interest rate.

Quite surprisingly, the results reported in table 13.6 show that, after controlling for borrowers' individual characteristics, the only significant difference between ARM and FRM contracts is the premium that banks charge over their cost of funds. In fact, although ARMs are slightly larger, have slightly higher interest rates, are used to finance the purchase of more expensive houses, and have a slightly longer maturity, none of these differences is statistically different from zero. The only significant difference is in the interest rate premium, which is much higher for ARMs than for FRMs. Such premium reflects borrower's riskiness and any markup that a lender enjoying some form of market power can charge. Taken together, this evidence suggests that lenders are pricing quite expensively the higher interest rate risk that ARMs pose on borrowers and borrowers are paying a high price for the benefit of low initial payments.

Table 13.6 Characteristics of ARMs and FRMs—matching model

Variables	*ARMs*	*FRMs*	*Difference (p-value)*
Mortgage size	67,634	66,368	4,056
			(0.91)
Interest rate	6.73	6.58	0.15
			(0.57)
House value	181,513	169,601	11,912
			(0.89)
Average value of installment	6,063	5,639	424
			(0.48)
Loan maturity	14.34	13.82	0.52
			(0.89)
Loan-to-value ratio	0.44	0.44	0.00
			(1.00)
Risk premium	1.25	−0.11	1.37
			(0.00)
No. of observations (common support)	222	181	
No. of observations	237	184	

Note: The table presents the results of a matching logit regressions of the characteristics of ARMs and FRMs. The mean of each variable is calculated for samples of comparable adjustable- and fixed-rate mortgages, where the matching is done using a propensity score function with the kernel option, controlling for characteristics of the household (age, gender, education and occupation of the head, marital status, and number of income recipients) and of the credit market (number of bank branches and household main bank dummies), and including geographical and time dummies. *Risk premium* is the difference between the mortgage rate paid by the household in the year of interview and the interest rate of one-year government bonds if it is an ARM or the interest rate of government bonds with a maturity as close as possible as that of the mortgage if it is an FRM. P-values for the test of significance of differences of means are reported in parentheses (significance is computed by using the bias-corrected confidence interval).

Concluding Remarks and Policy Implications

The stock of mortgages for home purchases in Italy and in most developed countries has risen substantially over the past decade. Understanding the functioning of this market is of increasing importance, because of the potential effects that changes in house prices, inflation, and interest rates can have on the investment and consumption choices of the growing number of indebted households. The evidence presented in this chapter, although preliminary, has provided a basis to answer some questions that are still open.

A first issue is that of the determinants of the recent surge in home-related borrowing. Based on our results, in Italy, both demand and supply factors have mattered. Among the demand factors, the reduction in the interest rates appears to have favored an increase of the number of mortgage holders—although the size of this effect is not as significant as expected. Among the supply factors, the positive coefficient on the number of bank branches points to the increase in bank diffusion and competition as a factor explaining the increase in house purchase financing.

A second important question that we address concerns the characteristics of households with different types of mortgages. Contrary to the indications of the theoretical literature, household characteristics proxying for risk aversion and exposure to other non-mortgage-related risks seem to have very low explanatory power on the choice between ARMs and FRMs. Indeed, the only significant individual characteristics explaining mortgage choices are the age of the head and whether there are children in the house: both reduce the probability of taking on an ARM.

What seems to matter the most in the choice are the price variables. FRMs are less likely when the interest rate spread is high and when, given the spread, the adjustable rate is high, consistent with the hypothesis that borrowers expect interest rates to be partly mean-reverting. Households buying houses in expensive areas are more attracted by ARMs, possibly because they are cheaper in the short run. However, the higher the per-square meter price relative to their income, the less likely borrowers are to take on an ARM, possibly because they fear they will be unable to repay the loan if interest rates rise. On the supply side, stronger bank competition seems to favor ARMs, as shown by the positive coefficient of the number of branches per inhabitants.

Overall, these results provide evidence consistent with the hypothesis that ARMs are a significantly more attractive form of loans for those households that are currently liquidity constrained. These households attribute a particularly high value to the level of the initial payment (which is generally lower on ARMs), tend to overlook the overall cost of the mortgage, and do not fully take into account the risk of a rise of the reference interest rates. On the other hand, lenders price quite expensively this risk and borrowers end up paying a high price for the benefit of low initial payments. In fact, after controlling for borrowers characteristics, the only significant difference between ARMs and FRMs is in the premium that lenders charge over their cost of funds. Hence, overall, some attention should be paid to the negative effects that an increase in interest rates might have on ARM holders. On the contrary, on the side of banks, there seems to be no evidence of excessive risk taking.

Notes

We thank for their comments and suggestions participants at the XIV International "Tor Vergata" Conference on Banking and Finance (Rome, December 2005), at the Finance and Consumption Workshop on Consumption and Credit in Countries with Developing Credit Markets (Fiesole, June 2006), at the 62nd Congress of the International Institute of Public Finance (Paphos, August 2006) and at the XLVI Annual Conference of the Società Italiana degli Economisti (Verona, October 2006). The views expressed are those of the authors and do not necessarily reflect those of the Bank of Italy. Address for correspondence: Monica Paiella, Bank of Italy, Research Department, Via Nazionale 91, Roma 00184, Italy, tel. +39.06.4792.2595, fax. +39.06.4792.3723. E-mail addresses: monica.paiella@bancaditalia.it;pozzolo@unimol.it.

1. In the last decade the ratio of Italy's residential debt to GDP rose from slightly more than 6 percent to almost 15 percent of GDP. In 2004 it was about a third of the EU15 average and less than a fifth of the ratio for the United States. From a supply side perspective, loans to households accounted for just over 15 percent of bank total loans versus an EU average of about 30 percent.
2. The Survey is biannual with the exception of the 1998 wave, which was run three years after the previous one. For a description and assessment of the survey, see Brandolini and Cannari (1994). The overall quality of the data has also been analyzed more recently by Battistin et al. (2003).
3. From the original sample, we exclude those households whose head is less than 20 or more than 70 years old (19 percent of the sample), those who do not own, nor pay cash rent for their home (7 percent of the sample) and those with non-positive income (0.4 percent of the sample). Furthermore, we exclude about 7 percent of mortgage holders whose mortgage information are completely inconsistent. After dropping all those mortgage holders with incomplete or inconsistent mortgage information, we are left with a sample where the share of mortgage holders and homeowners is somewhat lower than in the population.
4. The interviews are run in the spring of the year following that covered by the survey.
5. See Rubin (1979). For a recent survey, see Blundell and Costa Dias (2002).
6. The results are available from the authors upon request.

References

Battistin, E., R. Miniaci, and G. Weber. 2003. "What Do We Learn from Recall Consumption Data." *Journal of Human Resources* 38: 231–40.

Blundell, R., and M. Costa Dias. 2002. "Alternative Approaches to Evaluation in Empirical Microeconomics." Cemmap working paper n. CWP10/02. IFS and University College London.

Brandolini, A., and L. Cannari. 1994. "Methodological Appendix: The Bank of Italy's Survey of Household Income and Wealth." In Ando, A., L. Guiso and I. Visco eds., *Saving and the Accumulation of Wealth: Essays on Italian Household and Government Saving Behavior*. Cambridge University Press: Cambridge UK.

Brueckner, J., and J. Follain. 1988. "The Rise and Fall of the ARM: An Econometric Analysis of Mortgage Choice." *The Review of Economics and Statistics* 70: 93–102.

Campbell, J., and J. Cocco. 2003. "Household Risk Management and Optimal Mortgage Choice." *Quarterly Journal of Economics* 118: 1449–94.

Dhillon, U., J. Shilling, and C. Sirmans. 1987. "Choosing between Fixed and Adjustable Rate Mortgage." *Journal of Money, Credit and Banking* 19: 1.

Fabbri, D., and M. Padula. 2004. "Does Poor Legal Enforcement Make Households Credit Constrained?" *Journal of Banking and Finance* 28: 2369–97.

Magri, S. 2002. "Italian Households' Debt: Determinants of Demand and Supply." Bank of Italy, Temi di Discussione No. 454.

Rubin, D.B. 1979. "Using Multivariate Matched Sampling and Regression Adjustment to Control Bias in Observational Studies." *Journal of the American Statistical Association* 74: 308–29.

CHAPTER 14

INTEREST RATES IN THE SUB-PRIME MORTGAGE MARKET

Souphala Chomsisengphet and Anthony Pennington-Cross

Introduction

Sub-prime lending has grown rapidly in the mortgage market. According to Inside Mortgage Finance (IMF), sub-prime mortgage lending increased from approximately 65 billion dollars in 1995 to over 213 billion dollars in 2002. This growth accelerated in 2003 as the market grew by another 119 billion dollars to reach 332 billion dollars (IMF 2004).[1] By providing access to credit to those otherwise denied a mortgage in the traditional prime market, the sub-prime market can enhance welfare by completing the mortgage market (Chinloy and MacDonald 2005). Sub-prime credit gives more households the opportunity to become homeowners, as well as providing better access to equity held in the home through refinances and second mortgages. Despite the growth in sub-prime lending, little is known about the pricing of the sub-prime credit. This chapter helps fill this gap by examining the determinants of interest rates charged to sub-prime mortgage borrowers.

The most unique characteristic of sub-prime mortgage lending is that it charges more than the prime mortgage market and the charges include a wide variety of prices (interest rates and fees).[2] The growth of the sub-prime mortgage market suggests that risk-based pricing is a viable method of lending in the mortgage market. Sub-prime has introduced into the mortgage market risk-based pricing by sorting borrowers into a dozens of categories, each with its own interest rate. Hence, sub-prime mortgage lenders can move further away from the traditional accept-reject decision, which dominates prime lending, closer to identifying the correct risk-based price for each potential borrower. In this chapter, we find that interest rates in the sub-prime mortgage market are strongly impacted by a complicated interaction of downpayment and borrower credit history. This is in contrast with the prime market where interest rates are primarily driven by downpayment, given that minimum credit history requirements are satisfied.

Background

The growth and maturation of sub-prime has been accompanied by lender consolidation and a change in the type of institution originating loans. IMF reports that the market share of the top 25 originators in sub-prime[3] grew from 39.3 percent in 1995 to 93.4 percent in 2003. This rapid consolidation has been a function of individual firm failures, as well as mergers and acquisitions by traditional lenders seeking to move into the potentially lucrative sub-prime market. Table 14.1 lists the top ten sub-prime originators reported by IMF for 1996 and 2003. Most of the firms listed in 1996 are not included in the 2003 list.[4] In 1996 most of the originators were independent finance companies, but by 2003 Household Financial Services was the only finance company to remain independent and survive market consolidation and entry of traditional prime lenders.

In addition, the prevalence of sub-prime loans in the secondary market has changed as well. The securitization rate[5] of sub-prime home mortgages has grown from 28.4 in 1995 to 58.7 percent in 2003. While the rate is still below the prime market rate (75.9 percent in 2003), it has helped bring the sub-prime market into a form more closely resembling the prime market (IMF 2004). In fact, the securitization rate exceeds the rate in the conventional market rate in 1995–1997. Perhaps due to information asymmetries between primary and secondary markets, sub-prime lenders are less likely to securitize mortgages if they come from locations with improving but poor economic conditions (Pennington-Cross 2002). Furthermore, Fannie Mae and Freddie Mac have started to impact the structure of sub-prime securities. Trade magazines even refer to GSE class securities, which contain AAA-rated tranches backed by loans below the conforming loan limit.[6] In 2004, IMF reports that Fannie Mae and Freddie Mac purchased 43.7 percent of total sub-prime issuances, up from 39.8 percent in 2003.[7]

Table 14.1 Top ten originators

Rank	*1996*	*2003*
1	Associates First Capital, TX	Ameriquest Mortgage, CA
2	The Money Store, CA	New Century, CA
3	ContiMortgage Corp, PA	CitiFinancial, NY
4	Beneficial Mortgage Corp, NJ	Household Finance, IL
5	Household Financial Services, IL	Option One Mortgage, CA
6	United Companies, LA	First Franklin Financial Corp, CA
7	Long Beach Mortgage, CA	Washington Mutual, WA
8	EquiCredit, FL	Countrywide Financial, CA
9	Aames Capital Corp., CA	Wells Fargo Home Mortgage, IA
10	AMRESCO Residential Credit, NJ	GMAC-RFC, MN

While more traditional lenders have entered the sub-prime market, sub-prime lending remains fundamentally different from that of prime lending. Sub-prime lending is used more often in high-risk locations (Calem et al. 2004; Pennington-Cross 2002). Sub-prime borrowers are also typically less knowledgeable about the mortgage process and have a higher credit risk. However, it does not look like the transition into sub-prime is a permanent one. For instance, of those sub-prime borrowers who get a subsequent mortgage, 39.6 percent successfully made the transition into the prime market (Courchane, Surette, and Zorn, 2004). This result is consistent with the notion that the sub-prime market often provides a fairly temporary source of credit to households when they are in financial trouble.

Interest Rate Categories

In the prime market, a minimum credit score is required or else the applicant will be rejected. If the credit score or credit history requirement is met, the cost to the borrower is largely determined by the amount of the downpayment. The lowest cost prime loans go to those with downpayments of at least 20 percent of the home value. Those who provide less than a 20 percent downpayment must either purchase mortgage insurance or have a second mortgage. Both of these tools provide more flexibility to the borrower in terms of downpayments, but they also include an additional cost or premium, which varies according to how small the downpayment becomes.

By contrast, a three-step process is typically used to identify the interest rate in sub-prime. First, the loan grade is identified. This is most often referred to as A, B, C, or D, though each lender uses its own descriptive name.[8] Second, given the loan grade, the interest rate is determined by the downpayment in conjunction with the credit score. Third, loan-specific information such as points and fees paid, prepayment penalty, level of documentation, lien position, loan purpose, and so on, are used to adjust the base interest rate.

Table 14.2 provides a summary of the requirements used to sort borrowers into different loan grades.[9] In table 14.2, a borrower with two 30-day delinquencies in the last 12 months can qualify for the A grade, as long as the borrower has not experienced a foreclosure in the last 36 months, has discharged a Chapter 7 bankruptcy in the last 36 months, has discharged a Chapter 12 bankruptcy in the last 24 months, and has a total debt to income ratio up to 50 percent. For B grades, two 30-day delinquencies are acceptable and a Chapter 13 bankruptcy must have been discharged more than 18 months ago. In general, the lower grades allow more mortgage delinquency and more recent resolution of foreclosures and bankruptcies.

Within each loan grade, borrowers who provide larger downpayments pay lower interest rates and borrowers with lower or worse credit scores pay more. The highest rate is paid by borrowers with the worst credit scores and the smallest downpayment.[10] However, not all LTV-Credit Score combinations are available. For instance, the Countrywide California B&C rate sheet (www.cwbc.com downloaded on November 2, 2005) does not report an interest rate for loans with a 10 percent downpayment and a credit score of 520. Therefore, this applicant is rejected unless a downpayment of 20 percent can be provided. For grade B, lenders

Table 14.2 Underwriting and loan grades

Credit History	*A*	*B*	*C*	*C−*
Mortgage delinquency in days	2 × 30 × 12	1 × 60 × 12	1 × 90 × 12	2 × 90 × 12
Foreclosures	>36 months	>24 months	>12 months	>1 day
Bankruptcy Chapter 7	Discharged >36 months	Discharged >24 months	Discharged >12 months	Discharged
Bankruptcy Chapter 13	Discharged >24 months	Discharged >18 months	Filed >12 months	Pay
Debt ratio	50%	50%	50%	50%

Source: Countrywide, download from www.cwbc.com on November 2, 2005. 2 × 30 × 12 indicates two times 30 days delinquent over the last 12 months.

require a larger downpayment to compensate for the higher credit risk. Therefore, while sub-prime has introduced risk-based pricing through the many different categories based on loan grade, downpayment, and credit score, many loans can still be rejected.

Sub-Prime Mortgage Data

Our data comes from LoanPerformance (LP), Incorporated and includes loan-level information on securitized loans. LoanPerformance indicates that the data covers 61 percent of the outstanding sub-prime market. Our sample of loans originated from 1996 through July of 2003, therefore, includes loans that were originated in the different stages of the growth and maturation of the sub-prime industry.[11] The data is also dominated by loan grades A and B. Therefore, the analysis focuses on a higher-quality portion of the sub-prime market.

To create a homogeneous sample, only first-lien purchase, owner-occupied, 30-year fixed-rate mortgages are included. This will reduce any bias caused by different and unobserved product mix and pricing.[12] Observations with missing credit scores or missing loan grade are dropped from the sample.[13] The final dataset includes over 51,000 loans, of which 39,780 are A grade and 11,937 are B grade.

Given the definitions of the interest rate categories, three variables are of main interest: the contract interest rate, the downpayment (LTV), and the borrower's credit history. The dataset provides detailed information on the loan and includes direct measurement of the interest rate on the mortgage at origination, the LTV at origination, and the Fair Isaac's FICO score. The FICO score is a consumer credit score typically used in both the prime and sub-prime market. It is used to define the interest rate given the LTV and the loan grade. However, loan grade is determined using more specific credit history information such as bankruptcy and previous numbers of missed payments on a mortgage or rental payment. While the dataset does not include this detailed information, it does provide a loan-grade classification. Therefore, the empirical approach used in this chapter will be to segment the loans into loan grade, then examine the impact of downpayments, credit scores, and the interaction of downpayments and credit scores on the interest rate charged to sub-prime borrowers at origination.

Table 14.3 provides the mean and standard deviation of each variable by loan grade. In general, the LoanPerformance data is consistent with interest rate categories and the risk-based pricing example provided earlier. For example, A grade loans have on average better credit scores, provide smaller downpayments, and pay lower interest rates than B grade loans.

It may be also informative to compare the interest rate of the loan to the prevailing rate in the prime market, essentially providing an estimate of the premium paid by sub-prime borrowers to reflect both credit and prepayment risks borne by the lender and other investors. We define the spread as the difference between the interest rate on each sub-prime loan at origination and the prime interest rate (Freddie Mac's Primary Mortgage Market Survey (PMMS)) for the month in which the sub-prime loan is originated.[14]

Figures 14.1–14.3 present the average spread or premium over the 1996–2003 period. Figure 14.1 shows that the premium ranges from 2.5 to 3.5 percentage points, but peaked at approximately 3.3 points in 2001. For the same sample of loans, the contract interest rate on the mortgage averages from 10 to 11 percent from 1996 through 2000, and has been declining since. On the other hand, the premium has remained fairly steady through a period of volatile and declining interest rates.

Loans with better credit scores should on average have lower interest rates and hence lower premiums. Figure 14.2 shows that the average premium across credit score categories for loans originated in 1996 and 1997 are very similar, almost within half of a percentage point. By 2001, the premiums varied across credit score categories by almost 2 percentage points. Again, this finding is consistent with earlier observations, which illustrated conforming underwriting and risk-based pricing in sub-prime.

Table 14.3 Mean characteristics by loan grade

	A Grade		*B Grade*	
Variable	*mean*	*std. dev.*	*mean*	*std. dev.*
Interest rate	9.7	1.5	11.1	1.2
Premium	2.7	1.3	3.8	1.2
FICO	632	60	574	46
LTV	84	10	81	9
PMI	0.08	0.28	0.04	0.20
Low Doc	0.27	0.44	0.09	0.28
No Doc	0.01	0.09	0.00	0.04
Yield Curve	1.21	1.09	0.72	0.89

Figure 14.1 Interest rates and premiums

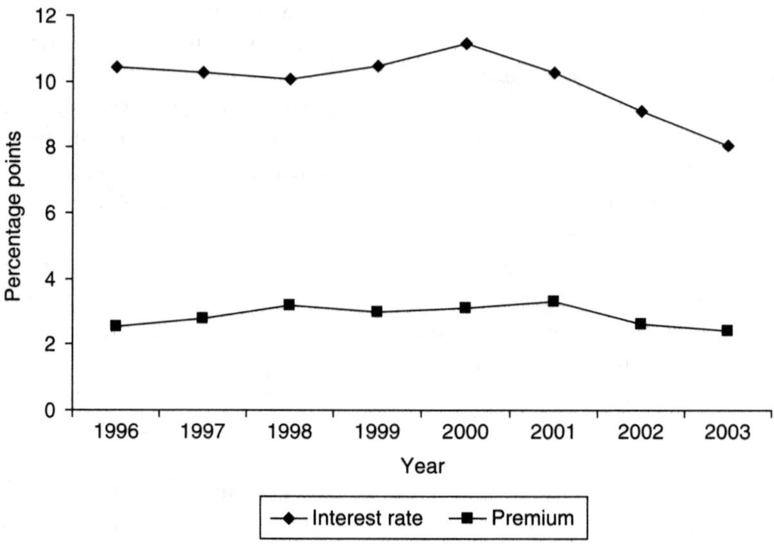

Figure 14.2 Premiums by FICO

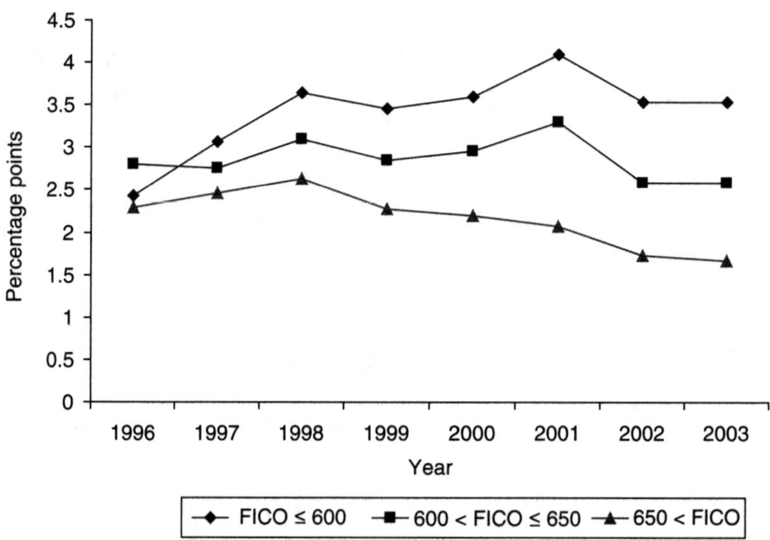

Figure 14.3 also provides the average premium through time, but by LTV category. Since smaller downpayments increase credit risk, the marginal impact of providing a smaller downpayment should lead to a higher interest rate. This is the general pattern shown in figure 14.3. For example, loans that provide 20 percent or less for downpayment tend to pay a premium just about 3 percentage points

Figure 14.3 Premiums by LTV

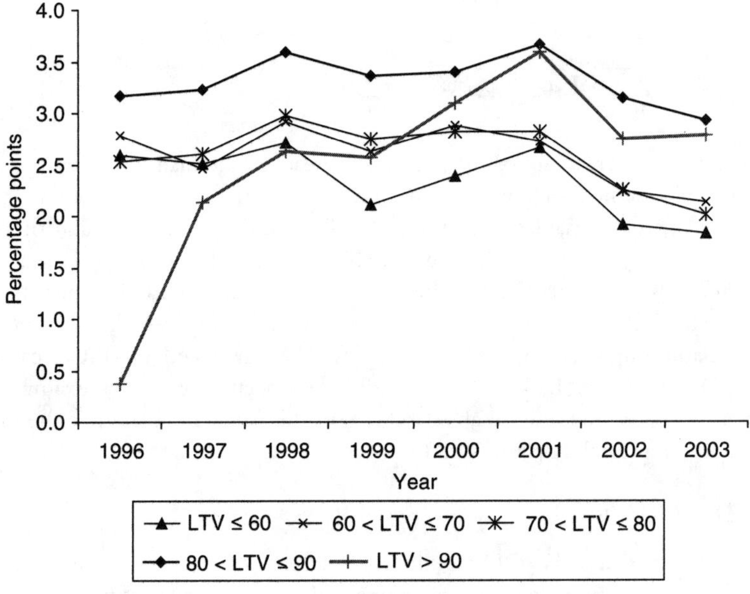

in 2003, while all other categories tend to pay a premium of approximately 2 percentage points in 2003. In general, figures 14.1–14.3 also indicate that the pricing of loans may have changed over time and any estimation should attempt to control for these potential time-varying impacts.

Specification and Empirical Results

Lender underwriting standards and risk classifications indicate that within each loan grade, borrowers are sorted into risk categories, each with a unique interest rate. Each category is primarily a joint function of downpayment and credit score. Therefore, any specification must account for the effect of LTV and FICO jointly. The most expensive group, or those with the highest interest rate, should be those with credit scores equal to or less than 600 and LTVs greater than 90 percent (FICO $<=$ 600 and LTV $>$ 90), because they provide the smallest amount of equity to compensate for the poor credit history. The group that should pay the lowest interest rate should be those with the highest credit scores and largest downpayments (FICO $>$ 650 and LTV $<=$ 70).[15]

Furthermore, Ambrose and Sanders (2005), who examined loans in the high LTV (LTV $>$ 100) market, and Ambrose, LaCour-Little and Sanders (2004) include measures of the yield curve, proxied by the difference between the ten-year constant maturity treasury rate and the one-year constant maturity treasury rate. In addition to these variables, theory indicates that the interest rate on a loan is sensitive to the termination profile, loss severity, capital requirements, origination fees and costs, servicing costs, cost of funds, and time discount rates (Fortowsky and Lacour-Little 2002). Hence, we estimate the following model of interest rates using ordinary least squares (OLS):

$$I_i = \beta_c + \sum_l \sum_f \beta_{lf} F_{if} L_{il} + \sum_x \beta_x X_{ix} + \sum_o \beta_o O_{io} + \sum_t \beta_t T_{it} + \varepsilon_i \qquad (1)$$

where I is the interest rate or the premium spread on the loan, i indexes the individual loan, F is the f categories of FICO scores, L is the l categories of LTVs, X is other explanatory variables (e.g., the level of documentation, PMI, and the yield curve),[16] O is the originator dummy variables with small and missing as the reference, and T is the t time dummies for each quarter (with 2003:Q3 as the reference time period). The interaction of the FICO and LTV categories allows for a nonlinear relationship between the two variables. The reference LTV-FICO category is FICO > 650 and LTV <= 70. Additional specifications also examine the relationship between these variables and the spread between the interest rate on the loans and the prevailing prime rate (S_i).

Base Model Results

Table 14.4 provides the OLS results for interest rate and premium spread for A grade loans and B grade loans, respectively. The interest rate results in table 14.4 show that credit scores and downpayments interact in the expected manner. Relative to the reference category (FICO > 650 and LTV <= 70), all other categories pay more. Loans providing the smallest downpayment and the worst credit scores have the highest interest rates and are charged 2.04 percentage points higher interest rates than the reference group. In general, holding all else constant, smaller downpayments and lower credit scores are associated with higher interest rates.[17] Consistent with Ambrose, LaCour-Little and Sanders (2004), a steeper yield curve is associated with lower interest rates. In addition, low and no documentation are also associated with higher interest rates. Loans with PMI have lower interest rates. This is the expected result because borrowers should receive a price break for insuring the lender against potential losses.

Table 14.4 also provides results that are very similar to the interest rate results except that the dependent variable is the spread between the interest rate on the loan and the prevailing prime interest rate. Again, loans with the best credit scores and largest downpayment pay the smallest spread and those with the worst credit scores and smallest downpayments pay the highest spreads.

Endogeneity Issues

The OLS results clearly show that the interest rate that a borrower is charged is sensitive to the size of the downpayment. Since interest rates are derived from a set of categories, there is not a linear or smooth function between downpayments and interest rates. As a result, if a borrower can find a few more dollars to move to a less expensive category, such as reducing the LTV from 81 percent to 80 percent, the interest rate will be substantially reduced. In addition, the

Table 14.4 Interest rate and spread results

	Interest Rate				*Spread*			
	A Grade		*B Grade*		*A Grade*		*B Grade*	
Variable	*Coeff.*	*Standard Error*	*Coeff.*	*Standard Error*	*Coeff.*	*Standard Error*	*Coeff.*	*Standard Error*
Intercept	6.69	0.12	9.12	0.27	2.48	0.12	4.73	0.27
FICO <= 600 and LTV <= 70	1.07	0.05	0.52	0.11	1.07	0.05	0.53	0.11
FICO <= 600 and 70 < LTV <= 80	1.57	0.04	0.92	0.11	1.57	0.04	0.92	0.11
FICO <= 600 and 80 < LTV <= 90	2.04	0.03	1.11	0.11	2.04	0.03	1.12	0.11
FICO <= 600 and 90 < LTV	1.74	0.05			1.75	0.05		
600 <= FICO <= 650 and LTV <= 70	0.67	0.04	0.25	0.13	0.67	0.04	0.26	0.13
600 <= FICO <= 650 and 70 < LTV <= 80	0.87	0.03	0.43	0.11	0.87	0.03	0.44	0.11
600 <= FICO <= 650 and 80 < LTV <= 90	1.57	0.03	0.94	0.11	1.57	0.03	0.95	0.11
600 <= FICO <= 650 and 90 < LTV	1.79	0.04			1.79	0.04		
650 <= FICO and 70 < LTV <= 80	0.23	0.03	0.2	0.13	0.24	0.03	0.21	0.13
650 <= FICO and 80 < LTV <= 90	0.91	0.04	0.6	0.13	0.91	0.04	0.6	0.13
650 <= FICO and 90 <= LTV	1.01	0.04			1.02	0.04		
PMI	−0.11	0.02	−0.19	0.05	−0.12	0.02	−0.2	0.05
Low doc	0.25	0.01	0.36	0.03	0.25	0.01	0.36	0.04
No doc	0.02	0.06	0.71	0.27	0.03	0.06	0.75	0.27
Yield curve	−0.06	0.04	−0.24	0.07	−0.56	0.04	−0.67	0.07
Observations	39,780		11,937		39,780		11,937	
Adjusted R^2	0.5753		0.3086		0.3709		0.2666	

Note: Dependent Variable interest rate on the loan at origination or interest rate spread on the loan at origination and the prevailing prime rate. Quarterly and originator dummies are included and are available upon request from the author. The excluded categories are 2003:Q3, unknown or very small originator, and 650 < FIC0 and LTV <= 70.

lending process can be viewed as a negotiation between the borrower and lender to find a mutually acceptable interest rate on the loan. Therefore, even in the prime market, Ambrose, LaCour-Little, and Sanders (2004) treat LTV as an endogenous variable. However, they treat LTV as a continuous variable and ignore the natural tendency for borrowers to clump at the border of downpayment requirements.

To control for this endogenous relationship, we estimate a multinomial logit model of LTV, broken down into the relevant categories. We estimate a multinomial logit specification where there are J ($j = 0, \ldots, J\text{-}1$) options available and the vector of variables that explain the decision made for loan i is z_i. The probability of observing a particular outcome of a loan is given by the following:

$$Prob(Y_i = j) = \frac{e^{\beta'_j z_i}}{\sum_{k=0}^{J-1} e^{\beta'_k z_i}}. \tag{2}$$

The parameters, β_0, are normalized to zero for identification purposes. The other β parameters are chosen to maximize the log-likelihood function:

$$\ln L = \sum_i \sum_{j=0}^{J-1} d_{ij} \ln Prob(Y_i = j) \tag{3}$$

where d_{ij} is a dummy variable equal to 1 if j is the outcome on loan i. Since we do not observe borrower risk factors beyond the credit score, we use the median income for the county as a proxy for household income, a series of time dummies to capture the national economic conditions, and a series of state dummies to capture local economic impacts such as historical house price appreciation and the stability of house prices.

Table 14.5 provides the results for the A and B loan grades. The excluded LTV category are loans with LTVs greater than 70 and less than or equal to 80 (70 < LTV <= 80). Higher FICO scores are associated with a higher probability of providing small downpayments (LTV > 90) and average downpayments (70 < LTV <= 80). Locations with higher median incomes are more likely to provide typical downpayments (70 < LTV <= 80) and least likely to provide very small downpayments (LTV > 90). Dummy variables for each time period and location control for local and national economic trends that could affect downpayments and originator dummies control for originator specific effects. For grade B loans, most of these factors have little impact on the LTV category.

Simulated LTV Results

The multinomial logit model estimates the probability of a loan having a particular size of downpayment (by LTV category). Using the estimated probabilities, the LTV for each loan in the sample will be randomly assigned to one of the five categories for A grade loans and to one of the four categories for B grade loans.[18]

Table 14.5 Multinomial logit LTV results

	Grade A		*Grade B*	
Variable	*Coefficient*	*Standard Error*	*Coefficient*	*Standard Error*
LTV <= 60				
FICO	−0.35	0.05	−0.07	0.11
Prime rate	0.26	0.22	−0.22	0.36
Income	0.01	0.03	0.20	0.06
Constant	−1.87	1.31	−1.03	2.25
60 < LTV <= 70				
FICO	−0.35	0.05	−0.03	0.09
Prime rate	0.34	0.20	0.05	0.28
Income	−0.02	0.03	−0.01	0.05
Constant	−2.31	1.16	−1.33	1.73
80 < LTV <= 90				
FICO	−0.74	0.02	0.03	0.05
Prime rate	0.05	0.09	−0.14	0.16
Income	−0.08	0.01	0.02	0.03
Constant	3.70	0.55	0.11	0.99
90 < LTV <= 100				
FICO	0.16	0.03		
Prime rate	0.11	0.12		
Income	−0.13	0.02		
Constant	−2.55	0.71		
Log of Likelihood	8,583		2,277	
Number of Observations	39,780		11,937	

Note: Quarterly and originator dummies are included and available upon request. The excluded reference categories are CA, 2003:Q3, unknown or very small originator and 70 < LTV <= 80.

This LTV will be referred to as the simulated LTV ($sLTV_i$). This process is repeated for all the loans in the sample and completes one draw.

For each draw the model is estimated just as in equation 1, except the simulated LTV categories are interacted with the credit score categories. The results provide an estimate of the coefficients for one draw. Five hundred draws are conducted and the mean estimated coefficient is reported along the standard deviation of the coefficients over the 500 draws. Table 14.6 reports the results using the simulated LTV categories and the 500 draws for A grade loans and B grade loans using the interest rate of the loan as the dependent variable. Table 14.7 provides a summary of the impacts of the originator and time dummies.

In general, the simulated results are similar to the base model results. For example, interest rates for the A grade loans are higher for loans with lower credit scores and smaller downpayments. The reference category (650 < FICO & sLTV <= 70) has the lowest estimated interest rate, while loans with the worst credit scores and

Table 14.6 Simulated interest rate and simulated spread results

	Interest Rate Results				*Spread Results*			
	A Grade		*B Grade*		*A Grade*		*B Grade*	
Variable	*Coeff.*	*Std. Dev.*	*Coeff.*	*Std. Dev.*	*Coeff.*	*Std. Dev.*	*Coeff.*	*Std. Dev.*
Intercept	7.35	0.03	9.32	0.12	3.13	0.03	4.95	0.13
FICO <= 600 and sLTV <= 70	1.16	0.05	0.67	0.13	1.17	0.05	0.68	0.14
FICO <= 600 and 70 < sLTV <= 80	1.21	0.03	0.74	0.12	1.22	0.03	0.75	0.13
FICO <= 600 and 80 < sLTV <= 90	1.30	0.03	0.75	0.12	1.31	0.03	0.76	0.14
FICO <= 600 and 90 < sLTV	1.32	0.04			1.33	0.04		
600 <= FICO < 650 and sLTV <= 70	0.66	0.04	0.35	0.14	0.67	0.04	0.35	0.15
600 <= FICO < 650 and 70 < sLTV <= 80	0.68	0.03	0.43	0.12	0.69	0.03	0.44	0.14
600 <= FICO < 650 and 80 < sLTV <= 90	0.79	0.03	0.52	0.13	0.79	0.03	0.53	0.14
600 <= FICO < 650 and 90 <= sLTV	0.86	0.04			0.87	0.04		
650 <= FICO and 70 < sLTV <= 80	−0.03	0.03	0.12	0.15	−0.02	0.04	0.14	0.16
650 <= FICO and 80 < sLTV <= 90	0.15	0.04	0.15	0.15	0.15	0.04	0.16	0.16
650 <= FICO and 90 <= sLTV	0.07	0.04			0.08	0.04		
PMI	0.10	0.00	−0.17	0.00	0.08	0.00	−0.18	0.00
Low doc	0.04	0.00	0.17	0.00	0.04	0.00	0.17	0.00
No doc	0.07	0.00	0.42	0.01	0.08	0.00	0.46	0.01
Yield curve	−0.09	0.00	−0.23	0.00	−0.59	0.00	−0.67	0.00
Observations (loans)	39,780		11,937		39,780		11,937	
Number of draws	500		500		500		500	
Adjusted R^2	0.526		0.281		0.2983		0.2378	

Note: Dependent Variable: simulated interest rate on the loan at origination or simulated interest rate spread on the loan at origination and the prevailing prime rate. Coefficients and adjusted R2 is the mean from the 500 random draws and standard deviation is the standard deviation of the coefficients over the 500 draws. Quarterly and originator dummies are included and available upon request. The excluded categories are 2003:Q3, unknown or very small originator, and 650 < FIC0 and sLTV <= 70.

Table 14.7 Summary of simulated interest rate and simulated spread fixed effects

	Interest Rate Results				*Spread Results*			
	A Grade		*B Grade*		*A Grade*		*B Grade*	
	Originator	*Quarter*	*Originator*	*Quarter*	*Originator*	*Quarter*	*Originator*	*Quarter*
Mean	0.12	1.91	0.05	1.20	0.12	−0.59	−0.06	−1.11
Standard deviation	0.41	0.65	0.87	0.45	0.40	0.58	0.87	0.87
Minimum	−0.81	0.19	−1.46	0.18	−0.81	−1.60	−1.57	−2.31
Maximum	1.05	2.84	2.29	1.82	1.05	0.55	2.36	0.33

Note: The excluded categories are originators with small (less than 10 observations) or missing in the data and 2003:Q3.

smallest downpayment (FIC0 <= 600 & sLTV > 90) had the highest interest rates. However, the magnitude of the impacts is smaller using the simulated LTV. In addition, the impact of a loan having PMI switched signs. Results in table 14.7 indicate that there is substantial variation specific to both the time period and the originator that is not captured by any of the other variables. These results are as expected because lending standards and the application of standards are likely to have changed over time as the sub-prime market has matured. In addition, originators may use different pricing and sorting mechanisms, which should lead to originator-specific heterogeneity.

The results for the B grade loans are also consistent with the base model results. Loans with better credit scores and larger downpayments pay the lowest interest rate. Again, the magnitudes of the interest rate differentials are more subdued. The impacts of documentation and the yield curve are also consistent across all specifications. However, the explanatory power of the results is lower for the B grade loans.

Tables 14.6 and 14.7 also provide a similar set of results using the spread between the interest rate on the loans and the prevailing prime rate (S_i) as the dependent variable. Again, the impact of credit scores and downpayment meets expectations with low credit score and small downpayment loans paying the highest spread, while good credit score and large downpayment loans paying the lowest spread for both A and B grade loans.

Conclusion

Sub-prime lending in the mortgage market has grown rapidly while introducing risk-based pricing into the lending process. The results in our chapter show that interest rates in the sub-prime mortgage market are strongly affected by a complicated nonlinear interaction of loan grade, consumer credit scores, and downpayments. After controlling for all other factors, the interest rate on A grade loans, for example, can vary by as much as 132 basis points due solely to credit scores and downpayments. In addition, the marginal impact of downpayments (credit scores) on interest rates depends on the borrowers credit history (downpayment). Other factors such as the level of documentation and the yield curve can also have substantial impact on the interest rate on a loan.

Future work on the cost of credit, in both the prime and sub-prime mortgage markets, should include all the costs associated with borrowing (in particular all ongoing and upfront fees) to refine our ability to identify the full cost of borrowing in the sub-prime market.

Notes

The views expressed in this research are those of the individual authors and do not necessarily reflect those of the Office of Comptroller of the Currency, or other officers, agencies, or instrumentalities of the United States Government.

1. This growth has occurred despite public policy concerns and regulatory restrictions The coverage of the Home Ownership and Equity Protection Act (HOEPA) was expanded in 2002 by lowering points and fees triggers, and at least 24 states had in effect by the end of 2004 HOEPA style predatory lending laws that cover a larger potion of the market and are typically designed to restrict prepayment penalties and balloon loans as well as requiring some form of credit counseling. See http://www.butera-andrews.com/state-local/b-index.htm, http://www.mbaa.org/resources/predlend/, and Standard & Poor's Anti-predatory lending update (September 2004) for more details.
2. For more details on sub-prime mortgage loans, see Chomsisengphet and Pennington-Cross (2006).
3. The volume number for sub-prime are reported for loans label B&C originators by IMF.
4. For example, Associated First Capital, the largest originator in 1996, was acquired by Citigroup. Long Beach Mortgage was purchased by one of the largest thrifts, Washington Mutual. United Companies filed for bankruptcy, while Aames Capital Corporation was delisted after significant financial difficulties and exited the market.
5. IMF calculates the securitization rate as securities issued divided by originations both measured in dollars. Therefore, this rate should be viewed as a rough estimate due to potential aging of loans before being packaged into securities.
6. The conventional conforming loan limit sets the maximum loan amount that Fannie Mae and Freddie Mac are allowed to purchase. It was set to 333,700 dollars for 2004.
7. In contrast, Fannie Mae and Freddie Mac are not in the top ten issuers of sub-prime securities for 2003 or 2002 (IMF 2004). Therefore, both firms have acted primarily as demanders not suppliers of sub-prime securities.
8. For instance, IndyMac Bank refers to loan grades as levels (1 to 5), while Countrywide uses the more typical letters (A to C).
9. This example drawn from Countrywide, one of the largest prime and sub-prime lenders, is representative of the basic approach used in the market. All of the information relates to the borrower's history of paying or not paying debts in the past. Therefore, it is very difficult for a borrower to be dynamically qualified for different loan grade requirements in the short term. However, if a potential borrower waits and cures past delinquencies, foreclosures, and bankruptcies, then he should be able to qualify for a better loan grade.

10. For example, grade A- borrowers pay 8.7 percentage points with a 10 percent downpayment and a credit score of 540. For grade B, the interest rate goes as high as 9.2 percentage point, which is 300 basis points higher than the lowest reported rate.
11. While this data set does not represent all of the subprime market, it is reasonable to assume that since these loans have become securitized, they represent the participation of the larger financial institutions in the subprime mortgage market. Small institutions with limited access to the secondary market, as well as portfolio lenders, will be sparsely represented.
12. While adjustable-rate loans do constitute a nontrivial portion of the sub-prime market, it becomes difficult to compare rates because adjustable-rate loans can have much different terms that are not reported in the available datasets. For example, it will be necessary to know what the interest rate is indexed on, the teaser rate, minimum and maximum interest rates, and minimum and maximum monthly, quarterly, and annual steps in the interest rate.
13. For the year 1995, the majority of the loans did not have a credit score reported. Therefore, all loans originated in 1995 are dropped from the analysis. By 2000, almost all loan records include a credit score. Therefore, the results from the earlier years of the study should be considered less representative of the whole market.
14. This spread between prime and sub-prime rate may include factors such as points and fees, prepayment propensities, duration, default propensities, and loss severity differences. However, the premium allows the empirical results to focus on those attributes that make the interest rate on a sub-prime loan higher than the typical prime loan.
15. Literature on interest rates in the prime market has also focused on the impact of Fannie Mae and Freddie Mac (the GSEs) (e.g., Ambrose, LaCour-Little, and Sanders 2004; Cotterman and Pearce 1996; Hendershott and Shilling 1989; Mckenzie 2002). Most of the studies in this literature use the Mortgage Interest Rate Survey (MIRS) compiled by the Federal Housing Finance Board. This data provides information on the contract or origination interest rate of a loan, fees paid, effective interest rate or yield on the mortgage, loan amount, LTV, and other attributes. However, no information on credit history or credit scores is used. On the other hand, using data from a single large lender, Ambrose, LaCour-Little, and Sanders (2004) are able to also include credit history or FICO scores.
16. In sub-prime lending, some borrowers do not fully document the source of income or wealth used for the downpayment. These loans are typically called "Low Doc" and "No Doc," depending on the level of documentation. Since neither the income nor the wealth of the borrower is fully verified, it is likely that these loans pose a higher credit risk and will be charged a higher interest rate. In addition, the Private Mortgage Insurance (PMI) reduces the exposure of the lender/investor in the event that a borrower goes into default. In the prime market, Fannie Mae and Freddie Mac require all loans with LTVs greater than 80 percent to have PMI. Since the borrower must pay for the insurance, we should expect the observed interest rate to be lower than otherwise. Since Fannie Mae and Freddie Mac do not dominate the securitization of sub-prime loans, the use of PMI seems to be more ad hoc or loan specific. For example, there is not a clean break where all loans over 80 percent LTV have PMI. In the sample, 6.9 percent of loans with LTVs between 60 and 70 had PMI. The rate does increase to 16.6 percent for loans with 10 percent downpayments, but there is no clear delineation by LTV category.

17. Note that the B grade results do not break down estimates separately for the $80 < LTV <= 90$ and $LTV > 90$ categories, because there were very few B grade loans with $LTV > 90$.
18. A uniformly distributed random number (R_n) ranging from 0 to 1 is compared to a series of cut-off values determined by the estimated probability of each LTV category. For example, assume only three (low, medium, and high) categories are included in the multinomial logit and the probability point estimates are 0.25 (π_l), 0.45 (π_m), and 0.30 (π_h), respectively for low, medium, and high LTV categories. If $R_n <= \pi_l$ then the loan is simulated as a low LTV category. If $\pi_l < R_n <= \pi_l + \pi_m$ then the loan is simulated as a medium LTV category. If $R_n > \pi_l + \pi_m$ then the loan is simulated as a high LTV category. As this experiment is repeated it will converge to the same proportions in each category as the estimated probabilities.

References

Ambrose, Brent W., and Anthony B. Sanders. 2005. "Legal Restrictions in Personal Loan Markets." *The Journal of Real Estate Finance and Economics* 30(2).

Ambrose, Brent, Micheal LaCour-Little, and Anthony Sanders. 2004. "The Effect of Conforming Loan Status on Mortgage Yield Spreads: A Loan Level Analysis." *Real Estate Economics* 32(4): 541–69.

Calem, Paul S., Kevin Gillen, and Susan Wachter. 2004. "The Neighborhood Distribution of Subprime Mortgage Lending." *Journal of Real Estate Finance and Economics* 29(4): 393–410.

Chinloy, Peter, and Nancy MacDonald. 2005. "Subprime Lenders and Mortgage Market Completion." *The Journal of Real Estate Finance and Economics* 30(2).

Chomsisengphet, Souphala, and Anthony Pennington-Cross. 2006. "The Evolution of the Subprime Mortgage Market." *Federal Reserve Bank of St. Louis Review* (January/February 2006) 88(1): 31–56.

Courchane, Marsha J., Brian J. Surette, and Peter M. Zorn. 2004. "Subprime Borrowers: Mortgage Transitions and Outcomes." *Journal of Real Estate Finance and Economics* 29(4): 365–92.

Cotterman, Robert, and James Pearce. 1996. "The Effects of the Federal National Mortgage Association and the Federal Home Loan Mortgage Corporation on Conventional Fixed-Rate Mortgage Yields." In *Studies on Privatizing Fannie Mae and Freddie Mac.* Washington, DC: U.S. Department of Housing and Urban Development (HUD).

Fortowsky, Elaine, and Michael LaCour-Little. 2002. "An Analytical Approach to Explaining the Subprime-Prime Mortgage Spread." Presented at the Georgetown University Credit Research Center Subprime Lending Symposium.

Hendershott, Patric, and James Shilling. 1989. "The Impact of the Agencies on Conventional Fixed-Rate Mortgage Yields." *Journal of Real Estate Finance and Economics* 2(2): 101–15.

IMF. 2004. "Mortgage Market Statistics Annual, 2004." Inside Mortgage Finance Publications, Inc., Bethesda Maryland, www.imfpubs.com.

McKenzie, Joseph. 2002. "A Reconsideration of the Jumbo/Non-jumbo Mortgage Rate Differential." *Journal of Real Estate Finance and Economics* 25(2–3): 197–213.

Pennington-Cross, Anthony. 2002. "Subprime Lending in the Primary and Secondary Markets." *Journal of Housing Research* 13(1): 31–50.

CHAPTER 15

DEFAULT AND PREPAYMENT RISK IN RESIDENTIAL MORTGAGE LOANS: A REVIEW AND SYNTHESIS

Michael LaCour-Little

Introduction

How long will payments under a residential mortgage loan continue? This question is central to pricing mortgages and mortgage-backed securities, now one of the largest sectors of the bond market. In this chapter, I review the research, identify major themes, and attempt a synthesis: what do we know and what do we not know?

It is axiomatic that the value of an asset is the present value of its expected future cash flows. But what are the expected cash flows from a contract that can terminate at virtually any point in time? Research on this topic is part of a broader literature on loan performance, which includes consideration of delinquencies, losses, and related topics, all of which are beyond our scope here. The narrower question is also a necessary, but not sufficient, input to asset valuation, since pricing has its own issues, including term structure model selection, choice of model parameters, and calibration of outputs to market conditions, all topics that are also beyond our scope here.

In the next sections I trace out the research, beginning with the most general theoretical work, and then turn to limitations of the theory, empirical analyses, and finally methodological research. Articles surveyed are mostly academic; although a few describe models used by investment houses or lenders, or compare predictions to those generated by such models. This review is necessarily limited, but I hope to present a reasonably comprehensive summary of the three main areas.

To begin, it may be helpful to briefly characterize each area. The theoretical literature focuses on asset pricing and tends to assume a homogenous group of rational households who can borrow without incurring transaction costs and who are motivated solely by financial considerations. In such models, level of financial sophistication, credit standing, institutional constraints, and transaction costs rarely come into play.

Empirical work may be categorized into research focusing on prepayments, research focusing on defaults, and research that addresses both. Applications may be termination risk prediction or termination functions may be used in asset pricing. Focus often depends on the particular asset under consideration. For example, since Government National Mortgage Association (GNMA) securities are government-insured, the consequences of default are minimal to the security holder, except as they produce unscheduled returns of principal. Since GNMA securities were the first traded mortgage assets, much early research focused on their pricing.

Methodological research may focus on either theoretical or empirical issues. When theoretical, the topic often centers on computational methods, whether backward-solving or forward-solving Monte Carlo techniques. On the empirical side, work tends to focus on modeling techniques and/or model specification.

Theoretical Framework

The theoretical framework originates with Merton (1973) on option pricing. Central is the insight that an option represents a contingent claim that will be exercised under certain states of the economy and not otherwise. For mortgages, two sources of uncertainty are the future level of interest rates and value of the collateral property. Accordingly, fixed-rate mortgages may be viewed as non-callable bonds containing two embedded options: the option to prepay and the option to default, either of which will terminate the mortgage. Under this view, prepayment constitutes a call option allowing the borrower to repay the mortgage at the then-current remaining balance and default constitutes a put option allowing the borrower to extinguish the debt by transferring the property to the lender.

Conceptually, if one could value the two embedded options, the value of the mortgage would be the difference between the option-free instrument and the joint value of the two options. Early references include Findley and Capozza (1977), Dunn and McConnell (1981), Foster and Van Order (1984), Buser and Hendershott (1984), Hall (1985), and Dunn and Spatt (1985). Hendershott and Van Order (1987) provide a summary of these first-generation mortgage pricing models.

Kau et al. (1992) is the most frequently cited work presenting a general model of fixed-rate mortgage valuation, recognizing that default and prepayment are substitutes. Kau et al. sets out what has become the standard two-factor valuation methodology for mortgages, allowing for both interest rate and house price uncertainty, but assuming optimal options exercise and zero transaction costs. The value of the mortgage can be shown to satisfy a partial differential equation for which no closed-form solution is available. By specifying boundary conditions, however, a solution can be obtained using the finite difference method and numerical procedures. Kau et al. note that unless initial LTV or house price volatility is high, the effect of default risk on mortgage valuation is small compared to prepayment risk.

Kau and Kim (1992) extend this work to focus on the timing of prepayment again absent transaction costs and nonfinancially oriented prepayment. Using similar numerical procedures, they derive an expression for the expected time to prepayment. Kau, Keenan, and Kim (1994) focus on default probabilities rather than option values and derive probabilities that depend on the interest rate environment, level of house price volatility, coupon rate, and initial loan-to-value ratio. Default probabilities over time are mainly a function of initial LTV and house price volatility. Kau and Keenan (1995) provide a summary of much of this theoretical work.

Stanton (1995) relaxes some of these assumptions and develops a model of mortgage prepayments assuming rational decisions by borrowers who face heterogeneous transaction costs and make prepayment decisions at discrete intervals. These two model features produce the "burnout" effect noted in empirical work.

More recently, Hilliard, Kau and Slawson (1998) apply a bivariate binomial options pricing technique to value default and prepayment options in a fixed-rate mortgage contract. This technique is relatively simpler than the finite difference technique yet results are quite similar.

Empirical Complications

Several problems arise from the option-theoretic approach. First, the values generated do not generally match observed market prices. In particular, the theory does not explain why mortgages, or mortgage-backed securities, trade at prices well in excess of par value. For example, Dunn and Spatt (2005) document GNMA prices in the 100–115 range during the mid-1980s and the Federal National Mortgage Association (FNMA) premiums currently trade in the 105–110 range. Second, the implied default and prepayment rates do not match those observed in empirical data. In particular, the option-theoretic approach predicts default and prepayment rates that are much higher than actually observed.

Evidently borrowers do not exercise options as theory would predict. Of course, borrowers may have other, nonfinancial, motivations for prepaying their mortgage prior to maturity, including household mobility. The extent to which borrowers fail to exercise in the money options has been a topic of much empirical work, especially for prepayments. For example, Quigley and Van Order (1990) examined data on loans originated during 1976–1980 and observed through 1989. Despite several waves of refinancing, only about 40 percent of mortgages had prepaid. Quigley and Van Order argue that while the degree to which the option is in the money has a great effect on prepayments, the option is not ruthlessly exercised.

Borrower heterogeneity is a possible explanation for the apparent under-exercise of mortgage options. Borrowers are likely to have heterogeneous holding periods, so the expected benefits of refinancing may vary across households. Researchers have attempted to adapt models to address such issues. For example, Follain, Scott, and Yang (1992) use binomial option pricing methods to develop a prepayment behavior when borrowers have heterogeneous holding periods. In their model, the point at which prepayment is triggered depends on transaction costs, interest rate volatility, and borrower holding period. Using data from the 1980s, they provide additional evidence on the extent to which prepayment options are not ruthlessly exercised.

Analogous under-exercise occurs when borrowers do not default when the value of the house falls below the value of the loan. Foster and Van Order (1984) found default probabilities of less than 10 percent using Federal Housing Administration (FHA) data even when equity was estimated to be quite negative. Similarly, Quigley and Van Order (1995), using data on conventional loans originated between 1975 and 1989, find that at low levels of negative equity the option to default is not exercised immediately. Nevertheless, there is strong relationship between default rates and original LTV.

Under-exercise of the default option spawned significant debate as to whether such behavior constituted nonrational behavior. Vandell (1995) addresses this question, summarizing arguments in favor of a trigger event-based theory, in which negative equity may be a necessary, but not sufficient, condition for default. He also raises the issue of lender-specific influences, since it is the lender who initiates foreclosure. For later work on trigger-event theory, see Elmer and Seelig (1999), who argue that default must be viewed in the context of the borrower's entire financial position.

The alternative view on under-exercise of the either option is that borrowers rationally delay to avoid forfeiting the right to exercise the option in the future. Support for this view may be found in Kau, Keenan, and Kim (1994), Kau and Kim (1994), Ambrose, Buttimer, and Capone (1997), and Ambrose and Buttimer (2000). Of course, a borrower refinancing into a new mortgage immediately obtains a new pair of options replacing those forfeited, so this cost may be relatively small.

Institutional Constraints—Prepayment

Institutional constraints represent another explanation for the under-exercise of the prepayment option. Archer, Ling, and McGill (1996) examine the effect of income and collateral constraints, finding that these constraints account for nearly all of the explanatory power otherwise attributable to borrower characteristics. Archer, Ling, and McGill (1997) consider the role of mobility-related factors, which affect call option exercise in two opposing fashions. First, households with high mobility may call their mortgages when the option is out of the money; second, households with short expected tenure may fail to call their mortgages even when the option is in the money.

Also focusing on constraints limiting prepayment, Peristiani, Bennett, Monsen, Peach, and Raiff (1997), argue that poor credit or low levels of equity limit refinancing, even when borrowers would benefit. Their empirical analysis concludes that borrowers with poor credit are much less likely to refinance and that the combination of low equity and poor credit significantly reduces prepayment probability. Likewise, Green and LaCour-Little (1999) examine the failure to refinance, attributing it to both transaction costs and low levels of housing equity. Caplin, Freeman, and Tracy (1997) extend this perspective to include its macroeconomic implications, arguing that the house price declines that produce defaults and constrain prepayments have the additional effect of exacerbating regional recessions.

In recent years a sub-prime mortgage segment has developed, allowing borrowers with various credit, debt, documentation, or collateral problems to readily obtain loans, although at higher rates. Presumably this development has reduced constraints on refinancing. Interesting research in the area of sub-prime loan performance is being done by Pennington-Cross (e.g., Pennington-Cross and Danis 2005). Related work by Kelly (1995) considers whether there are racial and ethnic differences in prepayment rates.

Prepayment—Other Factors

Assessment of specific factors or particular economic environments that are predictive of mortgage prepayments is another large area of research. A review of a few of these may be illustrative.

Green and Shoven (1986) use proportional hazard methods to empirically analyze the prepayment experience of a set of mortgage loans over the rising rate time period of 1976–1982, noting the lock-in effect of below market rates that presumably inhibits mobility, an element of prepayments. Quigley (1987) addresses similar issues, using PSID data from 1979 to 1981 and proportional hazards methods to assess the lock-in effect of below market rates on household mobility.

Bartholomew, Berk, and Roll (1988) address prepayments on adjustable-rate mortgages reporting that ARM prepayments differ from FRM in some significant ways. They attribute much of this to switcher effects, with ARM borrowers switching to FRM when they expect rates to rise.

Schwartz and Torous (1989) focus on valuation of default-free mortgage pass-through securities utilizing proportional hazard methods to estimate an empirical prepayment model that can be integrated into a valuation framework. They illustrate the effect of prepayments on security valuation by computing values of a non-callable security, one called optimally, and one based on an empirical prepayment function, with the empirical model producing prices that are closer to market prices.

Scott and Roll (1989) outline the four-factor prepayment model then used by Goldman Sachs for fixed-rate mortgage-backed securities, incorporating refinancing incentive, loan age, seasonality, and burnout. They argue that the ratio of the coupon to current market rate is a better measure of refinancing incentive than the difference and that accounting for burnout is essential in empirical prepayment models. Hall (2000) specifically focuses on burnout as a phenomenon, arguing that it occurs as a result of unobservable predictive variables.

Other research describing Wall Street prepayment models includes Patruno (1994), Hayre and Rajan (1995), and Hayre, Chaudhary, and Young (2000). These articles qualitatively describe model factors and graphically depict predictive power, but do not report regression techniques, specification, or parameter estimates.

McConnell and Singh (1991) consider the valuation of mortgage-backed securities (MBS) backed by ARMs using an empirical prepayment function. They show the effect of prepayments on valuation and the relative effect of altering ARM features, such as teaser discount, margin, and lifetime caps.

Schwartz and Torous (1992) focus on MBS valuation, noting that although losses from defaults are typically covered by a financial intermediary, default does affect the timing of cash flows and hence security value. As in Kau et al. (1992) they allow for two state variables, interest rates and house prices. In contrast, however, they allow for suboptimal prepayment exercise, incorporating an empirical prepayment function.

Chinloy (1993) develops a model of consumer behavior to explain the multiple choices available to the mortgage borrower: prepay the loan in its entirety, prepay only partially (curtailment), default, or continue with payments. This article appears to be the only one to consider curtailment as a distinct borrower option, although there is at least one dissertation on the topic (Fu 1998).

Schwartz and Torous (1993) propose Poisson regression to estimate a proportional hazards model of mortgage default and prepayment. They argue that Poisson regression is particularly efficient given the time-varying nature of many of the explanatory factors.

Institutional factors may also play a role. LaCour-Little and Chun (1999) focus on mortgage brokers, finding that loans originated by brokers are about three times more sensitive to refinancing incentives. A related analysis by Alexander, Grimshaw, McQueen, and Slade (2002) focuses on mortgage brokers and default rates.

Recently researchers have sought to more carefully disentangle prepayments arising from mobility from those due to refinancing. This problem persists because lenders do not receive any explanation for prepayments; they simply receive a payoff request. Work in this area includes Clapp, Harding, and LaCour-Little (2000), Pavlov (2000), Clapp, Goldberg, Harding, and LaCour-Little (2001), and Deng, Pavlov, and Yang (2005). For example, Pavlov (2000) uses data on real property transfers merged with mortgage terminations to determine whether prepayments occurred due to borrower mobility or in-place refinancing. Among his conclusions are that borrowers in high-income areas are more likely to refinance while lower-income households are less likely to refinance but more likely to move or default.

In a related piece of work, LaCour-Little (1999) examines prepayment behavior using a unique dataset that contains information on both the refinanced loan and the new loan, completely eliminating mobility-motivated prepayments. LaCour-Little argues that the role of borrower characteristics is overstated and may simply reflect differences in borrower mobility.

The effect of contract design on prepayment risk has been another topic. For example, work on prepayments has focused on adjustable-rate instruments with teaser rates (Green and Shilling 1997; Ambrose and LaCour-Little 2001), and hybrid mortgage design (Ambrose, LaCour-Little, and Huszar 2005). These studies suggest that unique contract designs produce distinct prepayment patterns.

The role of house prices has been another topic of interest. Rising house prices facilitate cash-out refinancing, which may be motivated by entirely different factors from those traditionally associated with prepayments. Mattey and Wallace (2001) and Downing, Stanton, and Wallace (2005) explore these issues.

Constraints on Default

Factors constraining default have not been addressed nearly as thoroughly. Reputation costs are often mentioned, but rarely quantified. Recourse is another important issue identified by Vandell (1995). This issue has also not been adequately explored.

Moreover, while it is popular to treat default as a put option, it is clearly not a contract option in the way prepayment is. Rather, default represents a breach of the contract, not the exercise of a contract right. Moreover, forfeiture of the property is not an option exercised by the borrower at all, rather it is the remedy exercised by the lender in the event of borrower default. This suggests that lender heterogeneity may be as important as borrower heterogeneity in explaining default. And it is not simply the lender's decision, given the reallocation of credit risk to specialized institutions. When a loan has been securitized, there is an investor, a loan servicer, and perhaps a provider of credit insurance, all of whom have a stake in outcomes.

Other Factors Affecting Default

Default has been subject to much empirical research and there are at least two survey articles, Quercia and Stegman (1992) and Vandell (1993). Early references include von Furstenburg (1969), Campbell and Dietrich (1983), and Vandell and Thibodeau (1985).

Quercia and Stegman characterize first-generation studies as focusing on loan characteristics, including loan-to-value, housing payment-to-income, and debt-to-income ratios. They distinguish these from second-generation studies that model the borrower's decision to default, and third-generation studies that focus on institutional perspectives. They argue that the role of loan characteristics is relatively well understood whereas the role of borrower characteristics, including transaction costs, is not.

Vandell (1993) provides another survey. Several outstanding issues are identified: (1) the degree of ruthlessness in mortgage default; (2) the effect of recourse; (3) default timing and loss severity; (4) workouts, modifications, and other alternatives to foreclosure. Other studies focus on particular contract types or features. A few examples are illustrative.

Cunningham and Capone (1990) compare termination risk between ARM and FRM contracts, finding that expected rate adjustments and large lifetime caps positively affect ARM termination probabilities. They also found higher default but lower prepayment probabilities for ARMs, though this latter finding is not consistent with later studies.

Similarly, Phillips, Rosenblatt, and Vanderhoff (1996) use data from 1986 to 1992 to estimate default and prepayment probabilities using multinomial logit methodology. Results differ for 15-year versus 30-year FRM, and for ARM. Like other empirical studies, they report higher rates of prepayment for ARMs but, unlike other studies, lower rates of defaults. ARMs are generally thought to have greater inherent default risk due to payment shock when rates rise. Of course, if lenders adjust underwriting accordingly, differential default rates may never appear.

Deng, Quigley, and Van Order (1996) address default risk on zero downpayment loans, a policy option to boost homeownership. They develop a competing risks model estimated with semi-parametric techniques using data on loans originated from 1976 to 1983 and tracked until 1992. They conclude that program costs, were the additional default risk not adequately priced, would be as much as 10 percent of the total funds made available for loans.

Capozza, Kazarian, and Thomson (1998) focus on the distinction between the conditional, and unconditional, default probabilities, characterizing the link between the theoretical models and the empirical tests as weak. Theoretical models focus on the unconditional probability of default, which should be tested using data on the cumulative defaults on mortgage loans over an entire 30-year term, data that is almost impossible to obtain. In contrast, empirical work focuses on conditional probabilities over short horizons, since individual loan or pool data is readily available.

Another issue that is largely unexplored is the effect of appraisal error on mortgage defaults. LaCour-Little and Malpezzi (2003) address the issue, arguing that poor-quality appraisals may lead to understated loan-to-value ratios and, hence, elevated default risk. This hypothesis has yet to be empirically tested with a large dataset.

Secondary Financing

Another issue is the effect of subordinate financing, a phenomenon that is largely prohibited in the commercial mortgage market. With the recent growth in home equity, second mortgage lending has exploded and home equity lines of credit now account for a large portion of bank lending. Home equity lending was also the genesis for the sub-prime segment, in which borrowers with poor credit and/or excessive debt levels could recapitalize using home equity (Weicher 1997).

LaCour-Little (2004) addresses the effect of junior liens on first mortgage loan performance, noting that all the theoretical models assume that the borrower has only one mortgage loan. Subsequent junior liens raise the effective contemporaneous loan to value ratio (CLTV) and reduce borrower equity, a phenomenon labeled "equity dilution." LaCour-Little (2004) provides some limited evidence that borrowers who are more likely to have junior liens are also more likely to default, though this hypothesis has yet to be more completely tested.

Other recent research focuses on home equity lending. Agarwal, Ambrose, and Liu (2005) find that borrowers taking out home equity credit lines have an elevated risk of future credit deterioration. Moreover, borrowers who experience negative credit events use higher fractions of their available credit line. Likewise, Agarwal, Ambrose, Chomsisengphet, and Liu (2006) examine the performance of home equity lines versus loans, finding considerable difference in default and prepayment rates. Unfortunately, their data does not contain information about the underlying first mortgage loan. While an important area for future research, the data requirements to jointly analyze the performance of first and junior loans are quite daunting.

Methodological Issues

Methodological research may address either theoretical or empirical issues. For pricing, the major methodological choices are backward-solving versus forward-solving Monte Carlo techniques, with significant methodological choices in each.

In empirical work, survival models such as proportional hazards model are popular choices for modeling termination risk. Such models must allow for time-varying covariates since post-origination events have considerable effect. For simplicity, researchers usually specify time in either monthly or quarterly units of observation.

While time to termination is the dependent variable in the usual hazard model, the conditional probability of termination at each point in time is the output necessary for most applications. Transforming loan-, or pool-, level data into event histories, which creates multiple observations up until time of termination or censoring, is another popular approach. Once so transformed, a variety of modeling techniques can be applied. Other interesting innovations are described later.

Deng (1997) applies semi-parametric hazard model methods to analyze default and prepayment risk when the term structure is stochastic. The forward term structure is simulated to compute option values at each observed termination point.

Nonparametric methods are another area of innovation. Maxam and LaCour-Little (2001) use kernal density regression model prepayments. Notable in this article is a comparison between model predictions and those by a parametric model used by a major mortgage lender during the early 1990s. Similarly, LaCour-Little, Maxam, and Marschoun (2002) show how kernal density regression may be used to improve parametric models.

Deng, Quigley, and Van Order (2000) is the most widely cited article in this area and presents a new methodology for estimating competing risk hazard models with unobserved borrower heterogeneity. Applying their technique to data on conforming loans, they jointly model the competing risks of default and prepayment, including baseline hazards, the effect of covariates, and of unobserved heterogeneity. Results indicate significant heterogeneity among borrowers, particularly with respect to prepayment. Accordingly, failing to model prepayment as a competing risk may produce serious errors in estimating default risk. Clapp, Deng, and An (2006) extend the modeling of unobserved heterogeneity to the multinomial logit model and provide an excellent overview of modeling choices.

An entire issue of *Real Estate Economics* was recently devoted to innovations in mortgage modeling. Wallace (2005) characterizes models as follows: (1) rational structural models applied to pool-level data; and (2) loan-level, reduced form, or behavioral models. Structural models link option exercise to the underlying dynamics of asset prices or interest rates whereas reduced form, behavioral models emphasize empirical estimation of the timing of option exercise.

Major Themes in the Research

We have seen that the main objective of mortgage termination research has been asset pricing. Theoretical approaches emphasizing the competing risks of default and prepayment may be solved in backward time by numerical procedures, but yield values that seldom align with market prices. Alternative valuation approaches include forward-solving Monte Carlo approaches, though these generally ignore default and simulate only interest rates. Resulting values may be calibrated to market prices by varying term structure or prepayment model parameters.

Much research has focused on explaining the mismatch between theoretical and actual termination rates. The effect of particular borrower or loan characteristics and the effect of the economic environment fall into this category. Major themes include the following six broad categories:

(1) The effects of default and prepayments on mortgage valuation
(2) Empirical determinants of defaults and prepayments
(3) Constraints on prepayments; constraints on defaults
(4) The effect of borrower mobility and other trigger events on termination risk
(5) The effect of unobserved borrower heterogeneity
(6) Methodological issues in valuation algorithms and estimation problems in empirical models

Many unanswered questions remain, including the following:

(1) To what extents are mobility differences the real source of borrower heterogeneity?
(2) Given the equity dilution option, how much of the error in predicting default is attributable to errors in measurement of current equity, as opposed to borrower heterogeneity?
(3) What role does recourse play and how often is that lender option exercised? To what extent do lenders differ in exercising the foreclosure option, versus workouts and other alternatives, and how do those differences vary across market segments and borrower types?
(4) What role does appraisal quality play in predicting future loan performance, especially default?
(5) Have constraints on prepayment declined with the advent of sub-prime lending?
(6) What will be the default and prepayment experience with new products, such as the payment-option ARM?

Ongoing research is essential to address these and related questions.

References

Agarwal, Sumit, Brent Ambrose, and Chunlin Liu. 2005. "Credit Lines and Credit Utilization." *Journal of Money, Credit, and Banking* 38(1): 1–22.

Agarwal, Sumit, Brent Ambrose, Souphala Chomsisengphet, and Chunlin Liu. 2006. "An Empirical Analysis of Home Equity Loan and Line Performance." *Journal of Financial Intermediation* 15(4): 444–69.

Alexander, W., S. Grimshaw, G. McQueen, and B. Slade. 2002. "Some Loans are More Equal than Others: Third-Part Originations and Defaults in the Subprime Mortgage Industry." *Real Estate Economics* 30(4): 667–97.

Ambrose, Brent W., and Richard J. Buttimer, Jr. 2000. "Embedded Options in the Mortgage Contract." *The Journal of Real Estate Finance and Economics* 21(2): 95–111.

Ambrose, Brent W., and Michael LaCour-Little. 2001. "Prepayment Risk in Adjustable Rate Mortgages Subject to Initial Year Discounts: Some New Evidence." *Real Estate Economics* 29(2): 305–28.

Ambrose, Brent W., Richard J. Buttimer, Jr., and Charles A. Capone. 1997. "Pricing Mortgage Default and Foreclosure Delay." *Journal of Money, Credit and Banking* 29(3): 314–25.

Ambrose, Brent W., Michael LaCour-Little, and Zsuzsa Huszar. 2005. "A Note on Hybrid Mortgages." *Real Estate Economics* 33(4): 765–82.

Archer, Wayne, David Ling, and Gary McGill. 1996. "The Effect of Income and Collateral Constraints on Residential Mortgage Terminations." *Regional Science and Urban Economics* 26: 235–61.

———. 1997. "Demographic Versus Option-Driven Mortgage Terminations." *Journal of Housing Economics* 6(2): 137–63.

Bartholomew, Lynn, Jonathan Berk, and Richard Roll. 1988. "Adjustable Mortgage Prepayment Behavior." *Housing Finance Review* 7: 31–46.

Buser, Steve., and Patric Hendershott. 1984. Pricing Default-Free Fixed Rate Mortgages. *Housing Finance Review* 3: 405–29.

Campbell, Tim, and J. Kimball Dietrich. 1983. "The Determinants of Default on Conventional Residential Mortgages." *Journal of Finance* 38(5): 1569–81.

Caplin, Andrew, Charles Freeman, and J. Tracy. 1997. "Collateral Damage: Refinancing Constraints and Regional Recessions." *Journal of Money, Credit and Banking* 29(4): 497–516.

Capozza, Dennis R., Dick Kazarian, and Thomas A. Thomson. 1998. "The Conditional Probability Of Mortgage Default." *Real Estate Economics* 26(3) (Fall): 359–89.

Chinloy, Peter. 1993. "Elective Mortgage Prepayment: Termination and Curtailment." *Journal of the American Real Estate and Urban Economics Association* 21(3): 313–32.

Clapp, John M., John Harding, and Michael LaCour-Little. 2000. "Expected Mobility: Part of the Prepayment Puzzle." *The Journal of Fixed Income* 10(1): 68–78.

Clapp, John M., Yongheng Deng, and Xudong An. 2006. "Unobserved Heterogeneity in Models of Competing Mortgage Termination Risk." *Real Estate Economics* 34(2): 243–74.

Clapp, John M., Gerson Goldberg, John Harding, and Michael LaCour-Little. 2001. "Movers and Shuckers: Interdependent Prepayment Decisions." *Real Estate Economics* 29(3): 411–50.

Cunningham, Donald F., and Charles Capone. 1990. "The Relative Termination Experience of Adjustable to Fixed-Rate Mortgages." *Journal of Finance* XLV(5): 1678–703.

Deng, Yongheng. 1997. "Mortgage Termination: An Empirical Hazard Model with a Stochastic Term Structure." *Journal of Real Estate Finance and Economics* 14(3): 310–31.

Deng, Yongheng, Andrey Pavlov, and Lihong Yang. 2005. "Spatial Heterogeneity in Mortgage Termination by Refinance, Sale, and Default." *Real Estate Economics* 33(4): 739–64.

Deng, Yongheng, John Quigley, and Robert Van Order. 1997. "Mortgage Default and Low Downpayment Loans: The Costs of Public Subsidy." *Regional Science and Urban Economics* 26: 263–85.

Deng, Yongheng, John Quigley, and Robert Van Order. 2000. "Mortgage Terminations, Heterogeneity and the Exercise of Mortgage Options." *Econometrica* 68(2): 275–307.

Downing, Chris, Richard Stanton, and Nancy Wallace. 2005. "An Empirical Test of a Two-Factor Mortgage Valuation Model: How Much Do House Prices Matter?" *Real Estate Economics* 33(4): 681–710.

Dunn, Kenneth, and Chester Spatt. 1985. "An Analysis of Mortgage Contracting: Prepayment Penalties and the Due-on-Sale Clause." *Journal of Finance* 40: 293–308.

———. 2005. "The Effect of Refinancing Costs and Market Imperfections on the Optimal Call Strategy and the Pricing of Debt Contracts." *Real Estate Economics* 33(4): 595–618.

Dunn, Kenneth B., and John McConnell. 1981. "Valuation of GNMA Mortgage-Backed Securities." *Journal of Finance* 36: 599–617.

Elmer, Peter, and Steve Seelig. 1999. "Insolvency, Trigger Events, and Consumer Risk Posture in the Theory of Single-Family Mortgage Default." *Journal of Housing Research* 10(1): 1–25.

Findley, M.C., and Dennis Capozza. 1977. "The Variable Rate Mortgage: An Option Theory Perspective." *Journal of Money, Credit, and Banking* 9(2): 356–64.

Follain, James R., Louis O. Scott, and Tyler Yang. 1992. "Microfoundations of a Mortgage Prepayment Function." *The Journal of Real Estate Finance and Economics* 5(2): 197–217.

Foster, Charles, and Robert Van Order. 1984. "An Options-Based Model of Mortgage Default." *Housing Finance Review* 3(4): 351–72.

Fu, Qiang. 1998. "Mortgage Curtailment and Its Role in Mortgage Pricing: Theories and Estimates." Ph.D. Dissertation, University of Wisconsin, Madison.

Green, Jerry, and John Shoven. 1986. "The Effects of Interest Rates on Mortgage Prepayments." *Journal of Money, Credit, and Banking* 18(1): 41–50.

Green, Richard K., and James D. Shilling. 1997. "The Impact of Initial-Year Discounts on ARM Prepayments." *Real Estate Economics* 25(3): 373–86.

Green, Richard K., and Michael LaCour-Little. 1999. "Some Truths about Ostriches: Who Never Refinances Their Mortgage and Why They Don't." *Journal of Housing Economics* 8: 233–48.

Hall, Arden. 1985. "Valuing Mortgage Borrowers' Prepayment Option." *AREUEA Journal* 13(3): 229–47.

———. 2000. "Controlling for Burnout in Estimating Mortgage Prepayment Models." *Journal of Housing Economics* 9(4): 215–32.

Hayre, Lakhbir, and Arvind Rajan. 1995. *Anatomy of Prepayments: The Salomon Brothers Prepayment Model.* New York: Salomon Smith Barney.

Hayre, Lahkbir, Sharad Chaudhary, and Robert A. Young. 2000. "Anatomy of Prepayments." *The Journal of Fixed Income* 10(1): 19–49.

Hendershott, Patric, and Robert Van Order. 1987. "Pricing Mortgages: An Interpretation of Models and Results." *Journal of Financial Services Research* 1(1): 19–55.

Hilliard, James, James Kau, and V. Carlos Slawson, Jr. 1998. "Valuing Prepayment and Default in a Fixed Rate Mortgage." *Real Estate Economics* 26(2): 431–68.

Kau, James B., and Taewon Kim. 1992. "The Timing of Prepayment: A Theoretical Analysis." *Journal of Real Estate Finance and Economics* 7(3): 221–28.

———. 1994. "Waiting to Default: The Value of Delay." *AREUEA Journal* 227: 195–207.

Kau, James B., and Donald Keenan. 1995. "An Overview of Option-Theoretic Pricing of Mortgages." *Journal of Housing Research* 6: 217–44.

Kau, James B., Donald Keenan, Walter Mueller, and J. Epperson. 1992. "A Generalized Valuation Model for Fixed-Rate Residential Mortgages." *The Journal of Money, Credit, and Banking* 24(3): 279–99.

Kau, James B., Donald Keenan, and Taewon Kim. 1994. "Default Probabilities for Mortgages." *Journal of Urban Economics* 35(3): 278–96.

Kelly, Austin. 1995. "Racial and Ethnic Disparities in Mortgage Prepayment." *Journal of Housing Economics* 4: 350–72.

LaCour-Little, Michael. 1999. "Another Look at the Role of Borrower Characteristics in Predicting Mortgage Prepayments." *Journal of Housing Research* 10(1): 45–60.

———. 2004. "Equity Dilution: An Alternative Perspective on Mortgage Default." *Real Estate Economics* 32(3): 359–84.

LaCour-Little, Michael, and Gregory H. Chun. 1999. "Third Party Originators and Mortgage Prepayment Risk: An Agency Problem?" *Journal of Real Estate Research* 10(1/2): 55–70.

LaCour-Little, Michael, and Stephen Malpezzi. 2003. "Appraisal Quality and Residential Mortgage Default: Evidence from Alaska." *Journal of Real Estate Finance and Economics* 27(2): 211–33.

LaCour-Little, Michael, Clark Maxam, and Michael Marschoun. 2002. "Improving Parametric Mortgage Prepayment Models Using Non-Parametric Kernel Regression." *Journal of Real Estate Research* 24(3): 299–27.

Mattey, Joe, and Nancy Wallace. 2001. "Housing-Price Cycles and Prepayment Rates of U.S. Mortgage Pools." *Journal of Real Estate Finance and Economics* 23(2): 161–84.

Maxam, Clark L., and Michael LaCour-Little. 2001. "Applied Nonparametric Regression Techniques: Estimating Prepayments on Fixed-Rate Mortgage-Backed Securities." *Journal of Real Estate Finance and Economics* 23(2): 139–60.

McConnell, John J., and Manoj Singh. 1991. "Prepayments and the Valuation of Adjustable Rate Mortgage-backed Securities." *Journal of Fixed Income* (June): 21–35.

———. 1994. "Rational Prepayments and the Valuation of Collateralized Mortgage Obligations." *The Journal of Finance* 49(3): 891–921.

Merton, Robert. 1973. "The Theory of Rational Option Pricing." *Bell Journal of Economics* 4: 141–83.

Patruno, Gregory N. 1994. "Mortgage Prepayments: A New Model for a New Era." *The Journal of Fixed Income* 4(3): 42–56.

Pavlov, Andrey. D. 2000. "Competing Risks of Mortgage Prepayments: Who Refinances, Who Moves, and Who Defaults?" *Journal of Real Estate Finance and Economics* 23(2): 185–212.

Pennington-Cross, Anthony, and Michelle Danis. 2005. "A Dynamic Look at Subprime Loan Performance." *Journal of Fixed Income* 15(1): 28–39.

Peristiani, Stavros, Paul. Bennett, Gordon Monsen, Richard Peach, and J. Raiff. 1997. "Credit, Equity, and Mortgage Refinancings." *Federal Reserve Bank of New York Policy Review* (July): 83–99.

Phillips, Richard A., Eric Rosenblatt, and James H. VanderHoff. 1996. "The Probability of Fixed- and Adjustable-Rate Mortgage Termination." *Journal of Real Estate Finance and Economics* 13(2): 95–104.

Quercia, Roberto G., and Michael A. Stegman. 1992. "Residential Mortgage Default: A Review of the Literature." *Journal of Housing Research* 3(2): 341–79.

Quigley, John M. 1987. "Interest Rate Variations, Mortgage Prepayments, and Household Mobility." *The Review of Economics and Statistics* 69 (4): 636–43.

Quigley, John M., and Robert Van Order. 1990. "Efficiency in the Mortgage Market: The Borrower's Perspective." *AREUEA Journal* 18(3): 237–52.

———. 1995. "Explicit Tests of Contingent Claims Models of Mortgage Default." *Journal of Real Estate Finance and Economics* 11: 99–117.

Richard, Scott F., and Richard Roll. 1989. "Modeling Prepayments on Fixed Rate Mortgage-Backed Securities." *Journal of Portfolio Management* 15(3): 73–82.

Schwartz, Eduardo, and Walter Torous. 1989. "Prepayment and the Valuation of Mortgage Pass-Through Securities." *Journal of Finance* 44: 375–92.

———. 1992. "Prepayment, Default, and the Valuation of Mortgage Pass-Through Securities." *Journal of Business* 65(2): 221–39.

———. 1993. "Mortgage Prepayment and Default Decisions: A Poisson Regression Approach." *Journal of the American Real Estate and Urban Economics Association* 21: 431–49.

Stanton, Richard. 1995. "Rational Prepayment and Valuation of Mortgage-Backed Securities." *Review of Financial Studies* 8(3): 677–708.

Vandell, Kerry D. 1993. "Handing Over the Keys: A Perspective on Mortgage Default Research." *Journal of the American Real Estate and Urban Economics Association* 21(3): 211–46.

———. 1995. "How Ruthless is Mortgage Default? A Review and Synthesis of the Evidence." *Journal of Housing Research* 6(2): 245–64.

Vandell, Kerry, and Thomas Thibodeau. 1985. "Estimation of Mortgage Defaults Using Disaggregate Loan history Data." *AREUEA Journal* 13(3): 292–316.

Von Furstenburg, George. 1969. "Default Risk on FHA-Insured Home Mortgages as a Function of the Terms of Financing: A Quantitative Analysis." *Journal of Finance* 24: 459–77.

Wallace, Nancy. 2005. "Innovations in Mortgage Modeling: An Introduction." *Real Estate Economics* 33(4): 587–94.

Weicher, John. 1997. *The Home Equity Lending Industry*. Indianapolis, IN: The Hudson Institute.

PART V

REGULATORS PROSPECTIVE OF CONSUMER CREDIT

CHAPTER 16

STATISTICAL ANALYSIS AND MODELING FOR FAIR LENDING AND COMPLIANCE: THE OCC'S PERSPECTIVE

Mark Pocock, Irene Fang, and Jason Dietrich

Introduction

In 1989, the Home Mortgage Disclosure Act (HMDA) was modified to require lenders to gather and report data on applicants' race and gender. This data created opportunities for banking regulators to incorporate statistical techniques into analyses of disparate treatment during fair lending exams. Statistics provide an objective and efficient approach to identifying patterns in large volumes of data. Results from these analyses can be used to draw conclusions about disparate treatment as well as to identify areas of higher fair lending risk needing more thorough review. Overall, statistics have been an important complement to traditional manual file reviews during fair lending exams.

Beginning with the Boston Fed Study (Munnel et al. 1996), a number of articles, including some by banking regulators, have presented statistical approaches to analyzing mortgage markets for disparate treatment. Most of these studies focused on underwriting decisions, because that was where fair lending risk was thought to be the highest and government monitoring data was collected. However, a number of recent changes in mortgage markets have potentially shifted fair lending risk. All but one of these changes is directly linked to data availability, and, therefore, has a direct effect on how statistical analyses should be conducted. First, advances in data collection and availability have increased risk in pricing decisions. With better data, lenders can more accurately identify applicants' risk levels. As a result, underwriting is becoming more automated, and risk-based pricing is increasingly being used to ration credit. Second, risk-based pricing in turn raises potential concerns about redlining and steering. More extensive data allows lenders to develop rate sheets for smaller geographic markets. Correlations between geography and protected class status raise potential redlining risk. Similarly, risk-based pricing has benefited the sub-prime market, as marginal applicants who would previously have been denied are now being approved but at a higher price. For larger institutions active in both prime and sub-prime markets, there is potential risk of prime customers being steered to sub-prime pricing. Third, with recent increases in the amount of electronic data that lenders maintain, the Office of the Comptroller of the Currency (OCC) has transitioned from estimating models based on sample data to models based on population data. While this allows all observations to be incorporated into the analysis, data is typically available for fewer variables than if samples are used. As a result, omitted variable bias has become more of a concern. Finally, brokers have dramatically increased their presence in mortgage markets over the last ten years, with a current market share of originations near 70 percent. Brokers introduce an additional layer of fair lending risk, especially for pricing decisions. In addition, brokers complicate statistical analyses since data being analyzed consist of many different decision makers, each with its own policies and only small numbers of originations or applications.

All of these changes have affected the focus of fair lending analyses and the types of statistical approaches used. However, few studies addressing the statistical issues related to these changes are available. The objective of this article is to begin to fill this void from a regulatory perspective. Specifically, this article summarizes the statistical approach the OCC uses during fair lending exams of underwriting and pricing decisions. Given the size of banks the OCC regulates, it is a natural place to develop and use statistical methods that rely on large quantities of data. These large datasets allow the OCC flexibility in the types of statistical tools it can use as well as when statistics can be used.

The remainder of the article is as follows. The next section presents a brief summary of fair lending laws and regulations. This is followed with a brief overview of the evolution of the use of statistics during fair lending exams at the OCC. The next section details the current statistical approach the OCC uses to test for disparate treatment in underwriting and pricing decisions. The succeeding section highlights future directions and challenges for fair lending analyses. The final section concludes the discussion.

Overview of Fair Lending Laws

The starting point for any discussion of fair lending laws is the Civil Rights Act of 1964. The Civil Rights Act officially outlawed discrimination based on race, color, religion, sex, or national origin. The extent of the law was quite broad and general, applying to public facilities, government, employment, education, and housing. Shortly thereafter, the Fair Housing Act (FHA) (1968) and the Equal Credit Opportunity Act (ECOA) (1974) were enacted to officially prohibit discrimination in housing and credit markets. The FHA prohibits creditors involved in residential real estate transactions from discriminating against any person on the basis of race, color, religion, sex, handicap, familial status, or national origin. It covers any person selling or renting property, engaging in residential real estate related transactions, or providing brokerage services and other services related to the sale or rental of housing. The ECOA prohibits discrimination in any aspect of a credit transaction against persons on the basis of race, color, religion, national origin, sex, marital status, age (provided the applicant has the capacity to contract), the fact that an applicant's income derives from any public assistance program, and the fact that the applicant has in good faith exercised any right under the Consumer Credit Protection Act. In short, it covers applicants in credit transactions.

Together, the FHA and ECOA provided the foundation for building a fair lending and compliance program, and HMDA provided the necessary data to implement the program. Enacted in 1974, HMDA required lenders to report numbers of applications and originated loans by census tract. Data were originally required only at an aggregate level, because redlining was the primary concern at the time. In 1989, as part of the Financial Institutions Reform Recovery and Enforcement Act (FIRREA), HMDA was modified to require lenders to gather and report information at the individual level. Data to be reported included the race, gender, and income of the applicant as well as the type, purpose, occupancy, loan amount, location, and action taken on the application. In 2003, HMDA was modified again, requiring lenders to report pricing information for the first time. For high-cost loans, lenders must now report the rate spread, which is the difference between the annual percentage rate (APR) for the loan and the rate on a comparable treasury instrument. High cost is defined as 3 percent above a comparable treasury yield for first lien loans, and 5 percent above a comparable treasury yield for second lien loans. In addition to pricing data, lenders also are now required to report ethnicity and race as well as information on property type, lien status, and whether there was a preapproval.

The OCC's Use of Statistics in Fair Lending Supervision

Capitalizing on the availability of government monitoring data on home mortgage applications in the United States, the OCC began in the early 1990s to explore the potential use of statistically driven data analysis on fair lending examinations. Economists began providing detailed analysis of a bank's HMDA data to examiners, as an aid to determining the focus of an examination. The OCC also began exploring the use of statistical modeling as a potential tool for automating comparative file review, which had previously been conducted manually by trained fair lending specialists. As the result of an extensive study (Stengel and Glennon 1999) that pioneered the use of statistical tools in fair lending examinations, OCC economists determined that statistical models could be an effective tool for systematically comparing large numbers of application decisions that are based on multiple factors. In addition, Stengel and Glennon concluded that such models should be bank-specific, that is, tailored to the underwriting policies of the individual bank, for the individual product and time period in question. The OCC has used this approach consistently since the early 1990s. When statistical modeling is used on a fair lending examination, OCC economists participate with examiners in an interview of the bank, in which extensive information on the bank's underwriting and/or pricing policies is documented.[1] This information is used to build a detailed statistical model that follows those policies and that allows underwriting and pricing decisions to be tested for the potential existence of disparate treatment.[2] The OCC has found the use of statistical analysis and modeling to be a useful tool for fair lending examinations where there are sufficient numbers of applications.[3]

The OCC's Approach to Testing for Disparate Treatment in Underwriting and Pricing Decisions

OCC bank examiners evaluate national banks' compliance with the FHA, ECOA, and the Federal Reserve Board's Regulation B.[4] Given the large volume of applications and originations at many of these banks, statistics allow the OCC to conduct systematic analyses of disparate treatment that would not be feasible with only a manual review. OCC economists assist examiners in three steps of this analysis: targeting (to determine focal points), statistical modeling (automated comparative file review), and the selection of files for manual follow-up review.

Targeting Analysis to Choose Focal Points for Examination

As suggested in the name, the purpose of the targeting analysis is to identify areas within a bank that have the highest fair lending risk. Annually, the OCC uses a risk-based screening program to select banks for in-depth fair lending examinations. From this analysis, which uses the HMDA data along with other information such as supervisory experience and customer complaints, banks with relatively higher fair lending risk are identified. Once a bank is selected for a fair lending examination and if requested by the examination team, economists perform a targeting analysis using data that include the variables recorded in HMDA.[5] These targeting analyses are an important input for choosing the focal points, or scope, for a fair lending exam.

In a targeting analysis, OCC economists analyze both underwriting and pricing decisions by each of the application characteristics reported in HMDA: loan type, property type, purpose of loan, owner-occupancy, preapproval, ethnicity, and race.[6] Following OCC policy, economists conduct the analysis separately for race and ethnicity, that is, comparing Hispanics with non-Hispanics and comparing each non-Hispanic minority race with non-Hispanic whites.

Specifically, they compute denial rates for each protected class and their respective control groups. A denial is defined as an application that was "denied by financial institution" or that was a "preapproval request denied by financial institution."[7] An approval is defined as an application that was originated, "application approved but not accepted," or "preapproval request approved but not accepted." OCC economists then compare these denial rates by computing denial rate ratios and denial rate differences. A denial rate ratio of one means that both the protected class and the control group are denied at the same rate. A denial ratio greater than one means that protected class applicants are denied more frequently than control group applicants. Since this measure is sensitive to the number of applicants in each group and the magnitude of the denial rates, economists also compute the difference in the denial rates, which is an absolute measure of denial disparity. As with denial ratios, a larger denial rate difference indicates a larger fair lending risk. An example of the targeting analysis for underwriting is table 16.1. Using denial rates for subgroups defined by characteristics of the applicant and application, OCC economists then statistically test whether the denial rate for the protected class differs from the denial rate of the control group. They recommend to examiners to focus on groups that have relatively large disparities and a high level of significance. Economists also advise examiners as to whether there are sufficient numbers of observations for further statistical analysis.

In addition to data on underwriting decisions, HMDA data also includes the difference between the APR on the loan and the comparable Treasury instrument. This rate spread is reported by a bank only if the APR on the loan is 3 percent higher than the comparable treasury for first liens and 5 percent higher for junior liens. This information helps in choosing pricing focal points. Specifically, we consider both rate spread incidences and rate spread averages. For rate spread incidences, OCC economists compute the same statistics as for denial disparities, but now for rate spread incidence disparities. An example of the targeting analysis for rate spread reporting disparities is table 16.2. For rate spread averages, economists compute the average rate spread for protected class and control groups as well as the associated ratios and differences analogous to the description for underwriting, given earlier. For both rate spread incidences and average rate spreads, they test whether the disparities between protected classes and control groups are statistically different. An example of a targeting analysis for average rate spreads is table 16.3.

Clearly, much of the information about the underwriting and pricing decisions that are necessary to model those decisions and to test for a potential pattern or practice of discrimination are not contained in the HMDA data. Information on credit worthiness and repayment abilities of the applicant, such as credit score, loan-to-value (LTV) ratios, and debt-to-income (DTI) ratios, are important factors in the lending decision. On occasion, the OCC is able to obtain data on these factors before the focus of the exam has been decided. If such is the case, OCC economists can then perform a more detailed targeting analysis that includes these additional factors.

Based on statistical tests, magnitudes, and the sign of disparities, economists recommend to the examiner possible focuses for the exam. Because the robustness of further statistical analyses is based on large sample sizes, they advise examiners to select groups with a sufficient number of observations in the event that further statistical analyses are desired.

Statistical Modeling of Underwriting and Pricing Decisions

Once the focal points have been chosen, and in cases where examiners choose to use statistical modeling to test for potential discrimination, OCC economists begin gathering information relevant to the modeling process. They first review the bank's underwriting and/or pricing policies and then construct a statistical model to test for potential disparate treatment.[8] The statistical model is an automated

Table 16.1 Statistically significant denial rate disparities by Hispanic ethnicity and non-Hispanic race

	Protected Class Group				Control Group			Denial Disparity	
Subset	*Product*	*Group*	*# Applications*	*Denial Rate (%)*	*Group*	*# Applications*	*Denial Rate (%)*	*Ratio*	*Difference (%)*
A. Hispanic Ethnicity Results									
1st, 1–4 family, owner-occupied	Conv, Refi	Hispanic	38,390	37.4	Non-Hispanic	228,516	24.8	1.5	12.6
1st, 1–4 family, not owner-occupied	Conv, Refi	Hispanic	2,554	45.8	Non-Hispanic	17,759	30.1	1.5	15.8
2nd, 1–4 family, owner-occupied	Conv, Refi	Hispanic	2,166	56.7	Non-Hispanic	16,008	46.0	1.2	10.8
1st, 1–4 family, not owner-occupied	Conv, HP	Hispanic	2,083	20.5	Non-Hispanic	15,336	12.8	1.6	7.6
1st, mfctd housing, owner-occupied	Conv, Refi	Hispanic	602	69.6	Non-Hispanic	4,139	62.8	1.1	6.8
2nd, 1–4 family, owner-occupied	Conv, HP	Hispanic	376	43.4	Non-Hispanic	2,437	26.2	1.7	17.1
1st, 1–4 family, owner-occupied**	Conv, HP	Hispanic	272	41.9	Non-Hispanic	3,520	28.6	1.5	13.3
1st, 1–4 family, owner-occupied*	Conv, HP	Hispanic	263	63.1	Non-Hispanic	2,369	48.0	1.3	15.1
B. Non-Hispanic Race Results									
1st, 1–4 family, owner-occupied	Conv, Refi	Asian	13,444	20.8	White	184,009	22.6	0.9	-1.8
1st, 1–4 family, owner-occupied	Conv, HP	Black	5,820	21.1	White	74,028	9.8	2.2	11.3
1st, 1–4 family, owner-occupied	Conv, HI	Black	3,063	57.4	White	13,502	28.5	2.0	28.9
1st, 1–4 family, not owner-occupied	Conv, HP	Black	1,213	31.7	White	12,656	10.7	3.0	21.0
lien n/a, 1–4 family, owner-occupied	Conv, HI	Black	803	62.4	White	1,972	54.0	1.2	8.4
2nd, 1–4 family, owner-occupied	Conv, HI	Asian	769	44.2	White	17,574	39.2	1.1	5.0
2nd, 1–4 family, owner-occupied	Conv, Refi	Asian	558	50.9	White	13,589	44.1	1.2	6.8
2nd, 1–4 family, owner-occupied	Conv, HP	Black	146	48.6	White	2,086	24.5	2.0	24.1
1st, 1–4 family, not owner-occupied	Conv, HP	Indian	50	20.0	White	12,656	10.7	1.9	9.3
1st, 1–4 family, not owner-occupied**	Conv, HP	Black	41	46.3	White	623	22.3	2.1	24.0

Note: First and second liens are denoted by 1st and 2nd, respectively. Conventional loans are denoted by Conv, HP, HI, and Refi denote home purchase, home improvement, and refinance loans, respectively. The Ratio column is the denial rate of the protected class divided by the denial rate of the control group. The Difference column is the percentage point difference of the denial rate of the protected class less the denial rate of the control group. The data are from the 2004 HMDA dataset. One asterisk denotes groups that requested a preapproval; two asterisks denote groups that did not request a preapproval. All other groups are without preapproval reporting.

Table 16.2 Statistically significant rate spread reporting disparities by Hispanic ethnicity and non-Hispanic race

	Protected Class Group				Control Group			Reporting Disparity	
Subset	*Product*	*Group*	*# Originations*	*Rate Spread (%)*	*Group*	*# Originations*	*Rate Spread (%)*	*Ratio*	*Difference (%)*
A. Hispanic Ethnicity Results									
1st, 1–4 family, owner-occupied	Conv, Refi	Hispanic	20,301	5.5	Non-Hispanic	147,975	3.7	1.5	1.7
1st, 1–4 family, owner-occupied	Conv, HP	Hispanic	12,488	2.3	Non-Hispanic	74,390	1.5	1.5	0.8
1st, 1–4 family, owner-occupied	Conv, HI	Hispanic	1,578	12.4	Non-Hispanic	8,477	8.4	1.5	4.0
1st, 1–4 family, not owner-occupied	Conv, HP	Hispanic	1,520	6.9	Non-Hispanic	12,248	4.5	1.5	2.4
1st, 1–4 family, not owner-occupied	Conv, Refi	Hispanic	1,177	17.2	Non-Hispanic	10,792	10.7	1.6	6.5
2nd, 1–4 family, owner-occupied	Conv, HI	Hispanic	546	27.1	Non-Hispanic	4,204	22.9	1.2	4.2
2nd, 1–4 family, owner-occupied	Conv, HP	Hispanic	183	15.8	Non-Hispanic	1,497	8.9	1.8	7.0
1st, 1–4 family, not owner-occupied	Conv, HI	Hispanic	166	51.2	Non-Hispanic	969	40.0	1.3	11.2
B. Non-Hispanic Race Results									
1st, 1–4 family, owner-occupied	Conv, Refi	Black	12,324	11.0	White	122,852	3.2	3.5	7.8
1st, 1–4 family, owner-occupied	Conv, Refi	Asian	9,446	0.9	White	122,852	3.2	0.3	−2.3
1st, 1–4 family, owner-occupied	Conv, HP	Asian	7,122	0.3	White	61,656	1.2	0.2	−1.0
1st, 1–4 family, owner-occupied	Conv, HP	Black	4,065	7.1	White	61,656	1.2	5.7	5.8
1st, 1–4 family, owner-occupied	Gov't, HP	Black	1,781	0.4	White	12,730	0.1	5.0	0.3
1st, 1–4 family, not owner-occupied	Conv, Refi	Black	1,190	29.3	White	8,802	8.6	3.4	20.8
1st, 1–4 family, not owner-occupied	Conv, HP	Asian	834	1.6	White	10,396	3.4	0.5	−1.9
1st, 1–4 family, not owner-occupied	Conv, HP	Black	738	22.0	White	10,396	3.4	6.4	18.5

Note: First and second liens are denoted by 1st and 2nd, respectively. Conventional loans are denoted by Conv, HP, HI, and Refi denote home purchase, home improvement, and refinance loans, respectively. The Rate Spread column is the rate spread reporting rate. The Ratio column is the rate spread reporting rate of the protected class divided by the rate spread reporting rate of the control group. The Difference column is the percentage point difference of the rate spread reporting rate of the protected class less the rate spread reporting rate of the control group. These data are from the 2004 HMDA dataset.

Table 16.3 Statistically significant rate spread average disparities by Hispanic ethnicity and non-Hispanic race

	Protected Class Group				Control Group			Avg. Rate Spread Disparity	
Subset	*Product*	*Group*	*# Originations*	*Avg. Rate Spread*	*Group*	*# Originations*	*Avg. Rate Spread*	*Ratio*	*Difference*
A. Hispanic Ethnicity Results									
1st, mfctd housing, owner-occupied	Conv, HP	Hispanic	264	5.53	Non-Hispanic	3,028	5.46	1.01	0.07
2nd, 1–4 family, owner-occupied	Conv, HP	Hispanic	195	6.07	Non-Hispanic	925	6.19	0.98	−0.12
1st, 1–4 family, owner-occupied	Conv, Refi	Hispanic	169	3.68	Non-Hispanic	2,122	3.86	0.95	−0.19
1st, mfctd housing, owner-occupied	Conv, Refi	Hispanic	80	5.04	Non-Hispanic	1,093	5.04	1.00	0.00
B. Non-Hispanic Race Results									
1st, mfctd housing, owner-occupied	Conv, HP	Native	33	5.20	White	2,647	5.42	−0.2	−0.69

Note: First and second liens are denoted by 1st and 2nd, respectively. Conventional loans are denoted by Conv, HP, and Refi denote home purchase and refinance loans, respectively. The Ratio column is the average rate spread of the protected class divided by the average rate spread of the control group. The Difference column is the difference of the average rate spread of the protected class less the average rate spread of the control group. These data are from the 2004 HMDA dataset.

comparative file review of all applications or originations in the population. The statistical model also serves as a mechanism to identify specific files for additional manual review.

To understand how to model underwriting and pricing decisions, economists review both the written policies of a bank and interview bank personnel who are knowledgeable about bank underwriting and pricing practices.[9] The underwriter interview is an opportunity for the OCC to learn about the bank's underwriting and pricing polices and for the bank to provide any additional information on these policies. Though this process is important for establishing policy, often follow-up questions and further dialogue are necessary to clarify questions about the data or about the names and definitions of products.

The OCC receives a large amount of information from the bank that is not contained in the HMDA data set. Incorporating this information into the modeling process can explain much of the variance in underwriting and pricing disparities that a simple analysis of the HMDA data would attribute to potential illegal disparate treatment. For example, underwriting policy information could include cutoffs or threshold values for certain key variables. This often occurs for DTI where cutoffs may differ by product. As a result, two applicants may have the same DTI ratio but a lender may view one as too high, while the other may be acceptable. Information about these cutoffs is critical in order to accurately model the bank's underwriting policies. In addition, often a strong credit-worthiness variable may compensate for a weak credit-worthiness variable elsewhere; such trade-offs can be captured in a statistical model. Another crucial piece of information is whether or not the bank considers any factors to be "fatal" to an application (i.e., necessitating an automatic denial). Modeling such policies correctly is crucial to understanding and correctly identifying sources of variation in the bank's decisions.

For pricing examinations, the OCC requests from the bank information such as rate sheets, policies on underages and overages, and exceptions to pricing policies for the chosen focal points of the exam. The amount and detail of information that the bank provides is often more than what OCC economists can explicitly incorporate into a statistical model. While the model will probably not include every detail, it will reflect a full understanding of the decision process and the context for decisions.

OCC economists often model the underwriting and pricing decisions with logistic and regression models for binary and continuous dependent variables, respectively. These two specifications are the workhorses of applied empirical economics. The models may include indicator variables for different levels of LTV, DTI, or other cutoffs used by the bank, an indicator variable for changes in policy, categorical variables for different credit tiers, and the interaction of all or only some of these variables.[10] As underwriting and pricing policies may differ by bank, channel, and product, the exact model specifications vary bank to bank and exam to exam.

After reviewing all of the files with a statistical model, economists also focus on additional areas where discrimination may occur. For example, if a certain market is more competitive than another market, a bank may give brokers a large overage range for loans. Another example is loan products that are underwritten through processes that are less automated than other loan products. Where more discretion is allowed, there may be greater risk for discrimination, overt or otherwise. In addition to reviewing areas with greater discretion, OCC economists also review the automated processes for fair lending compliance.

With a statistical model of the underwriting and pricing decisions based on the bank's policy, OCC economists focus on the magnitude and significance of the coefficient on the protected class variable. As expected, these coefficients are usually much smaller and less significant than they may have been during the targeting stage, because more information about the credit worthiness of the applicant is included in the model. If the coefficient on the protected class indicator variable is still significant after these models, or as requested by the examiner, economists identify individual application files that have the highest fair lending risk for further review.

File Review

The statistical model is an automated comparative file review of all applications or originations in the population. After constructing models that follow the bank's underwriting and pricing polices, OCC economists then analyze influential applications and outliers.[11] There are two objectives in doing so; first, like in all empirical work, we want to know whether a few observations are causing the statistical significance and/or large coefficients. Second, we want to identify files for further review, perhaps drawing on more information from the bank.

Examiners may also request files that are similarly situated but where decisions were not the same, for example, a non-Hispanic black applicant who was denied and a non-Hispanic white applicant who was approved where credit factors appear to be similar. With de facto scoring models for underwriting and pricing, OCC economists can identify files for which the predicted outcome differ from the actual outcome. These matched files that economists provide for examiners are a better-quality match than a random selection of files out of the entire focus of the exam.

The use of statistical tools on fair lending examinations enables a risk-based and comprehensive approach. From the targeting analysis to the selection of files for the examiner to request from the bank, all of the applications are reviewed. Specifically, at the beginning of the process all of the HMDA reportable applications at the bank are reviewed by analyzing disparities in denial rates, rate spread reporting incidences, and rate spread averages. Areas that have the highest fair lending risk are then further analyzed with a statistical model that incorporate the bank's underwriting and pricing decisioning polices, credit-worthiness data, and additional variables used in the decisioning process. Groups of applications that show signs of continued fair lending risk are again analyzed by looking at the individual files, and then finally, by asking the bank for the entire file for that application for review by the examiner.

As OCC economists analyze thousands, and sometimes millions, of applications through statistical models, it may appear at certain stages of the analysis that evidence disparate treatment may be present. In such instances, the OCC probes those high-risk areas and requests more data to do further analyses on those data.

Future Direction and Challenges of Fair Lending Analyses

Recent increases in the availability and quality of electronic data has affected how lenders evaluate mortgage applications and decision loans. In turn, this has affected fair lending risk and how regulators conduct fair lending exams. In this section, we present some of these changes and discuss their potential impact on fair lending exams. Throughout the discussion, we highlight some approaches the OCC is currently developing to address these changes.

One major change has been the increasing number of lenders that rely on automated underwriting systems to decision applications. These automated underwriting models implement what consumer groups have argued for in the past, that is, an underwriting method based on credit worthiness that eliminates possible biases in discretionary underwriting. As a result, risk of disparate treatment in underwriting, in general, should be mitigated. However, this move toward automation has potential drawbacks. Marginal applications and applications with limited credit history may be more likely to be denied in an automated underwriting system. To the extent that these application characteristics are correlated with protected class status, the risk of disparate impact becomes an issue. Currently, statistical approaches and tests appropriate for detecting potential disparate impact are limited.[12] The challenge for the OCC is to develop such tools for future exams.

As underwriting has become more automated, risk-based pricing has also become increasingly popular. Subsequently, fair lending risk in pricing decisions has increased as well. Analyzing pricing for disparate treatment raises a number of analytical issues. At a basic level, there is the question of how to measure "price."[13] Possible measures include coupon rate, APR, fees (both individual and aggregate), points, rate spread, rate spread incidence, and overages/underages. For lack of a strong defense for using any one of these measures, the OCC currently conducts comprehensive statistical analyses, which analyze disparities in a number of different pricing measures.

Once a measure of price is chosen, the next issue is what determines price. Price consists of a deterministic portion and a discretionary portion. Following standard policy, the OCC focuses fair lending analyses on the discretionary portion. However, the deterministic portion needs to be accounted for first. In a multivariate analysis, one approach to accounting for this deterministic portion is to include control variables reflecting all factors on the rate sheet. This provides estimates of the true effects of each of the rate sheet factors, assuming that they have been modeled correctly. As an alternative approach, the OCC also analyzes an adjusted price measure, which is price cleansed of the deterministic adjustments from the rate sheets. In other words, any rate sheet adjustments applied to determine an applicant's rate are removed. This approach accounts for the effects of a portion of the deterministic components of price exactly.[14]

Possibly the most important issue regarding fair lending risk in pricing decisions involves brokers. Brokers introduce an additional layer of fair lending risk for lenders, because lenders are responsible for brokers' actions, but brokers are not directly regulated by the OCC. Given that the compensation brokers receive from lenders is tied to the rate on the loan, fair lending risk is especially high in pricing decisions, as brokers' incentives are to extract as much consumer surplus as possible from each applicant. Broker behavior, however, is difficult to analyze as typical datasets contain only a few observations per broker and only the applications that each broker submitted to that particular lender. As a result, it is difficult to apply standard parametric econometric techniques. As an alternative, the OCC is exploring various nonparametric techniques, which do not depend on asymptotic distributional assumptions, and, therefore, do not depend on large sample sizes. As an example, for any given broker, after adjusting for the deterministic components of price, the average APR for a control group should be similar to the average APR for a prohibited bases group. If the average APR by broker is consistently higher for prohibited bases groups than for the control group, this would indicate evidence of potential disparate treatment.[15]

Related to pricing is reverse redlining, where lenders lend to a particular geographic area but only at higher rates. With increased availability and quality of data, lenders are able to develop rate sheets for smaller markets. Given correlations between geography and protected class status, lenders must be able to justify systematic differences in rates across markets. In addition, care must be taken when accounting for market fixed effects in pricing analyses to ensure that market effects are not proxying for protected class status. One approach the OCC uses to address this issue is to interact protected class status with market and test the null hypothesis of no differences. Alternatively, analyses can be conducted by market when sufficient observations are available. The objective here is to determine whether applicants are being treated consistently within markets as well as across markets.

Increased reliance on risk-based pricing also increases fair lending risk related to steering. This is especially an issue for larger lenders active in both prime and near-prime markets. Fair lending risk is especially high if similar products are offered in both markets. Steering begins to get at the counseling or guidance lenders offer applicants during credit transactions. This customer assistance is a very important aspect of the process and potentially an area of higher fair lending risk. Unfortunately, it is difficult to isolate this effect analytically, primarily due to a lack of data. One potential approach is to apply standards for prime products to the sub-prime population to determine whether some applicants who received sub-prime loans would have qualified for prime loans. An alternative approach is to use information from the notes sections of mortgage applications to develop some measure or assessment of customer assistance that could be analyzed systematically across applicants. Again, these types of analyses may be aided by the continued advances in data collection and availability.

Finally, recent changes in HMDA that require lenders to separately report information on ethnicity and race have generated much discussion about the groupings various regulators use during fair lending exams. More extensive data create opportunities to improve upon current racial and ethnic groupings. As each applicant differs on a number of dimensions, so may their experience differ by broker, the application process, and possibly the bank.[16] Current OCC policy is to compare Hispanics with non-Hispanics and each non-Hispanic race with non-Hispanic whites. More precise definitions that define more homogenous groupings may improve tests for disparate treatment.

Fair lending risk is evolving and, as such, regulators need to adjust their statistical tools and methods accordingly. This section highlighted some of the statistical tools and methods economists at the OCC are currently working on as part of this evolution. These tools and techniques are in various stages of development, and they are part of the constant and ongoing process of keeping up with changes in fair lending risk in mortgage markets.

Conclusion

Interest and concern over fair lending in general, and specifically over proper fair lending regulation and enforcement, is at one of its highest levels in years. The recent Supreme Court case, *Watters v. Wachovia*, highlighted the tension between state and federal regulators.[17] Some critics claim that federal regulators are more concerned with safety and soundness and that states are more concerned with consumer protection, and hence states should have more regulatory authority over national subsidiaries (Tse 2006). Feeding the interest in fair lending and alleged fair lending violations is the inclusion of pricing information in HMDA, a dynamic housing market, and the flattening of the yield curve in 2005, which in turn triggered more rate spread reporting in HMDA (Avery, Brevoort, and Canner 2006; Do and Paley 2007).

With the spotlight on fair lending, this chapter presents a transparent look at how OCC economists assist fair lending examinations. We show that through a risk- based methodology the OCC reviews all mortgage applications through an initial screen, selects banks and areas within a bank with the highest risk, and then interviews and draws out information about a bank's underwriting and pricing decisions. With this information, OCC economists create statistical models to look for patterns or practices of fair lending violations. Following a detailed analysis of the data and multiple statistical tests, economists provide examiners with the highest fair lending risk files to review manually.

Through this detailed process, much is learned about a bank's mortgage underwriting and pricing process. Often times, but not always, additional information that is not in HMDA but is available to OCC economists, such as LTV, DTI, and credit scores, explains disparities that may exist in analyses based only on HMDA. In the cases where evidence of fair lending violations still exist, a manual review of files often demonstrates valid reasons for the bank's underwriting or pricing decisions.

The results of these thorough examinations are manifold. First, it provides a deterrent to banks that may consider violating fair lending laws. Banks know in advance to applying for a national charter that fair lending will be regulated and enforced at the highest standards. These rigorous regulation methodologies also provide another audit for bank investors and boards of directors. Lastly, cases that are referred either to the Department of Justice or to the Department of Housing and Urban Development have already been thoroughly analyzed. From initial screening to manual file review and from interviews with bankers to follow-up questions on specific applications, a fair lending examination is very rigorous.

Though the number of cases that the OCC refers may not be large, after all of the analysis, the cases that are referred are of a higher quality than are cases that do not go through such a rigorous process. Each of these outcomes of a strong fair lending examination procedure further strengthens the reputation of the national charter, the accessibility of the U.S. banking system, and the quality of service for the retail consumer.

Notes

1. See Part III of the OCC's "Fair Lending Examination Procedures," April 2006, which is available at http://www.occ.treas.gov/handbook/compliance.htm, accessed October 20, 2006.
2. Disparate treatment occurs when a lender treats a credit applicant differently based on one of the prohibited bases. It does not require showing that the treatment was motivated by prejudice or a conscious intention to discriminate against a person beyond the difference in treatment itself. It is considered by courts to be intentional discrimination because no credible, nondiscriminatory reason explains the difference in treatment on a prohibited basis. ("Fair Lending Examination Procedures," p. 6.)
3. For more, see page 18 of the OCC's "Fair Lending Examination Procedures."
4. For further information on the role of examiners in fair lending exams, see the OCC's "Fair Lending Examination Procedures."
5. This analysis is similar to the Federal Reserve Board's cell matching in their "step one" process in fair lending exams (Calem and Longhofer 2000). For more information about HMDA, see "A Guide to Reporting HMDA: Getting It Right!" by the Federal Financial Institutions Examination Council (FFIEC).
6. OCC economists may also look at gender and age discrimination or other protected classes. For more on gender and age discrimination, see Dietrich and Johannsson (2005).
7. The text for these definitions is the HMDA guidebook, "A Guide to HMDA Reporting: Getting It Right!"
8. See Stengel and Glennon (1999) for a comparison of underwriting models with and without incorporating information from a bank's policy guidelines.
9. The type of questions that OCC examiners and economists ask in an underwriter interview is listed in appendix J of the OCC's "Fair Lending Examination Procedures."
10. For a list of the variables used in previous exams, see Courchane, Nebhut, and Nickerson (2000).
11. To better understand the statistical results, economists consider the effect of outliers on the coefficient and the variance covariance matrix. Using an outlier algorithm, such as dfbeta, they identify outliers and then re-estimate the model of interest. For more on outlier analysis, see Dietrich (2005).
12. See LaCour-Little and Fortowski (2004) for a summary of these issues and potential test for disparate impact.
13. Longhofer (1998, 2000); Courchane and Nickerson (1997); Crawford and Rosenblatt (1999); and Jaworski (1996) summarize many of the issues related to measuring price for fair leading analyses.
14. We are only including rate sheet adjustments here, and not the factors, such as score and LTV, that typically determine the base rate from the rate sheet. Backing

out the effects of adjustments is relatively low cost, as they typically change little over time. Backing out the effects of factors such as score and LTV get you closer to overage and underage measures, but can be costly as these factors may change often.

15. This is an example of a Wilcoxon Signed Rank Test.
16. Race and ethnicity information is not available for all of the applications in HDMA. HMDA reporting banks are required to ask applicants for ethnicity and race information, but they cannot require the information to be provided. If the applicant does not report ethnicity and race, and the application is being taken in person, the bank is required to note the ethnicity and race of the applicant based on visual observation or surname.
17. The case is Linda A. Watters, Commissioner, Michigan Office of Insurance and Financial Services versus Wachovia Bank, N.A. et al., Supreme Court No. 05–1342.

References

Avery, Robert B., Kenneth P. Brevoort, and Glenn B. Canner. 2006. "Higher-Priced Home Lending and the 2005 HMDA Data." *Federal Reserve Bulletin*. September.

Calem, Paul S., and Stanley D. Longhofer. 2000. "Anatomy of a Fair-Lending Exam: The Uses and Limitations of Statistics." Finance and Economics Discussion Series Working Paper No. 2000–15.

Courchane, Marsha, and David Nickerson. 1997. "Discrimination Resulting from Overage Practice." *Journal of Financial Services Research* 11:133–151.

Courchane, Marsha, David Nebhut, and David Nickerson. 2000. "Lessons Learned: Statistical Techniques and Fair Lending." *Journal of Housing Research* 11(2).

Crawford, Gordon W., and Rosenblatt, Eric. 1999. "Differences in the Cost of Mortgage Credit Implications for Discrimination," *Journal of Real Estate Finance and Economics* 19(2):147–159.

Department of Housing and Urban Development (HUD). 2002. "Discrimination in Metropolitan Housing Markets: National Results from Phase 1, Phase 2, and Phase 3 of the Housing Discrimination Study." Available at http://www.huduser.org/publications/hsgfin/hds.html, accessed October 20, 2006.

Dietrich, Jason. 2001. "Missing Race Data in HMDA and the Implications for the Monitoring of Fair Lending Compliance." OCC Working Paper No. WP2001–1.

———. "Searching for an Optimal Strategy for Identifying Files to Review for Fair Lending Exams." OCC Working Paper No. WP2005–3.

Dietrich, Jason, and Hannes Johannsson. 2005. "Searching for Age and Gender Discrimination in Mortgage Lending." OCC Working Paper No. WP2005–2.

Do, Chau, and Irina Paley. 2007. "Explaining the Growth of Higher-Priced Loans in HMDA: A Decomposition Approach." OCC Unpublished Paper. January.

Federal Financial Institutions Examination Council (FFIEC). 2006. "A Guide to HMDA Reporting: Getting it Right!" Available at http://www.ffiec.gov, accessed October 20, 2006.

Jaworski, Robert M. 1996. "Overages: To Pay or Not to Pay, That Is the Question." *Banking Law Journal* 13(9):909–917.

LaCour-Little, Michael, and Elaine Fortowski. 2004. "Credit Scoring and the Fair Lending Issue of Disparate Impact." In Elizabeth Mays, ed., *Credit Scoring for Risk Managers: The Handbook for Lenders*. Mason, OH: Thomson/South-Western.

Longhofer, Stanley D. 1998. "Measuring Pricing Bias in Mortgages." *Economic Commentary* Federal Reserve Bank of Cleveland, August 1.

Longhofer, Stanley D. 2000. "APR Flawed for Fair-Lending Analysis." *Regulation* 23(1):12–13.

Munnell, Alicia H., Lynn E. Browne, James McEneaney, and Geoffrey M.B. Tootell. 1996. "Mortgage Lending in Boston: Interpreting HMDA Data." *American Economic Review* 86(1):25–53.

Office of the Comptroller of the Currency (OCC). 2006. "Fair Lending Examination Procedures, Comptroller's Handbook." Available at http://www.occ.treas.gov/handbook/compliance.htm.

Stengel, Mitch, and Dennis Glennon. 1999. "Evaluating Statistical Models of Mortgage Lending Discrimination: A Bank-Specific Analysis." *Real Estate Economics* 27(2):299–334.

Tse, Tomoeh Murakami. 2006. "Federal Oversight of Banks Risk Abuse, States Argue." *Washington Post*, November 30, 2006, p. D1.

AUTHOR INDEX

SUBJECT INDEX